BREAD
and
ROSES

ALSO BY BRUCE WATSON

The Man Who Changed How Boys and Toys Were Made

BREAD
and
ROSES

MILLS, MIGRANTS,
AND THE STRUGGLE
FOR THE AMERICAN DREAM

Bruce Watson

VIKING

VIKING
Published by the Penguin Group
Penguin Group (USA) Inc., 375 Hudson Street, New York, New York 10014, U.S.A.
Penguin Group (Canada), 10 Alcorn Avenue, Toronto, Ontario, Canada M4V 3B2
(a division of Pearson Penguin Canada Inc.)
Penguin Books Ltd, 80 Strand, London WC2R 0RL, England
Penguin Ireland, 25 St. Stephen's Green, Dublin 2, Ireland (a division of Penguin Books Ltd)
Penguin Books Australia Ltd, 250 Camberwell Road, Camberwell, Victoria 3124, Australia
(a division of Pearson Australia Group Pty Ltd)
Penguin Books India Pvt Ltd, 11 Community Centre, Panchsheel Park, New Delhi–110 017, India
Penguin Group (NZ), Cnr Airborne and Rosedale Roads, Albany, Auckland 1310, New Zealand
(a division of Pearson New Zealand Ltd)
Penguin Books (South Africa) (Pty) Ltd, 24 Sturdee Avenue, Rosebank, Johannesburg 2196,
South Africa

Penguin Books Ltd, Registered Offices: 80 Strand, London WC2R 0RL, England

First published in 2005 by Viking Penguin, a member of Penguin Group (USA) Inc.

1   3   5   7   9   10   8   6   4   2

Grateful acknowledgment is made for permission to reprint an excerpt from "O What Is That
Sound" from *Collected Poems* by W. H. Auden. Copyright 1937 and renewed 1965 by W. H.
Auden. Used by permission of Random House, Inc.

PHOTOGRAPH CREDITS: Collection of Lawrence History Center, Immigrant City Archives and
Museum: insert pp. 1, 2, 4 (two photos), 8, 9, 11 (two), 12, 16; American Textile History
Museum, Lowell, Massachusetts: pp. 3, 6 (top), 14, 15; Walter P. Reuther Library, Wayne State
Library: pp. 5, 6 (bottom), 7, 10 (top), 13; Library of Congress: p. 10 (bottom).

CIP data available

ISBN 0-670-03397-9

Printed in the United States of America
Designed by Nancy Resnick

For the billion people around
the world who still survive on a dollar a day

If I did not work,
these worlds would perish. . . .

—Bhagavad Gita

Contents

BREAD
and
ROSES

Introduction

During the winter of 1912, headlines from a Massachusetts mill town captivated the nation. The drama began on a bitterly cold Friday in January. Just after paychecks were passed out that morning, thousands of workers stormed out of the massive textile mills that lined the Merrimack River north of Boston. They were protesting a pay cut, but they were really on strike for their lives.

By noon that day, dozens of power looms that wove worsted wool and cotton cloth had been smashed. Thousands more were idle. Broad, expansive mill rooms that only hours before had roared with the drone of machinery were eerily silent, empty. Outside, police had responded to a riot call. Teeming crowds poured through the streets shouting "Strike!" in thirty languages. By the following Friday, fifteen thousand workers stood on picket lines that stretched for blocks, running all the way around some of the world's longest buildings. Facing them were whole battalions of state militia, their bayonets fixed. On both sides of the divide, stars and stripes waved in the drifting snow.

For the next two months, Americans followed the latest dispatches from Lawrence, Massachusetts. Lawrence was embroiled in a bitter labor standoff, newspapers reported. Radicals preaching "industrial revolution" were stirring up uneducated immigrants in a strike that could lead to nationwide anarchy. Rich mill owners and their hired militia were barely keeping order at bayonet point. America watched and waited. Wherever workers huddled together, from the lumber camps of Oregon to sweatshops on New York's Lower East Side, the talk turned to Lawrence. Workers pooled their wages and sent them to strikers. Rallies led by fiery speakers ended with coins raining down on the stage, coins for hungry families in Lawrence. Meanwhile, in the finer homes, men with trim mustaches and starched collars read about Lawrence and shuddered. Sometimes they even shared their fears with their wives. Any day now, they predicted, some radical would say something incendiary. Some fool would throw a rock. The militia would open fire and dozens would die. Any day, the name of Lawrence would become as notorious as that of Haymarket or Homestead, an inspiration for further anarchy.

But as the winter deepened and the strike dragged on, unprecedented events caused old certainties to falter. Police found dynamite stashed in the city's tenement district but soon became suspicious about its origins. Then the nation's most feared radical, "Big Bill" Haywood, arrived in Lawrence to join the strike. Ten thousand met him at the train station and twice that many heard his thunderous voice ring out over the Lawrence Common. Later, a protest turned violent and a woman was shot. The strike's leaders were arrested for inciting her murder even though they had been a mile from the scene. And state militia came by the thousand, turning Lawrence into an armed camp.

As journalists from around the nation flocked to Lawrence, they found a surprising scenario. Workers were not in despair; they were singing. On sidewalks, women locked arms and marched together, cheering, calling out to others to join them. Reporters who journeyed into the dark maze of tenements found similar surprises. Immigrants from fifty-one countries were not at each other's throats, as mill owners had hoped. Germans with Jews, Italians with Poles, Syrians with French Canadians, they were sharing food, translating speeches for each other, and creating a community rarely seen in the savage strikes that had scarred America since the 1870s. The *New York Sun* reported: "Never before has a strike of such magnitude succeeded in uniting in one unflinching, unyielding, determined and united army so large and diverse a number of human beings."[1] There was something different about this strike, reporters said. Their suspicions were confirmed in mid-February.

After nearly a month without work or pay, strikers tried a tactic used in Europe but never before in America. Scores of mothers dressed their children in their Sunday best, took them to the train station, bid tearful goodbyes, and sent them into the custody of total strangers. In New York, the

"Children of Lawrence" were paraded through the streets. Dirty-faced, malnourished, bewildered, they were housed by sympathetic families who gave them their first decent meals in a month and took them to the zoo, to museums, to wonders beyond their wildest dreams. The "Children's Exodus" made headlines around the nation and made Lawrence police determined it would not happen again. Two weeks later, when more mothers took their children to the train station, police were waiting. What followed shocked even the most jaded observer. And still, despite congressional hearings, hunger, sporadic violence, and bedrock solidarity, the strike went on. . . .

Through the mysterious process that propagates fable and folk song, what happened in Lawrence is now known as the "Bread and Roses" strike, although the slogan was probably never used during the uprising. "Bread and Roses" has also come to stand for labor's long struggle for decent wages and the eight-hour day. Activists of all stripes use the phrase with pride, yet in the decades following the strike, pride was hard to find in Lawrence. For two full generations after that headlining winter, a curious silence prevailed throughout the city. Fearing repercussions from mill bosses, few would talk about the strike. Children grew up hearing little about it from parents or teachers. Generations passed without a single anniversary. In the 1970s, when the strike's new name surfaced, it was deeply resented. Only in the last few decades has Lawrence begun holding annual Bread and Roses festivals on its common. The first few were attended by a handful of people in their nineties who shared memories. Then these witnesses died, leaving the strike to be pieced together by children, grandchildren, and historians.

What happened in Lawrence has been too often relegated to history's ghettos. But the so-called Bread and Roses strike is a quintessentially American event, one of which the entire nation can be proud. People from all over the globe, having packed their belongings and come to America, found themselves on the nation's bottom rung. They bore their burden well for a while, and then rose up. Once merely workers, they became citizens— in name or only in spirit—demanding a living wage and a little respect. Their story, even if they were afraid to tell it, is rife with heroes, a few notorious, most known only to their families. The story takes place in a quaint and curious year.

Though less than a century ago, 1912 lies on the far side of a fault line carved by radio, television, and world wars. Hence, the year seems to have occurred not just in a different century but in a different nation. How different? During the year in which Lawrence went on strike, went back to work, and went on, the *Titanic* sank. The Boston Red Sox won the World Series in their brand-new Fenway Park. America grew from forty-six to forty-eight states. In a hotly contested election, the incumbent president came in third and the Socialist candidate earned almost a million votes. That summer, the first full-length movie came to America, but most people still sought entertainment from vaudeville, the Ziegfeld Follies, or the waning strains of ragtime. Only a few Americans had even heard the names Freud or Picasso.

It was the last era in which kerosene lit more homes than electricity and horse-drawn carriages outnumbered automobiles. It was a highly moralistic age in which morals were just beginning to loosen. Despite proper principles that would forever be named Victorian, wholesale injustices were accepted as the nature of things. Women could not yet vote, and millions of children still toiled in factories, mines, and mills. Each week, a few black men were lynched, and aside from the black press, few beyond the scene of each crime seemed to care. Poverty and wealth lived side by side. The great rudder of a stable society, the middle class, had not yet been invented; hence, Americans faced each other across a chasm of mutual resentment. Glittering mansions sat on hillsides and seashores. Their inhabitants, adorned in top hats and jewels, enjoyed oysters and champagne at fine restaurants. Meanwhile "the other half" lived in tenements and boardinghouses, survived on bread and molasses, and imagined a future that would offer their children a better chance.

Progressives had begun enlisting the government to fight corruption and trusts, yet millions accepted things as they were, or else, while toiling sixty or more hours a week, had little time to change them. But there were some who believed things would only change when the "workers of the world" arose, and there were others who would stop at nothing to keep that from happening. When the two sides clashed in a Massachusetts mill town, the epic struggle wove a fabric of community that reminds us of what America can be. The weaving began at dawn.

BOOK ONE

The weaver-god, he weaves; and by that weaving he is deafened, that he hears no mortal voice; and by that humming, we, too, who look on the loom are deafened; and only when we escape it shall we hear the thousand voices that speak through it.

—Herman Melville, *Moby-Dick*

Babies cried for no reason and parents knew exactly how they felt. Finding what privacy they could, women squeezed into starched white shirtwaists while men elbowed for room at mirrors and began shaving with straight razors. Breakfast was served—molasses and bread in some homes, just bread in others. Then, with the city still dark as midnight and the rest of its denizens asleep, the workers of Lawrence headed for the mills.

From a warren of bleak alleys and decaying slums came Labor incarnate. Clusters of women, their long skirts billowing, their hair piled on their heads, emerged from wooden hovels and walked with arms intertwined. Whole families surfaced from homes that were little more than holes—eight, ten, twelve people stepping as if by magic from two rooms. Men in cloth caps rattled down fire escapes. Boys in knickers took shortcuts across flat roofs, dodging stovepipe chimneys, leaping the narrow gaps between buildings, hustling down rickety stairs and spilling onto the street. And within minutes, twenty-eight thousand people[2]—a city within a city—were on their way to work.

They were as miscellaneous as any populace on earth. Seven out of eight were foreign born or children of immigrants. Half had been in America less than five years. In the newly coined metaphor of the time, this "melting pot" contained the seasonings of fifty-one different nations.[3] There were Poles from Galicia, Italians from Sicily, Syrians from the Ottoman Empire. There were Jews from Riga, Odessa, and other exotic ports of call. Beside them marched Scots, Armenians, Portuguese, Belgians, Germans, English, French Canadians, Russians, Greeks, Irish, and dozens more nationalities. Their faces were coffee-colored, pale as the sky, and every shade in between. Dark bushy mustaches sprouted from the men, accentuating sad brown eyes, while women's faces—pretty, plump, or skeletal— were framed in shawls or crowned by flowery hats. Their given names were as rooted in the earth as the families they had left back in the "old country." Maria and Giuseppe. Hans and Helga. Sadie and Otto. Yet workers had many other labels. Mill payrolls cataloged them by job titles—doffers, spinners, weavers, spoolers, yarn boys, carders, pickers. Mill foremen called them Wops and Dagos, Sheenies and Kikes, Canucks, Polacks, Huns, and Micks. And to the upper crust of Lawrence, old Yankee families tracing their American heritage to colonial times, they were simply "*those* people."

As "those people" headed for work, age was another measure of their miscellany. They ranged from tall twelve-year-olds whose forged work papers claimed they were fourteen to men and women approaching fifty. Some were slightly older, but not many lasted that long in the mills. Inhaling fibers that floated through dank, humid mill rooms, a third died within a decade on the job.[4] Malnourished, they succumbed to tuberculosis, pneumonia, or anthrax, known as "the woolsorter's disease."[5] They were crushed by machinery, mangled by looms and spinners. In a single five-year span, the Pacific Mill had a thousand accidents, two for every three days on the job.[6] Those who avoided accident or disease just wore out like an old suit. Doctors and ministers in Lawrence lived an average of sixty-five years. Mill bosses could expect to live fifty-eight years. The typical mill worker died at thirty-nine.[7] Yet on this icy morning, defying the odds, Maria, Giuseppe, Hans, Helga, and twenty-eight thousand others were marching to work. In the eyes of the mill owners, this gave them a final generic name—Labor.

Like the streams that flowed into the Merrimack, Labor trickled through the streets. Passing alleys reeking of garbage, they followed grimy avenues with ironic names—Oak and Elm, Valley and Park. Then, emerging onto Essex Street, the workers flowed together into a torrent of heads, caps, and faces sweeping past the ornate five-story storefronts of downtown. With the start whistle just minutes away, they picked up pace, powered, it seemed, by rumors. The night before, the rumors had swept through alleys, up stairwells, into cramped tenements. The rumors were ominous, inspiring, amazing: two hundred Polish women had stopped work at the Everett Mill on Thursday afternoon![8] They did not shout or walk out, just stood like statues beside their looms. Through an interpreter, they were asked why. "Not enough pay," they replied. When they refused to work and were ordered out, they began shouting, urging others to join them. A thousand looms were shut down![9] All night, the rumors had flown through the tenements. Now they came into the dawning light and a single word circulated in dozens of tongues. *Sciopero* in Italian. *Greve* in French and Portuguese. *Strajkuja* in Polish. *Streikokim* in Lithuanian. *Shtrayken* in Yiddish. *Streik* in German. And in English—*strike*.

Fanning out toward the dozen mills that lined the river, the crowd flowed through the streets, across bridges, and along the menacing facades of redbrick buildings several blocks long. Pouring through the yawning gates, twenty-eight thousand workers seemed to melt into the mills. Past time clocks, up creaky wooden stairs, along aisles crowded with machinery, they made their way to their stations. Then each gate was locked. Final whistles signaled the morning "speedup." And with a great groan and surge of muscle, steam, and turbine, thousands of machines all over the city started up at once. Another workday had begun.

A mill room, with its panoramic perspective, resembled an Italian Renaissance sketch. The room's vast ceilings were latticed by overhead beams, each propped by pillars that receded—twenty, forty, a hundred yards—toward some distant vanishing point. Through rows of tall windows, filtered light caught airborne fibers like the sun breaking through the clouds. During winter months, this was the only sunlight mill workers saw from Sunday sunset to Saturday noon. The only sound they heard was an incessant din drummed into their brains. As the mills accelerated into the morning, workers knew something was up, yet they could not share their concerns because a mill at full bore was no place for conversation. No sooner had the machines started than talk abruptly ceased. Along each aisle, men in bib overalls and women in long dresses dutifully tended their machines in silence or with an occasional shout of instructions.

Each mill's weaving room was its nerve center. On lower floors, women and children cleaned cotton or wool, spun it, then wound it onto spindles and warps, but it all came together on the top floor. There stood the power looms. Shorter than a man but wide as a truck, a power loom was a steel scaffold from which hung three wooden warps, or frames, each laced like a harp. Hooked to pulleys that timed movements to the split second, frames raised and lowered in sequence. Up-down, clack-clack. With each lift, steel arms hurled a thread-bearing shuttle from one side to the other, whizzing it back and forth more than two "picks" a second. From below, the loom was fed by a spool four feet wide, like something a fairy-tale giant's wife might use to darn his socks. And rolling off the back end was the fabric—broad, smooth, and ready for inspection. Each loom moved so fast a weaver dared not avert his eyes, yet many had to watch a dozen at once, absorbed by their incessant clatter and clash. Take the noise of a single loom, multiply by hundreds of machines spread out across a room that spanned several acres, and the product was the cacophony of mill work. Some workers insisted they got used to the clatter,[10] others said it drove them mad, but many found something hypnotic about it. Instead of a random drone, a weaving room played its own sinister music. Few machines ran at the same speed, so their drumbeat was constantly changing. For half a minute, the room seemed syncopated—RA-ta-ta, RA-ta-ta. Then, when some machines caught up and others fell behind, the whole room marched in a steady clack-CLACK-clack-CLACK. Just when a worker adjusted to the new rhythm, the machines fell out of step and back into syncopation. RA-ta-ta, RA-ta-ta. Clack-CLACK-clack-CLACK. Ten hours a day. RA-ta-ta, RA-ta-ta. Clack-CLACK-clack-CLACK. Six days a week. A Sunday off was not enough to get the rhythm out of one's head, and it started again on Monday. It was still roaring on the morning of Friday, January 12, 1912. It was supposed to last ten hours but within two, the trouble began.

Shortly after the speedup at the Washington Mill, a crowd of young men and boys began gathering outside the gates along the North Canal.[11] No one paid them much attention. In the small office near the gate, the mill's paymaster, Charles Kitchin,[12] was finishing the payroll. As he did every Friday, Kitchin expected to spend the morning wheeling his small hand truck from room to room, doling out checks. But at 9:00 a.m., the paymaster heard a roar. Looking through his window, he saw a blur of arms and backs surging through the mill gates and into the courtyard. He immediately called the police. Nightstick in hand, the lone cop on the local beat arrived a few minutes later to find two thousand people swarming outside the mill.[13] Inside, pay time was approaching when above the steady slam of machinery, a dull roar echoed through several rooms on the ground floor.

The strike began "like a spark of electricity," one overseer recalled.[14] Racing into the mill, men and boys shouted, "Short pay! All out! All out!" Hundreds bolted past startled workers, heading deeper into the mill. Within minutes, more had left their machines. They stormed through the Washington Mill, shouting, whooping, calling to others. Pulling knives, a few slashed the belts that rose like giant rubber bands connecting machines to overhead camshafts. With a long, sickening zip, shreds of rubber and canvas fell to the floor. Machines coasted to a stop. Men tore bobbins from spinning frames and heaved them. Fresh-faced girls recoiled in terror. Boys grinned nervously. Several women fainted, but others left their stations and joined in.

Rampaging through the mill, the workers unfurled two flags—the Stars and Stripes beside the Italian red, white, and green. The flags were soon paraded along the aisles as workers stopped at stations, begging, threatening, pleading with others to walk out. Bellowing above the din, overseers tried to keep their "hands" from joining the frenzy.

"Tony, if you don't get back to your place, you'll lose your job!"

"To hell with the job! I'll pitch it!"[15]

Station by station, room by room, workers were told to "come out." Those who tried to intervene were beaten down. In the jack-spooling room, an overseer was hit with a spindle that sent blood gushing from his head. Another was struck by a flying bobbin. False rumors, the first of hundreds, spread like fear itself. One young woman had refused to leave her machine and was stabbed![16] Another had been shot! Unchecked by police, bosses, or those who just wanted to keep working, workers tore at the mill. They hammered motors. They slashed the threads laced on power looms. They ran knives through finished cloth, shattered lights, threw whatever they could grab. While most of the mill's employees stayed at their jobs, some eight hundred joined the strike or were dragged from their machines.[17] Outside, strikers from other mills began gathering at the gates. More calls went out to police, and two officers entered to find fights breaking out with wrenches and other tools.[18] But soon the mob decided the Washington Mill was not its prime target. Revenge would be sweeter if aimed at the most hated man in Lawrence. And so, enraged workers stormed into the street and headed for the Merrimack and the world's largest mill along its banks.

The most dramatic strike in American history was sparked by a pay cut of thirty-two cents a week. Yet as management would note again and again, hourly wages had not been cut at all. On January 1, 1912, a new labor law had taken effect in Massachusetts, reducing the workweek from fifty-six to fifty-four hours. Workers welcomed the reduction, but only if it came with no cut in pay. Throughout the first two weeks of January, Labor tried numerous ways to learn how the mills would deal with the new law. Some sent a special-delivery letter to American Woolen Company president William Wood, whom workers derided as "Billy Wood." American Woolen owned four of the largest mills in Lawrence, employing half the city's textile work-ers.[19] Billy Wood was too busy to answer the letter. Others met with mill management but could learn nothing. The last time the legislature had mandated a cut in hours—in 1909—weekly pay had remained the same. This time, however, with annual profits having since plummeted 44 per-cent,[20] mill owners were not feeling magnanimous. Notices of the new law posted above time clocks did not mention wages. If the handwriting was not on the mill wall, however, it could be found in newspapers and trade journals. The day before the strike erupted, an editorial in the *Lawrence Telegram* explained the mill owners' dilemma: "The demand that the mills pay the same weekly wage for fifty-four hours' work that they paid for fifty-six hours' work is a demand for more pay. We wish the mills could fur-ther reduce the working time and increase the wages . . . but they must run their plants in accord with the iron law of competition, a competition with mills in states that permit sixty or more hours a week as the working time."[21] The textile trade journal *Fibre and Fabric* was even more blunt:

> Plainly, the [fifty-four-hour] law is a direct interference with the liberty of the people. . . . When laws actually take away from the earning capacity of the working classes they are detrimental to the welfare of the state where they apply. No women or mi-nors are or have been overworked in our textile mills, even from the time when 60 hours or more constituted a week's work. Hundreds and even thousands of the hale and hearty middle-aged and old people in our mill communities started work at 10 or 12 years of age, and spent a happy life in their work, until they could retire and enjoy the fruit of their labors.[22]

The message was unequivocal. Sensing the new law as a de facto pay cut, workers began talking of a walkout. Throughout the first week of 1912, noon meetings were held in many mills. Only skilled workers were invited. The vast army of unskilled workers were left to fend for themselves, yet some of them had their own fledging local. While weavers, spinners, and loom fixers met on January 3, Local 20 of the Industrial Workers of the World held its own gathering.[23] The IWW had a mere three hundred members in Lawrence.[24] All were as replaceable as bobbins. A walkout by a few hundred meant no more to mill bosses than a temporary power outage. Local 20 had tried two previous strikes but each had failed. Besides, the upstart IWW, founded just seven years earlier, did as much fighting at its raucous conventions as on the picket line. Folks called them "the Wobblies," though no one was sure why. They had their own songs, their own jokes, their own credo. Wobblies believed the working class and the employing class had nothing in common. Class warfare was coming, they preached, and the working class was bound to win. Chanting "One Big Union!" Wobblies staged head-busting strikes in the lead mines of Colorado and the goldfields of Nevada. This, however, was New England. The Wobblies had tried their tactics in some of the region's smaller textile towns,[25] but they had never organized a city the size of Lawrence. Thus, the possibility of a strike by the IWW was not taken seriously. A warning of a loom fixers' strike made the *Lawrence Tribune*'s front page,[26] but other headlines—MARY KENNEDY WINS FIRST WHIST PRIZE[27]—got equal weight. The IWW meeting was buried in the back pages. And no newspaper mentioned the doings of one lean, wiry Italian.

Throughout the first two weeks of 1912, much of the strike talk came from Italians, and much of their enthusiasm was fired by a single man. When the trouble began on January 12, however, that man was not among them. Instead, Angelo Rocco was in class at Lawrence High School. At twenty-eight, Rocco was the oldest student at Lawrence High. Short and feisty, with ink-dot eyes, high cheekbones, and curly black hair, he was fluent in Italian and French—"I knew French, I knew Italian and I knew my way about."[28] But he spoke a heavily accented, Chico Marx English, closing many sentences with "You unnerstan'? You unnerstan'?" Regardless of which language he was speaking, Rocco had a way of making himself understood, and even if he was not among the strikers that morning, he was with them in spirit. Those who had listened to him speak only two nights before knew that Angelo Rocco was no stranger to the mills. Those who knew him personally knew that his story was theirs.

When he was sixteen, Rocco had left the craggy village of Roccamonfina, forty miles north of Naples. In his home, Rocco's mother had made all the clothes for her husband and four children, weaving fabric on a hand loom, sewing every stitch. Rocco's first destination was France, but after working two years there, he went home for a spell, then took the big leap to the land Italian immigrants called "La 'Merica."[29] "I felt I could better my economic conditions by emigrating to the U.S.," Rocco recalled. "There was nothing wrong in Italy only I felt I could do better." He first saw the Statue of Liberty on December 13, 1902, his nineteenth birthday. No one knows whether he wept, sang "The Star-Spangled Banner," or got down on his knees, but he had no thought of turning back. He was in "La 'Merica" now and he did what he came for—he went to work.

For the next several years, Rocco's ambition sent him scurrying like the shuttle on a loom. He had an aunt in Pawtucket, Rhode Island, so he moved there first and got work in a mill. Higher pay soon lured him to Providence and then to the nation's largest textile city, Lawrence, where he lived with other Italians, five to a room. But his menial job—combing long from short fibers to make worsted wool for rich men's suits—drove him out of the city. "I said that's no job for me." Moving to Biddeford, Maine, he became a weaver, taking home ten dollars a week. He saved enough to send for his brother, then his mother, father, and two sisters. He settled them, got them jobs, moved on. Yorkville, Maine. Burlington, Vermont, then to adjacent Winooski. "We builded Winooski, we built up the economy. You unnerstan'? You unnerstan'?" Skowhegan, Maine, then East Madison. When William Howard Taft succeeded Theodore Roosevelt as president, Rocco looked forward to better times. Another Republican, he thought. Good for business. "We felt everything was gonna be good, you know, and I thought I was a good weaver at that time, knew all about the weaving. I could make section end supervisor. So I thought, 'Let's go to Woonsocket, Rhode Island.' I stopped over in Lawrence. It was December 1908, right after the election. People I knew in Lawrence told me to stay there."

Along with family and friends, Lawrence offered an ambitious young man another advantage—night school. The same month he settled in, Rocco enrolled in school, taking night classes after a full day's work at the Wood Mill. He was assigned to fifth grade; he was twenty-five. His family lived in a two-room flat with no running water. After a year in fifth grade, Rocco's natural quickness enabled him to jump to high school. Saving, always saving, he bought a three-floor tenement from "a Jewish fellow" and began collecting rent. For two decades, such dwellings had been springing up in "The Plains,"[30] Lawrence's spreading labyrinth of slumlord apartments. Two years after he bought it, Rocco sold his tenement, turning a profit that let him leave the mills and attend high school during the day, pursuing his dream of becoming a lawyer. Nearly eight thousand Italians lived in Lawrence,[31] but Rocco was the only Italian in his class; the rest were all at work. So on the morning of January 12, Angelo Rocco was in school. By night, however, he had been doing a different kind of homework.

Italians had a shady reputation in Lawrence. The first forty-two had been brought to the city in 1891 to break a streetcar strike. They spent their first night sleeping on straw beds in a condemned tavern, and the following morning awoke to find hundreds of people staring at them. Curious about this exotic breed, angry at their purpose, the crowd watched as the Italians shaved and washed. Some observers crowded so close that a few of the newcomers panicked and ran.[32] The rest went to work on streetcars. Ever since, they had been notorious scabs. "The Italian people, none of them could get a job," Rocco recalled. "They had to do the dirtiest work, that's the truth. For very little money. That's how they could get a better job, they had to be a scab, not a very noble thing." In a city where loyalty and labor were the measures of a people, scabbing made Rocco's fellow *paesani* the lowest of the low. Even worse, Italians were also known as anarchists.

A handful of anarchists met in small enclaves scattered throughout the "Italian and Polack district" near Union and Garden streets. There they were said to plot assassinations and bombings, but mostly they just talked about freedom. Scabs and bomb throwers—not much of a reputation, Rocco thought, yet the coming strike offered a chance for change. And word along Common Street, where all words were in Italian, said the strike would be a big one. If Italians again rushed into the mills to scab, Giuseppe and Maria might as well pack their bags and head back to Naples. They could continue to work in Lawrence but they would never be councilmen and ward bosses like the Irish, nor successful merchants like the English and Germans. In fact, they would never get out of the mills.

Rocco knew it would take leadership to get his friends to think of something bigger than a paycheck. The coming strike would need an organizer, someone from beyond Lawrence. Only an outsider, someone above the snake pit of nationalities, could turn patriotism into a weapon on the picket line. So on the Monday before payday, Rocco had a flyer printed and posted along Common Street. It invited all Italians to come to Paul Chabis

Hall, 109 Oak Street, in the heart of The Plains. Wednesday, January 10, at 8:00 p.m. "The craft unions that were organized made a vote that if the mill owners were going to cut off, they were going on strike," Rocco remembered. "The craft union, that means the Germans, the French, the English, they decided to go on strike. 'Now,' I said to myself, 'now is the time to have the Italian people join the other workers and not try to break the strike.'" On Wednesday night, when he slipped into the back of the hall, Rocco squinted in the dim light. A thousand people filled the place. Everywhere he looked, men were seated together or standing against walls, talking, gesturing, sculpting the air with their hands. Rocco skirted one wall and headed toward the stage. Stepping before the rumbling crowd, he pulled himself up to his full height and called for order. "I put the question to them. These other people go out on strike, what are you going to do?" Across the hall, cries rang out. "*Sciopero! Sciopero!*" If there were any dissenters, they kept silent. Then Rocco told the crowd he might be able to get some help.

Only six months before, a smaller strike had hit the Atlantic Mill. IWW organizer James P. Thompson had come to Lawrence but quickly realized there was little he could do with such a meager strike. He told Local 20 that if a larger walkout began, to call Joseph Ettor.[33] Some of you know Ettor, Rocco told the crowd. He was the Italian organizer who had come through Lawrence the previous spring. Known as "Smiling Joe," Ettor had run strikes from the lumber camps of Oregon to the steel mills of Pennsylvania.[34] He would come and help, Rocco said. Everything would be all right. *Meno male. Tutto bene.* Fired by Rocco's speech, the Italians filed out into the night. Inside Paul Chabis Hall, the stage was empty. Outside, the stage was set.

As the hour approached ten o'clock on January 12, a vengeful mob marched out of the Washington Mill. Behind fluttering flags, they tramped along the North Canal, dwarfed by the brick canyons of the mills. Reaching Union Street, they might have aimed their wrath at the nearest mill, the Everett, whose flat face stretched for four blocks. They might have attacked the smaller Kunhardt Mill or the Duck Mill across the canal. But each worker knew his next target as well as he knew the name Billy Wood. With a fury unified into one driving force, the mob headed for the Merrimack and the Wood Mill on its south bank.

Reaching the river, Labor got a postcard view of the raw manufacturing that distinguished this muscular new country from the homelands left behind. Upriver to the west was the low, wide dam that had harnessed the Merrimack and turned Lawrence into an industrial powerhouse. The rest of the year, water spilled over the Great Stone Dam in a glassy curtain, but this morning, beneath leaden clouds that promised snow, the dam was a sheet of ice. When built in 1848, the structure had modified nature on a human scale, and the mills in front of it still seemed modest, for mills. The view toward the east, however, revealed nature harnessed to the twentieth century's harsher demands. Downriver, the landscape seemed built of brick. Brick cliffs were lined by long queues of black windows stretching beneath towering brick smokestacks. Brick facades stretched to the horizon, as if Lawrence had once been solid brick before the river cut a shimmering strip through it. Brick formed a veritable universe of labor, suggesting nothing beyond, no way to escape, no boundary at all to the colossal mills.

Shuffling in step, the mob spent a few minutes crossing the trellised Duck Bridge. Reaching the south bank, they swept past the stately arched portico of the Wood Mill on the left and the handsome clock tower of the Ayer Mill to the right. From each mill's windows astonished workers watched. The crowd shouted to them—"Come out! Come out!"—then turned toward the rising sun and began trudging alongside a building longer than six football fields. Far down Merrimack Street watchman Louis Berry was chatting with a friend at the Wood Mill gate when he heard deep guttural shouts and the sound of tramping feet.[35] Seconds later the mob was upon him. Scrambling to protect the city's flagship enterprise, Berry tried to bar the gate but thrashing arms reached through the bars and wild-eyed faces pressed against them. The gate had been locked since the start-up whistle, but as Berry watched in horror, men lifted the grillwork off its hinges and sent it clattering to the ground. Clamoring, waving flags and sticks, the mob swept past the gateman.[36] Stampeding onto the ground floor, workers smashed down one door and streamed through others. In the front office, cashier Frank Sherman was just getting off the phone with his counterpart from the Washington Mill when he heard "the most ungodly yelling and howling and blowing of horns." Seconds later, the mill's paymaster, his face white with fear, rushed in shouting, "For God's sake, Mr. Sherman, they have broken in the doors and pulled over the watchmen and are loose in the entire mill!" Sherman phoned police several times before getting an answer.[37] Meanwhile, the paymaster, having placed some six thousand checks in his wagon for dispersal that morning, quietly wheeled the pay slips back into his office safe.[38]

As they had at the Washington Mill, workers spread through the Wood urging others to join in the melee. But threats were now backed by bludgeons—two-foot-long picker sticks used in weaving, steel handles ripped from machinery,[39] and chunks of iron. Brandished over bare heads, the weapons left workers little choice but to leave their looms and spinners.[40] "I didn't walk out," one man remembered decades later. "I tried to work but they wouldn't let me. They threw pepper in my eyes. They were a lot of foreigners. They wasn't Americans that'd throw pepper in your eyes."[41] One woman was driven from her post at knifepoint; two others were beaten.[42] A foreman in the machine shop was stabbed in the hand.[43] Yet for all its frenzy, the mob drew little blood. Many had waited years for this moment, a chance to strike back at bosses, owners, an entire industrial system that seemed designed to grind them into dust. But like England's Luddites, they took their rage out on the machines. Roaming through the sprawling rooms, the mob slashed belts, cut wires, tore at power looms, hurled loose bobbins and warps.[44] Cries of "Come out!" and "Short pay!" rose above the din. At the entrance to the mending room, one young woman saw the throng approaching. She fainted. Carried off, she could not be revived for a full hour. Several other women fled to the mill office where they found secretaries cowering in a corner, recoiling from the maniacal shouts and the crunch of scrap metal thrown into moving machinery.[45] No one knows who turned on the sprinklers but the move saved the mill. Water drenched several departments. Minutes later, the superintendent shut off all power, and six thousand employees, some still boiling with rage, others wishing they could go back to work or at least get paid before leaving, began filing out. Reckoning had come to the man whose name was on the mill.

∽∾

Carnegie. Rockefeller. Mellon. The magnates whose names stood for wealth at the turn of the century made their millions in brawling businesses. William Madison Wood was nearly their equal in dominance, yet because textiles never captured the public's fancy as did the swashbuckling worlds of steel, oil, and finance, he did not share their fame. And if William Wood is forgotten today, it is because, unlike his peers, he rarely shared his fortune with the public. There are no Wood foundations, institutes, or universities to commemorate the man. Instead, Wood lavished riches on his wife and spoiled his four children, buying them mansions, yachts, and European vacations. He was generous with personal loans—at his death, acquaintances owed him some six hundred thousand dollars.[46] Yet aside from a senior citizens' home[47] and an upscale planned community he bankrolled toward the end of his life, Wood kept most of his fortune among friends and family. For this reason, it is easy to caricature him as a greedy capitalist, a poster boy for the excesses of the rich. The mill workers of Lawrence found this caricature all too tempting, and throughout the strike, "Billy Wood" acted the part well. Yet William Wood was more complex than either his fortune or his good fortune suggested.

In the manner of his American Woolen Company, formed by merging eight textile firms, Wood was an amalgam of a man. He was equal parts J. P. Morgan, Horatio Alger, and Rumplestiltskin. Like Morgan, Wood made decisions that affected thousands of stockholders. Like an Alger hero, he had risen through "luck and pluck," climbing from four-dollar-a-week office boy to a life of luxury. And like the fairy-tale dwarf who spun straw into gold, Wood spun cotton and wool into the world's largest textile conglomerate. By the time he killed himself in 1926, Wood was one of America's richest men. His annual salary topped one million dollars, making him the second highest paid executive in the United States.[48] American Woolen owned sixty mills employing forty thousand people.[49] The trajectory of Wood's career explains why, when his employees smashed his machines and stormed into the streets, Wood was shocked and offended. Hadn't he been poor once? Hadn't he worked in mills? Hadn't he risen? "You can't keep an able man down!" he insisted with typical aplomb. "He is bound to rise."[50]

When the dawn whistled on January 12, a light was already burning in the second-story window of Wood's mansion in Andover, just south of Lawrence. The president of American Woolen had been up since 3:00 a.m., working. A short, stocky man with a bushy mustache and penetrating eyes, Wood kept a coffeepot by his bed. When ideas occurred to him, regardless of the hour, he summoned an aide, dictated an order, and made certain it would be put into practice the next day.[51] Wood had nothing but scorn for workers who griped about their hours. Fifty-six hours a week or fifty-four, either would have been a vacation for him. He routinely worked seventeen-hour days, six days a week.[52] While he enjoyed opera and playing the violin,[53] his real hobby, a friend noted, was "work and more work."[54] It was the recipe for success in his time, and few had followed it with greater diligence.

Back in the 1850s, Wood's parents had emigrated from the Azores, following a common route of Portuguese immigrants. His father, whose surname was either Jacinto, Madeira, or Silva,[55] booked passage on a whaler bound for New England. Arriving in Martha's Vineyard, the new immigrant changed his name to William Jason Wood, married an eighteen-year-old Portuguese girl, and began working menial jobs. During the next fifteen years, Amelia Christiana Wood bore ten children. Only six survived. Her second child and first son, William, was born in 1858.[56] Three years later, the family moved to New Bedford. For a while, Wood's father worked as a steward on a steamer running between the old whaling port and Martha's Vineyard. His mother toiled as a scrubwoman on the same ship. Then in 1870, when Wood was twelve, his father died of consumption.[57] "I started to work," Wood later recalled. "That was where my good fortune began. Work is whatever you make it: hardship or happiness, a punishment or a pleasure. I have worked practically all my life and I love it. A man who doesn't work not only shirks his duty but misses the greatest satisfaction."[58]

Quitting school, where he had been near the bottom of his class, Wood got a job in a mill office and soon began dropping by the mill itself. Amazed by the lightning-fast looms, drawn to the power of the men at the top, he regularly made a nuisance of himself. "I asked questions of everybody—superintendents, foremen, operators," he recalled. "From the very beginning, I was curious about the cost of things."[59] After three years in the office, he requested a transfer to the mill, where he toiled twelve-hour days[60] and asked more questions. "I used to look at two pieces of goods and wonder how much of the general mill cost each one bore. Any boy could have done this. A man who does no more than sweep the floor can learn *by* sweeping the floor, if he wants to learn."[61] Despite all he was learning, mill work made Wood restless. At eighteen, he quit to travel along the East Coast, visiting the nation's 1876 Centennial celebration in Philadelphia before returning to Massachusetts, first to New Bedford and then to the mill town of Fall River.[62] For the next decade, he worked in banks and mill offices, soaking up the principles of accounting and cost analysis in the cotton trade. By 1886, instead of four dollars a week, he was making seven times that much and had developed a taste for more.

During the frantic industrialization that followed the Civil War, textiles were as volatile as any other business, even railroads. Huge mills rose along the rivers of the Northeast, inhaling rawboned farmhands who learned to knuckle under to bosses, to run a loom or a spinner, and to punch a clock. Many textile firms folded during "panics" that seemed to strike at random. Having weighed risks and potential profits, Wood yearned to start his own mill, but first he was hired to rescue one. While in Providence, Wood met Frederick Ayer. A pompous man with a bushy white beard, Ayer boasted a New England pedigree that dated to the Puritans. He had made his fortune peddling Ayer's Proprietary Medicines—hair restorers and sarsaparilla, the latter advertised as the best remedy ever devised "for the cure of lassitude, debility, and all disorders peculiar to the Spring."[63] Ayer also sold *Ayer's Almanac*, whose annual run of twenty-five million copies earned it the billing "second only to the Bible in circulation."[64] When he met Wood, Ayer was squandering his fortune in textiles. His Washington Mill in Lawrence was bleeding money. Ayer hired Wood to supervise his cotton production but the department was soon shut down. Wood jumped to the wool division, but wool demanded a distinct expertise. In over his head, Wood was fired. Walking the gritty streets of Lawrence, he touched that lonely bottom all Alger heroes hit sooner or later, then pushed up. He walked back to the mill and offered to work as a traveling salesman. In an industry accustomed to having customers buy on-site, this was a radical idea. Within a year, Wood had sold two million dollars in worsted wools. Within three years, he was in charge of the Washington Mill. He had also married the boss's daughter, Ellen Ayer.[65]

Throughout the boom and bust of the early 1890s, Wood's financial acumen kept the Washington Mill afloat. Then in 1895, he devised a system of labor that delighted stockholders and wearied workers until they were threadbare. Wood's bonus system rewarded employees with extra wages for meeting production quotas. The system interlinked the performance of each worker, making the weaver's bonus hinge on the output of the spinner, whose bonus depended on the work of the doffer, and so on down the production line. But there was another catch. Workers only earned premiums if they missed no more than one day a month. Hence, day after day, whether sick, exhausted, or injured, workers marched into the mills to chase their small monthly bonuses. With pay as his carrot, Wood then speeded up his looms. And speeded them up again. By 1912, power looms that had run at 90 picks per minute in 1890 were racing at 140 picks per minute,[66] making the spindles of Lawrence the most productive in the country.[67] Despite the slight salary boost, workers loathed the bonus system and every one of them knew just whom to blame. Wood's system turned mill work from a distance race into a sprint. "They used to drive you like a hoss," one worker remembered. "That's what the whole trouble was, you know."[68]

With Wood's mills churning out fabric, his star continued to rise until, in 1899, he was ready for his masterstroke. That February, two years before Carnegie and Morgan formed United States Steel, Wood stunned the textile industry by merging mills from Lawrence to upstate New York into the American Woolen Company, valued at twelve million dollars. Wood became treasurer, then in 1905, when Ayer retired, president.[69] That year, he made an even bolder move. On the south bank of the Merrimack, he spent $3.5 million to build what the people of Lawrence dubbed "the eighth wonder of the world," the Wood Mill. The size of the building simply boggled the imagination. The mill had two parallel wings each 1,937 feet long, 500 feet longer than the Empire State Building if laid on its side. The mill's sprawling floors housed 1,470 power looms along sixteen miles of aisles.[70] All its machines were state-of-the-art. Between each of six floors, Wood installed new devices called escalators,[71] which his younger workers enjoyed climbing in the wrong direction but were fired if caught.[72] Enclosing thirty acres under one roof, employing a small city of six thousand workers, the Wood Mill was to textiles what Pittsburgh was to steel—the very symbol of consolidation and power. Skeptics doubted such a mammoth mill could function efficiently, but Wood, constantly barking out orders in his Boston office, made certain it did. By 1907, turning a million pounds of wool per week into blue serge for suits,[73] the mill had already paid for itself.[74] Two years later, Wood built the Ayer Mill across the street, hiring two thousand more immigrants just to spin enough yarn to keep the Wood Mill running.

In his spare time, Wood enjoyed the "conspicuous consumption" of the age. He might easily have afforded his own Newport mansion alongside those of the Astors and Vanderbilts, but he could not be satisfied with one opulent home. To complement Arden, as Wood called his green and white Carpenter Gothic manor in Andover,[75] he built new palaces. He bought a six-hundred-acre island off the coast of Martha's Vineyard and put a hill-top summer home there, complete with a dozen bedrooms and two bowl-ing alleys. From its windows, he told guests, he could see the sound where his parents had once toiled on steamers. Later he built The Towers, a four-story mansion in Palm Beach, Florida. The family also owned an estate in Beverly, Massachusetts, a gift of Frederick Ayer.[76] Then there were fleets of fine automobiles, so many, Wood said offhandedly, that he couldn't count them all.[77] And yachts, servants, and private train cars. It was an empire that seemed to grow of its own accord, yet on the morning of the strike that would rock it, Wood was up early devising plans to expand his holdings further.

William Wood was not the only mill owner in Lawrence, not even the stingiest. He had raised wages four times in the last ten years. (He had also drastically lowered them during one recession so that, by 1912, wages stood about where they were in 1905.) Wood pointed proudly to housing he had built in Lawrence—seventy-eight units for his workers.[78] But these, too, made him a convenient target. With his name on both his tenements and his mill, Wood was a fixture in the Lawrence landscape; hence his workers loathed him with the same logic cynics reserve for God. As creator of this realm, either Billy Wood would not mitigate its evils or he could not. In any case, the man who considered himself a beloved symbol of the American dream had become the despised symbol of its nightmare.

✦

Lawrence on the eve of its great strike can be compared to a certain "unsinkable" ocean liner that was then being readied for its maiden voyage that April. Blithely unaware of its looming ordeal, the city plowed ahead as if nothing were floating in its path. Thirty years had passed since the city's last large strike, and small walkouts had since come and gone with little notice. Despite warnings in the papers, citizens seemed unconcerned; business went on as usual. In a typical American city of 1912, business meant a wealth of small concerns. "The mills *are* Lawrence,"[79] it would later be written, but along with its thirty mills, the city also boasted 110 barbers, nineteen pool halls, a dozen blacksmiths, more than one hundred boardinghouses, fourteen bootblacks, thirty-four cigar and tobacco merchants, two corset shops, four dozen dry goods dealers, ten horseshoers, sixty-two saloons, fourteen steamship agencies, three hundred grocers, and eighty-one tailors.[80] Throughout the week of January 12, these businesses finished New Year's sales while the rest of Lawrence ran like clockwork. Milkmen made their daily rounds and doctors made house calls. The Colonial Theatre on Essex Street hosted *Echoes of Broadway,* a vaudeville show featuring PRETTY GIRLS, BEAUTIFUL SCENIC EFFECTS, TUNEFUL MELODIES.[81] The regular meeting of the Lawrence Women's Club, at the home of Miss Irene Butler, featured an illustrated lecture on the Parthenon.[82] Such society events were a fixture of Lawrence's newspapers, which interspersed ads for stomach pills and hair tonics with stories of crime, scandal, and the latest dirt about city government.

At city hall, whose bell tower overlooked the common, business was not proceeding as usual. Lawrence was nearly bankrupt and had not paid its bills for several months.[83] In order to meet its payroll, the city had asked property owners for an advance in taxes.[84] Just across the street from city hall stood the police station and courtroom, each recently condemned because of shoddy ventilation and lighting. But a new mayor had just been sworn in, promising to clean up Lawrence. Talk of progressive reform and the hope of a new year made it easy to downplay the imminent strike. "It seems to us that the employees of the mills make a serious mistake in striking at this season of the year," the *Lawrence Tribune* told its readers on January 10. Throughout 1911, times had been slack with many workers laid off. The return of steady work, the paper guessed, would be welcomed by

mill hands who "need the employment."[85] Recent strikes in other Massachusetts textile towns, each protesting two-hours-less pay, had broken
down in a few days,[86] and leading citizens of Lawrence, the ones who never
set foot in the mills, could not imagine workers risking their jobs for a pay
cut of thirty-two cents a week.

Pay, however, was only a pretense. The strike was also caused by posters,
some found on tenement walls,[87] others preserved only in memory. One
poster showed textile workers leaving mills carrying bulging bags of gold.
Another depicted a family of ten, father holding the gold, entering the
Wood Mill. "No one goes hungry in Lawrence," the poster read. "Here all
can work, all can eat."[88] The posters had been put up throughout southern
Europe. They were signed by the American Woolen Company. Each morning when they rose hungry and went to work, each week when they brought
home checks for $4, $6, or $8.50, workers remembered the posters that had
lured them to Lawrence, and they hated Billy Wood that much more.

Another cause was "huddle fever," a term coined by *The Report of the
Lawrence Survey*, a 1912 study of living conditions in the city. Huddle fever
described the prickly rage that came from living like human sardines,
packed into slums. On Valley Street, the average two-bedroom apartment
housed six people; on Common Street, typical occupancy was eight per
flat. With such crowding, kitchens doubled as living rooms and every
room was a bedroom.[89] Each alley, each street corner was crammed with
grubby girls and gangs of surly boys. In each kitchen mothers, aunts, uncles shouted while fathers drew the shades around their emotions. One
could never be alone. "I used to hear my mother call me from the kitchen
and the smell of food told me it was time to eat," one woman remembered.
"But when I'd get there sometimes, it wasn't my mother, but a voice from
next door, through the window! I could reach out and eat off my neigh-
bor's table, we were so close."[90]

Chapter titles in *The Lawrence Survey* painted a bleak picture of life in
the tenements: "Windowless Rooms." "From Darkness to Death." "Houses
That Trap Men Like Animals." Talk of a strike could be heard wherever
such conditions prevailed, but the talk was loudest on blocks where six
hundred lived in a single acre, where people slept four to a bed and a single
case of consumption quickly became an epidemic. "My people are not in
America," one local priest said. "They are under it."[91] In the finer stores

along Essex Street, the strike would later be blamed on "outside agitators," but the finer customers there did not know that the city's most radical agitator was death, which camped outside tenement doors, waiting.

The week before the strike was a typical one. On January 9, a fourteen-year-old boy had his leg crushed in an elevator at the Arlington Mill. The leg had to be amputated. He died the next day.[92] That same week, an Italian who worked in the Everett Mill left his family one evening and checked into a hotel on Essex Street. The following morning the maid knocked on the door. She knocked again. When she opened the door, the smell of gas soured her face. The man lay on the bed. He was revived and taken to the hospital, and was soon back on the job.[93] Such stories were given just a single inch in the paper, so it's unlikely anyone outside family and immediate bystanders noticed when a worker from the Wood Mill walked into a store on Essex Street the Saturday before the strike and dropped dead.[94] But other workers noticed.

When mill workers died, word spread through the tenements along a network linked by clotheslines and gossip, a network largely ignored by men but nurtured by women. Even before news reached the papers, women heard the names, just as they heard every time another infant died. The obituaries were hidden deep in the papers, but the names and ages were known in the keening circles that gathered at wells. Again, in a single week: Cara Meola, age one year and five months. Patricia Madden, sixteen days old. Margaret Burns, three months old. Ida Kappanan, nine months.[95] Disease stalked The Plains. Diseases now easily cured—diarrhea, measles, whooping cough, croup—killed hundreds, most of them children. During the year preceding the strike, 1,524 people died in Lawrence. Almost half were under the age of six,[96] and more than 500 had not yet reached their first birthday. These cold statistics gave Lawrence one of the highest infant mortality rates in the nation and gave the strike the urgency of war.

Immigrants had come to Lawrence lured by posters promising bags of gold, yet in packing their belongings and crossing the ocean crammed into steerage, few expected to get their hands on gold. Most expected only what they could not find at home—jobs. Perhaps some dreamed of being the next Billy Wood, but none wanted to be his next victim. Even if two hours' pay was granted, it would not compensate the workers for the shame of their condition and the threat of death hovering over their children. Nor would it restore the dignity denied them daily by overseers who constantly berated them, swearing at women and children, using racial slurs to keep men in their place. "They treated us like dumb cattle," one worker said.[97] And so, on January 12, as the mob tore through the Wood Mill, thousands more continued to work, not knowing whether they would walk out but increasingly certain that they could stand no more.

At 10:03 a.m., Cornelius Lynch, commissioner of public safety, gave the order to pull fire alarm box 333—the riot call. Despite previous strikes and racial unrest, there had not been a single riot call in the history of Lawrence. The last time alarm box 333 had been pulled, several years earlier, had only been a test. Lynch, then the city's mayor, had sounded the call to keep his "bluecoats" alert. So although the city crackled with impending chaos, many off-duty officers thought the commissioner was just crying "wolf" again and did not respond until phoned.[98] But before noon, as snow began to fall, William Wood was drafting a statement to the press blaming "mistaken labor interests" for cutting workers' hours. The *Lawrence Daily American* was preparing an inch-high banner headline for its afternoon edition: FRENZIED, ARMED MOB DESCENDS UPON MILLS.[99] And dozens of police, their nightsticks flailing, their faces cut by flying chunks of ice, were fighting a pitched battle with two thousand strikers at the Duck Mill. The police had been summoned from city hall by the riot call, the tolling of bells.

CHAPTER TWO

Immigrant City

How great is the responsibility of a rich man.

—Abbott Lawrence[1]

In the vision of its namesake, Lawrence was not foreseen as the setting of bloody battles and brutal strikes. It was instead designed to be a utopia, the efficient, rational, American answer to England's squalid textile cities. Lawrence began as a planned metropolis graced by parks, open waterways, and modest housing for contented workers. The dream soured quickly. All through the late nineteenth century, it continued to fester, and by 1912 it had been all but forgotten. Once the strike began, some blamed mill owners; others pointed fingers at immigrant workers and their radical leaders. But another culprit was the river whose power was too seductive to be ignored.

When Americans speak of rivers, they mention the Mississippi and its steamboats, the Ohio that slaves crossed to freedom, or the Missouri whose tendrils led Lewis and Clark across the West. Almost no one talks about the Merrimack. Stretching just 110 miles from New Hampshire's White Mountains to the coastal dunes and marshes north of Boston, the Merrimack is a mere stream compared to more fabled rivers. It is neither muddy like the Platte nor wild like the Columbia. Unlike the Colorado, it has carved no canyons, grand or humble. For most of its route, the Merrimack is a stepladder, barely flowing for miles, then crashing over white-water rapids, then barely flowing again. Yet because "energy is eternal delight," as William Blake observed, the Merrimack's falls drew power-hungry men to the river in the 1820s. And for the next half century, before water power gave way to steam and electricity, it was this river that jump-started the nation's industrial revolution. For this alone, the Merrimack deserves a prominent place among American rivers.

On the last day of August in 1839, when Henry Thoreau and his brother, John, set out on the Merrimack in a homemade rowboat, they saw only hints of things to come. For most of their weeklong journey, they saw the river much as the Pawtucket and Algonquin nations had seen it, teeming with shad and sturgeon, roiling into the occasional rapids that gave the river its name. In Algonquin, Merrimack means "rapid waters." In *A Week on the Concord and Merrimack Rivers,* Thoreau observed:

> It is worth the while to make a voyage up this stream, if you go no farther than Sudbury, only to see how much country there is in back of us: great hills, and a hundred brooks, and farmhouses, and barns and haystacks you never saw before, and men everywhere. . . . You shall see men you never heard of before, whose names you don't know, going away down through the meadows with long ducking guns, with water-tight boots . . . and they shall see teal—blue-winged, green-winged—sheldrakes, whistlers, black ducks, ospreys, and many other wild and noble sights before night, such as they who sit in parlors never dream of.[2]

Though intoxicated by nature, Thoreau was sobered by one stretch of the Merrimack. At the Pawtucket Falls, where the river tumbled thirty feet in less than a mile,[3] a city unlike any other on the continent had begun to grow. Lowell, Massachusetts, incorporated just sixteen years earlier, had grown from a mere bend in the river into the Xanadu of the modernizing world. Nicknamed "Spindle City," Lowell boasted six miles of canals, forty textile mills, ten thousand looms, and as many workers.[4] These were the fabled mill girls, New England farm daughters living in company housing and governed by strict codes that promised moral uplift and education as a reward for toil. In their spare time, mill girls wrote their own newspaper and enjoyed visiting lecturers such as Ralph Waldo Emerson.[5] But a mill girl did not have much spare time, for she rose six mornings a week to begin work at 5:00 a.m.[6] Processing raw cotton picked by Southern slaves,

Lowell's mills turned out more than one hundred million yards of cloth each year.[7] The planned city drew effusive praise from visitors ranging from President Andrew Jackson to England's own expert on industrial squalor, Charles Dickens. In *American Notes*, Dickens favorably compared Lowell to Britain's filthy, crime-ridden textile cities, likening the contrast to that "between good and Evil, the living light and deepest shadow."[8]

Unlike Dickens, Thoreau didn't care for Lowell but he tried to be optimistic: "Perhaps, after a few thousands of years, if the fishes will be patient, and pass their summers elsewhere meanwhile, nature will have leveled the Billerica dam, and the Lowell factories, and the Grassground River [will] run clear again."[9] Few of Thoreau's contemporaries shared his concern for "the freedom of the Merrimack."[10] More common in antebellum America were countless others, men "whose names you don't know," men whose living depended on manufacturing. These men so transformed the Merrimack that had Thoreau spent a week on its waters in 1912, he would have found few "wild and noble sights." From the mill town of Franklin, New Hampshire, on through Lowell, Lawrence, and all the way to the Atlantic, the Merrimack was lined with factories, stained with dyes, choked by dams. The river had flowed freely for eons. Within just a few decades, it had been tamed by some of the nineteenth century's richest and most puritanical men.

The tycoons who built America's first textile mills worked in bold defiance of the early American dream. The Founding Fathers were ambivalent about industry. Benjamin Rush, physician and signer of the Declaration of Independence, wanted Americans to have their own mills. "A people who are entirely dependent upon foreigners for food or clothes must always be subject to them," Rush wrote.[11] Alexander Hamilton promoted factories as a means of employing "persons who would otherwise be idle (and in many cases a burden on the community)."[12] Yet in 1814, when Francis Cabot Lowell built the nation's first self-contained mill on the Charles River in Waltham, Massachusetts, the ideals of Thomas Jefferson still prevailed. Jefferson rejected the very notion of "American industry." "While we have land to labor then," he wrote, "let us never wish to see our citizens occupied at a work-bench, or twirling a distaff. . . . For the general operations of manufacture, let our workshops remain in Europe."[13] Newspaper accounts of British textile cities, where children as young as four[14] trudged to work beneath shrieking steam boilers and belching smokestacks, made many shudder to think of an American cloth industry. The same year the Waltham mill opened, Congressman Daniel Webster warned against a future "when the young men of the country shall be obliged to shut their eyes upon external nature . . . that they may open them in dust, and smoke, and steam, to the perpetual whirls of spools and spindles."[15]

Yet Jeffersonian ideals proved no match for the power of the Merrimack and the profits of its mills. Once Lowell paved the way, others were bound to follow despite growing controversy over the hardships of making cloth. By the 1840s, conditions in the Lowell mills were hotly debated in Boston. The mills were said to be dank and dangerous. The mill girls, Thoreau said, were "wage slaves."[16] Others protested the grinding fourteen-hour days, the regular "speedups" of machinery, and the mill girls' unsteady health. The girls themselves had begun periodic "turnouts," walking off the job to protest low wages and long hours. Throughout Massachusetts, mill workers were sending massive petitions, some of them 130 feet long,[17] urging the state legislature to mandate a ten-hour day.[18] Ignoring the controversy, several of Lowell's early investors sought a site for another model textile city. Late in the winter of 1845 they gathered at a wide, rushing falls a dozen miles down the Merrimack to begin planning. Foremost among the planners was Abbott Lawrence.

For a man who came within eight votes of becoming president of the United States, Abbott Lawrence cast a short shadow. But then as the youngest of five sons, Lawrence had learned to pull strings behind the scenes. By the time he threw his prestige and fortune behind the city that would bear his name, Lawrence had seen as much tragedy as triumph in the textile trade. His oldest brother, Amos, one of Boston's richest men, was giving away more than a half billion dollars,[19] enriching Harvard and Williams colleges and sending religious tracts to poor clergymen.[20] Brothers Samuel and William were winding down careers that had seen them make fortunes in Lowell. Yet the mills had made quick work of another brother, Luther Lawrence. In April 1839, shortly after being reelected mayor of Lowell, Luther was touring the Middlesex Manufacturing Company, one of several mills owned by the Lawrence brothers. Gazing down into a pit that housed a mammoth power wheel, Luther slipped and tumbled into the works.[21] The wheel crushed his skull. Despite Luther's death, Abbott Lawrence remained optimistic about textiles. He and his brothers were staunch boosters of the "moral purity"[22]

Lowell's founders touted as the by-product of their boardinghouse system. The regulations of the Lawrence Company, whose five Lowell mills made underwear and stockings,[23] required that employees "on all occasions, both in their words and in their actions, show they are penetrated by a laudable love of temperance and virtue, and animated by a sense of their moral and social obligations."[24] This was not idle preaching: Abbott Lawrence's own life suggested what "laudable love of temperance and virtue" could accomplish.

Born in 1792 to a father who had fought at Bunker Hill, Abbott spent his childhood on the family farm in Groton.[25] At sixteen, he came to Boston to work for his brother Amos, a pious teetotaler given to Bible reading and preaching against work on the Sabbath. Unlike Amos, Abbott was not bothered by the wealth the brothers' dry goods business soon began to rake in. "If you are troubled with the belief that I am growing too rich," he wrote to a friend, "there is one thing you may as well understand: I know how to make money."[26] So did his tight circle of friends and family. The Lawrence brothers were charter members of a group historians call the "Boston Associates." In the 1840s and 1850s, these eighty tycoons held industrial New England in their hands. Their interests included thirty-one textile companies controlling one-fifth of the nation's spindles, banks commanding 40 percent of Boston's capital, insurance companies indemnifying two-fifths of the state's ships and three-quarters of its buildings, and railroads responsible for one-third of the region's railroad mileage.[27] The Lawrence brothers were heavily invested in all of the above. Of the Associates, a Unitarian reformer observed, "This class . . . can manufacture governors, senators, judges, to suit its purposes, as easily as it can manufacture cloth. This class owns the machinery of society."[28]

An ulcer convinced Amos Lawrence to retire in 1830, but his youngest brother was only getting started. In 1834, Abbott was elected to Congress. He declined to run for reelection, but in 1838, friends persuaded him to try again. A short, balding man with twinkling eyes and enormous charm, Lawrence was returned to Washington where the swampy climate gave him typhus fever, forcing him to resign.[29] After surviving a shipwreck off Nova Scotia in 1843, he was back in Boston when a man named Daniel Saunders, having bought the water rights to some falls on the Merrimack east of Lowell, approached him with the idea of starting a new textile city. The million-dollar deal[30] that created the city of Lawrence was done over dinner. On March 20, 1845, the state chartered the Essex Company "for the purpose of constructing a dam across the Merrimack river . . . to use for manufacturing and mechanical purposes."[31] The next day, the fourteen company founders, including Abbott, Samuel, and William Lawrence, took a carriage to Deer Jump Falls.[32] Enchanted by the raw power of the flowing water, the group went to the Merrimack House in Lowell for dinner. There they made plans to buy up farms, build a dam and canals, and issue stock. Abbott Lawrence became the largest stockholder, purchasing one thousand shares at one hundred dollars each and becoming Essex Company president. Then the hard work began.

We think of antebellum America, drawn by carriage and powered by waterwheel, as a plodding horse, but the era was greased lightning when it came to getting a city on the map. Within a year after the dinner deal, Lawrence was a boomtown to rival anything on the western frontier. To power the new city, engineers built the world's longest dam. Hauling granite from New Hampshire and timber from Maine,[33] they laid the dam's first stone on September 19, 1845. Three years later, on exactly the same month, date, and hour, the final stone was laid. When completed, the Great Stone Dam stretched 1,629 feet across the Merrimack. Water spilling over its 30-foot drop provided 150 "millpower." (The ambient term for measuring hydraulic energy, one millpower equaled between sixty and seventy horsepower.)[34] While the dam was being built, laborers dug the North Canal. The mile-long trench formed an island in the Merrimack from which mills could tap water power on both sides.[35] And all along the river's banks, merchants, peddlers, blacksmiths, and machinists set up shop on the newly laid out Essex Street. During 1846 alone, the city's first druggist, attorney, doctor, and grocery store opened their doors. Construction of the first two textile mills was begun that summer, which also saw the founding of four churches, a newspaper, and assorted hotels. The following year, 450 buildings went up.[36] By 1848, the city, now officially named Lawrence, had grown from a handful of farmers to six thousand people. More than a third were Irish, but the population also included one German, one Italian, three French, two Welsh, nine Scots, twenty-eight British, and sixteen Negroes.[37]

Abbott Lawrence was not on hand to appreciate the boom. In 1848, he was again flirting with politics, this time at the highest level. Other Massachusetts Whigs were backing Daniel Webster for president, but Lawrence was not among them. Webster was fighting the extension of slavery, the South's "peculiar institution" that kept cotton flowing into the mills. Lawrence, while opposed to slavery, thought its end to be in Southern, not Northern hands,[38] so he threw his weight behind Mexican War hero Zachary Taylor. When Taylor won the nomination, Lawrence was said to be a shoe-in for the vice-presidential slot, but last-minute desertions by Webster's men left the mill mogul just eight votes shy of the ticket. Taylor went on to the White House, where he died of acute indigestion in 1850. His vice president, Millard Fillmore, became the new chief executive. Abbott Lawrence, by then serving as ambassador to England, had come *that* close to the Oval Office.[39] He never complained, in either public or private, of his near miss. And his city continued to grow.

In 1854, a painting of Lawrence showed a farmer, with dog and cow at his side, gazing from pastoral Prospect Hill down on a city of fifteen thousand,[40] replete with smokestacks, row houses, and needle-sharp steeples. Yet for all its growth, Lawrence was still small enough to embody its founder's righteous principles. Donating a thousand dollars to a library, Abbott urged that the gift improve the common laborer's lot. "Let the standard be high in Religion, Moral and Intellectual Culture, and there can be no well grounded fear of the results," he wrote.[41] The Essex Company, too, made plans to assure that its city would not decay like the already overcrowded Lowell. Buildings on Essex Street had to be made of brick and stone, rising to a maximum of three stories. On residential Haverhill Street, limits were set—one house per lot, one family per dwelling. Along Canal and Methuen streets fronting the river, boardinghouse doors closed at 10:00 p.m. House supervisors reported to mill agents when boarders skipped Sunday services. The Pacific Mill could fire a worker for "lack of capacity and neatness," "unfaithfulness," "intemperance," even "profanity."[42]

Charmed as his life was, Abbott Lawrence did not live to see his dream darken. In 1854, he suffered a relapse of typhus fever just two months after Lawrence hosted its first riot. The melee had begun on a hot July day as anti-immigrant fever swept the nation. Sometime that afternoon an American flag was raised upside down above an Irishman's house. Outraged members of the nationwide Know-Nothing Party, whose credo demanded they answer "I know nothing" when asked about their secret anti-Irish, anti-Catholic society,[43] began parading in protest. Bystanders followed, picking up stones. Come nightfall, a crowd of two thousand had gathered in the Irish enclave on Common Street. Stones flew, and one newspaper reported shots fired. The house was badly damaged, but no one was hurt before the mob dispersed.[44]

There is no evidence that Abbott Lawrence heard of the riot. That fall, he was confined to his bed, where he lived until the following summer. His death brought a flood of tributes and a well-attended memorial in Boston's Faneuil Hall. Former Massachusetts governor Edward Everett eulogized Lawrence's founding father: "He heard in advance the voice of a hundred streams, now running to waste over barren rocks, but destined hereafter to be brought into accord with the music of the water-wheel and the power loom."[45] Abbott Lawrence bequeathed $150,000 to various public institutions, including the Boston Public Library and the Lawrence Scientific School he had founded at Harvard. He left another $50,000 to build lodging for the poor in Boston.[46] And he left behind a hot-tempered city, already home to eleven mills, each hungry for labor that would soon come in such numbers as to overwhelm his utopia.

The Irish had come first. Fleeing the Potato Famine in the late 1840s, nearly one million flocked to America. In Lawrence, where they helped build the dam and canals, they were soon known as "shanty Irish." The name was derived from the shacks made of rough lumber with stovepipe chimneys that rose by the hundreds in "New Dublin,"[47] the vacant land west of the Great Stone Dam. One such shanty was one hundred feet long and housed a single family and seventy-seven boarders.[48] On the heels of the Irish came the British. After the Civil War, textile workers from Manchester and Leeds heard of a cleaner mill city where they could earn a third more pay.[49] By 1868, British and Irish had turned Lawrence into the quintessential mill town, a reputation enhanced by a Winslow Homer illustration in *Harper's Weekly*. Entitled "Bell Time," Homer's engraving portrayed a flock of Lawrence workers, many haggard, others stoic and defiant, all carrying lunch pails as they headed home from their thirteen-hour day in the mills lining the river in the background.[50]

In the 1870s, it was the French Canadians' turn. Mechanization of dairy farming and widespread soil depletion[51] sent thousands south from Quebec to Lowell and Lawrence.[52] Next came the Germans. As their industry moved from Bavaria to the Ruhr Valley in the 1880s, German textile workers crossed the ocean and became American textile workers.[53] Arriving in Lawrence, each nation of immigrants settled into a frantically industrializing country glad to have their labor but suspicious of their foreign ways.

As if fulfilling the ancient Chinese curse "May you be born in interesting times," Lawrence had the mixed fortune to come of age during America's wildest economic roller-coaster ride—the Gilded Age. In the closing decades of the nineteenth century, America drove itself from a largely rural country into the world's leading industrial power.[54] Lawrence hustled to keep up with the giddy, greedy era. Through boom and bust, its mills pumped out fabric to clothe an increasingly fashion-conscious nation. In the 1870s and 1880s, the Merrimack was left to power itself as first steam and then electricity drove power wheels twice as tall as a man.[55] These in turn sped larger mills, enormous, inhuman beehives that awed arriving immigrants. In the frenzy of competition, new mill owners had no time for Abbott Lawrence's concern for "temperance and virtue." In place of paternalism came neglect. Mill men in Lawrence shared the attitude of their peer in Fall River who claimed, "I regard my work people just as I regard my machinery. So long as they can do my work for what I choose to pay them, I keep them, getting out of them all I can. What they do or how they fare outside my walls, I don't know, nor do I consider it my business to know."[56] Closer to home, one Lawrence mill owner was more direct. His workers, he said, were "a pack of fools."[57]

The fools, however, were restless. Throughout the Gilded Age, workers were organizing, forming fledgling unions such as the National Labor Union and the Knights of Labor. Prior to 1877, strikes were few and mostly peaceful, but Lawrence's mill owners regarded any hint of unions as a menace. The movement for a ten-hour day had come to the city before the Civil War, the unrest confined to small walkouts, quickly snuffed out. Then in 1867, under the slogan "Ten Hours and No Surrender," the city's first small strike occurred. Its leaders were summarily fired and striking women were both dismissed and evicted from company housing.[58] Throughout the

1870s, Lawrence was widely known as a model mill town with contented workers who, if they dared strike, were "promptly discharged"[59] and their names added to a blacklist circulated among New England mill owners.[60] In contrast to nearby Fall River, which suffered protracted strikes every few years, Lawrence did not see its first major walkout until 1882. "I believe the operatives would not strike if they were starving," the treasurer of the Pacific Mill blithely observed early that year.[61] Then in March, the Pacific slashed wages by 20 percent. A small contingent struck on March 14, and within three days, five thousand more had joined.[62] While other mills worked at full bore, the Pacific strike dragged on through the spring. Strike committees collected funds, including a dollar from each policeman, but as spring gave way to summer, the Pacific Mill survived on scab labor. Hungry and disillusioned, more than half the strikers left town and by August the strike was broken. The two union locals adopted a new policy— "arbitration to prevent strikes"[63]—and work in Lawrence went back to normal, that is, nonunion.

As American labor organized in its two-steps-forward-one-back fashion, other workers in Lawrence—barbers, masons, typographers, carpenters— formed their own locals.[64] Yet whenever the cry of "Union!" was raised in the mills, the steady influx of immigrants gave mill owners a convenient answer. If Germans talked of strike, bosses assured them that French Canadians would be happy to take their jobs. So would children, thousands of nine-, ten-, and eleven-year-olds working full days in the mills. Anyone who did not like mill work in Lawrence was welcome to seek employment elsewhere. Few did. Massachusetts was full of mill towns, and word among workers was that Lawrence was not as bad as some. Its wages were higher than in Holyoke or North Adams. Job conditions were much better than in Fall River, where housing and mill work resembled conditions in England's textile cities more than New England's.[65] As Angelo Rocco would learn along his winding path from job to job, Lawrence was not the worst the textile industry had to offer. Still, as even more immigrants came, the city strayed further from its founder's ideals.

Until 1890, Lawrence managed its rapid growth. Despite swelling to a population of forty-five thousand, it had a lower death rate and longer average life span than ever before. It was a self-important, bustling city visited by presidents, famous generals, and inventors[66] who duly acknowledged its

place in the forefront of American industry. But then just after William
Wood came to the Washington Mill,[67] the wave of immigrants crested and
a human tide began to drown "the music of the water-wheel and the power-
loom." Led by those notorious scabs, the Italians, fifteen thousand more immigrants came to Lawrence during the 1890s. They were followed, between
1900 and 1910, by another twenty thousand, whole families with children,
cousins, aunts, and uncles in tow pouring into the city and into the cavernous mills.[68] The old Essex Company rules—one house per lot, one family per dwelling—had long been ignored, but now they seemed a cruel joke.
Slums rose across the city's center in a maze of four-story wooden traps
with roofs as flat as the ground itself, as if God had stepped on these tenements to grind them deeper into the city's soil. Like mice in some clinical
experiment, children swarmed through the maze, fighting, playing, cursing
each other in their native tongues. Garbage and raw sewage filled alleys and
spilled into the canals, inspiring a sign in several languages.

WARNING!
Do not drink this canal water—it will make you sick.

AVIS!
Il est défendu de faire usage de l'eau du canal pour
boire—elle pourrait vous rendre malade.

OSTRZEŻENIE!
Nie pijaj wody z kanalu tego, bo zachorujesz.

ACAUTELEM-SE!
Nao bebam a agua do Canal. Fas-te doente.

ΠΡΟΣΟΧΗ
ΜΗ ΠΙΝΕΤΕ ΝΕΡΟ ΑΠΟ ΤΟ ΚΑΝΑΛΙ:
Θ' ΑΡΡ'ΩΣΤΗΣΕΤΕ.[69]

Long gone was any lingering notion of mills as bastions of "moral purity." Such a goal had been designed by New Englanders for New Englanders. It might be extended to early immigrants, but these newest foreigners seemed so . . . foreign. Instead of Ireland, England, Canada, and Germany, these people came from Italy, Russia, Lithuania, Turkey, Greece . . . The poet Emma Lazarus, in her famous inscription on the Statue of Liberty, called them "huddled masses yearning to breathe free."[70] *New England Magazine* called them "the off-scourings of Southern Europe" who "will not be assimilated [and] have no sympathy with our institutions."[71]

Regardless of nationality, each immigrant wave followed a strict settlement pattern, as the historian Donald Cole noted. A group's first decade in Lawrence was a struggle for survival. Each new ethnic group instantly became the city's bête noire, degraded by nicknames, denounced by politicians, spotlighted in newspaper crime stories. After a decade, however, each group began to coalesce, settle in, and chalk up small signs of permanence. The first sign was a church. With religion as its toehold, a group began to rise. The second ten years in the city saw each nationality open social clubs and stores with goods from back home. Soon came indigenous holidays. The Irish had St. Patrick's Day. The Germans celebrated the birthday of the poet Friedrich von Schiller. The Scots had Robert Burns's birthday, and the Poles celebrated the anniversary of the Polish Revolution.[72] Come the third decade in America, groups established their own native-language newspapers, debating societies, and a political presence. Individuals acquired property and the status it brought. By the 1880s, Lawrence's first immigrants were taking over city politics. In 1882, the Irish elected their first mayor, an undertaker named John Breen.[73] Soon they had taken hold of enough wards to wrest control of the city council. Boardroom battles between "Micks" and "anti-Micks" were fierce,[74] but not as bloody as turf wars among the teeming masses who had yet to rise.

Tension tightened on Saturday nights when recent paychecks were spent in the city's countless saloons, and Essex Street surged with sporadic violence. Once words flew, the confusion of tongues led to the universal language of fists and knives. Wedding receptions—where liquor and memories flowed freely—often broke into brawls,[75] as did Sunday picnics when turf overlapped. There seemed no end to the permutations of petty hatred. Irish fought English. English fought Irish. French Canadians slugged it out with Poles. Italians slashed at Armenians. . . . During the two decades prior to 1912, 6 percent of the city's population—several thousand per year—were arrested, most for drunkenness or assault.[76] And yet, for all its crime and tension, Lawrence had a rare cosmopolitan air found elsewhere only in Manhattan.

Those who didn't mind the risk could wander much of the world without ever leaving the city. Between the serpentine Spicket River to the north and the straight, smooth Merrimack on the south lay a human blanket of cultures. Most streets were polyglot mixtures, but a few stood out for their homogeneity. Along Common Street, the flavor was a savory Italian. Posters were in Italian. Conversation was mostly in Siciliano, the Sicilian dialect. Store windows, festooned with awnings, featured rows of hanging salamis, balls of cheese,[77] *formaggio di capra,* and *olio d'olivo.* During the annual Columbus Day celebration, Common Street burst forth with colored lanterns and the plaintive music of accordions and gourd-shaped mandolins. Elsewhere in smaller ghettos, other immigrants clung tightly to their cultures. Beginning in 1895, five thousand Jews fleeing pogroms in Russia and shtetls in eastern Europe settled along Valley, Concord, and Lowell streets, where mezuzahs decorated doorways.[78] There a good mensch could shop for lox and kippered herring, choose among synagogues, or just appreciate the joys of Yiddish. Nearby, two thousand Syrians, refugees from religious violence between Christians and Muslims,[79] were on the fast track to success. The Syrians already had their own newspaper and school, and several churches. On the east side of the city near Prospect Hill, the Germans lived in an enclave they called Hallsville. Like the city's other ethnic groups, Germans had created a culture to nurture them from cradle to grave. A German in Lawrence could be brought into the world by a German-speaking doctor or midwife,[80] go to school at Die Deutsche Schule, get the news from the *Anzeiger und Post,* sing in a German choir or opera company, belong to German *Vereine*—clubs devoted to sports, politics, or debate—get lederhosen from a dozen different German tailors, enjoy German cuisine at Boehm's Café, or buy sauerkraut from seventeen different German grocery stores. Lawrence also boasted four German jewelers, one dentist, three druggists, five cigar makers, two churches, and a brewery. And when his days were finished, the good German could spend his waning years in Deutsches Altenheim, the city's German home for seniors.[81]

Above this goulash of cultures, stirring it when it threatened to boil, were the "Americans," native born to native parents. By 1912, only twelve thousand remained in the city, yet their home-court advantage—language, wealth, connections—gave them control. Less than a fifth worked in the textile industry, most as bosses or front-office personnel.[82] Others were carpenters, masons, or shopgirls, but most were white-collar. The natives were bankers keeping track of mill owners' investments. They were the teachers wondering why "those children" stared into space during lessons and fought each other at the slightest provocation. They were the doctors who stitched up gashes from Saturday-night fights or diagnosed another case of TB in the tenements. Among them were about 260 blacks. None need bother applying for mill work. Those who didn't get jobs as kitchen help or bellboys toiled as household servants, working for a dollar a day[83] in the fine homes of mill owners and executives. But to reach these fine homes, the hired help had to take trolleys out of town, for the mill owners themselves were nowhere to be found in Lawrence. Beginning in the 1890s, they had fled to mansions in nearby Andover or along the ivied boulevards of Boston's Back Bay. On the eve of the strike, not a single mill owner or textile stockholder[84] lived in the city.

By 1912, Lawrence was no puritanical politician's dream; it was a powder keg, an explosive mix of eighty-six thousand people tamped into just seven square miles. The combustible material included groups with deepening roots in America and newcomers still harboring hopes of returning to the Old World. There were women and children who knew little about the mills other than what husbands and fathers told them. And there were women and children whose daily grind gave them a visceral understanding of economics and power. There were men who believed in anarchy, but only a few. More common were men who believed in law and order and were willing to subvert the former to protect the latter. Together these factions formed "Immigrant City," a proud populace of workers toiling for indecent wages, hoping their children would someday earn decent wages, perhaps even salaries. Until January 12, 1912, these factions were as distinct as the colors on a flag. For the rest of that year, they would be as intermingled as the colors on the same flag in a rippling wind. And together these colors would turn the Merrimack, which had so peacefully borne Thoreau along its banks, into an American battleground.

CHAPTER THREE

The Battle of the Merrimack

Ring, clanging bells of Lawrence!
Send echoes o'er the land!
Shine out, fair lights of Lawrence!
To cheer each toiling band . . .

Above our hum of traffic,
Above our triumph song,
Hear the plain and stern inquiry
Are we doing right or wrong?
As a free, united people, come
This primal truth to know,
Communities, like every man,
Must reap the crops they sow.

—From "A City of Today," written for Lawrence's fiftieth
anniversary by former mayor Robert H. Tewksbury

J ust after 10:00 a.m. on January 12, police responded to the riot call—
three quick gongs repeated three times every thirty seconds.[1] The clanging
resounded through Lawrence, turning heads, bringing teachers to class-
room windows and merchants to sidewalks to see what the trouble might
be. Pouring into the mill district, policemen found that the mob had already fled the Wood Mill. Inside they found rooms empty, battered, with
full spindles and warps drenched by the building's own sprinklers. Outside
on Merrimack Street, which ran for blocks alongside the mill, thousands of

displaced workers stood in clusters, wondering what had happened. The mob had moved on.

A dozen police headed up the street toward the Ayer Mill, arriving just as thousands more workers, fleeing the anarchy on shop floors, spilled through the gates. The surge of bodies turned the plaza between the Wood and Ayer mills into an echo chamber. Bellicose cheers, jeers, and taunts rumbled off walls and porticoes as workers waved small American flags and brandished brooms and sticks. Fights were breaking out everywhere. Police nightsticks cracked skulls. Picker sticks lashed out like baseball bats. The crowd was still swarming through the plaza when more police arrived on the fringes. To gain some semblance of order, Assistant Marshal Samuel Logan decided to herd strikers back across the Duck Bridge toward downtown. Logan ordered his men to show their revolvers and begin shoving.[2] The crowd, which consisted of a hard knot of fighters and a large periphery of onlookers, moved with little resistance. Beneath wispy clouds of breath, a mottled morass of coats crossed the bridge without incident until reaching the small Duck Mill on the North Canal. There the real battle began.

With a new target before it, the crowd refused to be herded any farther. Commanding Union Street, workers began shoving police. Mill windows soon filled with faces gazing down at the horde blocking the intersection of Union and Canal streets, backing up trolleys, carriages, and a few automobiles, their horns honking. From below, strikers taunted onlookers. "Come out! Come out!" Only one man and woman did, receiving a zealous cheer.[3] Then, massed in front of the mill, the mob prepared to storm it. A dozen police with raised clubs stood with their backs to the gate. In the thick of the crowd, one man climbed onto another's shoulders. From his perch above bobbing caps and derbies, he shouted in Italian while another did the same in Polish.[4] The police, with surnames such as Donahue, O'Sullivan, and McCarthy,[5] assumed the men were telling the crowd to disperse,[6] but seconds later, the mob rushed. The police began swinging.[7] When a few pulled revolvers and threatened to shoot the next man who approached, the crowd drew back, daring and taunting. Men grappled with police while women screamed and waved their arms, goading husbands, sons, and brothers to attack.[8] On the edge of the brawl, more police arrived in trolleys, on foot, or climbing out of bulky black squad cars.[9] Just then, a lone man rushed the Duck Mill gate. Hands reached to boost him, others to drag him down, but the man scaled the grillwork and landed on the other side. This seemed to signal the crowd for another rush. Again police defended the mill, knocking men to the street, where they lay writhing or deathly still.

Sensing it could not break into the Duck Mill, the crowd attacked its facade. Through the drifting snow, a fusillade of rocks and ice smashed windows, raining broken glass down on the street.[10] Within minutes, nearly every window along Union Street was broken.[11] Still more police arrived, massing behind the mob to drive hundreds away from the building. Then, as quickly as it had begun, the battle was over. It had lasted only a few minutes,[12] but it would haunt the city for years.

Freed from the confines of bridges and brick chasms, the crowd dispersed. Many turned onto Essex Street and disappeared into downtown. Most went home to nurse wounds, share stories, and worry about what might happen next. Downtown, klatches of men and women remained on the street, talking and gesturing wildly. Police bloodied by flying shards of ice and glass ministered to each other and rounded up the seven—six men and one woman—under arrest. The men, all Italians, were charged with inciting a riot, the woman with assaulting an officer with a knife.[13] By noon, an uneasy calm prevailed in the mill district, but a high-voltage intensity gripped the rest of the city.

William Wood got the news at American Woolen's office in Boston's Shawmut Bank Building. Stunned, he did what any Alger hero would do—he remained upbeat. In a statement to the press, he claimed his fellow workers had misunderstood his good intentions.

> The manufacturers are the friends of the employees, and greatly regret that the reductions in hours of work, which the new law has forced, compels their taking home just that much less money. There has been no reduction in the rate of wages but it cannot be expected that people who work fifty-four hours should take home the wages equivalent to fifty-six hours of work. When one considers that there are mills in the country running from fifty-six to above sixty hours selling their merchandise in the same market, one can see how impossible it is for the Massachusetts manufacturers to compete against such odds.

Once his fellow workers understood that the legislature was to blame, Wood predicted, they would see the strike as "hasty and ill-advised. There is no cause for striking and when the employees find that justice is not on their side, the strike cannot possibly be long lived. I look for an early resumption of work."[14]

By 2:00 p.m., when five hundred workers at the Pacific Mill opened their checks and peacefully walked out,[15] nearly eleven thousand[16] were on strike or locked out of the Wood and Ayer mills. Thousands more continued to work in every other mill, but while they soldiered on, the morning's frenzy spread through the city. That afternoon, aldermen met in emergency session with Mayor Michael Scanlon, a dapper man with wire-rimmed glasses[17] who had been on the job just twelve days. The first topic on the agenda: preserving order. Mill agents urged that the state militia guard the mills,[18] but the mayor decided against it. Militias had brought bloodshed to strikes elsewhere, Scanlon said, and a city on the verge of bankruptcy could scarcely afford to pay the state for use of its soldiers. The mayor also opted not to close the city's saloons.[19] With order restored, neither measure seemed necessary. Meanwhile, police spread from mill to mill to defend the hulking buildings against further attacks. And throughout the tenements, the morning's battles were recounted, the next moves planned.

Scattering through their own enclaves, many nationalities handed out circulars. One, issued by the Italian branch of the IWW, took credit for launching the strike. "The Italian strikers have prominently shown on this occasion that they are not unworthy of the great Mother Country," the circular boasted. The strike would "impress the blood-sucking capitalists that there is a limit to their insolence and blood-letting." The circular cautioned against renewed violence and vandalism, which "might result in detriment to the strikers and in favor of the employers who have on their side money and the powerful backing of the constituted authorities."[20] Other flyers announced mass meetings, and Mayor Scanlon made plans to attend as many as possible to calm the workers. As the sun set and kerosene lamps lit tenement windows, those who had stayed on the job streamed home and a small evening shift headed to work. No one met them to turn them back. When darkness fell, a single searchlight beam swept the length of the North Canal,[21] its circular spot illuminating a light, fluffy snow falling before the black facades of the besieged mills. The searchlight helped police, patrolling in temperatures that fell to six below zero,[22] spot anyone with a lingering rage to vent. It was a long and lonely vigil. Throughout the night, the only sound was the mournful bell of the Ayer clock tower tolling to announce the nightly curfew.[23] No suspicious activity was reported.

Lawrence had been the scene of previous strikes, but none had begun with rock-throwing mobs. "The City That Weaves the World's Worsteds" had never seen anything like the chaos of that morning. Lawrence did not regard itself as a hotbed of radicalism, and the evening papers were already reassuring readers that the rioters were not longtime residents, not even Americans. "The trouble was started by a crowd of about 500 foreign operatives," the *Lawrence Telegram* wrote.[24] The *Boston Globe* added: "The textile operatives in many of the mills number a larger percentage of foreigners— Italians, Syrians, Poles, Portuguese and Armenians—than of any English-speaking race. Having been encouraged to come to Lawrence, these classes of men and women now overrun the place." Such workers, the *Globe* concluded, "are ignorant and easily deceived and more readily excited."[25] (The newspapers were correct in noting that recent immigrants were most prominent in the strike but wrong in blaming ignorance or innate volatility. Mill pay scales broken down by nationality reveal the most active strikers— Italians, Syrians, Armenians, Lithuanians, Poles, and Russians—to be the lowest-paid workers.)[26] Reassured that the strike had been led by just a few "troublemakers," city officials tried to remain calm. Even if a few dozen or a few hundred immigrants had no respect for the law, they told themselves, the majority did. Order would prevail. That was how things were done in Lawrence, "A City of Today."

Nine years had passed since the city founded by the Essex Company had celebrated the fiftieth anniversary of its incorporation. Those nine years had seen a nationwide surge of patriotism and civic pride. During the opening decade of the twentieth century, red, white, and blue flew throughout parades, picnics, and that newest of American institutions, the World Series. America's Great White Fleet circumnavigated the globe, serving notice that the United States, having extended its influence from Puerto Rico to Panama to the Philippines, was now a world power. Capturing the spirit, Lawrence was as proud as any city in the nation. The city celebrated its golden anniversary in 1903 in a photo album entitled *Views of Lawrence*. The album gave no hint that at the city's core sat one square mile crammed with some of the nation's bleakest tenements. The album showed no slums at all and pictured the mills only in sweeping panorama. Instead, *Views of Lawrence* portrayed a thriving city adorned with stately architecture. The tour began upriver at the Lawrence Canoe Club with its octagonal cupola, expansive docks, and crew teams on the Merrimack. Moving downtown, a viewer found the Lawrence Public Library equally impressive, like some medieval manor with soaring arches and turrets. The Essex County Courthouse featured a lofty spire whose ornate adornments were outdone only by city hall, where a 165-foot tower was graced by a hand-carved wooden eagle and two cannonballs said to have been fired at Fort Sumter to start the Civil War.[27] The state armory, where the local militia was quartered when needed, resembled an Arthurian castle. Even the county jail was striking, with vaulted windows more reminiscent of a cathedral than a lockup. Scattered throughout the city were steep church spires, Gothic windows, and other trappings of European heritage. Finally, on both Prospect and Tower hills sat dozens of posh Victorian homes, their gables touting affluence and tradition.[28]

During the dangerous months to come, Lawrence would earn a nationwide reputation as a radical, lawless city. Its residents would be accused of fomenting a workers' revolution. Yet on January 12, 1912, there was no more patriotic city in America than Lawrence, Massachusetts. Textbooks in city schools proclaimed Lawrence an "ardently American city." The school committee urged teachers to foster "genuine patriotism" and teach the "superiority of our institutions."[29] The city's newspapers promoted hard work, honesty, and "Americanism," while the local foreign-language press urged readers to become naturalized citizens, vote, and support what the Syrian newspaper called America's "magnificent constitution."[30]

Not everyone in Lawrence read the newspaper, however. Almost a quarter of the city's immigrants could not read at all.[31] For them, civic pride was written in the flag-waving parades that seemed to march weekly along Essex Street. When not on the march, flags flew from lodges, auxiliaries, and meeting halls. Citizens of Lawrence also displayed their loyalty at the polls. From 1900 until World War I, American voters supported the

Progressivism of the age. So, too, did the people of Lawrence. They backed President Roosevelt when he spoke of busting trusts. The city's more progressive voters also supported such newfangled ideas, not yet become law, as a federal income tax, direct election of senators, even women's suffrage. But only a small percentage went so far as to vote for a Socialist candidate. In November 1912, Socialist Eugene Debs would draw more than 900,000 votes for president, 6 percent of the electorate. Only 520 of those votes would come from Lawrence,[32] whose voters narrowly favored Democrat Woodrow Wilson.

As the new mayor of this proud and patriotic city, Michael Scanlon knew he had not been elected to allow mob rule. And on the morning after the strike began, William Wood was not the only one up before sunrise. On Saturday at 4:30 a.m., Scanlon and his aldermen met at city hall. By 6:00 a.m., the mayor had deputized twenty firemen as police officers and sent them, in their firefighting uniforms, to reinforce policemen protecting the mills.[33] Then, as if nothing unusual had happened the day before, another Saturday began. Morning whistles went off on schedule. Thousands rose and went to work, filing past police and through the mill gates. Every mill was up and running. Estimates of the number of strikers on this second day ranged from four thousand[34] to twelve thousand,[35] but heedless of the absentees, Saturday-morning mill work passed without incident. Under heavy police guard, paymasters handed out checks that had not been distributed the day before. Each pay slip reflected two hours' less work, but no one shouted "short pay." No one walked out. Mill agents reported calm and predicted that all workers would return on Monday.[36] The mood of the city, however, was edgier than many suspected.

Sometime that morning, a woman at the Wood Mill was found with a hatchet under her shawl. Another man carried a long knife. Both said they needed weapons to protect themselves from strikers.[37] At 9:00 a.m., a crowd of six hundred gathered at city hall. The civic auditorium that usually hosted school conventions, dog shows, and church services[38] resounded with angry speeches supporting the walkout. Whenever the American Woolen Company or "Billy Wood" was mentioned, the crowd booed and hissed.[39] That morning, Angelo Rocco led a picket line that circled the mill district. Arriving at the Prospect Mill, he met a group of Italians planning to break in to free a striker held inside. The crowd had already slashed a police car's tires,[40] and Rocco saw that if it tried to storm the mill, "somebody is going to be killed." So he took the situation in hand. Approaching the captain on duty, Rocco asked to go inside and see what was going on. "So the captain let me inside so I saw the guy inside and I came out, and I told the crowd, 'The boy has gone to the police station. He's not here now, he's gone. Let's go along.' From there we went to the Uswoco Mill on Broadway. We just passed by down there and disbanded."[41]

Following the noon whistle, streams of workers headed home. Only one scuffle broke out—at the Everett Mill. The combatants were all women—workers and strikers—pulling hair and tearing at dresses. But even before the incident, company officials, preferring a lockout to a strike, had voted to close the mill "in view of the fact that most of the women employed in the Everett mills are foreigners, and are in fear of their lives among strikers of their own nationalities."[42] Saturday's skirmishes meant little, however, compared to the moment, shortly after 2:00 p.m., when a short, pudgy man in a blue suit, his black hair curling above his smiling face, stepped to the podium at city hall and began addressing strikers. With all mills now closed for the weekend, more than fifteen hundred were crowded into city hall. The first speaker, Mayor Scanlon, had called for self-restraint. "I hope we have seen the last of the unpleasant scenes of yesterday," the mayor had said. "Let it be the end. . . . This is a law-abiding country and we are all subservient to the law." The city council, Scanlon told the crowd, had formed a negotiating committee that was ready to meet with both strikers and mill owners.[43] "I beg of you not to listen to those who have appeared among you preaching a certain doctrine and urging you to continued struggle and fighting."[44] The mayor had been followed by a Boston judge translating Scanlon's speech into Italian, and then by the man representing the "certain doctrine" the mayor feared.

On the afternoon before the strike, Joseph Ettor had been in the IWW's Manhattan office on East Twelfth Street when a telegram arrived for him.[45] The telegram read: "Strike on in Lawrence. STOP Your presence required there. STOP."[46] The telegram was signed by Angelo Rocco. Rocco knew the reputation of the IWW. He knew the Wobblies' talk of revolution would not sit well in Lawrence. He sent for Ettor anyway. "The Industrial Workers was a radical organization," he remembered. "For my part, I didn't care what they were. I was looking for the organizer of the strike."[47]

That evening, Ettor took the telegram to Manhattan's Cooper Union Hall, the same hall where, in 1860, Abraham Lincoln had given a stirring speech that made him a presidential prospect.[48] Cooper Union was hosting a debate on "Socialism and the Industrial Workers of the World," featuring William "Big Bill" Haywood of the IWW and Morris Hillquit, cofounder of the Socialist Party of America. Arriving at the cloistered old hall, Ettor met several friends, including an Italian poet named Arturo Giovannitti and twenty-one-year-old Elizabeth Gurley Flynn,[49] who had been rallying workers to Socialism since she was fifteen.[50] Ettor and his friends listened as Haywood drew a pithy distinction between his brawny union and the effete Socialists. "The industrial union is Socialism with its working clothes on," Haywood told the crowd.[51] When the debate was over, Ettor showed Haywood his telegram. Ettor was reluctant to go to Lawrence, but Haywood convinced him, saying he would come later if more help was needed.[52] After staying up all Thursday night editing a manuscript, Ettor took the train to Lawrence on Friday,[53] arriving as the searchlight began to sweep the mills. Carrying his suitcase full of IWW literature, membership cards, buttons,[54] and a gavel he had used during previous strikes,[55] he booked a room at the Needham Hotel on Essex Street a half block from the Boston & Maine railroad depot.[56] On Saturday morning, he attended the strikers' meeting at city hall but said he was not ready to speak.[57] Then that afternoon, he rose before the gathering and went to work. Depending on the politics of the listener, the strike had found its Caesar, its Gandhi, or its Robespierre.

Stepping to the podium, Ettor received a thunderous ovation. He was twenty-six, but from the front rows, he looked like a baby-faced boy. His nickname—"Smiling Joe"—was not ironic. Whether he was addressing an audience, posing for photos, or intensely involved in planning a strike's next move, a joyous smile was usually spread across his face. "When he talked he glowed like a beacon light," one journalist remembered.[58] As Ettor began, the crowd settled in, swayed by the self-assurance usually reserved for much older speakers. He spoke to this ragged, weary crowd of workers as no one ever had before—as if they mattered. He told them that they were the most important people in the mills. Their labor built the mills. Their hands crafted the cloth. Their toil made millions for men like Billy Wood. And therefore, the mills of Lawrence and all factories, mines, and other industries rightly belonged to them, the workers of the world. Ettor's claim must have caused some bewilderment among the crowd. Few had ever heard such talk; few had dared to think they might be worth more than a paycheck plus the small raise they were always hoping for. Few even wanted to own the mills; they just wanted more pay. But here was this plump, smiling man telling them that workers like them would soon own the earth. It was a heady message, and its messenger tempered it with jokes, anecdotes, and cautions. "If there is blood to be shed, it is up to the strikers to decide whether it shall be the blood of the working class or of your employers," Ettor advised. Then he singled out the enemy at the gates.

Just after forming the American Woolen Company, Ettor said, Billy Wood had offered fellow capitalists a solution to the "labor problem." "Gentlemen, take a dollar and place it on a shelf," Wood had told a banquet. "Look upon that shelf at the end of six months and you will find it is still there. But take the working man or woman and place them on a shelf for six months and you will find a skeleton, will you not?" Waiting for the hisses to die out, Ettor continued. "Wood endorses that method of starving you into submission. The argument advanced for the cut in wages is that you will do less work. He knows that is not the case. The reduction of wages in New England a few years ago was claimed to be due to the Panic of 1907. Still we find there was never a day when the industries paid greater dividends than in 1907." His voice rising to a crescendo, Ettor concluded, "Fifty cents buys ten loaves of bread. Every one of you has that much invested in this struggle. It is a question as to whether you will get more or less bread."[59]

Ettor impressed one reporter as having "all the tricks and trite sayings of the street corner agitator."[60] The observation was couched in a sneer, but to Ettor, street-corner agitation was both a career and a calling. Before coming to Lawrence, he had traveled the hard roads of itinerant workers, speaking in lumber camps, outside steel mills, wherever labor needed him to simplify complex issues and unify warring factions. Details of Ettor's life prior to 1912 are sketchy. He was born in Brooklyn, but his family soon settled in Chicago. In 1886, his father was injured during the notorious Haymarket incident.[61] On May 4, a bomb thrown during a rally for an eight-hour day killed six policemen in Chicago's Haymarket Square. Other police opened fire, mowing down an unknown number of workers and wound-

ing hundreds more.[62] Though the incident occurred when Ettor was just a
year old, he knew its details as well as he knew his heritage. Ettor's father, a
militant Italian immigrant, had often regaled him with the story, perhaps
even showing him a scar. "The old man was proud to be a striker in those
stirring times," Ettor recalled.[63] While other children grew up on *Alice in
Wonderland* or *Little Lord Fauntleroy,* Ettor's father told his son bedtime
tales from the triumvirate of infamous American strikes in the late nineteenth century—Haymarket, Homestead, and Pullman. At his father's knee,
he learned the names of the four Haymarket martyrs hanged for the crime
of throwing the bomb despite lack of evidence. He thrilled to stories of
Homestead where, in 1892, strikers had waged an all-day gun battle with
Pinkerton detectives in the Carnegie steel town of Homestead, Pennsylvania. Before he was ten, Ettor could recite minute details about the 1894
Pullman Strike, in which a nationwide railroad walkout was snuffed out by
federal troops and militia. With such stories as his inspiration, Ettor har-
bored few illusions about the country where he came of age. His boyhood
convictions were confirmed at the age of nine when his mother died[64] and
he left grade school to work. He toiled as a cooper,[65] a railroad water boy, a
shipbuilder's assistant, and later in foundries and lumber mills.

Ettor's linguistic talents finally freed him from menial work. Speaking
fluent English, Italian, and Polish, conversant in Yiddish and Hungarian,[66]
he took to the road as a labor organizer for the IWW. He traveled throughout the West, speaking on soapboxes, forging dedicated strikers out of a
hardscrabble mass of immigrants, hoboes, and migrant labor. He was often driven from labor camps at gunpoint.[67] In 1909, he came east to run a
steelworkers' strike in McKees Rocks, Pennsylvania. Thirteen people were
killed and five hundred injured,[68] but the IWW won the strike[69] and Ettor
stayed in the Pittsburgh area, organizing Poles, Germans, Czechs, Croats,
and other nationalities. His work done, he moved on to organize shoemakers in Brooklyn and made the city his base. The previous summer,
while managing a small textile strike in New Bedford, Massachusetts,[70] he
had visited Lawrence. Staying in the home of Angelo Rocco,[71] Ettor had
studied conditions in the mills but seeing no incipient uprising, he had
departed.

Wherever he spoke, Ettor was accused of inciting violence, and violence occurred in nearly every strike he ran. But his father's stories ce-

mented his belief that violence was labor's worst enemy. Regardless of whether it was caused by strikers, police, or detectives hired to make trouble, bloodshed cost labor any support it might have among press and public. The only force Ettor advocated was passive resistance. "As long as the workers keep their hands in their pockets," he often told strikers, "the capitalists cannot put theirs there. With passive resistance, with the workers absolutely refusing to move, laying absolutely silent, they are more powerful than all the weapons and instruments that the other side has for protection and attack."[72] Though nonviolent, such rhetoric was as sharp and fixed as a bayonet, and it sent chills through the capitalists at whom it was aimed. But it was not Ettor's eloquence that frightened Mayor Scanlon. It was the gang he represented.

On paper, the Industrial Workers of the World was a union, but on skid-row street corners, in seedy meeting halls, and all along the rails where hoboes carried its red membership card, the IWW was an article of faith. Seen through the long lens of history, the Wobblies are often romanticized. They resemble some lovable, cantankerous Grandpa, the kind that sits on the back porch nurturing his memories and ranting about politics when anyone sits beside him. But during its heyday, from 1905 to 1917, the IWW was the most feared organization in America. Its numbers were always smaller than its opponents or Wobblies themselves claimed. Dues-paying membership nationwide was less than fifteen thousand when the Lawrence strike began[73] and never topped one hundred thousand.[74] But thousands more drifted in and out of the union, depending on whether they had jobs worth fighting for. These members were fiercely devoted, idealistic, relentless, often noble, occasionally violent, and always in the news. They seemed to show up wherever labor unrest began to smolder. Best known for their strikes in western mines, Wobblies also organized in Maine textile towns and Louisiana lumber camps, in the silk mills of New Jersey and on the bountiful farms of California.[75] Judged by their actions, which ranged from the first sit-down strike to civil disobedience campaigns for free speech, Wobblies now seem relatively harmless. But the powers that would ultimately crush the IWW did not judge the union by its deeds. They did not notice when organizers like Joseph Ettor molded angry mobs into singing crowds or when Wobblies compromised their credo to settle for less than revolution. "The final aim . . . is revolution," one member said.

"But for the present, let's see if we can get a bed to sleep in, water enough to take a bath, and decent food to eat."[76]

Instead, their opponents took the Wobblies at their word. And one didn't have to dig deeply through IWW speeches, songs, and journals to find words chosen to awaken workers and alarm their bosses. The Wobblies' gift for incendiary phraseology began at their founding convention. On June 27, 1905, in a smoky auditorium on Chicago's north side,[77] Big Bill Haywood stepped to a podium, grabbed a loose board to pound as a gavel,[78] and called for order. "Fellow workers!" Haywood boomed. "This is the Continental Congress of the Working Class. We are here to confederate the workers of this country into a working class movement that shall have for its purpose the emancipation of the working class from the slave bondage of capitalism."[79] The convention's two hundred delegates included such leading lights of labor as Eugene Debs and the grandmotherly Mary "Mother" Jones, whose fierce advocacy during miners' strikes had earned her a reputation as "the most dangerous woman in America."[80] The delegates spent twelve days devising a platform, bickering about the fine points of Socialism, and hammering out a constitution. The preamble to the IWW constitution did not begin "We, the people." Instead it stated:

> The working class and the employing class have nothing in common. There can be no peace so long as hunger and want are found among the millions of working people and the few, who make up the employing class, have all the good things in life. Between these two classes a struggle must go on until all the toilers come together on the political, as well as on the industrial field, and take and hold that which they produce by their labor.[81]

Within a year of throwing down this gauntlet, the IWW was under attack from all sides. Idealistic young organizers like Ettor were in the thick of bruising strikes. Haywood was on trial in Idaho for conspiracy to murder former governor Frank Steunenberg.[82] Harassed and hounded, the IWW was also tearing itself to pieces in endless arguments over ideology and tactics. Yet during that embattled first year, 384 IWW locals had been organized from Schenectady to Chicago to Spokane.[83] Joining the IWW was easy. Monthly dues were fifty cents, sometimes cut to a quarter. Any twenty workers signing a charter and scrounging ten dollars could start their own local, joining a union with its own journals and jargon. To the card-carrying Wobbly, a bedroll was a "bindle." A "fink" was a strikebreaker or an informer. An "idiot stick" was a shovel, all a "stiff" could expect to wield if he had dropped out of the "knowledge box," or school. A "scissor-bill" was an unenlightened worker, some "bushwa" (bourgeois) who still believed in "Pie in the Sky," i.e., capitalist promises of a better life ahead. Cops were "bulls," detectives "dicks," and the police station where they took a "Wob" who got "sloughed" was the "can." Hovering in the future was "O.B.U.," slang for the dream of "One Big Union" that would lead to the "Cooperative Commonwealth," a society of equality and justice where everything was just "jake" (fine).[84]

To understand the IWW's allure, one must consider how the West was really won. At the turn of the twentieth century, much of the West was be- ing built on the fly. Raw industries demanded muscle, but most were sea- sonal. Miners, loggers, and fruit pickers had no year-round jobs, no workmen's compensation, no unemployment insurance, no permanent homes. Many had no families, at least none they were eager to claim. (Wobbly slang for a wife was a "ball and chain.")[85] So they roamed through a West far wilder than the one that later made it into the movies, marked by explosive tension between Capital and Labor. Capital hired detectives to "investigate" and stir up trouble.[86] Labor hired saboteurs. Capital was backed by cops and militia who herded strikers into "bull pens," outdoor cages where men were kept for weeks, rotting, starving, dying.[87] Labor was backed solely by its numbers—tens of thousands who worked their hides off for months, then had nothing to do for a full season or, if times were hard, a full year. It was a West where a common crime on police logs was vagrancy—just hanging around. It was a tough, merciless West no more forgiving than a rattlesnake, with muddy streets and clapboard houses, ri- fle butts and dynamite, and the Wobblies were its union. Cutthroat western industrialists and radical Wobblies deserved each other. Both were spoil- ing for a fight.

The Wobblies filled a need that had gone begging for decades. The West's migrant laborers had no other union. Back in the late nineteenth century, the Knights of Labor might have let them in, but that pioneering union had disappeared shortly after the Haymarket bombing.[88] In its place rose Samuel Gompers's American Federation of Labor, which by 1912 had nearly two million members, organized trade by trade.[89] The AF of L had no use for unskilled laborers. It eschewed strikes, courted management's favor, and fought the Wobblies at every turn. The Wobblies, Gompers said, were "schemers" and "enemies of our movement."[90] Conservative and discriminatory, the AF of L's "pure and simple unionism" was too pure and simple to organize women, blacks, or immigrants. By contrast, the IWW was happy to have anyone who labored and dreamt of laboring less. "We are going down in the gutter to get at the mass of the workers and bring them up to a decent living," Haywood boasted.[91] The Wobblies' motto, adapted from an old Knights of Labor slogan, stated, "An injury to one is an injury to all."[92] "The I.W.W.," one of the organization's leaflets added, "is not a white man's union, not a black man's union, not a red man's union, but a working man's union."[93] And so, from its tumultuous beginning, the IWW's ranks grew by fits and starts while its reputation spread among hoboes and scissorbills alike.

To down-and-out workers with nicknames like "T'Bone Slim"[94] and "Haywire Mac,"[95] the Wobblies were as inspiring as any church. And in contrast to Communism, the IWW was quite comfortable with religion. Its journals evoked Christ as the "hobo Carpenter from Nazareth" and "Jerusalem Slim," who in the modern world "would be a member of the Building Constructors' Industrial Union."[96] But the IWW also served as its own diocese with its own martyrs, liturgy, and creed. The road to Wobbly heaven was paved by the general strike. According to the eschatology, once all workers had joined "One Big Union," they merely had to stop working. All at once. All over a city, a country, the world. Haywood wrote that the general strike would bring a day when "control of industry will pass from the capitalists to the masses and the capitalists will vanish from the face of the earth."[97] Precisely where all those vanishing capitalists would go was never explained, nor did Wobblies say much about how their "Cooperative Commonwealth" would be run. "There will be nonpolitical government," Haywood hinted. "There will be no States, and Congress will not be composed of lawyers and preachers as it is now, but will be composed of experts of the different branches of industry, who will come together for the purpose of discussing the welfare of all the people."[98]

The Wobblies' philosophy sounds something like Communism, which, with the Bolshevik Revolution still several years away, remained an untried theory. The IWW also contained trace elements of anarchism, the idealized government-free society based on voluntary altruism and absolute individual freedom. But technically the Wobblies were Syndicalists. A dream then inspiring massive strikes in France and England, Syndicalism promoted a utopian society in which trade unions would run industry and all other sectors would miraculously take care of themselves. Few Wobblies cared for "isms," however. As one worker noted, it was not philosophers or theorists "who count the most—it is the obscure Bill Jones on the firing line, with stink in his clothes, rebellion in his brain, hope in his heart, determination in his eye and direct action in his gnarled fist."[99] To Bill Jones and other weary workers, the IWW's gospel sounded like an archangel's trumpet. To the capitalists who would be asked to hand over all their capital and kindly vanish, it was tantamount to treason. And wherever the Wobblies went, their credo was waved in the press like a bloody shirt.

"Violence is the only stock in trade of the I.W.W.," reported the *Duluth News Tribune*. In Goldfield, Nevada, where the Wobblies led a miners' strike, the *Goldfield Gossip* suggested all Wobblies be "hanged . . . to telegraph poles."[100] Editorial cartoons featured IWW speakers with dynamite in one pocket and a bomb in one hand preaching to a crowd from a soapbox labeled "Sabotage!"[101] The initials IWW were said to stand for "I Want Whiskey," "Irresponsible Wholesale Wreckers," and, most often, "I Won't Work."[102] IWW journals defended the faith, but the Wobblies' own words tarred and feathered them. Haywood, who had seen the law twisted and stretched to incarcerate him and his fellow workers, proclaimed, "I despise the law. I am not a law-abiding citizen. And more than that, no Socialist *can* be a law-abiding citizen." The press was also happy to quote employers enraged by IWW strikes. To such men, the Wobblies were "subversive radicals"[103] and the strikers who followed them mere "tools . . . of anarchistic and socialist agitators from other states."[104]

In reality, the Wobblies never advocated murder or violence, but neither were they especially Gandhian by nature. Hard-bitten workingmen, they exploded at the slightest crackdown during a strike, leading to headline violence wherever the IWW banner was raised. And Wobblies did seem fascinated with sabotage. The international symbols of sabotage—a black cat and a wooden shoe called a *sabot*[105]—turned up frequently in their songs and cartoons. Wobblies explained that theirs was a broader version of sabotage, even encompassing nonviolent strikes, but the distinction was lost on potential targets. So when Joseph Ettor stepped to the podium on January 13, anyone in Lawrence who had followed the labor issue saw him as the avatar of a radical, violent union that had sown seeds of chaos out west and had now come east to use their patriotic city as a Bastille for launching a revolution. Ettor's closing statements that afternoon did not change their minds. As Mayor Scanlon listened onstage, his eyebrows must have risen above his glasses.

"Monday morning you have got to close the mills that you have caused to shut down, tighter than you have them now," Ettor told the city hall gathering. He cautioned strongly against any more violence, noting that "all the blood that is spilled in a strike is your blood. . . . It is up to you to encourage all to stand by the cause of the workers and get them not to go to work Monday morning. If you want to avoid bloodshed, remove the cause. You cannot win by fighting with your fists against men armed, or the militia, but you have a weapon they have not got. You have the weapon of labor and with that you can beat them down if you stick together!"[106] Ettor repeated his speech in Italian and was followed by others addressing the crowd in French, Polish, and Lithuanian.[107] Then, he formed a strike committee of fifty-six people, four from each of fourteen nationalities.[108] (Angelo Rocco, having decided not to attend classes while the strike continued, was among the Italian contingent.)[109] Conspicuous in their absence were the Irish, English, French Canadians, and Germans, who, with a few exceptions, had not backed the strike.[110] The committee would meet on Sunday morning, Ettor announced. Workers then filed out into the cold.

Sunday was as calm as any other Sunday in Lawrence, except behind closed doors. From pulpits throughout the city, ministers and priests prayed for law and order.[111] The city's most influential priest was not in town, however. The night before the strike began, Father James T. O'Reilly, spiritual leader to most of the city's thirty thousand Catholics,[112] had left on a Florida vacation given him for his twenty-five years of service.[113] While Lawrence erupted, its spiritual leader was basking in Palm Beach[114] and in no hurry to return to the cold. A less powerful priest, Father Mariano Milanese of the Holy Rosary Catholic Church, announced that he would visit the mills on Monday morning to help mediate any disputes.[115]

While churches held services, the strike committee met as planned at Franco-Belgian Hall on Mason Street, a block from the Merrimack. From then on, the hall, an old two-story wooden beam structure, would be the strike's headquarters. That Sunday, the newly formed committee named Ettor as its chairman and appointed subcommittees to deal with finance, publicity, investigation, organization, and relief efforts. Each member also named an alternate in case of illness or arrest.[116] Later that afternoon, three men with their heads bandaged from Friday's melee spoke to a gathering of Italians, and many other nationalities held separate meetings, some with plainclothes police in the audience.[117] Ettor issued a press statement noting that if any blood was shed on Monday morning, "the strikers would not draw it first. We desire peace as much as anyone and our men will only act when they are provoked, but if they are I cannot stop them."[118]

Frightened by Ettor or perhaps by rumors of dynamite and disorder, Mayor Scanlon changed his mind about the militia. On Sunday afternoon, the mayor ordered three companies to report to the state armory. The following morning at 6:00 a.m., Companies L and F of the Ninth Regiment, and Battery C—250 Lawrence residents in all—reported for duty. But before the troops could be quartered, the strikers answered Ettor's call. At 5:00 a.m. Monday morning, hundreds began gathering outside the city's smaller mills while five thousand clogged the gates to the Wood and Ayer plants.[119] When start-up whistles blew, these advance troops put Ettor's plan into practice. Ignoring his plea for peaceful picketing, they accosted anyone carrying a lunch pail. Hadn't they heard? There was no work today. The mills were closed. Those who pressed on were jostled, sometimes roughed up, but allowed to pass.[120] Not many reached their machines, however, because by 7:00 a.m., clashes were raging across the city.

At the Wood Mill, watchman Louis Berry, ready this time, kept the gate shut against repeated battering. But a few strikers slipped in somehow and roamed through the empty, echoing mill for an hour before being rounded up by police.[121] Elsewhere, the fighting was furious. At the Pacific Mill, workers charged the gates, were driven back, and charged again. Frustrated, they raided a nearby railroad yard for wooden slats and chunks of coal. Soon the shattering of glass was heard up and down Canal Street. Police pulled their guns and fired in the air but the mob did not disperse. Finally, mill managers opened three fire hoses. Graceful arcs of ice-cold water cut through the falling snow, drenching the front ranks. With the temperature again in the single digits, half-frozen people began spilling back from the mill. A few, however, plowed through the oncoming spray, knelt down, pulled revolvers, and fired at the men behind the hoses.[122]

While peaceful crowds roamed along the Merrimack, a skirmish was under way at the Arlington on the north edge of the city. Clubs. Nightsticks. Fire hoses. Sporadic fighting also broke out at the Washington Mill. The Pemberton. The Prospect. The Atlantic. Across the mill district, the few hundred who somehow managed to reach looms or spinners found them idle. Mills that had started up soon shut down while others never even attempted the morning's speedup.[123] Strikers had followed Ettor's instructions to the letter. Midmorning arrived on Monday in the world's leading textile city, but not a single spindle was turning, not a single power loom did a weaver's work. Strikers had shut down the mills. Now it was the owners' turn.

CHAPTER FOUR

Stars, Stripes, and Bayonets

I can hire one half of the working class to kill the other half.

—Jay Gould, railroad tycoon[1]

The 250 militiamen who reported to the state armory at 6:00 a.m. on January 15 were all volunteers. Most were idealistic young men who had never heard a shot fired in anger nor aimed sharpened steel at a human figure not stuffed with straw. They had not enlisted for the pay—$1.55 a day[2]—but more likely in hopes they would be sent to some exotic place to fight for freedom. Yet militia duty, of late, had been mundane. Since the Civil War, the Massachusetts militia had been called out just thirteen times. There had been strike duty in Fall River and Cambridge, but more common were peacekeeping patrols following devastating fires in Boston, Chelsea, and Deerfield. The militia had come to Lawrence in 1890[3] following a cyclone that killed six and splintered dozens of homes.[4] Keeping the peace was a worthwhile public service, but it did not live up to the legend of a militia whose history was the noblest of any in the nation.

These were the descendants of the Minute Men. In 1775, the Massachusetts militia had fired the first shots on the Lexington green and the "shot heard 'round the world" that repelled the Redcoats at Concord Bridge. Sons of the Minute Men had guarded the New England coast during the War of 1812, and grandsons had fought in the Mexican War. When the Civil War began, the militia's Sixth Regiment, calling themselves the "Minute Men of '61," fought their way past rebel snipers in Baltimore to become the first Northern troops to reach Washington, DC, in response to President

Lincoln's call. Thirty-seven years later, the Massachusetts militia fought in Cuba during the Spanish-American War.[5] It all added up to a vaunted war record. But on January 15, 1912, as strikers were shutting down the mills, the great-great-grandsons of men whose musket fire had started the American Revolution shouldered arms in a different kind of conflict, one the enemy proudly called "class warfare."

Hearing alarming reports of raging mobs, Mayor Scanlon ordered the militia onto the streets at 9:45 Monday morning. Deploying from the armory, Company F marched along Amesbury Street and crossed downtown at Essex. The battalion of local men, many recognized by onlookers, turned heads with its martial step and slap of boots on asphalt. Minutes later, another hometown regiment, Company L, swung into action. Approaching the canal, Company L turned right and quickly dispersed a crowd in front of the Atlantic Mill, leaving Company F face-to-face with the drenched, angry mob at the Pacific. Captain Charles Randlett halted his company, then ordered them to drive the crowd back across the railroad bridge and onto the river's north bank.[6] After the initial retreat, the crowd regrouped and stood, jeering the soldiers. Captain Randlett, standing before a long line of men in olive drab uniforms, held his revolver over his head and told the strikers to disperse. Hissing and catcalls answered back. The captain then gave the order to fix bayonets. "Ready!" he shouted. "Charge!"[7]

The previous Friday when Mayor Scanlon had refused mill owners' requests to call out the militia, he had not been unduly cautious. Throughout America's era of industrial violence, militias had quelled many strike-related riots but only at the cost of scores of lives. The chaotic era began in the summer of 1877, when a deep recession and a series of pay cuts triggered a nationwide railroad strike sometimes known as the "Great Upheaval." As gangs of workers paralyzed rail transportation from Albany to San Francisco, militias battled strikers and casualties mounted. State militias were the first to respond. In Baltimore, troopers opened fire on a rock-throwing crowd, killing ten and wounding twenty-three.[8] In Pittsburgh, strikers, including men, women, and children, stoned militiamen who fired back, killing twenty.[9] Ultimately, state militias proved insufficient—many sided with the strikers[10]—and federal troops were required to put down the uprising. In 1894, a year when 750,000 workers went on strike,[11] Illinois militia struggled to maintain order during the walkout at the Pullman Car Works near Chicago. Strikers were protesting wage cuts of 33 percent coupled with a rising cost of living in the company town, which controlled prices of workers' food, water, gas, and rent. Violence flared when federal troops were called out on the Fourth of July. Over the next few days, strikers set fire to railcars, leaving a cloud of smoke hanging over Chicago,[12] while federal troops and militia killed eleven and wounded fifty.[13] During the next decade, the violence moved west, where militias battled striking miners. Then, three years before Lawrence's uprising, two hundred state constables had evicted striking steelworkers from company housing at the Pressed Iron Works at McKees Rocks, Pennsylvania. The mounted militia, whom the strikers reviled as "Cossacks," charged workers and their wives while foot soldiers fired into the crowd, wounding a hundred. A month later, after the IWW had taken over the strike, workers and the militia waged another gun battle. Several troopers then tied the wounded to their horses and dragged them through the streets.[14]

Was this what Lawrence now faced? With battle lines drawn just a few yards apart, the city seemed poised for a massacre. On one side of Canal Street stood thousands of enraged workers, some with guns, others wielding knives or bludgeons. On the opposite side stood a full company of militia each with thirty rounds of ball cartridges.[15] A single shot might start the slaughter; a single accident could cost dozens of lives. And yet, the moment when Company F charged the mob was the height of the bloodshed during the strike's opening days.

Faced with advancing steel blades, the crowd wheeled and raced back across the bridge. Scuffling, scurrying, falling underfoot, strikers were driven through a freight yard and onto Essex Street, where they scattered like insects. Only one man was hurt. Pierced by a soldier's blade below his ribs, Dominic Rapradi was taken to the hospital.[16] Six others were hospitalized with head injuries, and thirty were arrested, including an Italian man carrying a .38 revolver, an ammunition belt, a dagger in one pocket and a stiletto in the other.[17] By noon, lines of soldiers stretched from the Wood Mill to the Prospect, and across the river to other mills. Additional police were on their way from Lowell, Lynn, and Haverhill.[18] Come early afternoon, American Woolen's four mills were running. Other mills also limped along with half or more of their workers out, but owners announced that all would open again Tuesday morning.[19]

During the week that followed, the city beefed up its security, adding an additional five militia companies. Except for a few isolated incidents, little violence occurred. Heeding Ettor's advice, workers kept their hands in their pockets, but the jittery stillness was enforced by more than bayonets. In court, Judge Jeremiah J. Mahoney served notice of how he would deal with strikers who did more than carry a picket sign. Each morning, the judge sat in the dimly lit, condemned courtroom while defiant strikers stepped before him. A buttoned-down, exacting man known in Lawrence for his wit and keen legal mind, the fifty-five-year-old judge had grown up in the city after his family emigrated from Ireland during the Civil War. He had practiced law for twenty-one years and been on the bench for seven.[20] Not one to brook even the slightest breach of the law, he came down hard on strikers. Even minor offenses—obstructing a sidewalk or causing a disturbance—drew fines of five to fifteen dollars,[21] one to three days' wages. And when faced with charges that smacked of anarchy, the judge's justice was swift, severe, and not always just. On Tuesday, his docket included twenty-four men arrested for rioting at the Pacific Mill. Spending less than five minutes per case, the judge sentenced each man to a year in jail.[22] The previous day, Vicenzo Lamastro, the man found carrying a gun, an ammo belt, and two knives, had been given two years.[23] And each convicted striker was given a lecture. "This is an epoch in our history," Judge Mahoney said. "Never can any of us remember when such demonstrations of lawless presumption have taken place here. These men, mostly foreigners perhaps, do not mean to be offenders. They do not realize the gravity of their offense and do not know the laws. Therefore the only way we can teach them is to deal out the severest sentences in this court."[24]

While the judge was laying down the law, Joseph Ettor demonstrated why the IWW had entrusted him to lead this volatile strike. All week, Ettor was everywhere, meeting with everyone involved. He stood at podiums, pounding the gavel he had used at McKees Rocks. He rallied strikers on street corners. He spoke to crowds while standing on fire hydrants.[25] "You may turn your hose upon the strikers," he told one gathering, "but there is being kindled a flame in the heart of the workers, a flame of proletarian revolt, which no fire hose in the world can ever extinguish."[26] While keeping his room at the Needham Hotel, Ettor slept in a different tenement each night in order to meet strikers and understand their concerns.[27] Early

Tuesday morning, when more violence was expected, he donned a thick overcoat and fedora[28] to take a walking tour of the mill district. Ambling through the urban gorges past militia lining the slushy sidewalks, Ettor was trailed by hundreds of strikers. As if playing the Pied Piper of Lawrence, he led them along the Washington Mill where his mere presence calmed strikers shoved by militia now wielding wagon spokes as clubs. Then Ettor conducted the crowd across the Merrimack and around the Wood Mill. Wherever he went, all remained peaceful. Only when the tension of the morning's start-up had subsided did he stroll out of the mill district to begin another hectic day.[29]

On one day alone Ettor met with Italians at 9:00 a.m., the strike committee at 10:00, the Perchers, Menders, and Burlers Union at midday, militia colonel E. LeRoy Sweetser at 3:00 that afternoon, city aldermen at 4:30, Franco-Belgians at 7:00 p.m., and Italians again at 9:00. While the rattled mayor predicted further rebellion would lead to "an awful slaughter,"[30] Ettor stood before cheering crowds, projecting a cool, defiant solidarity. Wherever he spoke, Ettor urged strikers to be peaceful yet unrelenting. "Order can be kept," he told one crowd, "but I never saw order maintained by the glistening bayonets of soldiers." Shouts of "Bravo!" rang out and Ettor let them ring before continuing. "I want you all to understand that the cause cannot be won by spilling blood. . . . Peaceful persuasion is the only weapon advocated from this platform."[31] Acknowledging the militia, Ettor cautioned, "Remember these toy soldiers. They have nice toys in their hands and they want to stab and have all the fun they can. Don't give them a chance."[32] Above all, Ettor urged strikers who had been traditional enemies—Greeks and Turks, Turks and Armenians, French and Germans, Italians from rival regions[33]—to stick together. "Forget that you are Hebrews, forget that you are Poles, Germans, or Russians,"[34] he said. "Among workers there is only one nationality, one race, one creed."[35] He admonished classes as well as nations to unite. "You are the skilled of the mills," he told perchers, menders, and burlers. "Do not play the aristocrat because you speak English, are habituated to the country, have a trade and are better paid. Throw in your lot with the low-paid. You must either reach down and lift them up or they will reach up and pull you down."[36]

With the strikers in his thrall, Ettor made a convenient target. And because he was from the IWW, his opponents included everyone from the press to politicians to other labor leaders. On Monday evening, John Golden, president of the United Textile Workers, came to Lawrence. Golden, a tall, stately former weaver from Fall River who had risen through the ranks of the AF of L, despised the IWW, branding it "an outlaw organization without the slightest standing in the world of labor."[37] As New England's top textile union boss, Golden cared little for unskilled labor[38] or immigrants, whom he considered "foreign to our institutions."[39] Lawrence was *his* turf and the IWW would not invade it without a fight. Golden instantly denounced the strike as "a revolution led by men whose hold upon the wage workers lies in the fact that they stir up bitter class hatred."[40] Calling Ettor "a bad actor,"[41] he advised workers not to be swayed by "smart talkers" and began a campaign to keep skilled workers off the picket lines.[42] Newspapers also singled out Ettor for contempt. The *Lowell Courier* claimed strikers were being deceived by "a little knot of wild-eyed proletarians."[43] The *Boston Herald* labeled Ettor an "imported agitator."[44] William Randolph Hearst's *Boston American* called him "the principal instigator of violence."[45]

Mayor Scanlon, however, preferred direct action. And like Ettor, the mayor had built his career on confrontation. For six years prior to the strike, while Ettor had roamed the country organizing, Michael Scanlon had been fighting to clean up city hall in Lawrence. Swept up in the progressive tenor of the times, Alderman Scanlon had challenged rampant featherbedding of city contracts. In 1910, he exposed a conspiracy that rocked city hall. Republican mayor William White went to jail, while Scanlon went on to draft a new city charter that replaced the corrupt system of ethnic ward bosses with a citywide election and also included provisions for recall and referendum. Voters overwhelmingly approved the new charter and, just five weeks before the strike, chose Scanlon as the new Democratic mayor of Lawrence. The election capped the remarkable rise of a reserved but righteous politician.

Born in Nova Scotia to Irish immigrants, Scanlon had lived in Lawrence since he was two. He left school to become a printer's apprentice, but poor eyesight forced him to try other jobs. During the 1890s, Scanlon sold insurance and real estate to Irish fleeing The Plains as new immigrants filled them. In 1901, he was appointed the city's milk inspector and five years later was elected alderman. Shocked by backroom deals between business and government, the meticulous Victorian cast dozens of lone votes against padded city budgets. He fought for fairness in police hiring, better pay for city workers, and a variety of urban improvements, including sidewalks, parks, and playgrounds. Having devoted his life to civilizing his city,[46] Michael Scanlon was not about to let Lawrence fall prey to an "imported agitator." A few hours after Monday's uprising, the mayor met with Ettor and several strikers at the police station. After listening to their demands, the mayor confronted the IWW leader.

"Don't you think, Mr. Ettor, that you are responsible for this trouble today?" Scanlon asked. "Don't you think that this is all due to the speech you made at the mass meeting last Saturday?"

"I am responsible for what I do, and I am responsible for what I said," Ettor answered. "I am not responsible, however, for what people do who have been provoked as these textile workers have. I am not responsible for what men do when they have been downtrodden, when their faces have been ground into the dirt so that they no longer resemble human beings." Ettor blamed the riot on starvation wages and fire hoses, but Scanlon, peering at the Wobbly leader through his wire-rimmed glasses, pressed his point.

"We agree with you that these people are not getting what they should," the mayor said. "There is no doubt that you have a right to more than you are getting, but that does not justify violence. We have never had a strike of this kind before in Lawrence. We have had strikes, but we never had to call the police to suppress disorder, let alone send for the people of other cities to help us and employ the militia. I believe that if you had not made that speech to the textile workers Saturday afternoon, Mr. Ettor, we would not have had this trouble today. . . . Now if you will call off the men who are making this trouble and will take the first train back to New York where you came from, I believe we can settle this strike very quickly."

Ettor replied that he had every right to be in Lawrence. "I shall stay here and do what I can for these people," he insisted.

"We do not intend to deprive you of any rights," Scanlon shot back. "All we ask is that you remain peaceful and cease destroying property and causing damage for which the city must pay. You can hold all the meetings you want if you will only counsel peace."[47] The mayor appeared calm, but underneath he was truly frightened by the resolve and charisma of the strike's leader. The militia could control the strikers, but who would control Ettor? Shortly after their meeting, Scanlon phoned the Sherman Detective Agency in Boston. By the end of the day he had contracted the services of "an Italian speaking operative able to take shorthand notes in either Italian or English conversations and capable of doing 'roping' if deemed advisable."[48] *Roping* was detective slang for tricking someone into incriminating himself. A detective began trailing Ettor wherever he went.

Just after meeting with the mayor, Ettor addressed thirteen hundred strikers at city hall, telling them of Scanlon's attempt to run him out of town. Assuring the noisy crowd that he would not desert them, Ettor said, "The only thing they can do to me is to put me in jail and within two hours after they do this there will be another man here defending you just as I am. They would jail me in a moment if they thought by so doing they could take the life out of the strike. The life of the strike does not depend upon me, and don't forget that."[49]

But throughout that first week, the life of the strike did depend on Ettor. As he tirelessly rallied workers, the early violence and venting of rage gave way to a steely determination that spread through the tenements, across meeting halls, and along the picket lines circling each mill. Disorder was limited to occasional shoving. On Tuesday, January 16, small skirmishes broke out between militia and strikers, but the only bloodshed came when a militiaman slipped in the snow, fell on his bayonet, and wounded himself in the groin.[50] Day after day, the mills continued to operate, but each succeeding speedup saw fewer on the job. "Our entire room didn't do one fair day's work this whole week," one woman complained. "We were so nerved up and excited, we couldn't. We simply could not sit still and the overseers didn't try to keep us at work. We just sat in groups talking things over most of the time. We expected to be blown up at any minute, and at the slightest unusual noise everyone would jump up and there would be a regular panic."[51] For "nerved up" workers, pressure intensified as strikers took Ettor's advice "to make life miserable for the scabs." The term *scab* soon joined *yes* and *no* as one of the few English words known to everyone in multilingual Lawrence. Strikers surrounded certain tenements chanting "Scab! Scab!"[52] Ominous Black Hands were painted on tenement doors. All along the picket lines, placards and coat buttons repeated a mantra— "Don't be a scab!"[53] Each morning, workers still bent on crossing the picket line were handed a circular:

To all workers, men and women, and to all those who sympathize with their aspirations for a better day:

We, striking textile workers, who in the past suffered untold exploitation, outrages, and insults, have reached the limit of human resignation and endurance. We submit to a candid world in brief our grievance and reason for revolt. Our wages have been gradually reduced, machines have been speeded up to the point that in order to keep up with them we have to strain to the limit of endurance. . . .

We had to rebel because we had drunk of the cup to the very dregs.

Our enemies are making an effort to blind the issue by making a cry of "foreigners," "rioters," to which we may reply we were not considered foreigners when we meekly consented to being robbed of our labors and opportunities; we were considered good citizens as long as we were traitors to our best interests; now that we dare to stand erect and demand but some of our rights, there is no name too foul for our exploiters and their kept men to anathemize [sic] us with. . . .

We urge and plead with all who wish our cause well to express themselves in words and deeds in no mistaken way.

Workers! Remember! An injury to one is an injury to all. Strike all together! Stick together! All to victory!

—STRIKE COMMITTEE[54]

As the week went on, Ettor's committee tallied the strike's steady growth at its morning meetings. With its multitude of languages and interpreters, the strike committee resembled a precursor to the United Nations as, one by one, ethnic representatives stood to make their reports. The Syrians were all out. Lithuanians—all out. The Polish would not return to work. The Italians? "No need to tell us about them," Ettor joked.[55] Franco-Belgians were crossing picket lines at the Arlington but more had joined the strike. Russians—all out. Portuguese—the same. Groups of Armenians[56] and Jews[57] had also voted to walk out. Even the few American-born workers, a majority of them at least, had joined the strike.[58] Across the city, small spontaneous walkouts took place at each mill. Strikers claimed the new recruits had willingly joined the cause, while overseers complained that loyal workers were being scared away from their jobs.[59] Whatever their motivation, by the end of the first week, additional walkouts brought the strikers' masses to at least the fifteen thousand cited by the *New York Times*,[60] but probably closer to the twenty thousand that Ettor claimed.[61] And after the strike committee voted unanimously to affiliate with the IWW,[62] some forty-five hundred had joined the union,[63] paid their twenty-five cents in dues, and received their red cards. The dues were immediately deposited in a strike fund.[64]

The strikers had more than solidarity, however. They also had a list of demands. The strike had begun for two hours' pay, but now that they were out workers wanted more. They demanded (1) a 15 percent across-the-board pay increase; (2) double pay for overtime—more than a fifth of the operatives worked overtime, always at the standard rate of pay;[65] (3) an immediate end to Billy Wood's grueling bonus system; and (4) no recriminations against strikers once they went back to work.[66] Though Ettor was opposed to outside arbitration, the strike committee overruled him, voting to send their demands to the state board of arbitration and conciliation.[67] Strikers hoped to meet with the board soon, but mill owners refused.[68] At first, William Wood issued no formal statement, merely telling Mayor Scanlon, "There is no strike in Lawrence, just mob rule."[69] When Wood finally responded, addressing the workers through the press, he sounded more like a jilted lover than a textile tycoon.

> Last Friday many of you left our mills and have since remained away. This action was wholly a surprise to me. You sent me no notice of what you were intending to do and you stated no grievances and made no demands. I learned from the papers that the reason for your staying away is that the company paid you for only fifty-four hours work. . . . Ever since you left I have had no word from any of you as to what you desire, but I have read in the newspaper that among other things, you want your wages raised so that you will receive as much for fifty-four hours work as you did for fifty-six.

Citing stiff competition, a recent recession, and a need to consider stockholder dividends as much as wages, Wood flatly refused any pay raise.[70] He did not mention the strikers' other demands.

With the two sides entrenched, each began a campaign for public sympathy. The focus was wages. How much did Lawrence textile workers really earn? Ettor told the press that the average mill wage was $6 a week; mill owners countered that it was $9.[71] The difference depended on who did the math, and how. Ettor was using a mathematical mean, dividing the mills' $150,000 weekly payroll by twenty-five thousand workers.[72] Mill owners relied on what statisticians call the median. Taking a weaver's average wage of $13 a week and a doffer's average of $4.50, they found the midpoint, then rounded up. Strikers protested. For every weaver, they pointed out, there were dozens of doffers, sweepers, and bobbin boys earning $4.50 a week or less. Mill owners countered that such low pay was earned only by the least skilled workers, few in number and not prime wage earners. But neither weekly wage figure factored in the several weeks each year that work was slow and thousands were laid off.

To settle the dispute, the *Lawrence Tribune* asked workers to send in their pay stubs. The paper received eighty-six in one day, ranging from $3.06 to $7.05 a week. Many of the stubs featured a local bank's ad telling workers to "begin to save money now and place it in this bank where it will grow steadily."[73] The *Tribune*, generally sympathetic to the strikers, noted that salaries of $3.06, $4.50, $5.25 represented a full week's wages of "male adults, many of whom have families."[74] Mill owners denounced the survey, claiming it was skewed by low-end pay stubs submitted "for the good of the cause."[75] Adding fuel to the dispute, local politicians charged that immigrants lived several to a room because they were used to such conditions or else were sending huge portions of their salaries to families back home. As the pay controversy dragged on, William Wood claimed that since 1906, mill workers in Lawrence had sent $800,000 overseas.[76] Yet he did not stop to calculate that $800,000 in six years came to $5.33 a person per annum. Offering a global perspective, the National Association of Wool Manufacturers correctly noted that pay in Lawrence was high when compared with that in other textile cities. "The Lawrence mills are modern, with the best equipment and being highly efficient, the operatives are well paid, that is, for textile workers," a spokesman said. Textile wages in Massachusetts were double those in England and much higher than in the American South, where a warp spinner could work sixty-six hours a week for $3.50.[77] Yet as the trade association had conceded, mill work was the bottom rung on any economic ladder.

Every grim statistic in Lawrence—high infant mortality, low life expectancy, a Calcuttan population density—was mirrored in textile towns from Maine to Georgia. No matter how you figured their wages, textile workers were falling behind their fellow laborers. Nationwide, paper mill operatives averaged $10.58 a week, shoemakers $11.42, and steelworkers $13.88.[78] Even Lawrence's garbagemen, pushing two-wheeled carts along Essex and Broadway, earned $12 a week.[79] But mill workers, whether they earned just above or just below a dollar a day, lived on the edge of hunger, selling unskilled labor in a free market whose "invisible hand" threatened to push them over the edge at any minute. Consider a typical family—the Bleskys.

Before going on strike, John Blesky cleaned raw cotton in the Pacific Mill. His weekly salary of $7.50—equivalent to $140 in contemporary figures— was the sole support for Blesky, his wife, and four children too young to work. Given such tight pockets, Blesky's wife kept an accurate record of expenses. One week's budget included:

Rent	$1.25
Kerosene	.12
Milk	.77
Bread	1.68
Tea	.05
Coffee	.15
Cabbage	.84
Meat	.50
Sugar	.07

The expenses left the family $2.07. They did not send any portion of this to relatives back in Poland. Instead, the money was spent on shoes, medicine, clothing, and various necessities for the couple's one-year-old son. Had their flat been larger, the Bleskys, like their neighbors, could have packed it with boarders each paying a dollar a week, but they had only two rooms and a kitchen. John, his wife, and the baby slept in one room while the three older children slept in the other, in iron beds. Most of their neighbors heated with coal, storing it in bathtubs,[80] but the Bleskys could not afford coal bought in bathtub-sized quantities, which cost twice the price paid in bulk by home owners with coal bins.[81] Instead, they stoked their kitchen stove with wood scraps their children gathered on the street. When the children came home empty-handed, there was no heat. Nowhere in the Bleskys' budget were such luxuries as butter (18 cents a pound) or eggs at 38 cents a dozen.[82] Like most mill workers, the Bleskys could not afford clothes fashioned in Manhattan sweatshops from fabric made in Lawrence. An overcoat cost $10.98. A skirt sold for $1.98, two to three days' earnings. And anyone who had to ask the cost of a suit ($15) couldn't afford that either.[83] The Bleskys each wore the same clothes until they wore out. When the strike began, Mrs. Blesky was still wearing the shawl, skirt, and shirtwaist she had bought in Poland three years earlier, just before coming to Lawrence. Ashamed of her shabby appearance, she almost never left her home.[84]

Mill owners and mill workers had their own separate statistics, but for Louis Brandeis, both sums were disturbing. The strike was not yet a week old when the eminent Boston lawyer and future Supreme Court justice warned that America was raising "a race of slaves." Describing deplorable working conditions and declining real wages, Brandeis offered only one remedy—stronger unions. He denounced efforts by big business to "eradicate every thing that even looked like unionism in any of their shops. . . . Social unrest is manifesting itself more and more as a result of this inequality," Brandeis told members of the Boston City Club, "and its terrible effects are being felt by the American people. Such outbreaks of violence as those in Lawrence are the result of this unjust use of power."[85] In 1912, Brandeis was only one of many voices calling for the taming of unbridled capitalism. Long before Theodore Roosevelt denounced "the great malefactors of wealth," concerned citizens had grown wary of power in the hands of a few fantastically rich men. Articles in major magazines such as *McClure's*, *Collier's*, and *Cosmopolitan* blasted away at corruption and collusion. The journalists Roosevelt derided as "muckrakers" exposed the evils of the steel trust, the oil trust, the sugar trust . . . and as the American Woolen Company flexed its political muscle, it came under fire as the bellwether of "the wool trust." The trust's secret weapon—secret because no one from the average citizen to the president himself could understand it—was the tariff.

Tariffs, the duties a federal government levies on imported goods, are not usually the stuff of everyday discussion. Yet beginning in 1910 and continuing through the strike, talk of the wool tariff filled parlors, smoking clubs, and saloons. Throughout the Gilded Age, Democrats had favored lower tariffs to keep prices down; Republicans had backed higher tariffs to protect domestic industries and, cynics said, to help the rich get richer. The GOP controlled Congress and the White House through most of the period, keeping tariffs historically high. Populists and Progressives protested but their complaints drew little attention because few Americans could hope to master a tariff's niggling details. Even President Taft admitted he didn't understand the tariff. "Why, it is just like Choctaw to a man who is not an expert," he said.[86] Then a slight woman from Pennsylvania's oil fields stepped forth to explain.

Six years after publishing her landmark *History of the Standard Oil Company,* which led to the trust's breakup, Ida Tarbell exposed how the wool tariff had helped men like William Wood acquire mansions, yachts, and more automobiles than he had time to count. In three articles published in *American Magazine,* Tarbell charged that the wool trust had used its political clout to preserve exorbitant tariffs on imported wool.[87] Thanks to the wool tariff, American wool cost twice as much as British,[88] was often adulterated with cotton, and had created a trust as wealthy and arrogant as any other cartel. The wool trust had several senators in its hip pocket, Tarbell wrote, among them Massachusetts senator Henry Cabot Lodge, "the chief apostle of protection," and Rhode Island senator Nelson Aldrich,[89] whose daughter Abby had married John D. Rockefeller Jr.[90] As for the trust's leaders, Tarbell mentioned Wood but zeroed in on William Whitman, president of the Arlington Mill in Lawrence. Tarbell cited Whitman as the author of the wool tariff, a levy so outrageously high that even President Taft called it "indefensible."[91] After hearing Whitman testify before a congressional committee, one congressman called the wool trust "the only first class trust I have ever seen."[92]

How did Lawrence's leading mill owners get a tariff that varied between 100 and 200 percent?[93] Perhaps, Tarbell suggested, because Whitman himself had written many of the wool tariff provisions.[94] Or maybe because the secretary of the National Association of Wool Manufacturers also happened to work on the Senate Finance Committee. And wasn't it interesting, added another exposé, that this wolf among the committee's sheep got a five-thousand-dollar bonus after the tariff was retained in 1909?[95] The result was Schedule K, the wool tariff Congress had promised to reduce, then approved without any substantial changes. Tarbell's crusade made Schedule K a whipping boy for the press. During the two years leading up to the Lawrence strike, two dozen magazine articles[96] and dozens of newspaper editorials around the country[97] attacked the wool trust. Wool manufacturers fought back. American Woolen spent one hundred thousand dollars for magazine ads[98] explaining "The Truth About Schedule K." The ads, signed by William Wood, tapped the nation's patriotism and vanity. The wool industry had helped win the Civil War by providing the Union's blue uniforms,[99] the ads reminded readers, adding that "American men and women are the best dressed individuals in the world" thanks to American Woolen.[100] Wood also explained why wool executives had written much of Schedule K. "A tariff law must, necessarily, deal with complicated phases of many businesses—phases which are understood only by those engaged in those businesses."[101] The campaign was too little, too late.

During the 1909 congressional debate, Republicans were warned that if they did not cut the tariff, the country would go Democratic. "Let the country go Democratic. What the hell do I care if it does?" replied GOP senator Reed Smoot, who later coauthored the tariff that deepened the Great Depression.[102] And in 1910, that's just what the country did, electing a widely Democratic House that promised to slash Schedule K. The summer before the Lawrence strike, Congress passed a bill cutting the wool tariff in half.[103] Taft, having lamented that "the woolen manufacturers together control so many votes" in Congress,[104] vetoed the bill.[105] Yet the near miss had shaken the vested assurance of William Wood and William Whitman. Six months later, when Lawrence's workers stormed out, mill moguls claimed they couldn't give workers the same pay for two hours less work. Among other reasons, they cited an expected plunge in revenue caused by a "tariff smashing Congress."[106] So as workers' wages were debated, it was the complex tariff, descending from the lofty heights of Capitol Hill, that hit the streets of Lawrence with a vengeance. No strikers, however, mentioned the tariff as the strike's first week went on. They were too busy parading.

By midweek, Lawrence resembled an urban bivouac, its streets commanded by armed companies who marched every few hours to and from their duty. Mayor Scanlon had ceded control of the mill district to Colonel Sweetser,[107] whose eight companies now lined both banks of the Merrimack. Shoulder to shoulder, more than five hundred men—from a dozen to sixty per mill—stood guard.[108] This was not heroic duty, but the descendants of Minute Men performed it with martial efficiency. Militia kept strikers from entering mills, arrested anyone harassing scabs, and stopped the slightest suspicious character. Keeping crowds constantly moving, militia barked "Move on!" whenever a pedestrian so much as paused to light a cigarette. Standing for hours in the numbing cold, militiamen wore special-issue wool caps, mittens, and overshoes. They slept each night in cots[109] laid out in makeshift encampments inside the mills. The only thing militia could not guard against was rumors. And like some epidemic disease, rumors spread through the city, growing wilder as the week went on. One rumor said that guns were stacked up in the mills, at the ready.[110] Another said the strike was nearly over, that Colonel Sweetser and Massachusetts governor Eugene Foss, who owned cotton mills elsewhere in the state, had agreed on a settlement.[111] But the most portentous rumor hinted of dynamite, said to have been shipped to Lawrence to blow up the mills.[112] Ettor laughed off the dynamite stories. "They are too ridiculous to dignify with a reply," he said. "Tell the people not to believe them till they hear the explosion."[113] Ettor's denial meant little to city officials, who continued to tighten their clamps. Saloons were closed.[114] Sharpshooters perched in the towers of major mills.[115] The whole fortified city seemed to be waiting, watching. But amid all the advance warnings of violence that had yet to occur, the jubilance of the strike's first parade caught everyone by surprise.

The parade grew like gossip. On Wednesday morning, January 17, strikers got Ettor's permission to march, and at 11:00 a.m., a few dozen gathered on Elm Street in the thick of The Plains. Rallying behind a large American flag, they set out, cheering and shouting to everyone they passed. Elm Street divided the Italian and Polish districts, each teeming with women toting groceries, men chatting on street corners, children throwing snowballs. As the parade went by, hundreds joined it. Passing the snowy fields of the common, they turned south onto Union Street. As they approached the Everett Mill, where workers were still locked out, many feared the parade would continue toward the line of militia, but the throng turned right onto Common Street and entered the heart of the Italian neighborhood. From deli counters and barbers' chairs, cobblers' shops and cafés, Italians came out waving, applauding. Many more joined, some carrying their own Stars and Stripes, and by the time they came under the clock tower of city hall, the revelers numbered three thousand. Doubling back, the procession swept again through The Plains picking up more people—women, children, teenagers, each with little to celebrate lately. Passing the yellow brick edifice of Lawrence High School, the procession drew cheers and catcalls from students hanging out of windows. At the police station, where calls from concerned citizens were urging that the parade be stopped at once,[116] paraders spotted the balding pate and snow white mustache of City Marshal James T. O'Sullivan.[117] Rather than hiss, they waved. By the time it turned onto Essex Street and flowed into downtown, the parade numbered ten thousand, all making what to some sounded like ovations, to others a war whoop. An Italian band blared the hymn of Garibaldi,[118] and through the cacophony, some heard a Franco-Belgian band strike up the worldwide hymn of workers' revolution, "The Internationale." Hundreds joined in, each in his native language.

Arise ye workers from your slumbers
Arise ye prisoners of want
For reason in revolt now thunders
And at last ends the age of cant.

Away with all your superstitions
Servile masses arise, arise
We'll change henceforth the old tradition
And spurn the dust to win the prize.

So comrades, come rally
And the last fight let us face
The Internationale unites the human race.

As the noon hour brought bankers and merchants onto Essex, the parade filled downtown from sidewalk to sidewalk for four full blocks. Streetcars slowed but were allowed to pass. Model Ts, horse-drawn drays, and pushcarts searched for other routes. For twenty minutes, the workers paraded past, flying flags, singing, showing "Immigrant City" that its immigrants had stifled their rage and become a tightly knit, unified army of labor determined to win. Then, having traversed the tenements and the business district, parade leaders decided to take their celebration to the source—the mills.

Reaching Broadway at the western edge of downtown, the parade turned south and headed for the river. Hearing them coming, Battery C moved into place across Canal Street. Jubilant paraders marched toward the line. As bayonets loomed ahead, the marchers stopped, but those in the rear kept pushing until word spread back through the crowd. The bands' blare faded and the crowd gradually stilled. Militia lowered rifles and aimed at the parade's advance guard. For several moments, the scene seemed frozen in time. Brandishing blades like the pickets on a fence, men in troopers' hats stared down the motley assortment of workers wearing shawls and cloth caps. Between them, above the snowy grit of Canal Street, American flags framed the standoff.[119]

When a few strikers hurled chunks of ice, the militia pressed forward. Several women, some holding babies, marched up to the jagged row of glinting knives and shouted their defiance.[120] One soldier drew his sword and struck down three people with its blunt edge. At the rear, some turned and ran but the rest could not. Beyond the militia, strikers could see the mills' squat facades and pencil-thin smokestacks. To their left was the dam that had created the city, its water still a solid sheet of ice, and in the distance across the Merrimack stood the blanched outlines of more mills. The showdown lasted one or two long minutes. Joseph Ettor was blocks away, too busy to join the parade, but his words seemed to haunt the scene. The night before, he had mocked the mayor's assertion that "Lawrence has ever enjoyed industrial peace." Yes, Ettor told his audience, "we have enjoyed industrial peace. The peace that fills the cemeteries and has brought thousands to a desperate stage. . . . They give you wages upon which you get a living that even a dog would not be jealous of. If that is industrial peace, what is industrial war?"[121] As if in answer to Ettor's question, the militia faced the swarm of strikers with the mills themselves as silent sentinels. Only the flags moved, unfurling in a slight breeze, until a car pulled up behind the soldiers. From it stepped Colonel Sweetser.

A lawyer by trade, a militia colonel in his spare time, the graying, mustachioed man marched quickly to the front of the line. Several strikers took their hats off to the colonel. After a moment of sizing up the scene, Sweetser sensed that this was not a mob, just a parade. He ordered Battery C to fall back. Cheering wildly, the crowd swept by them and onto Canal Street.[122] On past the crumbling boardinghouses built for workers in the 1850s, on past the Pacific Mill with its medieval turrets jutting into the sky, the paraders shouted and called to workers at windows. Then another confrontation occurred at the Duck Bridge, scene of the previous Friday's worst battle. When the militia barred the parade from crossing the bridge, one man leading the procession pointed to his flag. "This is the American flag," he said. "It can go anywhere." The lieutenant ordered his men to salute, and for a moment it looked as if the crowd might cross while the militia was paying its respects. But the lieutenant quickly ordered the bridge blocked again and the parade turned back up Union Street where, after two hours, it dispersed.[123]

On Thursday, another parade of ten thousand tramped through the snow,[124] but Friday dawned warmer, with heavy rains at last breaking the cold snap and leaving the mill district quiet and glistening. A full week had passed since the initial uproar. To anyone encouraged by the strike's growth, a grim reminder of the future came that morning when strikers received checks from the previous week, their last on the job. Under heavy militia guard, strikers filed through payroll offices, took their checks, and left, not knowing when or if they would return, and wondering how the checks, whether six dollars, nine dollars, or somewhere between, would feed their families as the strike ground on.[125] On Friday evening, Mayor Scanlon announced that he had not met with anyone—neither strikers, state arbitrators, nor mill owners—the entire day. There was no end of the strike in sight, the mayor said.[126]

Four more companies of militia reported for duty on Saturday, January 20, bringing the total to a dozen comprising eight hundred men.[127] All was peaceful that morning. With the addition of two thousand English-speaking strikers,[128] no one disputed that almost twenty thousand were off the job, as many participants in this single strike as in all the strikes throughout Massachusetts during 1910 and 1911.[129] At 8:00 a.m., a Polish man, said to be distraught and crazed by hunger, jumped from the third-story window of his tenement. He was taken to the hospital with a fractured spine.[130] Then shortly after noon, word spread through the streets, word that seemed like another rumor but proved to be true. Acting on tips from detectives, a team of police from Boston and Lawrence had entered the tenement district, searched in three locations, and discovered packages containing assorted fuses, percussion caps, and twenty-eight sticks of dynamite.[131]

CHAPTER FIVE

Dynamite

Industrial contests take on all the attitudes and psychology of war, and both parties do many things that they should never dream of doing in times of peace.

—Clarence Darrow[1]

T he discovery of dynamite sent ripples of fear through the city. Clustered in their tenements, residents were suddenly afraid to open their windows, draw their shades,[2] or let children out on the street. The strike's initial bedlam had endangered only strikers and police who got in each other's way, but twenty-eight sticks of dynamite could bring tons of brick crashing down on hundreds of innocent people. Lawrence knew the suffering a mill's collapse could cause. Fifty-two years before the strike, on January 10, 1860, a full shift of workers was approaching the end of the day when weak pillars gave way in the Pemberton Mill. Within seconds, five floors telescoped to the ground, bringing the entire structure down in one horrible, apocalyptic wave. The city's oldest residents still remembered the cries from the rubble, the fire that burned trapped victims alive, and the toll—88 dead, 116 crippled for life.[3] Through stories of heroism and loss, "the Lawrence Calamity" lived on in the city's lore.[4] And now dynamite raised the specter of another mill's collapse. Who was behind the plot? What could they possibly hope to gain?

But before fear came its inevitable prelude—fascination. Shortly after noon on Saturday, January 20, a crowd assembled outside the modest three-story home at 292 Oak Street where seven sticks of dynamite had been found wrapped in blue paper and hidden in a closet.[5] As onlookers traded rumors, detectives hurried outside, piled into their black cars, and sped off to find more explosives. Before the evening papers hit the streets, the sinister details had spread throughout the city. That morning, led by Inspector William Rooney of Boston, police had fanned out through The Plains. They had known exactly where to look, stopping at precise addresses, going to the exact churchyard cemetery where dynamite was found.[6] The plotters were "outsiders" who had obviously come to Lawrence for the purpose of blowing up something. The targets were said to be all the largest mills, the state armory, the police station, and the homes of William Wood and mill agent Walter Parker.[7] Among those arrested were two women, several Armenians, and a "Porto Rican Negro."[8] The mastermind of the scheme was Farris Marad, the tailor who had led the Syrian contingent during the week's parades.[9] When arrested, one man had a pair of brass knuckles and Marad was carrying a .38. The Syrian was led away with a downcast look on his face.[10] Police were hunting for two more men, Italians, seasoned dynamiters from Pennsylvania.[11] Dynamite was also found at a cobbler's shop next door to where Joseph Ettor picked up his mail. More dynamite was thought to be somewhere in the city, and newspapers were already denouncing "one of the worst dynamite plots in the history of this country."[12] All afternoon on Essex Street, anxious shoppers did errands, then hurried home.[13]

The most frightening aspect of the plot was its plausibility. Throughout the previous decade, nearly three thousand strikes had disrupted American labor each year.[14] Only a small fraction involved an explosion, but each blast made national news, making dynamite infamous as labor's last resort. Ever since the Haymarket bomb in 1886, mysterious explosions had destroyed mines, bridges, and other targets of organized labor. Decades of isolated bombings came to a climax between 1906 and 1911 when 110 construction sites were dynamited. The sabotage campaign was waged by the International Association of Bridge and Structural Iron Workers against United States Steel, which had crushed every fledgling union in its plants. Finding dynamite readily available on construction sites, iron and bridge workers used small explosions to drive the company to the bargaining table.[15] The campaign failed utterly but it made dynamite a regular feature of labor headlines. On the same morning it was found in Lawrence, dynamite made news in Indianapolis, where federal investigators were uncovering the union's sabotage campaign, and in Pueblo, Colorado, where a nonunion laundry was blown up.[16] But in Lawrence and the rest of America, all talk of dynamite instantly called to mind the plot that had been resolved just six weeks before the strike had begun.

Shortly after 1:00 a.m. on October 1, 1910, the night shift at the *Los Angeles Times* was putting the morning paper "to bed." From "Ink Alley" near the rear of the building came a dry, crackling sound. Suddenly an explosion ripped a hole in the plant. Within minutes, more explosions, some heard ten miles away,[17] set the building ablaze. The *Times* plant was destroyed and twenty people were killed. The next morning's paper, printed in an auxiliary plant, hit the newsstands with a banner headline: UNIONIST BOMBS WRECK THE TIMES.[18] The paper did not hesitate to point a finger because its publisher had battled unions as fiercely as he had fought for the Union during the Civil War.[19] A belligerent, blustering man who drove around L.A. with a cannon on the hood of his car, General Harrison Gray Otis and his archconservative paper had spearheaded the drive to keep Los Angeles an "open shop," nonunion city. "The General" was in Mexico when the dynamite left his headquarters in ruins, but upon returning he fired back in an editorial. It began: "O you anarchic scum, you cowardly murderers, you leeches upon honest labor, you midnight assassins . . ."[20] The tone did not get any softer. Otis hired his own detective, and rewards totaling three hundred thousand dollars were offered for information. Then as the case dragged on into 1911, it became labor's greatest cause célèbre in a generation.

A mayoral election was scheduled for Los Angeles and the Socialist candidate stood a good chance of being elected. While a mayor's committee and a grand jury investigated the bombing, the candidate's own inquiry revealed that *Times* employees had been sickened by gas fumes prior to the explosion.[21] A gas leak seemed a plausible explanation. Then in April Otis's detective, William Burns, caught two brothers, James B. and John J. McNamara, both higher-ups in the bridge and structural iron workers union. When the McNamaras were spirited to L.A. without any pretense of an extradition hearing,[22] the entire labor movement rose as one to assert their innocence. For the next five months the case aroused waves of indignation and self-righteousness. In Los Angeles, the public largely believed in the

Begun as a nineteenth-century utopian mill town, by 1912 Lawrence had become "Immigrant City," home to eighty-six thousand people from fifty-one nations, crammed into seven square miles.

The massive Wood Mill in Lawrence (1,937 feet long) was the chief target of strikers on January 12, 1912.

On January 15, when strikers stormed the Pacific Mill in single-digit temperatures, they were drenched by fire hoses. The battle for Lawrence intensified.

By the end of the strike's first week, eight companies of militia occupied Lawrence, marching to their duty from makeshift encampments inside the mills.

Standoffs between strikers and militia became daily events as the strike dragged on.

As a world of nations was molded into one, spontaneous parades of ten thousand strikers marched through Lawrence.

The son of Portuguese immigrants, William Wood rose from menial mill work to become the nation's most powerful textile tycoon and the most hated man in Lawrence.

While encamped in the mills, the fifteen hundred soldiers of the Massachusetts Militia kept up their spirits with songs, dances, and boxing matches.

A new tactic in American labor history, the marching picket line, was debuted in Lawrence in February.

HARPER'S WEEKLY

A JOURNAL OF CIVILIZATION

Vol. LVI.   New York, February 10, 1912   No. 2877

Copyright, 1912, by HARPER & BROTHERS. *All rights reserved*

MARTIAL LAW IN NEW ENGLAND

Disorders in Lawrence, Massachusetts, created by striking mill-hands, resulted in the occupation of the city last week by the military forces of the State. The strikers carried American flags in the belief that the troops would not fire upon them when thus protected. The arrest of the strikers' leader was followed by the murder of four strike-breakers in a tenement on the night of February 2. The photograph shows troops protecting a mill entrance

After two deaths and a dynamite plot, muckrakers and other journalists from around the country began covering the strike in Lawrence.

McNamaras' innocence and, in sympathy, made the Socialist the leader in the mayoral race. Samuel Gompers, who usually avoided controversy, visited the McNamaras in jail and called on all AF of L members "in the name of justice and humanity"[23] to work for the brothers' release. Nearly every American city had its own McNamara Defense League, while massive Labor Day parades called for the brothers' freedom. "A social revolution seemed at hand," Detective Burns later recalled.[24] Finally, in October 1911, with celebrated attorney Clarence Darrow heading their defense team, the McNamara trial began. Jury selection took nearly a month. In the meantime, Darrow, who had been reluctant to take the case, hired his own investigators to check out the evidence. He was appalled. "My God," he told the brothers. "You left a trail behind you a mile wide."[25]

On December 1, four days before a Socialist was likely to be elected mayor of Los Angeles, the city and the nation were stunned by events in the courtroom. Withdrawing pleas of "not guilty," Darrow submitted the McNamaras' confessions. "It was my intention to injure the building and scare the owners," James B. McNamara said. "I did not intend to take the life of anyone." Across the silenced courtroom, a reporter blurted out, "Jesus, ain't it fierce!"[26] The legacy of the fourteen-month case was especially fierce for the labor movement. The Socialist lost the election. Gompers wept in public.[27] The McNamaras went to San Quentin, and seven weeks later when dynamite was found in Lawrence, not a single newspaper editor, policeman, or citizen concerned about America's industrial strife doubted that it was part of a massive strikers' plot to blow up the mills. Joseph Ettor disagreed. "Anybody with any amount of sense can find a thing he has planted," Ettor told strikers that Saturday afternoon. "They can find it very easily if they have planted it only a couple of days before. I have had lots of tricks played on me before, but this is the first time a thing like this has been worked."[28] Yet Ettor's accusation had to swim upstream against popular opinion and recent headlines. Wasn't a frame-up just what Labor had sanctimoniously asserted throughout the McNamara affair?[29]

Fear continued to grip the city on Sunday, January 21, while fascination drew more than a thousand visitors to Lawrence. Taking the train from Lowell, Haverhill, or Boston, Sunday strollers disembarked beneath the towering campanile of the railroad depot and set out along Essex Street to see the scenes they had been reading about in the dailies—impassioned strikers speaking in various halls, lines of men in trooper's hats, and the mills themselves, like castles of labor guarded by feudal armies. A divide in public opinion was already opening. To workers who took their only day off to visit, Lawrence seemed like a dream of the future—labor rising up in one inspiring multitude. If this strike succeeded, workers everywhere would have hope. But to proper Victorians, the women in feathered hats, the men in their Sunday suits, Lawrence looked like their worst nightmare—a city under siege, its mobs held in check by the military, its future menaced by radicals preaching revolution. If Lawrence succumbed, what city would be next?

That morning, local clergy gave more considered sermons on the strike. Opinions in the pulpit varied as widely as interpretations of scripture. The Baptist minister called for "law and order at any cost."[30] The Presbyterian preacher prayed for peace, and many ministers urged parishioners not to be gulled by the evil IWW. Only a few clergymen sided with the strikers. The Unitarian minister, taking his sermon's title from Matthew 10:10, "The Laborer Is Worthy of His Meat," denounced the war between capital and labor, concluding, "It is a time when every one of us must seek for light on the great question of industrial democracy."[31] From his pulpit at Holy Rosary, the balding, bespectacled Father Milanese shared a personal letter from William Wood saying strikers should return to work and expect a wage increase once the economy improved.[32] Rejecting Wood's advice, Father Milanese urged strikers to remain firm, then solicited strike funds in the collection plate.[33] Congregational minister Robert W. Beers accused mill owners of forgetting that they were their "brothers' keepers,"[34] and the Syrian priest, Father Vasile Nahas, told strikers in his parish to remain out until all demands were won.[35] Meanwhile in the state armory, militiamen attending their own services were urged to be disciplined during this "disagreeable" duty.[36] The city's most influential clergyman, Father O'Reilly, still on vacation in Florida, sent back no advice to his flock.

As another week began, the mayor and an ad hoc Citizens' Committee shuttled back and forth between Lawrence and Boston, seeking a settlement. They were encouraged on Sunday when mill owners said they might meet employees, mill by mill,[37] but the strike committee quickly rejected such a piecemeal approach.[38] Longer picket lines formed behind signs reading: THE FIGHT IS ON—JOIN THE IWW AND STAY WITH US.[39] As leaders of both sides refused to talk, city officials seemed desperate, but strikers behaved as if, arisen from their slumbers, they saw no need to punch anyone's time clock. Their meetings, as precisely programmed as any at American Woolen headquarters, lasted entire mornings. Men chatted throughout while women sat patiently beside their children listening to the latest news and rumors. The committee drafted defiant letters to Billy Wood, voted to keep a booklet with names and photos of scabs,[40] and charted the steady growth of the strike fund. From beyond Lawrence, money had begun to trickle in. A fifty-dollar check from a woman in Arlington.[41] One hundred dollars from shoemakers in Haverhill, then another seven hundred dollars.[42] Contributions in kind came from within the city. Polish bakers offered bread at reduced prices while Polish barbers said they would not shave any scabs. Armenians served free food to Armenian strikers at their boardinghouses.[43] And on Tuesday, January 23, the first soup kitchen opened at Franco-Belgian Hall.

Twice a day, mornings and afternoons, three long tables in the creaky, shedlike hall[44] filled with hungry people. While women cooked in the back, men carried steaming bowls of soup, glass mugs of black coffee, and thick slices of rye bread to the tables. Children and adults, coming from tenements heated solely by kitchen stoves, drank in the warmth as much as the nutrition. A babble of tongues filled the room as adults shared news while children, their faces[45] lean and dirty, gobbled down bowls of soup and asked for more. Unlike Oliver Twist, they were given it. "Give them all they want" was the kitchen's unofficial motto. Across the hall, a long line of children, dinner pails in hand to take soup home to their families, eyed the steaming bowls.[46] The soup kitchen, which would eventually serve nearly four thousand meals a day,[47] was a spin-off of a cooperative the Franco-Belgians had been running in Lawrence for years.[48] It quickly became the model for relief efforts in other ethnic neighborhoods, each feeding thousands more.[49] Like the strike itself, soup kitchens broke down barriers. "I didn't dare go at first because I came from an Orthodox family and it was Gentile food," one man recalled. "Well, the first day I went to the soup kitchen, run by a Belgian organization, I got a ham sandwich. Which, I had never tasted ham before. And a frankfurter. When I got back from the soup kitchen, my mother said, 'Here's a cup of tea and some bread.' I said, 'I already ate, mother.' She says,

'Where'd you eat?' and I told her, 'In the soup kitchen.' She immediately washed my mouth out with kosher soap and water and I was told not to go back. But being hungry, I went along with the boys."[50]

While their children were being fed, strikers continued to parade. They had also begun singing—on the picket line, on the march, during meetings. "It is the first strike I ever saw which sang!" one seasoned reporter wrote. "I shall not soon forget the curious lift, the strange sudden fire of the mingled nationalities at the strike meetings when they broke into the universal language of song." Strikers soon had songbooks provided by the IWW, including the "Eight Hour Song," the "Banner of Labor," and "Workers, Shall the Masters Rule Us?"[51] They also wrote their own songs, including a parody of "In the Good Old Summertime."

> In the good old picket line, in the good old picket line
> The workers are from every place, from nearly every clime
> The Greeks and Poles are out so strong, and the Germans all
>   the time,
> But we want to see more Irish in the good old picket line.[52]

Following strict orders from Ettor, parades did not approach the mill district, but sometimes when sighting militia, strikers shouted "Boo!" and marched on, laughing and joking.[53] Despite the revelry, the rest of the city remained on edge and fear of dynamite darkened discussions. Was there really a McNamara plot in Lawrence? Would a mill or municipal building be leveled at any moment? Police questioned suspects but did not know what to make of what they were told. Especially puzzling was testimony from two Armenians, roommates of the Syrian tailor accused of leading the plot. At 10:30 p.m. the night before dynamite was discovered, a knock on the door had awoken David Rashad. Opening the door, Rashad faced a strange man carrying a package. Rashad spoke little English but noted that the stranger did not know the names of anyone at 292 Oak Street. The package, the stranger said, was for "the man in the house." Rashad had put the bundle on the table and gone back to bed. A half hour later, his roommate had come home. Opening the package, Joseph Assef found sticks "like sausage or candles." "I was thinking of touching a match to one of the things to see if it would light," Assef told police. The next morning, he took

the sticks to a local coffeehouse where a friend identified them as dynamite. A neighborhood druggist told him to call the police right away. Returning home, Assef set the dynamite in the closet, intending to take it to
the police station after lunch, but "the officers came and saved me the trouble." This seemed an unlikely story, but when police questioned the druggist, he corroborated the details down to the minute. Police moved on to
question cobbler Urbano da Prato. A thin man with a handlebar mustache,
da Prato told of a stranger delivering a bundle to his shop on Saturday
morning. The stranger was a stout Irishman in a black derby who "talked
good English."[54] Assuming the bundle contained shoes, the cobbler had set
it in his shopwindow[55] beneath large lettering that read SHINE 5¢.[56] And
that was just where police found it, wrapped in a magazine.

As these stories spread, some began to wonder why investigators, having discovered nothing in their initial search of the church cemetery,
returned with a map detailing exactly where to find the third cache of dynamite.[57] On a sandbank. Concealed beneath a bush. Wrapped in paper.[58]
Then on Sunday evening, a stranger carrying a bundle knocked on another door on Oak Street. A Syrian woman answered. The bundle, the man
told her, was for her brother-in-law. Having heard David Rashad's story,
the woman screamed and the stranger fled. When the "man of the house"
came home, he notified police, whose suspicions were already deepening.[59] In court on Monday morning, January 22, Judge Mahoney held the
dynamite cases over until Friday. The city's assistant marshal had asked for
the continuance, noting, "There are some things not satisfactory to the police,"[60] while the judge saw "indications to show that the men and women
arrested, charged with having cached dynamite in this city are innocent
victims of a plot, and dupes of some persons interested in maintaining a
reign of terror in this city."[61] But what persons? Other strikers? Anarchists
from Boston? Wobblies from out west?

The city tried to relax, but with an army on its streets and mill owners
getting gun permits for loyal workers,[62] the panic could only settle into a
pall of despair. The weather refused to relent. More snow fell on Monday
and Tuesday. All through the mill district, raw-faced militiamen stamped
their feet to keep warm, griping about the cold, their skimpy rations of
hash and stew, and the drudgery of this duty. Struggling to keep up their
spirits, each night they danced jigs, gathered around a piano to sing,[63] or

waged shadowboxing bouts in the spooky, echoing mills.[64] Along Essex Street, honking cars and hacks jousted for position while women in shawls, their children in tow, trudged beneath grimy skies.[65] Visitors from out of town noticed how few overcoats or even sweaters protected the children of Lawrence, whose faces and hands were tinted blue by the brutal winter.[66] Each morning, thousands of workers ran a gauntlet of hecklers and crossed lines of jeering pickets to enter the mills, which straggled along with two-thirds of their employees out.[67] Black smoke still spewed from smokestacks, and pickets could see silhouettes in a few mill windows, but even more windows were dark, shattered, or faceless, hiding whatever little work might be going on behind them. All day in the tired tenements, thousands clustered like rats, waiting for some sign of progress. The parades were exhilarating, the soup kitchens were open, and there was always another meeting to attend, but still there were hours on end to fill. Hours of bitter cold. Hours cooped up with whining children. Hours fighting the temptation to just end it all and go back to work. Who had suspected that once the dawn-to-dusk workday was removed from their routine, dawn to dusk could seem as wearisome outside the mills as inside them?

While women busied themselves at their second jobs—caring for children—men desperate to do *something* sought work elsewhere. On Monday, the Lawrence Ice Company advertised for men to cut chunks of ice from the Merrimack. In those days before refrigerators, nature's own refrigerant was peddled from drays whose drivers sold a thirty-pound block of ice for a dime.[68] Sawing ice was frigid, grueling labor, but nearly a thousand men responded to the ad; eight hundred were turned away.[69] On many days, dozens of strikers made the short train trip to Lowell only to be told that mills there did not need "floaters."[70] As the strike approached the end of its second week, every day brought another alarming report—a striker bayoneted in the arm,[71] a scab knifed, even a horse stabbed by accident. What was happening to the city and when would it end? Gathered in crowded kitchens, families asked each other hard questions. Should they go back to the old country? Go back to work? Stand firm and risk starvation and, if the strike failed, reprisals or dismissal? Politics became personal as younger strikers echoed an IWW flyer or an Ettor speech, only to be upbraided by an elder. Socialism might be fine for Europe, but this was not the old country. This was America. Didn't it promise a better life for all, a life of individual freedom? As decisions were debated, a certain indefinable resilience toughened the strike force. Having come this far, leaving their cultures and countries, crossing the Atlantic, being herded like cattle through Ellis Island, finding a job, learning it, enduring it, starting a new life, almost no one was ready to go back. Some could not, having fled violence or persecution; the rest would not. They had not come so far just to return, bitter and defeated. So they dug in, dug down, intensifying the strike and all its emotions. The constant shift of mood, from jubilation to anger to fear, crystallized in a single day, one that began in celebration and ended in betrayal.

At 9:00 a.m. on Wednesday, January 24, a crowd began to gather at the depot. More than a hundred passenger trains pulled into Lawrence each day,[72] but the crowd was not anticipating family or friends; it was waiting for a legend. By 11:30, ten thousand people milled around the ubiquitous American flags.[73] One young woman, not content to march with a flag, had fashioned a bonnet and shawl from the Stars and Stripes and now posed coyly for newspaper photographers.[74] Finally just before noon, another engine puffed into the station. Someone on the platform saw the familiar face—chubby, taciturn, seeming to squint—and great cheers echoed off the bell tower as William Dudley Haywood arrived in Lawrence.

Many must have been surprised to see that Big Bill was wearing a derby instead of his famous Stetson. And he was not as big as his nickname suggested. Newspapers had listed him "well over six feet," even "close to seven feet,"[75] but he actually stood five foot eleven. At 240 pounds,[76] his expansive waistline earned him his nickname,[77] but the moniker applied equally to his life. By the time he came to Lawrence, Big Bill had lived one of the largest lives in post–Civil War America. He had been a miner, a cowboy, and a homesteader. He had prospected for gold in Nevada and won and lost small fortunes at faro tables in Colorado saloons. He had lost one eye, and had his right hand crushed in a mining accident. Tried for a murder he did not commit, he had also gone free after shooting a detective in a street brawl. He had led his wife, a frail, sickly woman called Nevada Jane, on a palomino pony across 140 miles of desert to reach some natural mud baths to relieve her rheumatism. And when Nevada Jane began giving birth to a second child in their remote cabin, Haywood frantically skimmed a medical manual, then delivered his daughter himself, cutting and tying the umbilical cord. Later, when he rose to become a labor leader, this one-eyed ex-miner and street brawler was welcomed in London by George Bernard Shaw and in Copenhagen by Vladimir Ilyich Ulyanov, whom the world had not yet learned to fear as Lenin. Tough as rawhide, seasoned like a good bourbon, Haywood also memorized Shakespeare and whiled away idle hours playing chess. To workers from coast to coast, he was not just a leader; he was, as Eugene Debs called him, "the Lincoln of labor."[78] To mill bosses, mine owners, and police he was as dangerous as dynamite itself.

The most seditious man of his times came from the most American of circumstances. Haywood was the only leader on either side of the strike who was neither an immigrant nor the child of immigrants. He was born in an adobe house[79] in Salt Lake City just a few months before the golden spike completed the transcontinental railroad in 1869. His mother had come west in a covered wagon.[80] He had only one memory of his father, a former Pony Express rider. Home from a mining camp, Bill Haywood Sr. bought his three-year-old son candy and his first pair of pants, then carried the boy on his shoulders. Soon after returning to the mines, Haywood's father died of pneumonia. When Bill's mother took him to visit his father's grave, the boy fell on it. "I remember digging down as far as I could reach," he later wrote.[81] When his mother remarried, the family moved to a mining camp, where Bill witnessed gunfights, explosions, and a lynching. "These scenes of blood and violence happened when I was seven years old," he remembered. "I accepted it all as a natural part of life."[82] At nine, he lost his right eye when a knife, with which he was whittling a slingshot, slipped and sliced into it. Doctors kept him in a dark room for days, but to no avail.[83] The useless eye remained in its socket, giving him a menacing squint, which he concealed in photographs by posing in profile.[84]

Haywood quit school at twelve and went to work on a farm, where he soon waged his first strike. One day he stopped plowing to watch a den of mice. Spotting the squatting boy, his boss struck him with a whip. Haywood gathered his things and left for home, but the boss tracked him down and reminded his mother her son was under contract.[85] Haywood reluctantly returned to the job but left six months later and began ricocheting around Utah and Nevada, working in silver and lead mines. He might have remained a miner until, like thousands of others, he died young or was killed on the job, but in 1886, he began to question the way things were after reading about a bombing in Chicago. Haywood followed the Haymarket affair from a Nevada mining camp. "I was trying to fathom in my own mind the reason for the explosion," he remembered. "Were the strikers responsible for it? Was it the men who were their spokesmen? Why were the policemen in Haymarket Square? Who threw the bomb? . . . Who were those who were so anxious to hang these men they called anarchists?" The event, Haywood concluded, was "a turning point in my life."[86]

Before his life could turn around, however, Haywood had to spend another decade scraping out an existence for himself and his new wife. Failure met him at every turn. He tried homesteading on an abandoned federal fort, but lost his land when it became part of a new Indian reservation.[87] With his wife bedridden following the birth of their daughter, Haywood grew more desperate. During the Panic of 1893, the nation's worst depression prior to the 1930s, he left his family with in-laws and went to California. Roaming mining camps and railroad yards, he found no work. He joined Coxey's Army, a ragtag band of unemployed men riding the rails toward Washington, DC, to march for jobs, but got off the train in Nevada and returned to his family in Winnemucca. There, he read about the Pullman Strike and saw a union's power firsthand. When local railroad workers refused to handle boxcars packed with produce bound for Chicago, the cars sat on sidings in Winnemucca. Hungry men helped themselves to oranges and other bounty. Haywood saw Pullman as a "great rift of light."[88] If all workers could join into one big union, they could shut down mines, mills, the entire nation, refusing to work until they earned decent wages, fewer hours. They might even take over the means of production, owning everything they had made with their own hands. Pursuit of this dream, however, would have to wait until Haywood lightened his own workload.

After a full day rounding up cattle or digging ore, Haywood did all the housework and cared for his children while Nevada Jane lay helpless in bed. The harder he worked, the more embittered he became. Seeing striking miners clubbed, shot, or caged in "bullpens,"[89] he came to loathe "the capitalist class." "The capitalist has no heart," he would later say, "but harpoon him in the pocketbook and you will draw blood."[90] Finally, in 1896, he joined the fledgling Western Federation of Miners and began working his way through its ranks. By 1901, his strategic, chess-playing mind had made him the WFM's second in command. He moved his family to Denver,[91] where his size and reputation singled him out as the target of mine owners and their hired thugs. Haywood's explosive temper often got him in trouble, but in his many brawls he gave as good as he got. Once in Denver's Union Station, he spotted a mine owner and threw a punch. Knocked sprawling, Haywood came up facing the barrel of a gun. "Pull it, you son of a bitch, pull it!" he screamed. Bloodied and bedraggled, he was taken into custody, where he decked two deputies before being beaten senseless.[92] Another time, when he and fellow organizers left a saloon, they were met by deputy sheriffs. Words followed, then fists. Struck with a pistol butt, Haywood dropped to his knees, pulled his own gun, and fired. He was booked for attempted murder but released when the victim recovered and police labeled the shooting self-defense.[93] A few years later, not long after he pounded the loose board that called the first IWW convention to order, he was not so lucky.

Beyond mining camps and IWW meeting halls, the nickname "Big Bill" was little known until 1907, when Haywood was tried for the murder of Idaho's former governor. Prosecutors did not claim Haywood planted the bomb that killed Frank Steunenberg on December 30, 1905.[94] But when a drifter named Harry Orchard was offered immunity and a cushy jail cell, he confessed to the killing and was encouraged to go further. Who had hired him? Orchard fingered Haywood and two WFM associates, claiming the killing was payback for the governor's ruthless suppression of a miners' strike. Rounded up in Denver without any extradition hearing, Haywood was loaded onto a sealed train and whisked to a Boise jail. Behind bars, he read Tolstoy, Dostoyevsky, and Marx,[95] while an America growing more attuned to its smoldering class war learned his name. Legal challenges to Haywood's "kidnapping"[96] went to the U.S. Supreme Court. With one lone dissenter, the Court ruled that the arrest, though "hastily and inconsiderately done," did not violate the Constitution.[97] Haywood had to stand trial. On May Day, tens of thousands marched singing "Shall Moyer, Haywood, and Pettibone die? Here are 60,000 workingmen who will know the reason why."[98] And when President Roosevelt called Haywood an "undesirable citizen," marchers wore buttons proclaiming that they, too, were undesirable citizens.[99]

The trial began on May 9, 1907. Defending Haywood was Clarence Darrow, who would seem to be at every celebrated trial of the time. After a jury composed of farmers and ex-farmers was impaneled,[100] Harry Orchard began to tell his story, "and what a story!" as Darrow later noted.[101] Orchard recited a list of bombings he'd done at Haywood's bequest, giving precise fees he'd been paid, concluding with $240 to assassinate Governor Steunenberg. But there was no one to corroborate Orchard's story. Another drifter had earlier confessed to being at the meeting where the assassination was planned, but he later recanted and did not appear at the trial.[102] Orchard's testimony was left hanging alone in the courtroom, yet his startling recall and self-assurance convinced nearly everyone that Haywood would be found guilty.

In his eleven-hour summation,[103] Darrow summed up Haywood in a few sentences. "I don't claim that this man is an angel," Darrow told the jury. "The Western Federation of Miners could not afford to put an angel at their head. Do you want to hire an angel to fight the Mine Owners Association and the Pinkerton detectives and the power of great wealth? Oh, no, gentlemen, you'd better get a first class fighting man who has physical courage, who has mental courage, who has strong devotion, who loves the poor, who loves the weak, who hates inequity and hates it more when it is with the powerful and the great."[104] The jury deliberated for twenty-one hours. To this day, some think Haywood did hire Orchard,[105] but when the surprising verdict—not guilty—spread throughout the nation, miners lit fireworks, danced around bonfires, and set off tons of dynamite. The fiery anarchist Emma Goldman sent President Roosevelt a telegram reading: "Undesirable citizens victorious. Rejoice!"[106]

Haywood emerged from the courtroom a free man and a national symbol of defiant, uncompromising Labor. He spent the next four years touring the country, speaking to packed urban auditoriums and to disgruntled workers on the job. Travel and fame broke up his marriage. He never again lived with Nevada Jane, whose conversion to Christian Science appalled the atheistic Haywood,[107] yet steady speaking engagements made him a master at controlling a crowd. Haywood captivated audiences with his booming voice, his scathing rhetoric, and his wit. "Tonight I am going to speak on the class struggle," he often began, "and I am going to make it so plain that even a lawyer can understand it."[108] While on the podium, he often joked, "I'm a two-gun man from the West, you know." Then he would reach for his "guns," pulling his union card from one pocket, his Socialist

Party card from another.[109] Haywood was often criticized for his incendiary statements, which made the IWW look even more radical than it was: "Confiscate! That's good! I like that word. It suggests stripping the capitalist, taking something away from him. But there has got to be a good deal of force to this thing of taking."[110] Yet Haywood left no doubt about his sincerity or his vision. "They can't stop us," he told workers. "No matter what they do we will go on and on until we—the roughnecks of the world—will take control of all production and work when we please and how much we please. The man who makes the wagon will ride in it himself."[111]

On the Monday before his arrival in Lawrence, Haywood sent a letter to Ettor. Congratulating him on the job he had done so far, Haywood warned, "Keep the reins tight, Joe. They want you and will get you if they can. Get your committees in shape so that every detail of work will go on without interruption even if you are arrested."[112] Then putting the finishing touches on plans for his next speaking tour, he boarded the train out of Manhattan. When he pulled into Lawrence on Wednesday morning, January 24, the man used to holding crowds in the palm of his hand found the situation reversed. To the music of bands and the shouts of revelers, the crowd lifted all 240 pounds of Haywood and carried him on their shoulders. The reception was "the greatest demonstration ever accorded a visitor to Lawrence,"[113] the *Lawrence Tribune* proclaimed. Carried, shoved, escorted by self-appointed bodyguards, Haywood was in the crowd's hands throughout a half-mile[114] procession from the depot to 109 Oak Street. There he scurried into Paul Chabis Hall, where Ettor was meeting with the strike committee. The crowd continued to clamor outside until Ettor appeared at a second-story window. With a wave of his hand, he silenced them and told everyone to disperse and gather at the bandstand on the common at 2:00 p.m.[115] Then old friends Ettor and Haywood met to discuss the day's plans, which for the first time included a meeting with mill owners.

Only a half hour before, while the crowd had been waiting for Haywood, a car carrying Mayor Scanlon and Colonel Sweetser had pulled up in front of Paul Chabis Hall. The two men had great news for Ettor, who met them on the street. Mill owners had agreed to meet the strike committee that evening at 7:00 p.m. Ettor balked. He had other commitments—speaking engagements, mostly—but the mayor insisted. "We have been trying to bring this thing about for ten days," a desperate Scanlon told Ettor. From inside the car, Colonel Sweetser said, "Come down and you will be the most popular man in town." Ettor noted that he didn't need to be more popular than he already was but finally agreed. The car bearing the mayor and the colonel sped off.[116]

With Haywood in town and a meeting scheduled with mill bosses, Wednesday was progressing as if the strike would be over by the weekend. Strikers were also inspired by the appearance of Dominic Rapradi. Rumored to be near death after being stabbed near the Pacific Mill eight days earlier, Rapradi stood smiling before the strike committee, another symbol of endurance.[117] Even the sky seemed optimistic. That afternoon beneath a bright blue canopy, ten thousand assembled beneath the bare maples and oaks on the Lawrence Common. Speaking from the bandstand in the center of the expansive stretch of snow, Ettor introduced a new face in the strikers' pantheon—Arturo Giovannitti. A poet and editor of *Il Proletario*, an Italian Socialist weekly in New York, the bookish Giovannitti said a few words in his native tongue, then turned the podium over to the man everyone had been waiting for.

As Haywood stepped before them, his hard life and hard drinking made him look older than his forty-two years. Thinning hair, a prominent nose, and heavy jowls gave him an uncanny resemblance to W. C. Fields, but speaking without a microphone, he leaned forward and hurled his words like Teddy Roosevelt himself. For nearly everyone present, the speech offered a first chance to hear Haywood, but it was not Haywood at his best. Accustomed to tapping an audience's anger, he seemed nonplussed at the sight of such jubilation among so many different nationalities. What could he add that Ettor had not already said? Looking across the sea of industrial faces, Haywood cobbled together a speech of platitudes. He urged "sister and brother workers" to "keep a tight rein on yourselves. . . . You have been ground down terribly in these mills. I can see that by your faces." But he moved the crowd with tales of victorious general strikes in London and Paris, and announced he would soon tour the West, "and every city that I go into I will say to the unions, 'Help the strikers in Lawrence by sending provisions and money.'" The crowd cheered Haywood to the last word, then with "Big Bill" and "Smiling Joe" at the lead began yet another parade. At its conclusion back on the common, Haywood praised the group as "truly a parade of nations."[118] Only in the coming weeks, when jubilation had surrendered to rage, would Haywood live up to his reputation.

As if the parade and its grand marshal were not enough to lift spirits, another revelation brightened Wednesday's mood. Governor Foss's private secretary had written a confidential letter to a journalist. Leaked to the press, the letter appeared in print that afternoon. It blasted mill owners as being "more solicitous of their machines of steel and iron than they are of the human machines," and blamed the strike on one man. "Public sentiment points its finger in one direction—at him. Living conditions as he ordained them are intolerable."[119] The next day, the governor's secretary would express shock that his letter had been leaked, while the "one man," William Wood, objected to the "wicked and cruel" accusation.[120] But as the evening meeting with mill owners approached, strikers felt that even the mill-owning governor might be on their side. Then the meeting began.

At 7:00 p.m., Ettor, Haywood, and all fifty-six members of the strike committee entered the cramped aldermen's chamber in city hall. They were met by the mayor and other city officials. But where were the mill owners? A few mill agents sat in nearby seats, but when American Woolen's representative arrived, they all rose and retired to the mayor's office. And thus the strange encounter began. Willard Howland, chairman of the state board of arbitration, spoke to strikers about the urgency of the situation and the need for a quick settlement. A striker standing in the back interrupted.

"I would like to ask *who* is representing the other side here?"

"There is no other side," Howland replied. "We have invited you and the manufacturers to come—"

Strikers began muttering "no, no!" until Ettor calmed them. Outraged that he had canceled other meetings for this one, he threatened a mass walkout unless mill agents came out of the mayor's office immediately. Howland said the men still wanted to meet with employees mill by mill, but Ettor refused. "There is only one lash of hunger which the employers have wielded over these people," he said, "and now there is only one union for them to deal with." While Howland retired to the mayor's office to consult with the mill men, aldermen apologized to Ettor, saying they had been assured mill owners would be present. Moments later, Howland returned. He began stressing the importance of arbitration but Ettor cut him short.

"I want again to insist on the purpose for which we came here," Ettor said. "If the chairman of the state board wants to give us a lecture on the advantages of arbitration we can appoint a time and place for it. But now we are here for a purpose." Howland then revealed that the mill agents had refused to meet with strikers as a whole. Men and women began to walk out.

"Come back! Come back!" Mayor Scanlon shouted. "Ask Mr. Ettor when he will meet with the mill men in committee of the whole!" But Ettor, having wasted the evening, was reluctant to set a time. When Scanlon asked how much notice he would need for a meeting, Ettor replied, "I believe that the other side has more time than we have. They have more automobiles than we have at any rate. I can state no time." Pressed further, he granted that with a few hours' notice, the committee could gather again, but only to meet with mill owners themselves. An alderman returning from the mayor's office then announced that all but two of the mill agents had gone home. "We've been wasting our time," a striker said. "I move we adjourn." And with an echoing "Aye!" the meeting was over. Flanked by Haywood and Ettor, the committee shuffled out into the dark streets.[121] The day that had begun with such promise ended in another long walk back to the tenements, and the temperature was dropping fast.

Nothing was changing; both sides were as unyielding as the icebound Merrimack. As the week unraveled, Governor Foss called for a state probe of conditions in Lawrence,[122] while the city's small Socialist Party began gathering signatures to recall the mayor whose reform crusade had made recall possible.[123] Soup kitchens continued serving hot meals, and one downtown clothing store promised to donate 10 percent of its sales to the strike fund.[124] Then on Friday, January 26, another flutter of optimism surfaced. That afternoon, newsboys on Essex Street shouted the headline of the evening's *Lawrence Tribune*: SETTLEMENT IN SIGHT![125] William Wood had agreed to meet Ettor in person. Even before the news hit the street, however, the meeting was over.

It had begun cordially. At 3:00 p.m., in the somber, dark paneled offices of the American Woolen Company in Boston, the plump, pompous head of the wool trust—dressed in a natty suit with a pince-nez, spats, and a watch chain—shook hands with the quintessence of free-thinking radical-ism with his wild head of hair and perpetual smile. Then William Wood and Joseph Ettor sat and sized each other up. The two men had much in common. Both were short and intense, the sons of immigrants who had risen from menial labor. Both claimed to be the true representatives of twenty-eight thousand "fellow workers." Yet although they sat across a sin-gle table, they could not have been farther apart. Wood, with his attorney close by, credited Ettor with keeping strikers in line, calling him "a great lit-tle general."[126] Ettor had no time for cordialities. Instead, he pressed the strikers' demands—a 15 percent pay raise, double pay for overtime, no more "bonus system," no recriminations. Wood questioned the wage in-crease, causing Ettor to invoke free-market principles. When you sell your cloth, you ask a price for it, Ettor told Wood. If dealers don't want to pay that price they can't get the cloth. The wage increase was the new price of labor in Lawrence. If the president of American Woolen wanted to sell his goods, he would have to pay the price. Bayonets did not weave cloth.[127]

Wood and his attorney retired to another room, then returned. Ameri-can Woolen would not meet any of the demands, Wood declared. Strikers should rethink them. Ettor refused and the meeting ended. "Disgusted but not discouraged," Ettor told strikers to "prepare for a long struggle," while Wood issued a statement that mill owners would no longer meet with Joseph Ettor. "Negotiations along this line are at an end,"[128] he declared. And then, William Wood disappeared from the strike. Still hurt by being made into the villain, and appalled at the leadership his employees pre-ferred to his own, Wood stopped issuing statements to the press. He sent no more letters to strikers. He simply dropped out of sight, refusing to pontificate, threaten, or even posture. And his plan, if it was one, seemed to work. Strikers would soon stop berating "Billy Wood" in favor of more vis-ible enemies.

The morning after Wood met Ettor, police exonerated all those arrested for harboring dynamite. Word was leaked that "one very well known young man" was being questioned about "planting" the explosive.[129] That after-noon at dusk, residents living near the city's reservoir feared the worst when they heard three explosions. But the blasts turned out to be the confiscated dynamite being detonated by state police. Discovered to contain 75 percent nitroglycerin, with a highly sensitive cap that could have been set off by the slightest pressure, the dynamite was judged the most powerful ever found in New England.[130] A few hours later, Haywood boarded a train for Toledo, Ohio, where he had a speaking engagement. "There are no foreigners here except the capitalists," Big Bill told a crowd,[131] promising to return to Lawrence as soon as he could.[132] Throughout the weekend onlookers came and went, the militia donned capes to keep warm, and strikers planned a "monster" parade around the mills at 6:00 a.m. on Monday. After an exhausting second week, twenty thousand people remained without work or pay, yet the strike leader's unflappable mood kept hopes alive. Told that one mill overseer was meeting strikers at his home to persuade them to go back to work, Ettor quipped, "He must have a pretty big house."[133]

CHAPTER SIX

Spinning Out of Control

> *O what is that sound which so thrills the ear*
> *Down in the valley drumming, drumming?*
> *Only the scarlet soldiers, dear,*
> *The soldiers coming.*

—W. H. Auden

Despite thousands of witnesses, dozens of newspaper reports, and the testimony of a lengthy murder trial, what happened in Lawrence on January 29, 1912, remains shrouded in uncertainty. The most mystifying piece of the puzzle was the mob that attacked the city's streetcars two hours before sunrise.

Mobs know little of logic, yet they usually have their own motives for running riot. The chaos in Lawrence that morning, however, defied all common sense. For Labor, the strike was going as well as could be expected, well enough for its leader to declare victory. The previous Friday evening, just a few hours after meeting William Wood, Ettor had spoken at Faneuil Hall. Standing at a podium in the majestic old colonial building where the late Abbott Lawrence had been eulogized, Ettor made a bold assessment. "The preachers have been preaching the brotherhood of man for more than two thousand years," he told the Boston Socialist Club, "and we have more nearly realized it in this strike than it has ever been realized. Between you and me, this strike is won."[1] While premature, Ettor's boast seemed to mirror the strike's trajectory. The workers' initial overtures of anger, perpetrated without leadership or plan, had given way to unprecedented solidarity. Twenty thousand were forged into one, parading through the streets, celebrating, singing, mocking the mill owners who only a few weeks before had them beggared and beaten. State officials were weighing an investigation. The dynamite scare had dissolved into some dastardly scheme to disgrace the strikers, and under the national spotlight attracted by Haywood, a sizable strike fund was accumulating. Yet on Monday morning, Labor seemed willing to squander all these advantages just to keep more scabs out of the mill. As with the strike itself, this renewed violence began "like a spark of electricity." Police quickly rounded up two suspects, but no one would ever be sure who was to blame. There had, however, been fumes.

Throughout the weekend of January 27–28, strikers had shared the same disturbing story. Agents from American Woolen were combing the tenements, winding their way through muddy alleys, climbing gloomy staircases, knocking on doors. The strike was over, the mill men said. Come back to work on Monday. All demands had been accepted; all was forgiven. When Ettor learned of this tactic, he was furious. Fearing a wholesale return to the mills, he lashed out with incendiary rhetoric that would be quoted by his enemies for months to come. On Saturday afternoon, he told strikers how to deal with visitors from American Woolen. "If an overseer comes into your house and invites you to betray yourself into being either a 'scab' or a blacklisted man, throw him down the stairs!" Ettor shouted. Following wild applause, he compared the strike to a revolution, specifically the one that had recently overthrown China's centuries-old Qing dynasty. "The methods of the mill owners are not American," he said. "They lead straight to China. Now in China when they didn't like conditions, they got up a revolution lately and cut off the heads of the people who didn't agree with them. And if they go on grinding and grinding, you workers will have to do what they did in China and organize a head cutting expedition."[2] Speaking to nine separate meetings on Sunday,[3] Ettor proposed the Wobblies' most treasured tactic—sabotage. If strikers were forced to return to the mills, he said, they should fill their pockets with emery dust and throw it in the machines. "If they starve us back to the looms, God help their cloth, their yarn, and their looms when we go back!"[4] he said. Then for the first time in the strike, a crack appeared in Ettor's optimism. "This town won't be very happy in two days," he predicted. "Something is going to happen. There is going to be no dynamite, so don't get excited, but I'm telling you something is going to happen."[5]

The following morning, two hours before sunrise, strikers roamed through the tenements banging tin pans to wake their fellow workers.[6] By 5:15 a.m., more than a thousand people huddled together on Essex Street, waiting. Ettor had called for the parade to "close the mills tighter than ever before,"[7] yet he had also reminded strikers to "put your hands in your pockets and keep them there."[8] In the arctic blackness of early morning, with spotlights sweeping the mills and groggy militia already on duty, strikers obeyed Ettor's orders—at first. Then a single streetcar, its interior lights flickering, rumbled down Broadway toward Essex. Hands were pulled from pockets, and a hailstorm of stones and ice smashed into the trolley, shattering windows and bringing muffled screams from inside. Surrounded by the mob, the streetcar shuddered to a stop. A few men scrambled atop it to unhook the trolley from its overhead line, plunging the car into darkness.[9] Shouting "Scab! Scab!" strikers boarded and began dragging off anyone found carrying a lunch pail. Pails and bundles were thrown out of the cars, then stomped and kicked down the street. Passengers were stripped of overcoats, sweaters, and overalls. Twirling the clothes like flags of anarchy, strikers headed for the next unsuspecting trolley coming down the track.

As the sky lightened and start-up whistles resounded throughout the city, workers made their way toward the mills while strikers, most of them peaceful but dozens out for vengeance, roamed downtown. Ettor was seen here and there on the streets. He directed the mob away from mills[10] but not from streetcars or suspected scabs. Strikers cornered young women walking to work, forcing some to take refuge in the police station. Strikers smashed streetcar windows and dragged men out while hysterical women and children scurried behind seats. Stones and ice chunks flew everywhere. Struck in the face, one woman ran to the nearest militia screaming, "Shoot the cowards! Shoot them!"[11] But the mob stayed clear of the mill district and rarely encountered militia. When approached, militiamen locked their breech bolts with audible clicks. Strikers retreated, hissing and taunting. As Ettor moved from site to site, so did Colonel Sweetser, seen driving to strategic militia points. Meanwhile, all along Essex, police slugged it out with strikers while workers sought refuge on side streets or in shops that had opened early. As the sun rose on the melee, strikers "had full control of the streets of this city," the *Lawrence Tribune* reported.[12]

When it was all over, several policemen and workers nursed welts and gashes. A few trolley passengers had been cut by flying glass. Nine strikers were under arrest, and sixteen streetcars sat broken and battered.[13] But the damage to the strikers' cause could not be measured by numbers. Ettor had no idea of the morning's toll. As repercussions began to spread through the city, he spoke to a gathering on the common. "We turned one on the bosses this morning," he boasted. "They expected we would have a parade and instead we formed a picket line." Sending the crowd home, Ettor told a reporter that he was "perfectly satisfied with the situation." Asked about the attacks on streetcars, he said he had not seen any such thing and would have stopped it if he had.[14] Throughout the day, Ettor continued to make glib comments. When another reporter asked him about the violence, he said, "I don't know anything about that. That's none of my business. We fooled them, all right, by drawing up our separate picket lines, didn't we? They couldn't get by us."[15] At the strike committee's morning meeting, he added, "I will venture to say that there was more violence on the other side than on ours."[16] That was not how the other side saw it, however. Before noon, a score of the city's most reputable men, including the mayor and his aldermen, a committee of businessmen, several bankers, mill agents, and Colonel Sweetser met at the Bay State Bank to discuss putting the city under martial law, perhaps even closing the mills. Among many topics of discussion, the men quoted comments that Ettor and his assistant, the mysterious Arturo Giovannitti, had made to strikers and considered what might be done in response.[17]

By early afternoon, when Ettor realized the extent of the mob's damage, he began charging that, like the dynamite, the rioters had been planted. Neither police nor militia had stopped the riot, he asserted, because it was planned by mill owners to discredit the strikers. The cars under attack "were old, dinky cars not worth five cents," he told one audience, reminding them of the Pullman Strike when streetcar companies paid thugs posing as strikers to burn their old cars, then bought new ones with insurance money. Here in Lawrence, he said, undercover agents from the mills had infiltrated the strikers' ranks. "The work of these agents is to provoke trouble so that the strikers may be charged with rioting."[18]

Perhaps Ettor was covering his tracks. Or perhaps he was right. Coming in the wake of so many peaceful parades, Monday's violence seemed wholly out of character, as if a thriving merchant had been accused of torching his own store. Another suspicious element was the slogan carried by several men and women that morning—WE STRIKE FOR JUSTICE![19] The simplistic phrase can be found nowhere in any of the posters or flyers distributed by the IWW or by any striker throughout the ordeal. The hiring of detectives as agents provocateurs had been a common tactic in strikes. Though the Sherman detective hired by Mayor Scanlon remained clandestine, local newspapers had already reported detectives from both the Pinkerton[20] and Burns[21] agencies to be undercover in Lawrence. Months later, Alderman Cornelius Lynch, under oath during an investigation of the dynamite plot, would admit that police had provoked some of the strike violence.[22] Yet could dozens of hired thugs perpetrate such widespread mayhem without a single striker recognizing them as infiltrators? Had a few paid agitators started the destruction and let zealous workers do the rest? Or had Joseph Ettor, enraged by American Woolen's trickery, spoken too harshly, unleashing a wrath more destructive than he imagined? There are no clear clues to the cause of the riot on January 29, and no smoking gun proving it was caused by hired agents,[23] yet all morning and into the afternoon, the city simmered. By 4:00 p.m., when Ettor and Giovannitti were off to a meeting with German strikers,[24] the mood on the streets was even uglier than the morning's turmoil. The strike's last glowing embers of forbearance and restraint were about to be fanned into flames.

Precisely this much is known about Anna LoPizzo. She was thirty-three years old. She boarded at 18½ Common Street. She had dark brown hair and dark eyes.[25] She worked in a mill. On January 29, at about 5:00 p.m., she left her home and walked into the fringes of a brawl between strikers and police near the corner of Union and Garden streets. She was on strike but was not active in the picketing. She would not have been out at dusk had she not decided to visit a friend a few blocks away. It is difficult to imagine why, upon seeing strikers throwing ice at police who fought back with nightsticks, she would have gone anywhere near the free-for-all. Yet with a shawl over her head, she was standing on a street corner watching when the bullet struck her.

If America had a Tomb of the Unknown Immigrant paying tribute to the millions of migrants known only to God and to distant cousins compiling family trees, Anna LoPizzo would be a prime candidate to lie in it. Her name is known, but even that detail is debated. In the coming newspaper articles and history books she would be known as Annie LoPezzi, Anna La Piazza, Anna LaPizza, Anna Lopez, and several other variations. On Common Street, some said she was Anna LaMonica, having taken the surname of the agent who hired her for mill work.[26] One newspaper reported she wore a wedding ring,[27] though no husband turned up at her funeral. She had come to "La 'Merica" with the great wave of Italians that landed between 1890 and 1910. Ellis Island records list an Anna LoPizzo, age thirty, arriving on a twin-smokestack steamer from Naples on July 28, 1909.[28] There were no other LoPizzos on the ship. Perhaps one day, after quarreling with a husband back in the impoverished end of Italy's boot, she had seen a poster on some sepia-toned wall in her village. Perhaps the poster, with its bags of gold being carried from a mill, spoke to her of a better, or at least richer, life. Believing the promise, she made the crossing. Flushed from Ellis Island into the streets of Little Italy, she heard the word that circulated from Maine to Manhattan: "If you want a job, go to Lawrence."[29] She came to the textile city, and though she did not get much gold, she did get a job. She may have planned to send for other members of her family; she may have had no other family. Only one mourner, said to be an uncle, attended services at her grave. Yet thousands more filed past her casket, thousands who did not know any more about her than is known now—that she died an accidental martyr and that her death shook the city to its roots.

The battleship sky was darkening and the snow was coming down in buckets when a crowd began to gather at Union and Garden streets. The corner had been a strategic one throughout the strike. Union Street flanked the Everett Mill, which stretched for four blocks, north to south all the way to the North Canal. The Everett was still closed, but Union ran along its looming face before crossing the Duck Bridge leading workers to the Wood and Ayer mills. Because no militia patrolled as far north as Garden, strikers had free rein against workers passing the intersection carrying lunch pails. If approached by militia, anyone could easily escape into the safe haven of the Italian district. Thus, every morning at start-up and every evening at quitting time, the intersection was a rendezvous for those bent on finding scabs and, as Ettor had urged, making their lives miserable.[30] On this afternoon they were joined by hundreds of people eager to vent the rage of three weeks without work, of a mounting hunger, and of promises and posters proven to be lies.

Police received the call at 4:30 p.m. Only two patrolmen were on duty near the Everett, but given the morning's rioting, another dozen quickly responded. Colonel Sweetser, hearing about the impending riot, dispatched Company D. The militia arrived just as the police were beginning to use their nightsticks. "We used the clubs," the sergeant in charge later recalled. "We used them pretty hard and did not stop to count the ones we struck."[31] As the militia was spotted marching up Union, a cry went up. "The soldiers are coming!" Hundreds were soon pinned between police and militia. Many soldiers began clubbing heads and backs with rifle butts, hitting so hard that some rifles broke. Fallen strikers were carried from the scene, and the swift suppression did what it was supposed to do. The crowd scattered in all directions, but from nearby windows women screamed at police and goaded the strikers on.[32] The crowd regrouped and returned to the fray. Streetlights had gone on and, despite the heavy snow, the scene was as light as day, yet when the first shots were heard, no one knew who had fired. Moments later, a curious yelling came from the direction of several women standing off to one side.[33] Then in the fog of battle, events happened so quickly that they would never be sorted out.

As militia fought at one end of the mob, policemen found themselves surrounded by the group's northern flank. Dark figures streaked across brightly lit snow. Gray shadows followed. Shoving. Pushing. People falling, slipping on the slush and ice. Cries and the thud of wood on flesh. Surges of bodies heading in one direction, then another. More shots. Approaching a policeman, one man shouted, "Look out! They're going to get the police!" Another insisted the shots were blanks. Just then, one woman among the onlookers folded and fell to the ground. Before anyone could go to her, an officer felt a sharp pain in his back.

"I've been hit with a brick, I think," Officer Oscar Benoit said.

"Hit with a brick? You've been shot!"[34]

The officer was rushed to Lawrence General Hospital, a block up Garden Street, where a stab wound was found in his back. It was stitched up and he was sent home. The same ambulance carried Anna LoPizzo. A .38 caliber bullet had passed between her ribs, severed a pulmonary artery, and lodged in her right shoulder.[35] Doctors said she couldn't have suffered much. Some strikers later reported seeing a man fire at Officer Benoit but hit the woman by accident.[36] Benoit himself said the same.[37] Others, having seen a man firing at the ground, guessed that the bullet had ricocheted off the street, yet an autopsy revealed that it had been on a downward trajectory when it struck.[38] Whoever fired the shot, whatever the circumstances, the strike had claimed its first victim. No one knew her name—three Italians came to the hospital that evening but could not identify her—yet nothing would be the same again.[39] A somber hush lay over the strategic intersection of Union and Garden, where people clung to each other and stared at the red stain in the snow until more snow fell and covered it.

As the news spread through the city, tragedy was tinged by black humor and shock. At 9:00 p.m. Monday night, police arrested the man accused of planting dynamite. He was indeed "one very well known young man," as rumor had hinted. He was John Breen, an undertaker by trade, an ex-alderman and a current member of the school committee. He also came from one of the city's most prominent families, being the son of John Breen, Lawrence's first Irish mayor and frequent grand marshal of the city's enormous St. Patrick's Day parades.[40] Circulated with the report of Breen's arrest was gossip about how police had tracked him down. It was no Sherlock Holmes job. Breen had been the man who steered police to the dynamite, tipping them off, then drawing a map to help detectives whose first search of the church cemetery turned up empty.[41] But the smoking gun proved to be a magazine, though not the kind that holds bullets. Wrapped around the dynamite delivered to Urbano da Prato's cobbler's shop, the magazine was *Shadyside,* an undertaker's trade journal.[42] The magazine had a subscription label with a name—"John Breen"—clearly printed on it.[43] Lawrence was appalled and a little amused. "Maybe God intervened in that sense," Angelo Rocco later recalled. "In the stupidity."[44]

Breen was charged with conspiracy to destroy property and released on bail of one thousand dollars. Now that his good name was sullied, what was Lawrence to think of the new John Breen School dedicated during the strike's first week?[45] At least the grammar school had been named for Breen's father. And thank God the elder Breen, who had spent a lifetime building Lawrence's broad Irish political base, had not lived to see the family name on a court docket. But if John Breen wasn't the brightest alleged conspirator in the city, who had put him up to the plant? The conspiracy charge was leveled against "John J. Breen and a certain other person or persons whose name or names are not known."[46] One of the unknowns was thought to be a Syrian.[47] Strikers must have had their own guesses as to who else might be behind the plot. Some might even have suspected a man of Portuguese descent.

All that calamitous Monday Mayor Scanlon had been regretting an order he had given the day before. The previous afternoon, with the strike deadlocked, strikers jubilant, and an uneasy calm prevailing, the mayor had ordered the militia to stand down. Quartering and feeding eight hundred troops had already cost the city $10,500,[48] and the militia's full presence seemed unnecessary. On Scanlon's orders, three companies of militia had gone home, leaving only nine guarding the mills.[49] But on Monday evening, in the wake of riots and death, the mayor turned to Colonel Sweetser and offered him carte blanche. The colonel did not hesitate. Calls for militia went out all over eastern Massachusetts. All night, trains carrying troops rolled into the depot. From Wakefield. Stoneham. Charlestown. Newton. Waltham.[50] Two companies of cavalry, their chestnut horses groomed and prancing, came from Boston. Fresh ammunition was sent from an arsenal in South Framingham.[51] One company came from Harvard University, whose president excused militia volunteers from midterm exams in order to do their duty.[52] Harvard's new president had more than an academic interest in mill towns. Like his sister, the cigar-smoking poet Amy Lowell, and his brother, the renowned astronomer Percival Lowell, Abbott Lawrence Lowell was the grandchild of Abbott Lawrence.[53]

By Tuesday morning, January 30, fifteen hundred soldiers patrolled the streets of Lawrence. No longer guarding just the mills, lines of militia stretched past the storefronts of Essex Street, up Broadway, and through the tangle of tenements that clogged the city's center. Mounted police rode in formation, shouting out orders to "Keep moving!" Fifty-three of Boston's Metropolitan Police, brawny men in double-breasted light blue coats, were also on patrol. Eight sharpshooters from the U.S. Marines stood ready.[54] This was not martial law, as Colonel Sweetser, the lawyer, was careful to note. In Massachusetts, only the state legislature could declare martial law, and there was no time to wait for such a declaration.[55] Yet from here on in, the colonel decreed, there would be no more parades, no more meetings on the common, and "no more fooling."[56] Anyone on the street for any purpose would be considered a potential rioter and would be dealt with accordingly.[57] "If they think the soldiers are afraid to shoot," the colonel said, "they are making the biggest mistake of their lives. . . . Lawlessness will be repressed by whatever measures may be found necessary."[58]

That morning, militiamen fired their guns for the first time during the strike. Clamping down on security, especially near the mills, they had been told to watch for anyone crossing the frozen Merrimack. At about 5:00 a.m., they spotted a scrum of shadows heading onto the ice just beneath the Great Stone Dam and dangerously near the Uswoco Mill. Several soldiers fired warning shots. From the riverbank below, the men called to stop shooting. They were just going to work, they shouted. They had been hired by the Lawrence Ice Company.[59]

Yet in a city now on a hair trigger, serious trouble was not long in coming. An hour after shots were fired above the Merrimack, militia approached a group of Syrians all set to parade through their cloistered quarter. They had not heard of Colonel Sweetser's ban on parades, but militiamen quickly informed them. In the ensuing scuffle, many Syrians were chased through the streets. A few young boys stopped to throw ice. One who did was eighteen-year-old John Rami. With his mother and two brothers, Rami had come from a small village in the foothills of the Lebanon Mountains where cedars still grew on the slopes. Rami was employed in the Arlington Mill but actively supported the strike and had marched in the Syrian drum and bugle corps during parades.[60] His mother had begged him not to go out that morning, but he may have been planning to play in the parade. Witnesses reported that Rami and two

friends had been throwing ice at soldiers. Suddenly the boys found themselves running just a few feet ahead of advancing knives. At some point in
the chase, Rami slowed down. As the bayonets neared, he was trying to de-
flect one blade when another pierced his left shoulder. The wound did not
seem serious. Rami walked home and despite the blood on his shirt told
his mother not to worry. A doctor summoned to the house saw differently,
however, and sent Rami to the hospital. Rami asked if he might die and the
doctor said yes.[61]

When the citizens of Lawrence went out for their business on Tuesday,
January 30, they found an armed encampment. Soldiers and shoppers jostled on Essex Street. Several women had to remove their hats lest the large
feathers be knocked off by upright bayonets,[62] and everywhere one looked
stood a line of soldiers, their parallel weapons aiming skyward. Calm was
reported throughout the city. Mayor Scanlon saw the strike in permanent
deadlock, yet mill owners were more hopeful. Under an agreement with
the mayor, the mills had opened later than usual that morning. Because the
recent trouble had occurred in the darkness before the morning speedup,
the mills were put on daylight hours—7:30 a.m. to 4:30 p.m. All but two
were running and all reported substantial gains in their workforce.[63] Militia prevented any harassment of workers making their way to the mill
gates. The sounds of machinery echoed all along Canal Street, smoke
poured from chimneys, and the mills seemed to be churning away. It was
commonly believed that the strike was weakening, that death and mob violence had broken its back. Then two reporters peered behind the brick
curtain. A *Boston Globe* reporter stole into the Washington Mill spinning
room. He saw rows and rows of machines spinning but not a single worker
tending them.[64] The *New York Times* correspondent, posing as a mill executive driving a fancy car, entered the Arlington Mill and found the same
phantom scene. An enormous weaving room, usually hosting four thousand weavers, had just sixteen at work, and cavernous spinning, carding,
and combing rooms were empty, although their machines were running at
full speed.[65]

John Rami died that afternoon. The wound that had at first seemed
superficial had severed a major artery. This was just the latest blow to the
Syrians, who in the past two weeks had seen their leaders go on strike,

organize parades, and be accused of harboring dynamite. Throughout the Syrian quarter, grief mingled with hints of revenge.

"They kill that boy—all right," one man told a policeman that evening. "We get even tomorrow."

"Go home!" the policeman snapped. "Get in your house!"

"All right, I go home, but someone else won't go home tomorrow night."[66]

This second death within twenty-four hours numbed Joseph Ettor. All Tuesday afternoon he had conferred with Colonel Sweetser, negotiating plans for the funeral of Anna LoPizzo. Despite the colonel's ban on parades, Ettor had finally secured permission for a brief funeral procession.[67] Twenty thousand marchers were expected. And now strikers had another martyr to bury. Ettor emerged from the conference with the colonel more sullen than anyone in Lawrence had seen him.[68] For the last few days, he had been missing, in spirit at least. First uncharacteristically angry, then somber and serious, he had been a different man. But by evening when he spoke to two thousand Poles who had worked their way past militia to enter Paul Chabis Hall, he had recovered. Smiling, steely-eyed, at times even buoyant, he infused the crowd with his signature confidence. As he rose to speak, no one knew that this was to be Ettor's last speech during the strike. It opened with a renewal of purpose.

"I think this meeting is a denial that the strike is broken," Ettor began. "In their effort to win this fight they have got a few more soldiers and metropolitan police here and they will drown the strike in blood if possible. The mill owners now propose to argue. They will speak in the language of bayonets and dynamite. But the strike is won, there are no two ways about it." He recited the casualties, calling attention to a double standard. "To kill a striker is law, to cut a policeman's coat is murder. To us, murder is murder and mob rule is mob rule. If there has been any riot it is because their own men have started it. The only dynamite that we use is class solidarity. . . . We have but one issue—more bread for the strikers and less automobiles for the mill owners!" Ettor then dismissed strikers' fears of his imminent arrest. If arrested, he assured the crowd, he would soon be out on bail. "They have talked all night and they have talked all day and they are still talking," he said of his arrest. "That's all right. They know where to find me."[69] Ettor was right about the police; they knew just where to find him. He was wrong about the bail.

The Needham Hotel was one of those all-in-one Victorian hotels, the kind that might figure prominently in a novel by Theodore Dreiser. The Needham cut a low profile on Essex Street. It was a narrow cabinet of a building, six stories high but just four rooms wide, with white cornices above each window contrasting starkly with red brick.[70] But as the closest hotel to the depot, the Needham became the strike's unofficial base of operations. As was the custom at major urban hotels in 1912, businessmen booked rooms there for weeks at a time. Some men lived in the hotel, and others, including cops, reporters, and who knew how many undercover detectives hung out in its Rathskellar bar to get "the lowdown" on what was going on during the strike. The hotel boasted phone service, "electric and gas lighting," and "running water in every room." Except for the first week, when he had lodged with different strikers, Ettor had stayed at the Needham since arriving in Lawrence, setting up his headquarters in room 32. On Tuesday night, following his speech to Polish strikers, he returned to the hotel. Spotted by reporters in the lobby, he spent forty-five minutes answering questions, then excused himself, promising to return soon with a written statement. When his head of curly hair disappeared into the elevator, plainclothes police who had trailed him all day did their best to blend into the wallpaper. Reporters started a card game in the lobby. They were still playing when, at 11:30, a tall man wearing a derby and three-piece suit and sporting a walrus mustache[71] strode through the lobby and straight to the elevator. Moments later Ettor, fully dressed but weary and disheveled, opened his door, gazed up at Captain William Proctor, and was informed that he was under arrest. He asked to see the warrant. The charge was not inciting a riot, as he had expected. Two personal letters were taken from Ettor and he was handcuffed to Captain Proctor. Word soon spread through the hotel—"Ettor is pinched!"[72] As reporters scrambled, Ettor was led swiftly back through the lobby and into a police wagon. Two hours later, police knocked on the door of a tenement in the Italian district and arrested Arturo Giovannitti on the same charge—being an accessory to the murder of Anna LoPizzo.[73]

Early the next morning, Angelo Rocco came to the police station to see Ettor. Told that no visitors were allowed, Rocco left but returned moments later, insisting on seeing his friend. When Rocco gave his own name, Marshal O'Sullivan recognized him as one of the most influential Italian strikers. "He said, 'Lock him up! Lock him up!'" Rocco recalled. "I was locked up and they charged me with disturbing the peace."[74] As Rocco was going into his cell, the jail's more famous prisoners were being led out. At about 10:00 a.m. on January 31, Ettor and Giovannitti were booked. While the judge read the charge, Ettor studied his fingers, and Giovannitti, his face drawn, his large brown eyes sadder than usual, sat in silence. Both men pleaded not guilty. Had the charge been inciting a riot, they might have made bail, but no such grace was granted for those accused of murder, even as accessories. As they were being taken away, a woman charged with larceny walked over to Ettor and shook his hand.[75] Then with a dodge by police to skirt reporters and strikers waiting outside, Ettor and Giovannitti were hustled out a side door of the police station. The angry crowd that spotted them was promptly broken up by militia and the patrol wagon took them to the Essex County jail. Approaching the Gothic stone building with its multitiered tower and tall arched windows, Giovannitti remarked that it looked like a church.[76] They would not see the outside of it again until their arraignment the following week.

Without Ettor at the helm, the strike seemed like a tired dancer going through the motions. The Wednesday morning strike committee meeting was conducted by a local leader wielding Ettor's gavel. Strikers swore that Ettor's arrest had only strengthened their cause and the healthy attendance was encouraging, but after a mere forty-five minutes of the usual reports, the leaders retired to executive session.[77] Meanwhile, people struggled to go on in a city still reeling from the string of startling events. A shoe store on Essex Street put out word that it would distribute free bread that morning and militia had to keep order along a line that ran far down the sidewalk. In a single hour, five thousand loaves were shoved into grasping hands.[78] The mills continued to run in their ghostly fashion, and "absolute and universal peacefulness"[79] prevailed on the street, but it remained what Ettor had called "an industrial peace." From their perches high on horseback, mounted policemen caused the most tension. The clatter of hooves on the pavement deepened the winter's chill, causing children to gaze in wonder until they were hurried along by anxious parents. Stalking the tenements, men on horseback waved revolvers, scattered groups of people, and shouted at residents on doorsteps to go back inside.[80] The Harvard militia seemed more sporting. Though one said he was eager for a "fling at those people,"[81] the handsome Ivy Leaguers laughed and joked among themselves, posing for a group photograph as if they were a crew team. An unknown number of young women were especially taken by their uniforms. "Oh, they were dressed fancy," recalled Lillian Donohue, then a fifteen-year-old mill worker. "They wore blue capes and red satin linings!" Donohue eventually married a militiaman, though not one from Harvard.[82]

Early Wednesday morning, the last day of the month the strike had begun, undertaker Frank DeCesare laid the body of Anna LoPizzo in an open casket and opened his front doors. A line of people soon ran past the body, out the door, and for blocks along Common Street. Many in the procession were more outraged than mournful, and DeCesare was startled by talk of vengeance planned for the afternoon. Alarmed, he left for the police station. There he urged Ettor's attorney to get a statement from the leader calling off the procession. From his jail cell, Ettor sent a letter to the strikers.

> Fellow workers:
>
> In accordance with the desire on the part of mill owners to break your strike and that they may continue to spin and weave your lives into cloth, they arrested what they choose to call "the backbone of the strike."
>
> Let this serve you as a spur and determination to carry on the strike to a successful conclusion.
>
> Fellow Worker Yates has been advised what to do and in a day or two Bill Haywood and William E. Trautmann will be with you to give what aid they can to win your strike.
>
> Meanwhile, fellow workers, be of good cheer and remember the watchword is "No Arbitration. No Compromise." With greetings and cheer.
>
> Yours for victory,
> Joseph J. Ettor
>
> P.S. Am advising against funeral parade this afternoon. I am prevented from being with you in body but not in spirit.[83]

When DeCesare took Ettor's letter back to his funeral home, it seemed to calm mourners still filing past the casket. Yet the funeral director was taking no chances. Anticipating a riot or at least a demonstration, he hoped to remove the casket in secret, but all morning and into the afternoon, the faces just kept filing by. At 1:30 p.m., nearly one thousand people were milling outside the funeral parlor when mounted militia came around the corner of city hall and headed up Common Street. Halting before the crowd, the men on horseback pulled their revolvers, then slowly and ceremoniously loaded and locked them with clicks that could be heard even above the muttering of onlookers. The company captain ran inside and learned that the funeral had not yet been held. Emerging, he led his cavalry up and down Common Street. For more than an hour, the menacing standoff continued, the horses neighing, the men with revolvers at the ready, strikers and sympathizers booing and waving fists. Finally, at 3:40 p.m., when the crowd had thinned a little, DeCesare saw his chance. At his signal, a hearse pulled up ahead of a horse-drawn hack. The coffin was hustled outside. One lone mourner got in the hack and both vehicles drove to the Immaculate Conception Cemetery[84] on the northwest edge of town, within view of the Arlington Mill. There Anna LoPizzo was laid in a tomb to await the spring when the ground would thaw to enable her burial.

The following day, Thursday, February 1, hundreds of Syrians gathered for the funeral of John Rami. Filling the lime green Maronite church on Elm Street, women in black lace mantillas and men in dark suits chanted and sang. The air was sweetly scented with incense as the priest recited, "Fear not those who kill the body; fear those who kill the body and the soul." Father Gabriel Bastany suggested erecting a monument to Rami inscribed with the words "Killed in the Lawrence Strike," but none was ever built.[85]

And so the most baffling days of the strike ended with many marveling at how quickly the city's mood had darkened. It had been only a week since Haywood's celebrated arrival and just two since the first parade. Victory had seemed imminent then, but now many were expecting defeat any day. Toward the end of the week, two harbingers foretold even tougher times ahead. Portending yet another snowstorm, a delicate halo around the moon hovered over the city, as if one of the mill's chimneys had blown a smoke ring.[86] But a more reliable warning arrived in the form of military provi-

BOOK TWO

As we come marching, marching, in the beauty of the day,
A million darkened kitchens, a thousand mill-lofts gray
Are touched with all the radiance that a sudden sun discloses,
For the people hear us singing, "Bread and Roses, Bread and Roses."

As we come marching, marching, we battle, too, for men—
For they are women's children and we mother them again.
Our lives shall not be sweated from birth until life closes—
Hearts starve as well as bodies: Give us Bread, but give us Roses!

As we come marching, marching, unnumbered women dead
Go crying through our singing their ancient song of Bread;
Small art and love and beauty their drudging spirits knew—
Yes, it is Bread we fight for—but we fight for Roses, too.

As we come marching, marching, we bring the Greater days—
The rising of the women means the rising of the race—
No more the drudge and idler—then that toil where one reposes—
But a sharing of life's glories: Bread and Roses, Bread and Roses!

—James Oppenheim

CHAPTER SEVEN

A Nation Divided

America is in a period of clamor, of bewilderment, of an almost tremulous unrest. We are hastily reviewing all our social conceptions. We are profoundly disenchanted.

—Walter Weyl, *The New Democracy*, 1912[1]

Shortly after fifteen hundred soldiers settled in Lawrence, Mayor Scanlon received a letter from Nashua, New Hampshire.

> Dear Sir,
>   If you will engage me to help you in the strike in your town, I will guarantee you that I will do as much as three policemen, on condition that you will furnish me with one good horse and one Horn tree saddle, if possible, and one saddle whip or quirt and two (2) Colt revolvers. . . . I have just left the Navy about two months ago and would like to do something. I am a stranger around these parts of the country. I am a good shot and also a good horse rider as I had my training before I joined the Navy. I got my training in Penn and I can hit most anything with a Colt revolver, and . . . I have plenty of training in repulsing a mob. I await your answer.

The mayor's reply was tactful. While the offer was "duly appreciated," the city was already well guarded. Should the militia, Boston's Metropolitan Police, marine sharpshooters, and Lawrence's own officers fail to keep the peace in Lawrence, "chances are that your many qualifications will be considered."[2] The following day, two men were overheard in Manhattan discussing the arrest of Joseph Ettor. "Another damnable outrage by a lot of harebrained capitalists!" one said. "They have cooked their own goose. It will force an investigation into that death."[3] Lawrence, it seemed, was becoming the concern of the entire nation.

During the winter of 1912, America was accelerating into the twentieth century. Henry Ford's new Model T had made automobiles a more common sight, airplanes had just gotten off the ground, and railroads were approaching their peak of power and performance. The Panama Canal was evolving from a muddy ditch into the greatest engineering feat since the Pyramids. Manhattan and Chicago were scraping the sky. To the tinkling of a ragtime piano, nickelodeons showed short, flickering movies, including *The Lily of the Tenements,* directed by D. W. Griffith, and *Little Red Riding Hood,* starring "America's Sweetheart," Mary Pickford.[4] With expanded teletype coverage, newspapers ran headlines and photographs no one had ever seen in their own parlors—a race for the South Pole, Dutch girls standing before windmills, the crowned heads of Europe on parade. George M. Cohan and Ethel Barrymore starred on Broadway, while Buster Keaton, W. C. Fields, and some zany young brothers named Marx made the vaudeville circuit. The era was neither the best nor the worst of times, but many Americans did their best to portray it as one or the other. Whether preaching the imminence of a workers' revolution or defending the "white man's burden" to civilize a savage world, their conceits made it an age of high moral dudgeon.

Throughout January, two topics dominated the headlines. The first was the coming election. Republicans had held the White House for sixteen years and for all but two terms in the half century since Lincoln. In 1912, however, the incumbent was widely perceived as a big, fat pushover and the presidency seemed up for grabs. President Taft's veto of tariff revision still rankled the nation, while his habit of falling asleep at dinners, concerts, and cabinet meetings disquieted an energetic populace.[5] Even a fellow Republican saw the three-hundred-pound president as "an amiable man completely surrounded by men who know what they want."[6] This much everyone knew—Taft was no Teddy Roosevelt. All month, newspapers speculated on whether Roosevelt would try to recapture the White

House he had left three years earlier. Roosevelt wavered, making head-lines with each pronouncement. Meanwhile New Jersey's new governor, Woodrow Wilson, looked like a serious challenger, and Governor Foss of Massachusetts was considered a dark horse.[7]

The second topic of the times was the weather. Not since the blizzards of 1888 could anyone remember a worse winter. As temperatures hovered in the single digits, huddled masses shivered in their tenements and farm-ers were snowbound from Maine to the Midwest. Ice choked Boston Har-bor and the breadth of Long Island Sound.[8] At Niagara Falls, crowds walked daily out onto an ice floe sixty feet thick and a thousand feet long that had formed near the falls.[9] The winter overseas was warmer but even busier. China had just survived a revolution, while Cuba, Mexico, and Honduras boiled with rebellion, causing talk of sending U.S. Marines to protect the holdings of American fruit companies.[10] War was brewing in the Balkans while in imperial Russia, a hypnotic monk was said to have a mystical hold on Czarina Alexandra and her hemophiliac son, the heir to the Romanov dynasty.[11] But as February unfolded, in the wake of two deaths and a dynamite plot, Americans turned their attention to Lawrence.

This was a story anticipated for more than a decade. Well within the liv-ing memory of millions, America had changed beyond its own recogni-tion. Recently rural, it was now a nation of overcrowded, corrupt cities. Since the 1890s, reformers had been lecturing in quiet halls and cacopho-nous auditoriums, telling Americans that theirs was no longer the nation envisioned by its founders. It was not a "city on a hill" but a slum on a hill. The American dream had soured and a growing consensus held that gov-ernment alone could freshen it. Throughout the first decade of the twenti-eth century, "progressives" were elected to run major cities, and in the person of Roosevelt, the nation at large. Their aim was not to wage class warfare, as the IWW touted, but to prevent it, rolling back a rising tide of Socialism by blunting capitalism's sharp edges. Talk everywhere was of cleaning up urban political "machines," taming big business, and making cities livable for "the other half." By 1912, the reformers' zeal had peaked and what is now called the Progressive Era was ripe for its own morality play. The curtain went up in Lawrence. Here in a single venue was a strike that bared all the paradoxes of a divided nation, posing questions about la-bor unrest, rampant industrialization, high tariffs, immigration, Socialism, Syndicalism, women's rights, child labor. . . . Recognizing its appeal, the only media of the age—newspapers and magazines—jumped on the story. America had twenty-six hundred newspapers in 1912, an all-time high,[12] and their politics ran the gamut from hard-core Republicanism to unabashed anarchism. Each major city had several dailies. Competition was cutthroat, and with newsboys shouting out sound bites, headlines sold papers. The strike in Lawrence, with its sporadic violence, ethnic flavor, and warring factions, was tailor-made for massive media coverage.

Ever since January 12, local dailies—six in Boston and three in Lawrence[13]—had each devoted up to eighty inches of copy per day to the strike. Reports varied from the sober to the lurid. The most sensational came from New England's most popular daily, Hearst's *Boston American.* On the morning after the strike began, the *American* infuriated strikers with an unfounded accusation that they had threatened to dynamite the mills.[14] In subsequent reports, the *American,* known for its sensational headlines, abundant photo spreads, and tabloid treatment of celebrities, singled out each minor incident in Lawrence as evidence of anarchy at work. Strikers became especially suspicious when the paper reported the dynamite plot on January 18, two days before the explosive was even discovered.[15] Calling the *American* "an ulcer on society,"[16] strikers failed to notice its change in coverage come February. Once Hearst's reporters began returning from the tenements with stories of hunger and despair, the *American* backed the strikers. Though still reporting rumor as fact, Hearst's was the only Boston paper to criticize Ettor's arrest as "fishy"[17] and attack "the enormous profits which the protective tariff enables the manufacturers to make."[18] Other papers, while more accurate, were not nearly so sympathetic. The *Boston Transcript* and *Herald* sided openly with mill owners while the *Globe* ran almost no editorials about the strike and reported events with a cool detachment.

Lawrence papers were divided on the strike. The *Tribune,* billing itself as "The Representative Democratic Paper of Essex County," roundly criticized Ettor and Haywood but supported the strikers. "An able-bodied man who is worth anything to a corporation is worth more than a dollar a day,"[19] one editorial declared. The city's other dailies, both Republican-owned,[20] were plainly in the mill owners' camp. *Telegram* editorials championed law and order, cited mill owners' higher wage estimates,[21] and frequently reprinted other papers' denunciations of the IWW. The lurid *Lawrence Daily American* displayed its disgust with the whole situation in stark headlines: [ETTOR] SAYS THEY'LL TURN TOWN UPSIDE DOWN[22] and STRIKER WITH RAZOR ARRESTED.[23]

The Lawrence dailies, however, reported only to the city's English-speaking citizens. As it had grown into a mill town of many tongues, Lawrence hosted a potpourri of foreign-language papers. The Syrian *Al-Wafa* had recently folded, but the French *Courrier de Lawrence* and the German *Anzeiger und Post* were still in business[24] and both backed the strikers. The *Courrier* gave the strike a French twist. To its readers, Ettor was *le chef de la grève,*[25] Colonel Sweetser was *le Colonel,* and Mayor Scanlon simply *le maire.* At first, the paper merely reported events and sought contributions for *ceux qui souffrent,* "those who suffer." Yet as the strike ground on and more French Canadians walked out, the *Courrier* hardened its line, questioning America's entire economic structure. One editorial listed the nation's richest men, from Rockefeller on down, asking "is it possible that these millionaires who came from countries as poor as Job could have become rich so quickly by following an honest path?"[26]

The *Anzeiger und Post* covered the *Fabrikarbeiter-Streik* with equal empathy. "As much as one might long for a speedy settlement," an article noted, "one cannot blame the people who began the strike for clinging doggedly to their demands."[27] And like its French counterpart, the German paper grew more strident when more Germans struck in mid-February.[28] Beneath a headline proclaiming JEDER ARBEITER SEINE LOHNE (EVERY WORKER DESERVES HIS WAGE) the paper doubted mill owners were too poor to meet strikers' demands.

> One only has to look at the gigantic and expensive new factory buildings, which were constructed during the last few years. Has it happened that the rich owners have become poorer as a result? On the contrary, aren't most of them getting noticeably richer? The naked truth is probably that the big businessman in America has not yet learned to be satisfied with a moderate profit from his investment. All his hustle and bustle

is only about scraping together riches. And for what purpose? So that he can live in unlimited splendor and leave many millions to his frequently degenerate children.[29]

Lithuanians in Lawrence followed the strike in *Keleivis,* a Boston-based weekly. *Keleivis* detailed specific attacks on Lithuanians,[30] printed long lists of Lithuanians throughout America and Canada who contributed a few cents or a dollar to strike funds,[31] and blasted scabs as "evil people" taking bread out of the mouths of strikers.[32] In a typically vituperative article, *Keleivis* described the dynamite plot: "The free American capitalists with their dear government and their rabid dog tendencies, similar to those of the Russian police, have placed dynamite in several locations here in Lawrence."[33]

Beyond local foreign and English papers, the national press took a week or more to notice the strike but quickly caught up with coverage in Boston and Lawrence. A panoply of editorial opinions soon emerged.

- "The Lawrence strike . . . was intended to be only a part of a nationwide if not a worldwide strike in the textile trade and thus, as the plotters hoped, the beginning of a social revolution."
  —*New York Tribune*[34]

- "Why not have arrested, rather, President Wood of the American Woolen Company, as an accessory to the murder of a striker? He had as little and as much to do with it as Ettor."
  —*Topeka Capital*[35]

- "Doubtless the strikers make a pitiful figure before the guns of the soldiers, and the schedules of the wages bespeak hardships of life. . . . [But] the strikers are asking sympathy for anarchy in order to produce a scarcity of goods. It is plain that consumers of such goods cannot afford to sympathize with the enemies of production."   —*New York Times*[36]

And the *Los Angeles Times,* still raging against the McNamaras and the "cult" of Socialism, took special umbrage. Branding Ettor and Haywood "mob leaders,"[37] the *Times* asked, "Now in the name of the great Jeho-shaphat [*sic*], and the Continental Congress *tambien,* is it not about time that most of us conjured up courage enough to . . . tell these lawbreakers to go to Jericho?"[38]

Though mainstream press coverage was mixed, the nation's burgeoning Socialist press spoke with one voice. "Lawrence is a typical capitalist mill town," wrote *Appeal to Reason,* a Socialist paper out of Kansas that was America's most popular weekly. "Poverty, privation, the dread of idleness and starvation fall to the lot of the wage-earners there while a few who hold the titles to the mills put on all the airs and display all the arrogance of the feudal barons of the Middle Ages."[39] The Greenwich Village maga-zine *The Masses* called the strike a revolt. "A strike had not even been thought of by these poor mill slaves five minutes before they revolted be-cause of their decreased pay. They had been driven too hard to be able to think of organization, ballots, or anything else except bread, molasses, water, and the infernal whirring of the mills."[40] In Socialist publications, the strikers were always "starving,"[41] the mill owners "thieves" and "para-sites,"[42] and the strike itself a romantic reincarnation of the Paris Com-mune, the workers' government that ruled Paris for two months in 1871 before being crushed. Typifying this sentiment was *Il Proletario,* the Italian Socialist Federation weekly, whose editor, Arturo Giovannitti, was now in a Lawrence jail. Along with erratic reporting—the weekly's first dispatch from Lawrence reported militia gunning down strikers[43]—*Il Proletario* waxed eloquent about the glory of the fight, "too beautiful, too epic to fin-ish in cowardice."[44]

Magazines took longer to discover Lawrence but their coverage, emerg-ing in early February, was more nuanced. Magazines were the conscience of the Progressive Era. Many ongoing moral crusades, from cleaning up a "treasonous" Senate to reforming the tariff, had begun with long, detailed magazine articles, and many of the journalists responsible for those arti-cles now came to Lawrence. Disembarking at the depot to the alarming sight of soldiers patrolling an American city, muckrakers Lincoln Steffens, Mary Heaton Vorse, Ray Stannard Baker, and William Allen White roamed the streets penning articles. Walter Weyl, who would later staff the upstart *New Republic,* offered a typical tableau in *The Outlook:*

The militia, armed with guns and bayonets, guarded the streets and bridges in the mill district and challenged all comers. The hulking factories, with their iron gates and massive doors, appeared in the semi-darkness like fortresses, and along the face of these mills there played a strange, trembling light from the search lanterns opposite. There were soldiers inside the mills ready to pour out volleys of lead into any storming party.[45]

Journalists attended strikers' meetings, listening to impassioned speeches in a dozen languages. They interviewed Mayor Scanlon, Colonel Sweetser, and Haywood, then wound their way through the pestiferous tenements. *Harper's Weekly,* in an article that would cause American Woolen to cancel its advertising account,[46] described a family of Syrians.

There were six in the family, which lived in three rooms. The halls were dirty and full of ashes and unremoved garbage. The family were supported by the work of children—a boy of sixteen and one half years and a girl of seventeen, who earned between them $12.50 a week. The rent was $10 a month. It was this girl who cried . . . "Oh, that only we had never come away from Damascus."[47]

Magazines ran photographs showing children lining up for bread,[48] gaunt women holding babies,[49] standoffs between strikers and militia beneath furled American flags.[50] Awash in stories and statistics, the American public debated the strike, its causes, solutions, and significance. Soon the people of Lawrence began to feel as if their city were in a fishbowl. "Is there any person outside of Lawrence who does not know all the merits of the strike and how it should be settled?" asked the *Lawrence Tribune.*[51] Dispatches from Lawrence were read in studies and sitting rooms, sweatshops and mining camps, making the strike a story that rivaled even the weather and Roosevelt's ultimate decision to throw his hat "in the ring." And as the winter deepened, Lawrence became the lightning rod of a "profoundly disenchanted"[52] nation.

Americans at large seemed to know just what should happen next in Lawrence, but as the strike started its fourth week, all sides were as bogged down as the dray horses that stalled in snow and slush every morning on Essex Street.[53] Once strikers recovered from the carnage of late January, their first response was a barefaced defiance. On February 1, militia were herding crowds off Common Street when a soldier ordered a woman back inside a store. The woman refused. This was her husband's store. Her own sidewalk. The militiaman aimed his rifle at her. The woman began waving her arms and shouting. Onlookers froze. Finally, the woman's husband gently took her by the hand and led her inside.[54] Moments later, a Portuguese man stuck his head from a second-story window. Three rifles took aim. The man tore open his coat and bared his chest. "Go ahead and shoot!" he shouted. "Go ahead and shoot!" The man stood, his sallow chest an open target, until he was steered from the window.[55] With Billy Wood silent and sullen, such incidents made militiamen the strikers' new enemy of choice. Haywood, who had seen militia rout strikers out west, blasted them as "uniformed cowards,"[56] while strikers shared stories of drunken soldiers insulting or threatening them. Some, however, were happy to have the militia on duty.

One afternoon, Arthur Regan, known in his neighborhood as "Dude," was crossing the bridge near the Pacific Mill. Carrying lunch pails and pushing a wagon, the boy was spotted by three strikers. "They said, 'You're carrying dinners for scabs,'" Regan recalled. "I says, 'No, these are for engineers, firemen. They have to be there [in the mills] on account of the insurance.' Nothin' doin', so they took and threw my two full dinner pails and two empty ones over the bridge and then they threw my wagon. They started to push me. They didn't really hit me but was pushin' me around and everything, and I was only nine years old. And I looked up and there's a couple militia from Battery C with wagon spokes with holes drilled in 'em, and piece of rawhide put through 'em, on their wrists. They did a job on the three guys. One asked, 'Did they do any damage to you, Dude?'" When the tearful boy told the militia about his wagon, soldiers tipped the assailants upside down and shook them. Spare change clattered onto the bridge. Soldiers gathered the coins and gave them to the boy. "So I got $2.06 for a wagon I made from nothin'," Regan recalled. "Boy, talk about the good old days."[57]

As the mood of defiance hardened, strikers grew dangerously brazen. One morning, someone threw dynamite at a passing train. The single stick landed harmlessly on the tracks.[58] Every workday at dawn, strikers donned hoods and began visiting scabs.[59] "If there was a light early in the morning," one woman remembered, "six or seven o'clock—they come along, they rapped at your door and said, 'Put out the light! You can't go to work!'"[60] Stronger threats arrived by mail. When a Congregational minister praised mill owners and criticized immigrants who "have too many children,"[61] he received the notorious Italian "Black Hand" death threat.[62] The minister quickly apologized.[63] The strike committee was equally rebellious. Meeting before overflow crowds that made Franco-Belgian Hall's wooden floor sag ominously,[64] the committee issued another declaration:

> The strike is won if you, the workers, stay out as you are doing! The arrest of Ettor and others is simply a proof of the desperation of the bosses. Instead of breaking the strike, it has only strengthened the workers' determination to get what is due them. . . . The strike cannot be lost. Who will come here to replace strikers at $6 per week? Attend meetings. Don't be a scab! An injury to one is an injury to all![65]

Writing from his cell, Ettor urged strikers to "pay more attention to strengthening your defense than to me."[66] In the mills, where unfilled orders were piling up, looms and spinners churned on with the smallest workforce yet, just a quarter of the full payroll.[67] With donations coming from all over the country, and local IWW membership now topping ten thousand,[68] the momentum had shifted back to the strikers' side. When Haywood returned, he told crowds, "expecting from the newspapers to find the strike all over in Lawrence, I found it all over Lawrence!"[69]

Militia kept order in the streets, but citizens had to maintain order in their own lives. Amid the constant threat of bloodshed, ordinary diversions became more important than ever. Attendance at nickelodeons was much higher than usual.[70] Lodges and women's clubs assembled as if nothing strange were happening.[71] The North Essex Congregational Club went ahead with plans for a Lincoln's Birthday celebration featuring talks by two men who had met Lincoln while serving in the Union army.[72] Without a trace of irony, newspaper ads told "Factory Girls" suffering from "nervousness" to try Lydia E. Pinkham's Vegetable Compound, "guaranteed to be absolutely genuine."[73] But beneath this veneer of civility, many were fed up with the standoff. "I have a lot of sympathy for the strikers," said a grocer whose receipts for a full day totaled just four dollars. "I think they ought to have more wages. But this strike has got to be settled."[74]

On Friday, February 2, while a delegation of strikers journeyed to Boston to meet with Governor Foss, attention shifted to the courts. Before a crowded courtroom in Lawrence, Judge Mahoney heard witnesses tell how John Breen had steered police to the dynamite he had allegedly planted. Breen's trial was set for May.[75] That same morning, a Boston judge considered a writ of habeas corpus for Ettor and Giovannitti demanding their release from what their lawyer called "this most ridiculously trumped up case."[76] The judge postponed the hearing and the men stayed in jail, where Ettor received a telegram from Eugene Debs: "Congratulations! Victory is in sight! The slave pens of Lawrence under protection of America's Cossacks are a disgrace to American manhood and a crime against civilization."[77] As the day ended, strike committee members returned to Lawrence, angry that the governor had not shown "one bit of sympathy to us."[78]

That evening in Manhattan, the strike took center stage at Carnegie Hall. Haywood was supposed to moderate a debate on "Anarchism vs. Socialism" but he became the evening's star. Big Bill never looked so small as when he stepped onstage before the multitiered hall but his booming baritone never served him better. "I am here tonight representing 22,000 textile workers who are on strike in Lawrence, Massachusetts," Haywood began. He could not continue. At the mere mention of Lawrence, the audience stomped and whistled for several minutes. Casting his squinting gaze from the overhead chandelier to the well-dressed audience below, Haywood waited. When at last able to speak, he enthralled the sellout crowd with firsthand accounts of the strike everyone in Greenwich Village and the Lower East Side had been talking about.[79] The strikers "are fighting for their right to live!" he thundered. "They are the persons who clothe you and yet they are the persons who are naked." After victory in Lawrence, he promised, the IWW would extend the strike nationwide. And strikers would win if "not whipped back to the mills by the lash of hunger. It depends on you!" Sending ushers through the crowd for donations, Haywood said he expected a take of at least $300. People dug into purses, unfolded wallets. Contributions totaled $452.04. Astonished and grateful, Haywood made one final appeal. "I don't want a man or woman in this audience to go out of this place with more than carfare in his or her pocket!" At this, coins began to rain down onstage. Haywood and debater Emma Goldman gathered these and the bills that fluttered from upper boxes. The next evening, Haywood returned to Lawrence with $750. Arriving at Franco-Belgian Hall, he added his take to the money pouring in daily from workers and unions nationwide.

Something was happening in America and the strike was only its signal flare. The *New York Times* saw the shifting mood in the full house cheering Big Bill Haywood in the hall named for union buster Andrew Carnegie. As if playing anthropologist in this "remarkable" scene, the *Times* reporter described the crowd. It contained many nationalities and all ages, including elegant women "every whit as enthusiastic as were the poorer people in the top galleries in their applause of the anarchistic utterances of Emma Goldman."[80] Wealthy women applauding America's most infamous radicals? What was the nation coming to?

The nation was coming to a crossroads. Forty years of frantic industrialization had left America riven with fault lines. In 1912, Americans stood on the cusp between Victorian and modern times, torn between two opposing ideals of human behavior. Victorians had preached that character was self-made and the engine of one's destiny. Thus each person, no matter how downtrodden, got what he deserved. Emerging moderns countered that character was not determined by birth but by circumstances beyond one's control; hence, a just society should struggle to even out those circumstances. Adding to this fundamental schism were other divides. An influx of immigrants—thirteen million since 1890[81]—had stirred an outbreak of xenophobia. The NAACP had formed to protest weekly lynchings and tightening Jim Crow laws. Women, weary from more than sixty years of marching for suffrage, were ever at odds with men. But crosscutting all other divisions was the chasm of class.

The Gilded Age was over but its excesses lingered like interest on a debt. Enriched by decades of tax-free income, dividends, and vast inheritances, the richest 1 percent of Americans held *half* the nation's total wealth.[82] Per capita income in 1912 was $340 a year,[83] roughly $6,000 in contemporary figures, yet socialites were still throwing parties like the one in the nation's capital in early February, a $35,000 soiree whose hostess wore a half million dollars in gems, including the Hope diamond.[84] In each American city, islands of opulence—glittering mansions, posh restaurants, social registers listing the wealthy and their heirs apparent—were surrounded by a rising sea of slums. Observing the glaring divide, Eugene Debs proclaimed early in 1912, "Comrades, this is our year!"[85] A growing number of Americans agreed. Membership in Debs's Socialist Party had skyrocketed from 10,000 in 1901[86] to 118,000 in 1912.[87] In contrast to the IWW, which most Socialists considered recklessly radical,[88] the Socialist Party did not preach imminent revolution. From the platform of his "Red Special" railroad campaign car, Debs assured farmers and factory workers that Socialism would come through the ballot, not strikes and sabotage. Debs's platform included a progressive income tax, women's suffrage, municipal ownership of utilities, and an active federal government to curb corruption in housing, banking, and industry.[89] More than a thousand Socialists already held office,[90] including one congressman and the mayors of Milwaukee, Schenectady, St. Mary's, Ohio, and both Watts and Berkeley, California.[91] A 1911 *Atlantic Monthly* article urged readers to PREPARE FOR SOCIALISM. Its coming was inevitable, the *Atlantic* said, "because all of the wage-workers of the world are possible recruits to be won for Socialism."[92] *Harper's* offered the same prediction from H. G. Wells.[93] Respected Americans, including Helen Keller, Jack London, and members of the Harvard Socialist Club founded by student Walter Lippmann,[94] called themselves Socialists. So did more than a half million readers of *Appeal to Reason*.[95]

For all its rising popularity, however, Socialism itself was divided. The political left wing had wings of its own, ranging from the Wobblies on the far left to the saintly Debs in the middle to academic Socialists denouncing all the rest. Many wealthy women applauding Emma Goldman at Carnegie Hall had been moved to sympathize with workers, first by a violent garment workers strike, later by the 1911 Triangle Shirtwaist Fire, which killed scores of immigrant women trapped in the notorious sweatshop or leaping, with skirts ablaze, to their deaths.[96] Few wealthy husbands shared their wives' sympathies, however, nor were they comforted by the left's constant bickering. Men of property charted Socialism's numbers, heard the masses in Lawrence singing "The Internationale," and saw red. "I say to you that things are being said and printed similar to the incendiary speeches which aroused the peasants of France and caused the French Revolution," Judge Elbert Gary told a dinner crowd of fellow steel magnates. "Unless something is done the spark will burst into a flame."[97] Whether they made their millions in steel, oil, or textiles, the wealthiest Americans were not likely to "prepare for Socialism." So much more than income was at stake.

In *The Protestant Ethic and the Spirit of Capitalism,* German sociologist Max Weber seemed to know the Lawrence mill owners better than Joseph Ettor did. Ettor ranted against these "parasites and social sponges . . . too lazy and impotent to work,"[98] but Weber's landmark 1905 essay saw capitalism as the creation of relentless, exacting men. Among their common characteristics, Weber cited a sense of divine calling,[99] Calvinist asceticism,[100] and an unflagging faith in hard work, especially their own.[101] Weber's parameters needed little tailoring in order to fit New England's textile oligarchy. Capsule biographies of the region's mill moguls read like the *Plutarch's Lives* of their time.[102] Each executive had followed a similar path, from prep school to the Ivy League to a mill office with a title on the door. From there, the men's lives were linked on boards of insurance companies, banks, and mills.[103] Leading mill men belonged to the same social clubs, notably Boston's Arkwright Club, named for the inventor of the power loom. Since 1880, Arkwright members—each a mill owner or an executive—had banded together to oppose child labor laws, support high tariffs, and pool funds to win strikes.[104] When trouble arose, one club president said, members stood together "like a row of bricks."[105] These men shared not only power but religion (most were Episcopalian), politics (Republican), and breeding (Boston Brahmin). Sons of immigrants were accepted into the circle if they made slight alterations. By 1900, William Wood was denying his Portuguese ancestry, listing on a federal census form that his father had been born in Scotland.[106]

Underlying each man's accomplishments was a Puritan piety Abbott Lawrence would have found reassuring. Wool tariff mastermind William Whitman put it succinctly: "One thing, I believe, can honestly be put on my tombstone—I have always kept my word."[107] A natty gentleman with piercing blue eyes, snow white hair, and wire-rimmed glasses, Whitman idealized his rise from boyhood on a Nova Scotia sheep farm to textile tycoon. He often told of landing in Boston at age thirteen with ten dollars in his pocket, walking to Cambridge to save carriage fare, and talking his way into a clerk's job. After selling textiles during the Civil War, Whitman hired on as treasurer of the Arlington Mill in 1867, became director six years later, and mill president in 1902.[108] In 1912, at age seventy, he worked at his desk all day, taking only fifteen minutes for lunch.[109] Proud, thrifty, self-righteous, Whitman exuded Weber's "spirit of capitalism." "I believe I could almost preach a sermon on the subject of the rule of honor," he said. "Nothing develops any human being quite so much as meeting every single obligation, real or implied, that he ever assumes."[110]

The strike posed little threat to the personal fortunes of Whitman, Wood, or other mill owners. Only their pride and lifelong accomplishments were imperiled. These were men who had mastered commodities markets from Liverpool to Australia, charting the annual acreage of cotton and "clip" of wool, buying millions of pounds from Argentine ranches, Wyoming sheep farms, and southern plantations. They had built the world's largest factories, then automated them to turn out miles of finished fabric each year. The last few years had seen profits plunge but 1912 promised a return to the black. And now a group of radicals, men who had never worked in the mills, who believed the most unskilled rabble should own and run them, were threatening to take their empire away. Against such an unthinkable outrage, the row of bricks stood more solidly than ever.

Beneath the mills' upper crust, however, a slightly lower class had something more tangible than pride to defend. For stockholders in the mills, income was indeed threatened by the strike. "It can almost be said that the aristocracy of Boston is based upon the profits of the textile mills of New England," observed Ray Stannard Baker.[111] Throughout the strike, Wood and Whitman protested that they could not afford to pay workers more. Financial reports suggest why. Year after year, despite the recent decline in earnings, dividends in the textile industry had remained as expansive as the cloth it made. During the ten years prior to the strike, the Pacific Mill paid average annual dividends of 14.8 percent,[112] doubling a stockholder's investment every five years. Pacific, the world's largest cotton print mill, had just six hundred stockholders, not surprising since a single share sold for $3,800,[113] nine times the annual salary of a mill worker. American

Woolen was not quite so generous—holders of its preferred stock ($89 a share) enjoyed 7 percent dividends. Dividends at American Woolen had doubled since 1904, although net profits had risen only 22 percent.[114]

As dividends rose, stockholders came to expect no less. "There is no question of right or wrong there," a leading Bostonian said of Lawrence. "The whole matter is a case of supply and demand. Any man who pays more for labor than the lowest sum he can get men for is robbing his stockholders."[115] One mill executive was more diplomatic: "I've got to look after this property and to earn dividends for my stockholders—else I lose my job, and someone else comes in who *will* earn dividends. We are tied up by national laws, by state laws, by the still more sweeping laws of competition, in short, by the whole system under which we work. Neither my company alone nor I alone could any more essentially change conditions in the textile industry than the lowest Italian operative in our mills."[116]

Their hands tied, their principles and incomes at stake, mill workers and mill management faced each other across the Great American Divide of 1912. But between the poles of rich and poor were millions who found the new century more complicated than any single doctrine suggested. Reading about Lawrence, a growing cadre of white-collar workers,[117] having no income or cause at risk, were pulled in many directions. Common sense told them that no man should have to raise a family on a mill worker's wages, let alone send his wife and children into the mills. Yet an assortment of fears—of immigrant tides, of anarchists like the one who had assassinated President William McKinley in 1901,[118] of mounting havoc as strikes grew larger and more violent—left them terrified of the IWW. Starvation wages were not the American way, but was mob violence? Abolishing the wage system? And such radicalism was especially frightening given the strike's singular setting. Staunchly Republican Massachusetts was the bedrock of America, home of Plymouth Rock and Puritan Blue Laws, host to the nation's finest universities and wisest pundits.[119] Massachusetts also boasted some of the nation's most progressive labor laws.[120] If the IWW could take root there, nowhere in America was safe. With the lines drawn and the nation split into "haves" and "have-nots," the strike in Lawrence stood ready to serve as its litmus test. As Labor and Capital squared off, Americans could only choose up sides and read the daily reports. And on

February 3, startling news again lit up the Linotypes. In a tenement in the French Canadian quarter, four immigrants had been murdered.

Truth trickled out slowly, long after rumors—the victims were scabs,[121] the murder weapon was a bayonet![122]—had spread panic. But truth and rumor proved equally stark. In the black, silent hours of an early February morning, screams and groans from a second-floor flat awoke residents on Valley Street. Family fights were common in The Plains and neighbors went back to sleep. The next evening, when no one had come down from the second floor all day, a girl went for the police. Ascending the stairs, officers found the landlord knocking on the door. The morning paper was still on the landing. All was silent inside. After another knock, police bashed in the door. Their flashlights shone on a scene of Gothic horror. Scattered playing cards and whiskey bottles sat on a table. Bloody handprints were smeared on one wall. Sprawled across the kitchen floor lay three shadowed, inert forms in pools of blood. Each body had been brutally hacked. A fourth mutilated corpse was discovered in the bedroom.[123]

While a frenzied crowd gathered on the street, police fanned out through the neighborhood. Witnesses had seen a man in a derby, short gray coat, and dark pants fleeing the apartment early that morning. One witness saw a club or knife in his hand, silhouetted in the moonlight. On the street, there was loose talk that "Scab!" had been chalked on the door.[124] When that was proven false, a likelier motive emerged. The two women who lived in the flat were notorious in the neighborhood. They brought home men. Strangers. And one of the men they brought home that night had just withdrawn $485 from the Essex Savings Bank.[125] The cash, not found on him, instantly became the key to the crime, a con game that whiskey had escalated into murder. By Saturday morning, newspapers were reporting that there was "not an iota of fact to connect the murders with the textile strike."[126] Still, the murderer was at large.

As fear tightened its tentacles, middle ground was hard to find. The most promising—and the most threatening to the IWW—was staked out by AF of L textile head John Golden. Infuriated by the Wobblies' headway in Lawrence, Golden plotted to end the strike on his own terms. Longtime Wobblies had expected as much. Five years earlier, Golden had sent in "union scabs" to break an IWW textile strike in Skowhegan, Maine.[127] Now

Golden announced that the AF of L could not "silently permit the pernicious doctrine of brute force further to be spread by the would-be leaders of Lawrence."[128] On February 3, with the city jittery over the four murders, Golden and leaders of Lawrence's Central Labor Union invited weavers, spinners, and other skilled workers to formulate a separate set of demands. Once these had been determined craft by craft, they would be presented to mill owners. If craftsmen got slight wage increases, their return might cause a rush back to the mills. Then the IWW could be run out of town. Calling the move "a dagger in the back of the strike,"[129] Wobblies mounted a counteroffensive. Personal attacks became staples of meetings where strikers, regardless of their language, learned to boo and hiss whenever anyone said "John Golden."[130] Throughout the coming week, as IWW loyalists began wearing white ribbons of solidarity, skilled workers hammered out their separate demands.[131] And in another flanking move around the Wobblies, Golden and the CLU set up their own relief station.

Hunger prowled the city. Soup kitchens were serving a few thousand a day,[132] but that was just a fraction of those out of work. Churches also handed out meals, yet many families were ashamed to seek help,[133] and scrawny, shivering children had begun showing up at the back doors of restaurants begging for bread.[134] Bakers handed out thousands more loaves,[135] and schoolteachers sold bread to strikers' children for a penny a slice,[136] yet hunger would not be sated. On February 4, the AF of L sent out a nationwide call for donations,[137] an appeal that attracted those who did not want their good names tarred by ties to the Wobblies. One of the first contributors was Boston mayor John "Honey Fitz" Fitzgerald, grandfather of John F. Kennedy, who sent one hundred dollars.[138] The donations—nearly thirteen hundred dollars in the first week of February[139]—were channeled to the CLU's new relief station in Lawrence, which became a rallying point for social workers, suffragettes, and other good Samaritans from the Boston area.[140]

Each morning, meticulous women in shirtwaists and floor-length skirts arrived at the makeshift office on Broadway to find strikers trembling at the door. After letting them in to sit on old orange crates around a woodstove, the women reviewed a thick file of needy families. At 9:00 a.m., the interviews began. "Name? Age? Where do you live? What church do you attend? How many children have you? What do you need most?"[141] Interviews ended abruptly if the applicant admitted being "an IWW," but otherwise, the relief work went on well into the evening. By the glow of candlelight, the women handed out food, clothing, and coal, while marveling at the strikers' mettle. "I have been on picket duty where we had to implore the strikers not to return," said Mabel Gillespie of the Women's Trade Union League. "But here they are all firmly welded together."[142]

By the end of the strike's fourth week, the standoff was as solid as ever. Rumors of another murder had proven to be only a fright. A desperately hungry man had entered a woman's kitchen and fled out the back door.[143] Ettor and Giovannitti still sat in prison, their writ of habeas corpus denied.[144] Angelo Rocco was freed with a fine of fifty dollars. As a lawyer in the making, he appealed.[145] Police confessed they did not have a single lead to the four murders, and whole militia companies, having served their two weeks' duty, were replaced by fresh battalions marching from the depot down Essex Street to the armory.[146] On February 8, after weeks of stalling, the state legislature agreed to investigate labor conditions in Lawrence, sending one delegation to meet with strikers, another with mill owners. Heading the latter group was a shy, taciturn state senator from Northampton named Calvin Coolidge.[147] The future president found Wood and his cronies as intractable as ever, still refusing to meet with strikers as a whole.[148] But Coolidge had even more disdain for strike leaders: "Socialists and anarchists [who] do not want anybody to work for wages. The trouble was not wages," Coolidge wrote to his stepmother. "It is a small attempt to destroy all authority whether of any church or government."[149]

Not even John Golden's scheme could thaw the stalemate. After a week of meetings, skilled workers proved even more demanding than unskilled. Most wanted a 15 percent raise and weavers wanted 20 percent. Each craft also had stipulations far exceeding the IWW's four demands. Weavers at the Everett Mill wanted to be paid by the yard. Pacific Mill weavers wanted to run no more than fourteen looms. Wood Mill menders wanted to be paid for "bad work."[150] These grievances were sent to mill owners, who filed them away. Several meetings between mill agents and craftsmen were postponed as management pondered its next move. Golden threatened his own strike if mill owners did not respond.[151] They remained mute. Finally William Wood, suffering from tonsillitis and nagged by the press to break his silence, exploded. "Why make me the figurehead all the time?" he shouted at a reporter. "It isn't just my strike. I haven't anything to say and I don't want to say anything. Talk to someone else for a change!"[152]

The whole nation was watching, but Lawrence remained in an armed, edgy stalemate. Although there were hints that the strikers' children might soon be sent out of town, the biggest news at week's end was an exodus of adults. After a month of fear and frustration, 100 Russians, 350 Italians, and 350 French Canadians had had enough. Lugging trunks and small furniture to the depot, whole families began to reverse the process that had brought them to America. A few said they might come back once the strike was settled, but many more declared their solemn intention never to return. "We came to America thinking it a country of fine prospects," said Arturo Massavi, standing before two hundred countrymen as they changed trains in Boston. "We were urged to come here by posters spread throughout Italy by the American Woolen Company, describing how mill owners will treat us like their own children. It is a false pretense. We were treated like dogs. Our Italy is bad but your country's textile mills are worse."[153] Then Massavi and his fellow Italians took the train to Manhattan, where they boarded a steamer. The ship sailed out of New York Harbor, past the Statue of Liberty, which grew smaller as seen from the stern, and headed home.

CHAPTER EIGHT

The Children's Exodus

No strike was ever won that did not have the support of the womenfolk.

—Mother Jones[1]

As the sun rose over the mills on February 10, as militia marched in step to their morning duty, as the rest of Lawrence slept late on a Saturday, several dozen mothers and their children quietly gathered at Franco-Belgian Hall to give this bitter and vindictive strike a human heart.

Neither mothers nor children were prepared for the subzero temperatures that numbed noses and fingertips. Steaming in from the cold, red-faced children wore few gloves or mittens, just tattered sweaters and overcoats. Many mothers had no more than shawls over their long dresses.[2] Yet an unmistakable radiance filled the old hall, fueled by a sense of mission and a flurry of activity. In the hall's kitchen, women busily prepared hundreds of sandwiches. Others collected stray children, seated them at long tables, and warmed them with hot milk or coffee. Because a last-minute decision to depart well before noon had been spread through the tenements only the night before,[3] there was much to do in preparing 150 children to be sent into the care of strangers. Each child had to be registered and pinned with a paper listing name, age, address, and nationality. Permission letters had to be gathered and given to chaperones. Mothers had to be reassured that their children would be safe, that host families had been carefully screened, that this was all for the best. And above all, if the strike was to be won, tears had to be stifled. The children must not know the grief their departure would cause.

The children were supposed to catch the 8:20 train but by 8:00 a.m., they were nowhere near ready. Mothers fussed and children nagged—"When are we going to go?" Parents had told them about New York—the Statue of Liberty, the Lower East Side and Little Italy, the soaring buildings and bustling streets crammed with peddlers' pushcarts—all those wonders Lawrence had only in microcosm. And now the children were headed there, for a few days, a few weeks, who knew how long? But with so many details to finalize, the children did not leave Franco-Belgian Hall until 8:30. The cold did not dampen their spirits. As they strode two by two beneath cloudless blue skies toward the depot, they broke into song, first "The Marseillaise" and then, as their parents had also sung on parade, "The Internationale," each in his native tongue. Turning onto Broadway, the children passed crowds of cheering strikers and passengers gazing curiously out of trolley cars. The throng of two hundred adults and children arrived at the depot ten minutes before the 9:02 train to Boston was due. Ten minutes gave mothers a chance to reconsider, and by the time a train whistle was heard in the distance, more than two dozen women had taken disappointed children, tagged and still eager to see New York, home to the tenements.[4] But the rest began to press forward, and as the engine huffed to a stop, the price about to be paid became as clear as the reflections in coach windows, reflections that showed tight-lipped faces melting in the cold.

For the next few minutes, the platform bustled with farewells and embraces. Cautions—to be careful, to write—followed the oldest children onto the train while the littlest, some just two years old, were handed to chaperones on coach platforms. Men as well as women wept, and even the more adventurous children found good-byes catching in their throats. One toddler, suddenly realizing the finality of the morning's preparation, cried out, "Oh, mama, mama, mama!" Her mother gave the girl a last hug, loosened her grip, then handed her over and hurried from the child's sobs.[5] Other mothers engulfed the weeping woman, consoling her with reminders that the strike must be won.[6] Inside the car, children rushed for window seats and pressed their faces to the glass.[7] Then as the train began to pull out, the platform billowed with waving handkerchiefs[8] and the sadness gave way to a great shout. The children of Lawrence were on their way.

The idea had come from Europe by way of Manhattan. Members of the Italian Socialist Federation had heard of strikers in Italy sending their hungry children out of harm's way and into the care of supportive families. Freed of the children's appetites and the need to attend to them, workers had won strikes this way not solely in Italy but also in France and Belgium. Yet such an exodus had never occurred in America. During a meeting in Union Square, Italians suggested the strategy to Haywood.[9] The plan carried tremendous risk. The exile would doubtless draw plenty of attention, but if even one child was lost, injured, or abused, the IWW would lose all credibility in Lawrence. Still, Haywood liked the idea of sending the "kiddies" away. He would later call it "a war measure."[10] And beginning on February 7, the *New York Call*, a Socialist daily, advertised[11] for willing families:

TAKE THE CHILDREN

Children of the Lawrence strikers are hungry. Their fathers and mothers are fighting against hunger, and hunger may break the strike. The men and women are willing to suffer, but they cannot watch their children's pain or hear their cries for food. Workers and strike sympathizers who can take a striker's child until the struggle ends are urged to send their name and address to the *Call*. Do it at once.

Families flooded the *Call*'s offices with letters and phone calls pledging space for seven hundred young exiles.[12] Each applicant was screened through interviews and home visits.[13] *Call* headlines proclaimed SEND US YOUR CHILDREN! *Il Proletario* was even more accommodating. SIAN FIGLI NOSTRI read its front page[14]—MAKE THEM OUR CHILDREN. And by Saturday afternoon, while many of the children were enjoying their first train rides, a teeming crowd had gathered at Grand Central Station expecting them any minute. But when the 3:30 train from Boston arrived, no swarm of children emerged.[15] Telegrams went up and down the New York–Boston line. Where were the children of Lawrence?

Late for their first train, the "kiddies" had missed their connection in Boston. They had to wait ninety minutes, and in that time they filled the echoing concourse of South Station with songs and antics that delighted other passengers.[16] Upon learning of the children's purpose, however, not all were delighted. An elderly man assured bystanders that "good old Massachusetts can take care of her children," repeating this until a chaperone strode up to the gentleman. "Sure, good old Massachusetts! Ha ha!" the woman said. "Massachusetts send soldiers to shoot children's fathers. Massachusetts say to fathers, 'You work, work, all day you work.' Fathers say, 'No more I work and children hungry.' Massachusetts say 'Then we shoot!' Good old Massachusetts, ha ha!" The woman snapped her fingers, turned, and went back to watch the children.[17]

When time came to board, the Lawrence contingent filled a special coach added for their trip.[18] Rolling west out of Boston past snowy fields and fairy-tale forests, the children continued their adventure. Yet as the train crept toward Manhattan and the day dragged toward evening, many began to wonder just where they were bound. Up ahead, the crowd at Grand Central learned that the arrival time was now 6:30. A scheduled parade up Fifth Avenue had to be canceled. Some went home for dinner but by evening five thousand packed the Grand Central concourse to its bursting point. Then shortly before 8:00 p.m., as dozens of red banners waved above the crowd, an engine's headlight shone along the platform. As if on cue, the hum of "The Marseillaise" began to swell until the train pulled to a stop. Then suddenly, cheers and shouts erupted.[19] Caps and bowlers flew in the air. Seconds later, men emerged from the coach carrying little children, sound asleep. Moments later the older ones emerged and formed into two columns. Marching down a concrete ramp, they began chanting:

"Who are we? Who are we? Who are we?

"Yes we are! Yes we are! Yes we are!

"Strikers! Strikers! Strikers!"

Police tried to restrain the crowd, but in the confusion many shoved past, lifting kids onto their shoulders. Barriers of nationality fell before the commonality of class. Italian men carried Polish children. Germans bore young Italians aloft.[20] Big black mustaches bounced beneath towheads. Children too big to be carried marched through gaps cleared by police. Instead of a parade, they were escorted to the nearest elevated station, where a train took them to the Labor Temple on the Upper East Side. There many families had come to see if a Lawrence child might be "left over" to take home.[21] None were. The children devoured a hot meal of meat, soup, rice, and potatoes. Given warm clothes, pinched and prodded by doctors,[22] they were found to be alarmingly malnourished. One had chicken pox, another suffered from diphtheria, and almost all had swollen tonsils. Margaret Sanger, a nurse and future founder of Planned Parenthood, who accompanied the children, observed, "I have never seen in any place children so ragged and deplorable as these children were. . . . They were very much emaciated; every child there showed the effects of malnutrition. . . . When they had this supper, it would bring tears to your eyes to see them grab the meat with their hands and eat it."[23] The paperwork of assigning host families continued into the early morning until all 119 children,[24] exhausted and scarcely believing they were in the same country where they had awoken that morning, were in the homes of families who promised to care for them until the strike was over.

If there was one truth a divided America could agree upon, it was the sanctity of childhood. The early twentieth century was (and still is) regarded as childhood's golden age. Never mind that two million children worked in mines, mills, and factories,[25] while thousands roamed the streets in cutthroat gangs. The era's classic children's books, ranging from *Peter Pan* to *The Bobbsey Twins*, and the charming illustrations of Maxfield Parrish and N. C. Wyeth made childhood seem a sublime wonderland, innocent and sacred. Progressives protected childhood by creating juvenile courts and prolonging compulsory education. Academics pioneered child and adolescent psychology. If America could not provide for all its workers, it could at least shelter the children. Then on February 10, 1912, the news began to spread that a radical union had taken more than a hundred children from their mothers, tagged them "as cattle are tagged,"[26] and shipped them into the arms of Socialists carrying banners reading: YE EXPLOITERS, KNEEL DOWN BEFORE THE SONS OF YOUR VICTIMS.[27] The children may have been singing, adults throwing hats in the air, but the rest of America was not amused. The reaction was most pronounced closest to home.

Mayor Scanlon, who had two children and a third on the way,[28] was righteous in his indignation. Claiming parents must have been coerced into sending their children away, the mayor said, "I could scarcely believe that the strike leaders would do such a thing as this. . . . Lawrence could have very easily cared for these children."[29] Father Milanese, otherwise sympathetic to the strikers, termed the exodus "one of the greatest outrages connected with the strike. Many of the parents did not know just where their little ones were going and they did not want them to be taken away. But they have such great confidence in the leaders here . . . that they were led to think that it was for the best."[30] John Golden denounced the IWW for "tearing little children from their home ties for the sole purpose of exploiting them in order to raise funds."[31] In proper Boston, proper Bostonians called the move "insane foolishness,"[32] while the head of Massachusetts's Society for the Prevention of Cruelty to Children lamented he did not have the authority to intervene.[33] The press in both Boston and Lawrence universally condemned the exodus, describing the departing children as "dear little offspring"[34] and "pinch-faced, half starved, wondering eyed little folk."[35] More than one reporter flatly stated that some of the children would never return.[36]

If they were being exploited, the children of Lawrence did not seem to notice. One girl expressed the bewilderment of many when, upon surveying her host family's apartment, she turned and said, "I've seen it all now. Hadn't we better go home?"[37] Thirty-one children were sent to Hoboken, New Jersey, into the care of the Italian Silk Weavers' Union. The rest stayed in New York. Forbidding and mystical at first, the city seemed more accommodating when, on Sunday morning, many children ran into their peers at the aquarium, the Museum of Natural History, and the Bronx Zoo.[38] There they traded stories of warm homes and plush beds that did not have to be shared with siblings. While officials in Lawrence worried about possible neglect, the children were given free medical treatment, stuffed at every meal, and enrolled in local schools.[39] Within a few days, they wrote to parents asking "to stay for a year"[40] or saying they never wanted to come home.[41] One child, however, returned immediately.

Eleven-year-old Mary Sullivan did not have her parents' permission to go to New York, only to the depot to watch friends leave. But after being separated from her younger sister, Nancy, Mary decided it might be fun to see New York, so she asked an adult to go along. She was duly tagged and on her way. When Nancy Sullivan came home from the depot alone, Mary's anxious parents hurried to Lawrence police, who wired the NYPD but heard nothing. The following day, Mary wrote home: "I am having a lovely time here. Do not worry about me for I am happy and I have some hats and shirts, a new sweater, and five new croshayed hats. . . . Why did Nancy run home from the depot for nothing, because she was cold? She is missing a lovely time."[42] Alerted by authorities, Mary's father went to Manhattan on Monday night. Mary was back in Lawrence on Tuesday, telling anyone who would listen that "New York is a dandy place but I would rather stay at home and I won't go away any more."[43]

Poignant and unexpected, the children's exodus signaled to the nation that the strike in Lawrence was not just another brawl between Capital and Labor. And having helped pull off this daring chess move, Bill Haywood now stepped out of Joseph Ettor's shadow to earn his reputation as "the Lincoln of Labor." Taking up Ettor's old headquarters at the Needham Hotel,[44] Haywood, like his predecessor, proceeded to be everywhere at once. Often seen beside the strike's freshest face, that of Elizabeth Gurley Flynn, Haywood addressed up to ten meetings a day.[45] His speeches blended western grit with dogged will and a newfound respect for nonviolence. "I, for one, have turned my back on violence," he told strikers. "It wins nothing. When we strike now, we strike with our hands in our pockets. . . . Pure strength lies in the overwhelming power of numbers."[46] And as he had since his early speeches out west, Haywood displayed his unique brand of Americanism. Ettor had compared the strike to the French and Chinese revolutions, but Haywood's metaphors were as American as his favorite dessert—apple pie.[47] The strikers, he said, were "as firm today as Plymouth Rock"[48] and as "determined as were our Pilgrim fathers."[49] Quoting Patrick Henry, he told a Faneuil Hall crowd, "Human life is now the cheapest commodity in the market; we propose that human life shall be the most valuable asset on the planet. If this be treason, make the most of it."[50]

Big Bill's outsize personality won over strikers in need of a leader with the workingman's touch. He began to eat at their homes, devouring heaping plates of spaghetti and Turkish shashlik. After dining with Syrians, he was offered a hookah, which he smoked until his beefy face turned pale. "You're lucky, Gurley," he later told Flynn. "They don't expect the ladies to smoke."[51] At podiums, he showed that a notorious radical could also be a democrat with a small d. Before one audience, Haywood asked each nationality to choose a delegate, then brought the chosen onstage to say a few words. Some echoed Haywood's own phrases; others could barely speak.

When the audience responded with mock applause, he reminded them that great workers are not always great speakers. One Italian girl seemed about to bolt off stage, but Haywood escorted her to the front and presented her with a graceful bow. She managed to say a few words, then returned to the audience feeling that someone cared about her opinion.[52] Another evening, speaking in a Chinese restaurant, Haywood made his talk so simple that everyone in the audience—Chinese, Armenians, Greeks—understood although they spoke little English.

With Haywood at the helm, what was now being called "the strike for four loaves," because thirty-two cents a week bought that much bread,[53] entered its fifth week. On Monday morning, February 12, strikers debuted a new tactic. Instead of standing and shivering, pickets formed an "endless chain" that trudged all day along the slushy sidewalks fronting the mills. This endless chain stretching around the endless mills proved the perfect symbol for an endless strike. The chain allowed strikers to dodge an increasingly hostile militia, but it did not make picket lines any harder to cross.[54] After their numbers had peaked at twenty-three thousand following the death of Anna LoPizzo, strikers had begun trickling, then flowing back to their jobs. During the first two weeks of February, nearly three thousand returned to work,[55] so many that mill owners hired undercover detectives to watch for sabotage.[56]

Who were these people the strikers loathed as "scabs"? At first, most were skilled workers. Better paid, unionized, and justly proud of their craftsmanship, they were reluctant to join a bunch of "greenhorns" on strike. Others were just being loyal to their heritage. The Irish consistently opposed the strike, which they saw as an uprising by recent immigrants too ignorant or volatile to rise as they had. French Canadians, generally suspicious of unions,[57] had been late in joining, as had Germans. But as pickets marched around the mills and the strike slogged on with equal infinitude, fear and famine drove a wide range of people back to work. The children's exodus was euphoric, but it changed little back home. Mill owners were still silent. And once again word began to spread that the strike was breaking down. It looked as if it would soon be over anyway, so why not go back?

Nearly twenty thousand were still out,[58] but how long could they continue? The creeping sense of desperation escalated the strikers' ongoing war against scabs. On the night the children left the city, a mob gathered on Water Street along the Merrimack to throw stones through scabs' windows.[59] Death threats were commonly shouted at those crossing picket lines. One German who called another a "scab" found himself facing down the barrel of a revolver.[60] Torn by conflicting loyalties, each mill hand had to make a decision that might forever affect career, family, and reputation. The equation was painfully simple—remain on strike and stay hungry, or go back to work and be harassed and hated. One who decided to work was Romain Marcoux. Each morning, Marcoux endured vicious heckling while on his way to the Pacific Mill. Then one day he got a Black Hand letter, in his native French, giving him three days to walk out or be killed. He took the letter to police, who turned it over to the militia. Nothing was done and Marcoux kept working. "I can't stop work," said the father of nine. "I won't go around begging food and letting people take up collections to buy food for me or my children. I won't do that while I can work."[61]

By midweek, the *Boston Globe* saw the strike's spirit as "badly shaken."[62] The sudden shift in momentum worried Haywood, who knew that the IWW's own manifesto warned "a strike that is not won in four to six weeks cannot be won by remaining out any longer."[63] Management had more money and resources and the strikers more to lose by holding out. Another children's exodus might help, but Haywood had to do something right away to counter the sinking feeling. His answer: a downtown boycott. On February 14 at 2:00 p.m., hundreds gathered on Essex Street. Obeying soldiers' orders to keep moving, they marched up and down the sidewalk, women arm in arm, men side by side. To show merchants how much the strike was costing them, strikers entered small shops and department stores. They browsed for a few minutes, then walked out. Many were hustled along the sidewalk, even shoved by militia,[64] but in a city where public assembly was banned, Haywood's demonstration showed strikers the power that remained in their numbers.

Throughout the week, the war of words between the IWW and John Golden's affiliate, the Central Labor Union, escalated. When the CLU claimed to represent the strikers, the strike committee declared, "Such a proclamation can emanate only in the brains of idiots or in the offices of the mill owners."[65] Strikers were soon singing a song penned by Wobbly songwriter Joe Hill to the tune of the hymn "A Little Talk with Jesus."[66] The new song was entitled "A Little Talk with Golden."

> In Lawrence, when the starving masses struck for more to eat
> And wooden-headed Wood tried the strikers to defeat
> To Sammy Gompers wrote and asked him what he thought,
> And this is the answer that the mailman brought.
>
> A little talk, a little talk with Golden
> Makes it right, all right;
> He'll settle any strike if there's coin enough in sight;
> Just take him up to dine and everything is fine—
> A little talk with Golden makes it right, all right.[67]

Aside from his own craftsmen, however, no one was talking with Golden. Mill owners still refused to, finally claiming that the business climate and threat of tariff reform made it impossible to meet skilled workers' demands. Golden never heard from American Woolen.[68] With Wood flatly informing Coolidge that he would never meet with the IWW[69] and the strike committee voting unanimously to remain out until Ettor and Giovannitti were freed,[70] strikers faced weeks, perhaps months, more without pay. Only the militia was changing—for the worse.

On the day the children departed, Colonel Sweetser ratcheted his troops to a heightened alert. Anyone who gathered in "riotous assembly," brandished a weapon, or resisted arrest "may be fired upon without warning," the colonel announced.[71] Sweetser's edict turned even a casual stroll to the market into a dash through enemy territory. Another striker was wounded, his left forearm ripped open by a bayonet.[72] When one man walking a dog refused to hurry, a militiaman stabbed the dog.[73] In morning meetings, strikers complained of militia threatening to kill them, to run a bayonet "through the wop," at the slightest provocation.[74] Harassed and insulted, strikers started to fight back. On three consecutive evenings, soldiers marching beneath the searchlight of the Washington Mill were startled by the zing of air-gun pellets hitting an iron fence. No one was hit; no gunman was ever found.[75] It was just the beginning of a more blatant rebellion.

Amid the battlefield stress, some soldiers began to sympathize with strikers. Each day, IWW circulars posted in the mill district pleaded for soldiers' support, urging them to stand by their fellow workers, lay down their arms, and reject "the military ideal." "Young man," one circular began. "The lowest aim in your life is to be a good soldier. The 'good soldier' never tries to distinguish right from wrong. He never thinks, never reasons; he only obeys. . . . Young man, don't be a soldier—be a man."[76] One soldier gave a dollar to the strike committee. Haywood promptly had the bill framed.[77] Others—it was said as many as forty—refused to return to duty and were facing court-martial.[78] But for the vast majority of militia, such propaganda was not as demoralizing as the boredom, bitter cold, and resentment at being used. A militiaman later recalled his company's mood:

> There was too much of the feeling that we were fighting on the side of the mill owners. No one of us felt that he was like a policeman in the employ of the city to do justice to all its citizens. We were quartered at a mill and were fighting on the side of the mill men to protect them from the violence of the enemy. We had excellent accommodations at the mill and were constantly receiving favors from the mill men.[79]

And day after day, there was the deadening fatigue of duty. "Damn the strike!" a militiaman from Lowell said. "I only had three hours of sleep last night and I want to get home."[80] (Duty alone, however, did not tire the militia; many held dances in the mills lasting till the early morning, inviting young women until the city put a stop to them.)[81]

All that week crowds gathered outside police headquarters just off the common where the arraignment of Ettor and Giovannitti was in progress. Each morning, the two were led into the courtroom in handcuffs, Ettor smiling, Giovannitti downcast, disheveled, still a puzzle to the press.[82] Once when allowed to meet supporters at the railing of the prisoner's dock, the men shook hands and shared news with dozens of strikers. One Italian threw his arms around both men.[83] A reporter asked Ettor how he was feeling.

"Great! Why shouldn't I be?"[84] Ettor replied.

To convince a judge that the two leaders had incited the murder of Anna LoPizzo, the district attorney relied chiefly on testimony of reporters and undercover detectives. Phrases that would haunt the defendants were quoted and weighted with portent. Ettor: "This town won't be very happy in two days; something is going to happen." "We will keep the hardware stores busy giving out firearms."[85] Giovannitti: "Prowl around like wild animals looking for blood."[86] "To hell with peaceful picketing! If they don't stay out of the mills, we'll bust their heads!"[87] The prosecution also put the IWW on trial. Citing Wobbly literature, the district attorney accused the union of fomenting violent revolution. Two letters found on Ettor when he was arrested proved key to the case. One came from Vincent St. John, the IWW secretary-treasurer. The strike, St. John told Ettor, could never be won by outlasting management. "Get those 16,000 or 20,000 organized to break into jail and make the county feed them while they are on strike." The other letter, from a Wobbly in Rhode Island, advised extending the strike to American Woolen mills throughout New England.[88] Incrimination of the IWW was a familiar judicial tactic, and Wobblies ably defended their union. Smiling and triumphant in the docket, Ettor called the IWW "a child of history" and denied that it advocated force or violence. "What we mean by force is union solidarity," he said. "The I.W.W. does not believe in any violence. They believe in peace."[89] Haywood repeatedly took the Fifth Amendment, and Angelo Rocco supported the defendants insistently until ruled a hostile witness.[90]

The prosecution granted that neither Ettor nor Giovannitti had fired the shot that killed Anna LoPizzo. Who had, then? Turning to the events of January 29, testimony zeroed in on a tall dark Italian wearing a brown coat and carrying a long stick. In the snowy blur of bedlam, the man was seen resting his revolver on another's shoulder and aiming at Officer Oscar Benoit, the policeman stabbed that evening. Benoit then testified that he had seen a flash, felt the bullet whiz past, and saw the woman fall to the ground.[91] This account seemed to fit newspaper reports and was generally accepted as what must have happened. The prosecution rested its case on Tuesday, February 13.

That afternoon, Haywood, portly and commanding in his three-piece suit and bowler, entered the courtroom alongside a short, blue-eyed woman with plaited black hair. Since her arrival in Lawrence, Elizabeth Gurley Flynn had been only a marginal player. Now, she was about to become the strike's leading lady. Having just returned from New York, where she had accompanied the children, Flynn spoke all over Lawrence that day, bringing strikers news of their children and gathering support for another exodus. "This children's demonstration is the most wonderful that I have ever seen," she told strikers. "I have been in strikes and battles for free speech but I have never seen such an outburst of human brotherhood as I saw Saturday. I think that the capitalist class can well tremble on their thrones."[92]

Wherever she spoke, Flynn leaned over podiums, flailing one arm and projecting her voice in a manner common to seasoned speakers but surprising in a woman so young. At twenty-one, she was already infamous for her role in strikes nationwide. She had spoken in Lawrence the previous summer, and her arrival on January 20, as the dynamite scare terrorized the city,[93] had drawn hundreds to the train station, cheering as she and Ettor made their way through crowds.[94] Her tripartite name was confusing at first. Following her debut speech on the common, a strike committee member said, "I propose three cheers for Miss Elizabeth . . . er, whats-her-name."[95] To another she was "that wonderful little girl that speaks."[96] But the woman with three names was about to show Lawrence why, from Brooklyn to Spokane, she was considered "one of the most dangerous of the I.W.W.s."[97]

Joe Hill dedicated his song "The Rebel Girl" to Flynn, and its lyrics describe her importance to the union:

> That's the Rebel Girl. That's the Rebel Girl.
> To the working class she's a precious pearl.
> She brings courage, pride and joy
> To the Fighting Rebel Boy.[98]

"The Rebel Girl" came by her rebellion just as Ettor had—she inherited it. The daughter of steadfast Irish patriots, Flynn grew up in an impoverished household enriched by idealism. Her father, Tom Flynn, was a civil engineer whose passion for Socialism exceeded his will to work. "My long-suffering mother often felt that Pop overworked Karl Marx as an alibi for not looking for a job," Flynn remembered.[99] Flynn's mother, Annie Gurley, was a seamstress, a suffragette, and a fervent believer in the duty of women to speak their minds.[100] Bone-poor, the Flynns moved through mill and industrial towns where the sight of young mill girls with missing fingers "shocked me immeasurably,"[101] Flynn recalled. The family finally settled in Harlem, raising four children in a tenement with no heat or hot water but plenty of library books. "Ideas were our meat and drink, sometimes a substitute for both."[102]

As a teenager Flynn began reading Marx, Upton Sinclair's *The Jungle*, and the Russian anarchist, Prince Kropotkin. While still in high school, with her parents' encouragement, she took to speaking from soapboxes all over New York. Wearing a long dark skirt, white shirtwaist, and red tie, she told whoever would listen about the evils of capitalism and the coming revolution. One who listened was Theodore Dreiser, whose *Broadway Magazine* profile called Flynn "An East Side Joan of Arc" and "one of the most remarkable girls that the city has ever seen."[103] After she was arrested for speaking without a permit, a Broadway producer offered Flynn a stage debut. "I don't want to be an actress!" she replied. "I'm in the labor movement and I speak my own piece!"[104]

Flynn joined the IWW in 1906, when she was sixteen. The following year she hit the road as an organizer. While speaking in a mining camp, she met and married a miner, but marriage did not suit a "Rebel Girl." After bearing a stillborn child, she went off on her own again. In the summer of 1909, she organized throughout Montana, Washington, and Oregon, where she said, "I fell in love with my country—its rivers, prairies, mountains, cities, and people."[105] In labor camps teeming with hard-bitten "bindle stiffs," the blue-eyed teenage girl stood out like a rose in a thicket. Wobblies protected her from their own kind, insisting "Gurley is as safe with us as if she was in God's pocket,"[106] but they could not protect her from the laws of a country that would never appreciate her disparaging— some would later say "treasonous"—love.

In December 1909, the IWW was embroiled in a "free speech fight," one of many civil disobedience campaigns it waged throughout the West. Forbidden to speak on street corners in Spokane, Wobblies put out a call to "fellow workers" to come and fill the jails. More than six hundred flocked to Spokane to give speeches or just recite the Declaration of Independence[107] until police dragged them off soapboxes. In jail, they were beaten, crammed into sweatboxes, kept in ice-cold cells. Dozens were hospitalized and one died. "If men had murdered my own mother," a local reporter wrote, "I could not see them tortured as I saw the IWW men tortured in the city jail."[108] Arriving in Spokane that winter, Flynn was pregnant again, and the IWW would not let her speak. But as the editor of the union's journal, *Industrial Worker,* she was arrested on conspiracy charges, spent a long night in the lockup, and was brought before a judge. Asked on what she based her speeches, Flynn replied, "The Bill of Rights."

"But you're not a lawyer," the judge retorted. "How can you interpret them?"

"They are in plain English, your Honor, anyone can understand them," Flynn replied. "They were not written for lawyers but for the people." Acquitted,[109] she went back to her husband in Chicago, where in 1910 she bore a son. Soon divorced, she balanced motherhood and labor organizing until she was called to Lawrence. There she spoke to immigrants about their plight. They had been uprooted from the "old country," she told them, and lured to America for freedom, but "what freedom? To be herded into great prison-like mills, into slums in big cities, into tenements in these mill towns?"[110] She held special meetings for children to counteract school-teachers' negative comments about their parents, the strikers.[111] Rallying audiences in Lawrence, roaming the Northeast to gather strike funds, planning the next strategic move, Flynn became "the spirit of the strike," as journalist Mary Heaton Vorse remembered:

> When Elizabeth Gurley Flynn spoke, the excitement of the crowd became a visible thing. She stood there, young, with her Irish blue eyes, her face magnolia white and her cloud of black hair, the picture of a youthful revolutionary girl leader. She stirred them, lifted them up in her appeal for solidarity. Then at the end of the meeting, they sang. It was as though a spurt of flame had gone through the audience.[112]

Though she was the most visible, Flynn was not the lone female spirit of the strike. Lawrence, where more than half the mill workers were women and children,[113] had always had what the local press derided as "women agitators." The city's last big strike, in 1882, had been incited by a woman who complained to her boss about a pay cut, had a door slammed in her face, then led a walkout through The Plains.[114] The Wobblies only added fuel to this fire. Unlike the AF of L, the IWW welcomed women. "They cannot be driven back to the home," Flynn wrote in *Industrial Worker*. "They are part of the army of labor."[115] Now, with Flynn and her union backing them, the women of Lawrence were arming for battle, and not a metaphorical one.

From the strike's opening uproar, women had been as enraged and united as men. Come mid-February, with children in exile, men's endurance faltering, and a gnawing famine as near as each empty kitchen cupboard, women strode into the front lines. At first, men resisted the enlistment of their wives, mothers, and daughters,[116] but once women had proved themselves, their will drove the strike onward. Their collective character, a blend of feistiness, camaraderie, and humor, was embodied in one encounter between a female picket and a soldier. Militiamen often tried to "jolly" female pickets,[117] asking them out on dates. Most women just walked away, but one shared her response with the strike committee. She had been picketing when a militiaman approached and told her to move on. When she refused, the soldier asked if she would "make an appointment" with him. She replied, "No, I only make dates with men."[118]

Men were clearly in charge of the strike, yet beneath the masculine veneer women were their equals in influence. Throughout the tenements, women met in doorways or on street corners to discuss strategy.[119] They pooled their meager resources, cooking together, caring for each other's children. Peeling potatoes in soup kitchens, they broke into "The Internationale."[120] On sidewalks, they linked arms and swept up the street, singing and calling out to passersby. Policemen, raised to think of women as Gibson girls, were flummoxed and a few were even put to flight. Haywood recalled seeing women strip a policeman to his long underwear and dangle him, headfirst, above a canal before another officer intervened.[121] Women threw pepper in the faces of police and militia, cut their suspenders with scissors,[122] or sent them flying off horses jabbed by hat pins.[123] Police fought back, arresting 130 women during the strike,[124] but propriety prevented officers from treating women as roughly as men, at least at first. "One policeman can handle ten men," lamented Lawrence's district attorney, "while it takes ten policeman to handle one woman."[125] From the bench, Judge Mahoney criticized this "game the fellows are playing"[126] by putting women in harm's way, but women denied they were being used. "Women strikers are not being egged on by anyone or forced to go upon the picket line, as Judge

Mahoney has said," one woman clarified during a strike committee meeting. "We go there because we feel that it is but duty."[127]

Among the most active households of women was that of Consiglia Rocco, Angelo's sister. While her brother went to meetings, fourteen-year-old Consiglia followed her mother, whom everyone on Elm Street called "Grandmamma,"[128] around the Italian quarter. "She'd be in heated debates herself," Consiglia recalled, "you know, getting more food for the strikers, planning all the things that had to be done." The Rocco household was open "to all the kids on the block. She'd make bread or pizza and everybody would be there—all during the strike. My brother was very active, so we didn't see too much of him, you know he was in jail or at the I.W.W. So my mother make so no one goes hungry or cold, not on our block."[129]

While thousands of women picketed and sang, a few, as the historian Ardis Cameron noted, took more direct action and became local legends. There was Sara Axelrod, a.k.a. "the egg woman." A Russian immigrant and former mender in the Wood Mill, Axelrod had moved to a nearby poultry farm just before the strike but visited the city daily, bringing eggs to hungry families.[130] And there was Josephine Lis, who had worked with her father in the Wood Mill, each earning seven dollars a week, the sole support for a family of eight.[131] Fluent in Polish, conversant in Yiddish and Lithuanian, Lis became a valued interpreter, counseling arrested strikers and serving on the Polish delegation to the strike committee. But she only became the talk of the town when stopped by militia. One soldier clutched Lis's arm so tightly she screamed, then called her a whore.[132] When he lowered his bayonet, Lis shoved it away[133] and slapped him in the face with her muff.[134] Arrested for assault, she refused to pay her ten-dollar fine, telling the judge, "If I'm not free when I'm out, I'd just as soon be in jail." Another Josephine, Josephine Resnick, was arrested for striking a soldier with his own gun. Seems the soldier had impugned the femininity of female pickets.[135] The most dynamic female striker, however, was the one who had been the highest-paid worker in all the mills.

For her dexterity in weaving finely crafted "art squares," Annie Welzenbach earned $20.58 a week.[136] It was said that one word from the twenty-four-year-old weaver could shut down three mills in Lawrence. She and her husband, a mill foreman,[137] owned a home in South Lawrence, yet she joined the strike immediately because "I have been getting madder and madder for years at the way they talked to those poor Italians and Lithuanians."[138] Welzenbach was busier during the strike than she had been at the Wood Mill. Fluent in German, Polish, and Yiddish,[139] she attended court sessions, visited strikers' homes, and was the only female member of the strike committee's executive board. Like Lis, she became famous when arrested. Welzenbach called the arrest "a laughing affair,"[140] but strikers, especially women, were incensed. Just before midnight on February 16, police raided the homes of Welzenbach and her two sisters, taking them into custody in their nightgowns. They were charged with intimidating female workers, but many in Lawrence, and not just strikers, felt the police themselves were guilty of intimidation. Welzenbach was instantly lionized.[141] Protesting her arrest, two dozen members of the Progressive Women's Club of Lawrence,[142] each with respectable Anglo-Saxon surnames, signed a letter comparing the late-night seizure to "such actions in Russia."[143] Welzenbach was convicted and given a small fine but her fame grew. Easily recognizable in her flowing black dress and tall, jaunty hat, she drew thanks from total strangers. One day an Italian approached her. "Me no care if I die," he told her. "If any hurt you, I die for you."[144] Another afternoon, she was walking down Common Street when others began to fall in behind her until some two thousand strikers marched her home.[145]

With women united and Haywood and Flynn taking the reins, each day saw the jousting of hope and fear, solidarity and subsistence. Thanks to publicity from the children's exodus, relief was now arriving at the rate of several hundred dollars a day.[146] At Franco-Belgian Hall, strikers were kept busy opening letters from around the country, emptying out quarters, dimes, and dollars. Two dozen strikers served on the IWW's relief committee, distributing funds to eighteen soup kitchens run by separate nationalities.[147] Angelo Rocco handled much of the money for the Italians, spending some $5,000 on food throughout the strike.[148] The committee also provided vouchers for groceries. A single striker was given a $2.00 weekly voucher. Families got between $3.00 and $5.50, along with coal— enough to fill the bathtub bin twice—and twenty-five cents a week for wood.[149] Shoes and warm clothing were distributed when available. Across town, the CLU relief station took donations from unions—carpenters, shoemakers, musicians, bartenders, upholsterers—from as nearby as Lowell and as far off as Bakersfield, California. Individuals from Boston and

Chicago, Waco, Texas, and Grand Forks, North Dakota, also sent in a dollar, five, or fifty.[150] Outside relief helped strikers avoid eviction and starvation, yet each child begging at a restaurant, each weary mother lined up for bread, each ghostly old man wolfing down a hot meal at a soup kitchen proved that hunger was still rampant. To keep it at bay, those who could not give from their pockets turned to their pantries. In the nearby town of West Peabody, two men went door-to-door and collected two hundred dollars, an assortment of live pigs and chickens, and a cornucopia of vegetables, coffee, and tea.[151] Farmers from surrounding villages sent in provisions.[152] And as Haywood and Flynn planned the next exodus, offers came from throughout the East to care for the children of Lawrence.[153] Socialists in Boston proffered their homes as did workers in Lynn, Brockton, Philadelphia, Providence . . .[154]

On Saturday, February 17, 150 children were sent to two separate destinations. The first group left promptly at 7:21 a.m. to the waving of hats and handkerchiefs. In Boston, they were marched through the maze of streets leading from North to South Station, passing hundreds lined up to see the now-famous exiles.[155] The train to Manhattan was on time. Again under Flynn's supervision, the children were given a tumultuous reception—trumpets, drums, long lines of red-capped porters[156]—and then, finally, the promised parade up Fifth Avenue. At the head of the procession marched a curly-headed four-year-old girl carrying a sign: SOMEDAY WE WILL REMEMBER THIS EXILE. Behind her, other placards read: WE CAME FROM LAWRENCE FOR A HOME and A LITTLE CHILD SHALL LEAD THEM.[157] All along Fifth Avenue, children walked, bands blared, and women solicited strike funds.[158] Many shoppers donated but just as many sneered, called out, or urged police to stop this rank exploitation of poverty on parade.[159]

A second group of exiles, thirty-five Italian bambini, left Lawrence that morning bound for Barre, Vermont, where they had been requested by Italians working in the granite quarries of the Green Mountains.[160] At Barre's central station, sixteen hundred people, one-fifth of the town's population, met the children's train. Their parade may not have been up Fifth Avenue, yet without the catcalls of hostile onlookers, Main Street in Barre was more welcoming. No one knows whether the children carried signs saying they would remember, but eight decades later, one did. In 1993, looking back from the other end of his life, Ernesto Calderone, who was eight when sent to Barre with his sister, recalled a city and a family that opened their arms:

> I never seen a thing the way they treated us; it was mar-
> velous, marvelous. They brought us to a hall, a stage, then took
> us one by one and asked if anybody wanted this boy or girl. . . .
> When it came to me, the guy and wife took me, brought me
> home, showed me my bedroom, and started figuring out what
> to buy. They bought me a suit, a sled, some shirts and ties. I
> don't remember the name of the family. There was a girl my age.
> They bought me a sled and we used to go coasting, me and her
> every day. The only thing was we were young. We were wanting
> our families.[161]

From the mountains of Vermont and the canyons of Manhattan, the children's exodus seemed a startling success. But from city hall overlooking The Plains in Lawrence, it looked like a cheap publicity stunt that had to be stopped. Lawrence had already been branded a hotbed of radicalism; now it was being portrayed as a heartless city that could no longer care for its own children. City officials vowed to do more than denounce the departures. Two hours after the second exodus on February 17, Colonel Sweetser sent a letter to strikers announcing, "While I am in command of the troops at Lawrence, I will not permit the shipping off of little children away from their parents to other cities unless I am satisfied that this is done with the consent of the parents." Ignoring the letters of consent chaperones carried for each child, Sweetser said he had received complaints from parents coerced into parting with their children, and that some of the "little ones" did not even belong to strikers.[162]

When Sweetser's letter was delivered to Franco-Belgian Hall, the Saturday morning strike committee meeting was well under way. Strikers had just cheered Annie Welzenbach. "Colonel Sweetser is willing to have these soldiers, or whatever you may call these things in khaki suits, to insult ladies," Welzenbach charged. "Colonel Sweetser is no man." So when the colonel's letter was read aloud, hisses filled the hall. The meeting went on, as would plans to send more children.[163] Philadelphia was next, set to receive two hundred children the following Saturday.[164] By then Flynn, who had gone on from New York to raise funds throughout the East, was expected back in Lawrence, eager to make good on her goal to "leave this city. without a child."[165] And all through the tenements that week, mothers wrestled with their emotions, held their children as long as they could, then went out to another day on strike.

Near the mills one morning, two dozen women gathered outside a church. Stamping their feet in the cold, they chatted while pulling shawls around their shoulders. A cloud of breath rose above them as the eastern horizon turned salmon pink. Then steeling themselves, the women headed down the sidewalk toward the picket lines. Suddenly a detail of police, their badges glinting in the overhead arc light, loomed up ahead. The policemen surrounded the women, cursed them, pulled nightsticks, and sent them scurrying off into the morning. As she left, one woman called to a friend, "I go home. I nurse the little one. I be back yet."[166]

CHAPTER NINE

Crackdown

*No fear can stand up to hunger, no patience can wear it out, disgust sim-
ply does not exist where hunger is; and as to superstition, beliefs, and
what you may call principles, they are less than chaff in a breeze. Don't
you know the devilry of lingering starvation, its exasperating torment,
its black thoughts, its somber and brooding ferocity?*

—Joseph Conrad, *Heart of Darkness*[1]

On most afternoons in mid-February, when it was not snowing or cru-
elly cold, a young boy in the tenements stepped outside to play soldier. But
in contrast to boy soldiers elsewhere in America, Johnny Lane did not pre-
tend to storm San Juan Hill or reenact the fighting at Gettysburg. Instead,
he staged the battle in his hometown. Donning a blue uniform made by his
mother, with brass buttons and epaulets, Johnny got his gun—an air rifle—
and began pacing the corner of Hampshire and Myrtle streets a few blocks
north of the common. Throwing his chest out, he shouted at friends and
snapped at neighbors to "Move on!" Once when bemused militiamen
gathered around him, Johnny assured them he was going to be a real general
someday.[2] The soldiers hooted and egged the kid on, but in a city where
nerves were as tight as a close-order drill, the militia's presence was no
laughing matter.

Governor Eugene Foss was growing anxious about Lawrence. Still a
dark-horse presidential candidate, Foss knew that pundits were down-
grading his chances due to his handling of the strike.[3] In fact, he had not
handled it at all. Known throughout New England for his antilabor votes

while he was in Congress,[4] Foss had done little more than propose a thirty-day back-to-work truce flatly rejected by strikers.[5] A former Republican, Foss had recently switched parties, leaving him open to constant attacks from his opposition legislature.[6] Now this plump, amiable mill owner bore ultimate responsibility for Massachusetts's own army. Despite strikers' complaints, state and local officials felt the militia had handled a difficult situation admirably—so far. Yet with bayonets poised, some wholesale slaughter was just a shot away. So on February 13, Foss called Michael Scanlon to a meeting beneath the gold dome of the State House in Boston. There the governor told the mayor that Lawrence police must do more to patrol their city. The disagreeable duty should not be left solely to the militia. The usually self-possessed mayor emerged from the meeting in a feisty mood. The strike, Scanlon told reporters, was not a strike but "an incipient revolution. It is the beginning of a wage war which is to spread throughout the country." As for mill owners, he blamed them for starvation wages, blasting the "tremendous dividends that the mills declare and the immense salaries paid to their officials."[7] The standoff would continue, the mayor said. "There isn't a chance in the world that I can see to end this strike."[8] And the soldiers, despite rumors and headlines to the contrary,[9] would stay in Lawrence.[10] Then that evening, the militia's highest-ranking officer took his own shot at the mayor.

"The civic authorities in Lawrence are absolutely spineless and rely altogether on the militia to control the situation," Adjutant General Gardner W. Pearson said. "It's about time that the authorities make some effort to help themselves."[11] SPINELESS. Plastered on the front page of the *Lawrence Daily American,* the word echoed throughout city hall all that week. It still hung in the air when aldermen met on Thursday, February 15. That evening, Mayor Scanlon watched in dismay as his governing coalition, which had remained united in the face of a recall petition and withering criticism, started to crumble. Aldermen lashed out at police, calling officers demoralized, unfit, even afraid of strikers. Cornelius Lynch, the commissioner of public safety who had sounded the riot call on the strike's first morning, defended the force. "What are we doing here today, Mr. Mayor?" Lynch asked. "Trying the police department?"[12] But the arrows had hit their mark. Within days, the Lawrence police, under the command of a new marshal, would take control of all streets beyond the mill district.

Within another week, their crackdown—anything but spineless—would unhinge the city and shock the nation.

Whenever authority changed hands in Irish-dominated Lawrence, outsiders saw it as a mere shuffling of surnames. Aldermen named Finnegan and Flanagan, Casey and Collins came and went.[13] The strike's key public figures included an attorney named Roewer and a judge named Rowell, an attorney named Lynch and the alderman of the same name, and in the courtroom, four Mahoneys—two lawyers, a judge,[14] and a clerk.[15] Hence, few saw the significance when John J. Sullivan replaced James T. O'Sullivan as city marshal. Yet a generational shift had occurred. Retiring marshal O'Sullivan had first walked a beat in Lawrence in 1868. As marshal, he had helped capture bank robbers and small-time crooks, but handling teeming hordes of strikers seemed beyond the seventy-year-old's powers. Many felt it was time for fresh blood. The new city marshal was sixteen years younger and, it was hoped, much tougher. John J. Sullivan had been on the force for thirty years, most of them as captain of the night watch. Having been the man of his family since the age of five, when his father died, Sullivan was known as a "strict disciplinarian and an efficient officer."[16] He had also done battle with strikers. Sullivan had defended the Wood and Prospect mills against mobs, and was struck by ice chunks during the January 29 raid on streetcars.[17] With thin, determined eyes, chiseled cheeks, and a humorless countenance,[18] Sullivan looked the very picture of military discipline. Certainly it was this, more than his being Mayor Scanlon's brother-in-law,[19] which accounted for his promotion. With such a man at the helm, the *Boston Globe* predicted "a more vigorous civic policing."[20]

As the strike entered the dreary bleakness of late February in New England, all signs pointed to impending chaos. Reporters[21] and strike leaders[22] sensed that something would happen in the next week or two, something forcing mill owners to give in or else drive despairing strikers back to the mills. Small strikes had broken out in textile towns from Fall River to Maine,[23] and Lawrence was growing dangerously rowdy. Women, who had volunteered to take over all picketing, continued their surge to the forefront, becoming the rowdiest of all. Roaming outside the mills in packs, they openly berated scabs, and when arrested, furiously beat at militiamen or dropped to the sidewalk, thrashing and screaming.[24] Others seemed happy to be arrested, proudly entering squad cars to be taken to the station.[25] Negotiations did not seem likely to settle anything any time soon. Calvin Coolidge was finding his task "a very hard job to manage."[26] When his committee dared to suggest that mill men bargain directly with the IWW,[27] infuriated city officials rushed to Boston to squelch such a crazy idea.[28] Another thousand strikers had gone back to work,[29] renewing the rage against the strike's turncoats. Haywood and Flynn were planning the largest children's exodus yet, but the new marshal vowed to stop it using "all the force, power, and authority I possess."[30]

Into this hornet's nest stepped the Lawrence police. Still reeling from charges of incompetence, police were stung by testimony during the waning days of the Ettor-Giovannitti arraignment. Had a tall, dark Italian killed Anna LoPizzo? The defense offered its own answer when a slight fifteen-year-old Polish girl took the stand. Greta Zurweil lived at the corner of Union and Garden streets. At about 5:00 p.m. on January 29, she had gone outside to see what the noise was all about.

"Did you see a woman on the ground?" the district attorney asked.

"Yes, right near me."

"Did you see her before she fell?"

"Yes."

"How many shots were fired?"

"Four or five."

"Did you see anyone fire the shots?"

"Yes."

"Who?"

"A policeman."[31]

Zurweil identified Officer Oscar Benoit in the courtroom, saying, "I saw Officer Benoit raise his arm, fire his revolver, and the woman fell."[32] A friend who had been with Zurweil backed her testimony.[33] Like the charge of being spineless, the accusation reverberated through city hall. On Wednesday, February 21, Ettor and Giovannitti, denounced by the prosecution as "labor buzzards," were held over for the grand jury due to convene in April. Bail was denied. The two men went back to jail,[34] and the Lawrence police, now accused of murder as well as cowardice, went back on patrol.

The following day just before 1:00 p.m., eleven children and their parents appeared at the depot. The station was quiet, with no more than the usual milling strangers. The 1:00 p.m. train that would take more strikers' children to host families in Bridgeport, Connecticut, came on time. Mothers were beginning their sad good-byes when Officer Benoit and another patrolman stepped forward. Under orders from Marshal Sullivan, they announced, no more strike children would be allowed to leave Lawrence. A few parents protested that they were traveling with their children; they were allowed to board the train. The rest were taken to the police station, where the new city marshal asked parents why they were sending their children away. They all said they could not afford to care for them. Seated beside the marshal was a kindly, white-haired reverend who ran the city's charity mission. The Reverend Clark Carter assured parents they could come to him for relief. Lawrence took good care of its poor children, he said. Commissioner Lynch, also on hand, took a special interest in one mother whose six-year-old son kept rubbing his eyes. The woman had been promised her boy would receive medical attention in Bridgeport. Commissioner Lynch knew such poverty firsthand. Raised by a single mother of five, he had gone to work in the mills at age ten, earning fifty cents a day. Touched by the mother's story, Lynch personally took the sick boy to Lawrence General Hospital that afternoon.[35] Then with a stern warning[36] and fifteen dollars Lynch had given the parents, the families were released. The incident ended amicably, but with Haywood bellowing about charging the city with "false arrest,"[37] it was the low, distant rumble heralding a storm.

As opposing sides headed for their showdown, public opinion further braced Marshal Sullivan's spine. Since the first exodus on February 10, a protest had been mounting, in part due to relentless baiting by the *Boston American*. The Hearst paper compared the children's departure from Lawrence to the forced exile of Acadians in Longfellow's poem *Evangeline*. Calling the move "un-American and unjustifiable by any standpoint,"[38] the *American* claimed parents had been coerced into parting with their "little ones" for such "juvenile exploitation."[39] Several other papers printed letters from happy children writing home:

> Dear Mother:
>   I am having a good time. And I'll be home after the strike is
> over. And I am going to school. . . . Where I am there is a little

boy and I am playing with him. And I am going to the show. Will you please tell me when I was vaccinated? The people I am with bought me some clothes. I feel good and don't worry. And how is the baby and how are you getting along?

With love, Joseph.[40]

But the *American* ran daily interviews with distraught mothers who wondered if sending their children away had been the right move.[41] As public indignation mounted, Haywood fired back. Mocking Boston's "Back Bay polite society and the daily papers that cater to their ilk," he charged that the "plutes" (plutocrats) had said nothing about children's exploitation in the mills. "Afraid of losing their little slaves, in whom they have only a material interest, our smug Boston exploiters and their ladies now sound the alarm," Haywood said.[42] And in defiance of all police warnings, he made plans to send more.

On Friday morning, February 23, downtown Lawrence was unusually calm. Essex Street had its scattering of shoppers, but for the first time in twenty-five days, no militia pushed or prodded them. All fifteen hundred soldiers had returned to the mill district, where they easily handled a pack of women harassing scabs near the Everett Mill.[43] Throughout the day, there were no other incidents or arrests. Lawrence police could take care of everything, Marshal Sullivan assured the mayor. "By Monday morning," he said, "we shall be ready for them whatever they do."[44] The strikers, however, could not wait for Monday. They had a train to catch.

As they had on the previous two Saturday mornings, mothers and children rose before sunrise on February 24 and prepared for another exodus. By 6:30 a.m. the depot waiting room was crowded. Nowhere near the expected two hundred children were on hand, perhaps because police had visited tenements the night before warning parents against sending their little ones away. Yet forty-six children, along with parents and assorted chaperones, waited in the station. The chaperones bore credentials from the IWW's Children's Vacation Committee authorizing them "to take provision for the sending away of the strikers' children." Each child had an identification card signed by parents.[45] The children sat quietly on the benches. Adults waited. Haywood arrived, greeted the entourage, and went off by himself. Then at 6:45, Marshal Sullivan strode into the waiting room. Dressed in plainclothes but bearing his full, military manner, the marshal ordered all those not departing on the 7:11 train to leave. "If any of you women attempt to send your children away," he announced, "I will arrest both you and them."[46] A few parents grabbed their children and left,[47] but one woman strode up to the marshal and shouted, "I zend dem to mine friends! They is mine children, not yours! You mind your business!"[48] The rest stood, hushed and confused. Moments later, the marshal stepped outside to confer with policemen. On the far edge of the platform, four militia companies stood in waiting.[49] At the curb near the baggage office sat a large, open-backed military transport truck, sent from an arsenal in Watertown.[50] For the next several minutes, no one moved. No one spoke above a whisper. Then the huffing of a train was heard in the distance. The engine chugged in, and as it came to a stop all reason fled from Lawrence, as if it, too, had purchased a ticket and could not wait to escape this rancorous city.

As with the murder of Anna LoPizzo, accounts of what happened next remain uncertain. Were children dragged like dolls? Were women clubbed? Were pregnant women clubbed? Despite the presence of several reporters, there are no photographs of such brutality. In fact, there are no photographs at all from that morning. Words alone were enough.

The trouble began when police formed a gauntlet between the waiting room and the arriving train. Women and children were told to leave by the east entrance leading back to the street or else stay inside until the train pulled out. Angry and frightened, mothers turned to each other, to husbands, to their children, wondering what to do. Haywood might have told them, but he had slipped onto the train and taken a seat. After a moment, a Polish woman leading a small child by the hand approached police. Suddenly she made a break across the platform. Policemen hustled mother and child back into the waiting room.[51] The unknown woman proved to be the spark that set the morning ablaze.

Within seconds, mothers marched their children toward the train. To the horror of onlookers, police grabbed the women, tearing them from their boys and girls. Cries rang out in Polish, Russian, Lithuanian, Yiddish.[52] Children screamed as mothers were dragged away. The women fought back, fists flying, fingernails scratching bare cheeks. Fathers lifted children to take them to their mothers but police drove them back. Beneath the engine's billowing steam, the station platform was littered with floral hats. In all directions, bare hands stretched out, reaching, pleading, flailing. Disbelieving faces watched from train windows as officers continued their roundup, using two or three bluecoats to control each frantic woman. With hair disheveled, long skirts and scarves flying, bodies jackknifed over policemen's burly arms, the women groped for their children with one hand and hammered at their captors with the other. Though city officials would forever deny it, police were "compelled to use their clubs."[53] Battered and hysterical, the women were thrown into the open transport truck. As officers began to drag children away, a woman on the platform cried out, "Be careful of the children, you are killing them!"[54] But police threw several, some as young as six, in with their mothers. Women fought to get out, tearing at one policeman who cracked skulls to fight them off.[55] Another officer, about to fall off the truck, throttled a woman until she stopped her pummeling.[56] And then, while women screamed and children sobbed, while men stared daggers at police, while the militia watched from nearby, the 7:11 train slowly began to pull out. At one window, on his way to a speaking engagement, Haywood sat alone, livid with anger and racked with remorse at having had to dodge certain arrest. Not a single child from Lawrence was on board with him.

It was all over in seven minutes. As the police wagon pulled away, those remaining on the platform jeered. "Police no good," one man shouted again and again until he was arrested.[57] Then, faster than any vehicle could drive the half mile to police headquarters, an electric rage crackled through the city. When the arsenal truck pulled into the municipal plaza beside city hall, a hundred people were waiting, in no mood to let anyone pass. Police descended on the crowd, scattering them onto the common. Then those rounded up at the depot—five men, nine women, and fifteen children—disappeared into the police station,[58] and the word went out across the tenements, down to the picket lines, and all around the city. The word was not always accurate—the beatings at the train station grew more savage with each retelling—but the word was final. This would be avenged.

At 10:30 that morning, the strike committee gathered for its regular meeting at Franco-Belgian Hall. The word was humming through the clogged aisles when two police, in plainclothes but with badges clearly in sight, entered at the back. Instantly, the crowd exploded in hoots and jeers.

Fearing a riot, IWW secretary William Trautmann rushed to the podium. "The capitalists are desperate!" Trautmann shouted. "All they want you to do is to start something! Don't let them provoke you. . . . You have seen them use their clubs against women and children! Bear it with patience however as you know that with the next twenty-four hours the world will know of these outrages!"[59] With the pair of policemen standing in plain sight at the rear, the meeting went on. Delegates fresh from the train station described the scene. "I was in Russia when the revolution broke out," said Samuel Lipson, referring to the 1905 uprising against the czar, "but I never saw anything like I saw this morning." As witnesses drew Goyaesque images of nightsticks thrashing women, of children thrown like rag dolls, of pregnant women struck on their breasts and bellies, cries of "Shame!" resounded through the hall. Someone yelled, "Put out the spies and detectives!" But when reports of atrocities concluded, the meeting continued without incident, the chief business being a vote on whether to send more children. The committee unanimously approved another exodus, again to Philadelphia, on Monday. "The strike is only beginning," one member said. "It begins good today."[60] The publicity committee set to work on circulars to be posted around Lawrence that night. The two policemen thought it prudent to leave before the meeting ended.[61]

By noon, the steps of the police station were jammed with men whose wives were in custody. Along with the nine rounded up at the depot, twenty-five women had been arrested for picketing that morning. Waiting for news, some husbands were in tears, and many stood with toddlers in their arms.[62] When allowed to enter, they handed the children to chagrined policemen who took them to mothers in jail. Upstairs, Marshal Sullivan was boasting to a *Boston American* reporter, "We had no militia to help us today, you notice. That was arranged on purpose so that we might demonstrate to the world that we are able to control the situation here without help."[63] Downstairs, children as young as three months were being nursed behind bars.[64] At 2:45 p.m., many infants were still in their mothers' arms when the women were brought before Judge Wilbur Rowell—sitting in for Judge Mahoney, who had gone to Boston to urge the Coolidge Committee to blackball the IWW.[65] One by one the names of the women arrested for picketing were read. Maggie Jesocantz. Pauline Narack. Annie Rajak. Eva Glinconas . . .[66] Each woman denied she had done anything wrong, accusing the police of beating picketers. Each was fined one to five dollars. Each refused to pay and was taken back downstairs, except for one woman sent to the hospital with a broken arm.[67] Then Judge Rowell turned to those taken at the train station.

"When parents voluntarily allow their children to go from their custody to a city hundreds of miles away," the judge declared, "it appears to be nothing short of neglect."[68] The judge cited the Massachusetts Acts of 1903 under which parents could be charged with neglect of any child under sixteen found to be "growing up without education or without salutary control." Attorney George Roewer protested. All the departing children had parental permission. All were bound for homes where they would be better fed and clothed than they had ever been in their lives. If that was neglect, Roewer said, then the dictionary definition needed revision.[69] Ignoring the argument, Judge Rowell remanded all fifteen children to the City Home, a.k.a. the Poor Farm, a complex of three old farmhouses behind a white picket fence on the outskirts of the city.[70] There they would wait until Tuesday, when their cases would be continued.[71] He charged the mothers with creating a disturbance and fined each from one to three dollars.[72] Ruling from the bench was easy, however, compared to taking the children from their mothers again. When the city's probation officer began leading the children away, several mothers raced to their boys and girls and sheltered them in their arms. The women had to be forcibly separated, scuffling and screaming while the judge pounded his gavel for order.[73] An hour later, four horse-drawn hacks pulled up on Common Street and as crying children were led toward them,[74] a crowd of five hundred surged forward. It took police twenty minutes to fight off the mob while loading the children inside. When the carriages pulled away, many women fainted and had to be dragged into the police station. One man, however, having grabbed his children in the confusion, stole away with them across the common.[75]

That night hundreds fanned out through the city to tack up the strike committee's latest flyers. One issued a call to militia: "Cease all brutalities. Stop all provocations. Be human."[76] Another told scabs, "You still have time to repent and make good. . . . Rise up! Get back into the ranks! On to victory!"[77] And a third was directed to all the city's workers. The time had come, it said, for a general strike.

Workers, quit your hammers, throw down your files, let the
dynamos stop, the power cease to turn the wheels and the looms,
leave the machinery, bank the fires, shut the steam off, stop the
engines on the tracks, tie up the plants, tie up the town. Great is
the provocation; greater must be the answer of the workers to
the employing class. . . . The time has come, has come now. On
to the general strike of all workers, of all professions, of women,
men, and children.[78]

When Lawrence awoke on Sunday morning, the circulars papered the
city. They were posted on trees, telephone poles, buildings, and trolley
stops.[79] Fallen posters lay trodden in the snow. Struggling to capitalize on
Saturday's events, Haywood was playing his trump card, hoping the promise of a general strike could contain the strikers' rising rage. Further violence by strikers would only squander the widespread sympathy expected
from the beating of mothers and manhandling of children. But the IWW's
enemies had their own ace, and that Sunday, strikers at last came up against
the most powerful force in the city, a force not clothed in the blue coats of
police nor the olive drab of militia but in the frocked collar of Father James
T. O'Reilly.

To call Father O'Reilly an influential priest in Lawrence is akin to calling Napoleon an influential general in France. Though Father O'Reilly was
one of a score of priests in the city, he was, in the memory of one parish-
ioner, "the big boss."[80] The head of St. Mary's Catholic diocese was the spiritual bedrock of the city. For many, it was hard to imagine Lawrence
without him. In 1895, when Father O'Reilly traveled to Rome for a convention of his Augustinian order, his parishioners gave him twenty-one hundred dollars for the trip and celebrated his return with a "monster parade."[81]
When he spoke, Catholics listened out of obedience and everyone else listened to take a reading of the city's moral compass. When he made a decree,
it affected members of his eleven interlinked churches, children attending
several parochial schools, and dozens of Sunday-school programs tied to
various immigrant dioceses. A man of the cloth, Father O'Reilly was equally
a man of the flag. He arranged frequent patriotic displays in which a thousand children in starched white uniforms waved the Stars and Stripes. God
and country were one for Father O'Reilly, as he preached one Memorial

Day: "And two emblems, the cross upon the globe, and the noble stars and stripes shall speak to our children the truest of patriotism—loyalty to God and country. We are not ashamed to assert it—God first, country second! And he who serves God well, the better serves his country!"[82]

Father O'Reilly's unflinching devotion to his ideals was forged out of a sorrowful childhood. Orphaned when his mother died and his father succumbed to an illness while fighting for the Union during the Civil War, James T. O'Reilly was raised by his grandparents, Irish immigrants to New York's Hudson Valley. After attending a rigid parochial school, he entered Villanova College at age fifteen. There he heard the call to God and was ordained to the priesthood. He taught mathematics at Villanova and served as the college's business manager before seeking his own parish. In 1886, at the age of thirty-five, Father O'Reilly took over St. Mary's in Lawrence only to find the parish $425,000 in debt. The priest's business skills served him well in raising funds, securing loans, and almost single-handedly willing St. Mary's out of the red. He also began consolidating his influence, reaching out to social clubs, service organizations, and immigrants until, by 1900, the orphaned boy had become the undisputed leader of twenty-eight thousand Catholics, then more than half the city's population. In the decade before the strike, as immigrants poured into the city, Father O'Reilly bankrolled separate Catholic churches for Greeks, Syrian Maronites, Portuguese, and Lithuanians. His influence in Lawrence was not just Catholic but "catholic," from the Greek root meaning "universal." Father O'Reilly belonged to the city's board of trade. He cofounded the Merrimack Co-Operative Bank. He served on the school committee and the city's committee of arbitration on labor disputes.[83] He organized the Knights of Columbus and the Young Men's Catholic Association. He ran charities from the St. Vincent de Paul Society to the city's orphan asylum. He was even a trustee of the Lawrence Public Library. "Everything they did in the city," recalled one parishioner, "if he said no, it was no."[84]

Father O'Reilly had supported previous strikes. In 1894, he had intervened in a small strike at the Washington Mill, stating, "If any man cannot manufacture by paying reasonable wages, he has no moral right to manufacture."[85] That same year, he had backed the Pullman Strike, earning a reputation in Lawrence as "a champion of labor."[86] But on February 15, 1912, when the white-haired, bespectacled priest came home from his three-week vacation in Palm Beach, he found a city under siege. During the next ten days, Father O'Reilly spoke with civic and clerical leaders. What he heard confirmed his worst suspicions. A decade earlier he had warned mill owners of "the rumble of a socialistic battle between labor and capital" led by "those apostles of discontent who come from other cities to stir up strife and bad blood."[87] Now this Armageddon had engulfed his own beloved Lawrence. On Sunday, February 25, like a Christian soldier "marching as to war," Father O'Reilly delivered his first sermon on the strike.

The topic was Satan's temptation of Christ, but local parallels were not lacking. "We have heard this same demand on the part of Satan from the lips of the agents of revolution in our city," the priest said, his stentorian voice echoing through St. Mary's lofty nave. "The spirit of anarchy demands that labor shall fall down and adore it and promises in return the complete overthrow of present social conditions." Though he supported higher wages, Father O'Reilly said the strike no longer hinged on pay. Lawrence was at war. "It is a war against lawfully constituted authority—against religion—against the home—against the people. It is a world-wide war of class against class and the Lawrence trouble is only a flash in the pan." Father O'Reilly did not mention the IWW by name, but he thundered against "a revolutionary organization that has declared a general war on society and decided to make of Lawrence a test case for the whole country." Claiming that most mill workers wanted to return to their jobs and that mill owners were ready to grant small wage increases, the priest blamed the strike solely on the "anarchistic principles" of this "revolutionary organization." In conclusion, Father O'Reilly announced that the time had come for citizens of Lawrence to ask what they, as Catholics, should do. "Shall I be an element of strength in favor of law and order in my own limited sphere in life? Shall I be with Christ and His law or with revolution and chaos?"[88]

No one knows how parishioners answered these questions, but that afternoon, strikers made their own replies. Sundays had been quiet throughout the strike, but in the wake of Saturday's beatings, strikers ignored all pleas for calm. That afternoon, a crowd gathered outside Paul Chabis Hall on Oak Street. Breaking up the assembly, police arrested one man and suddenly had to deal with hundreds. Swarming, shouting, surrounding the policemen, the crowd struggled to rescue the arrested man. Men merely waved their fists, but women strode up to policemen and spat in their faces. Again the nightsticks descended, bashing heads and battering ribs. Some women fought back, swinging broomsticks or cordwood. One brandished a baseball bat.[89] Five more were arrested before calm was restored. Roaming the city that evening a *Boston Globe* reporter noted, "the foreigners are in an ugly mood tonight."[90] It was a mood shared by many across the nation who had read the latest news from Lawrence.

Whether they subscribed to *The Masses* or the *New York Times*, whether they worked in sweatshops or in the halls of Congress, whether Republican, Democrat, or Socialist, Americans were appalled by police conduct at the Lawrence depot. Denunciation in the press varied from polite criticism to outright censure. The crackdown, said the *New York Tribune*, was "as chuckle-headed an exhibition of incompetence to deal with a strike situation as it is possible to recall."[91] The *New York World* added, "The Lawrence authorities must be blind and the mill owners mad."[92] Recounting the incident, the *Miami Herald* marveled that "all this occurred, not in Russia . . . but right here in America, almost within sight of the cradle of our boasted liberties."[93] Elsewhere, the police action was condemned as "an inferno of law"[94] and "the worst of blunders."[95] Editorial cartoons depicted emaciated mill workers held at bayonet point[96] or cowering beneath policemen's clubs.[97] The Socialist press was not so much critical as apocalyptic. *Appeal to Reason* labeled February 24 "Black Saturday," an American version of czarist Russia's "Bloody Sunday" massacre of peaceful protesters in 1905. "Remember Lawrence, the Lexington of labor's struggle for liberty!"[98] the weekly told readers. The foreign-language press was only slightly less strident. The French *Courrier de Lawrence* predicted a revolution if the wealthy did not change "their princely habits,"[99] while the Lithuanian *Keleivis* denounced the "animal behavior" of the police.[100]

Censure from public figures cut across the political spectrum. Republican senator William Borah, who had prosecuted Haywood in Idaho, stated, "I know of no authority of law that would prevent parents from sending their youngsters out of reach of strike disturbances."[101] Cleveland's Democratic mayor warned, "America will not countenance such warfare against labor."[102] Samuel Gompers denounced this "crime staining black our national and Massachusetts history."[103] Telegrams flooded Congress demanding an investigation.[104] The Cincinnati Housewives Cooperative League blasted the police's "misuse of power,"[105] while on ladies' night at the Boston Rotary Club, the ex-speaker of the Massachusetts House of Representatives, a longtime friend of mill owners, regretted that the Lawrence police had "lost their heads."[106]

For those who cared about the city's good name, it was time to circle the wagons. Since early February, a small group of citizens had been meeting to discuss "the peril from the press."[107] Now they created an official body— the Lawrence Citizens' Association. Its mission: to refute "the absurd conceptions formed during the past six weeks of Lawrence."[108] Father O'Reilly was a member, of course, along with bankers, merchants, lawyers, ex-mayors, and other civic leaders.[109] Within ten days, the association would issue its first pamphlet, but in the meantime the *Lawrence Telegram* served as an advance guard. "Every scoundrelly betrayer of the people, every notoriety seeking pulpiteer and every writer for the yellow press is jumping on Lawrence," the paper complained on February 26. Just two days earlier, the *Telegram*'s own reporter had seen police "compelled to use their clubs," but in tune with city officials, the paper now denied all "alleged brutality." "Lawrence people do not believe that any of the police clubbed women at the railway station,"[110] the *Telegram* reassured its readers.

This would be the first of many denials. Over the next several years, even decades, the leaders of Lawrence would control their city's image and history, creating a parallel version of the strike. But not even a rigid police force could control the city itself once "alleged brutality" ignited what had always been the strike's most volatile time frame—Monday morning.

At 5:00 a.m. on Monday, a plodding horse[111] drew a baker's wagon slowly past the bare trees of the common. With the mills' first morning whistles still an hour away, all was peaceful. A few lights burned in tenement windows. The glow of searchlights sweeping the mills lit up the sky to the south while snow spread its muffling blanket over The Plains. Then the crystalline stillness was cracked by pistol shots.[112] The horse bolted. The echo of gunfire faded and a long, mournful wail rose above the trees.[113] As the clatter of hoofbeats faded, several men were heard chattering in Italian. More shots rang out. Three officers skirting the common felt bullets skim past, then wheeled to see men huddling in a shadowed doorway lit by the flash of gunpowder. Sprinting toward their assailants, the officers fired back. Two men fled but one waited until a policeman neared, then carefully aimed and fired at point-blank range. His gun jammed and he fled into an alley. Police gave chase on foot.[114] Another Monday had begun.

No children would be sent away that day, and despite the strike committee's call to "tie up the town," no general strike would break out. This was not Paris in 1871, nor St. Petersburg in 1905. This was Lawrence, not at all the revolutionary city Haywood and his fellow Wobblies thought it to be. Even after six weeks of bruising battles, it remained a city of loyal immigrants whose cause was not revolution but two hours' pay. An exodus of children, a general strike—either would have required organization and planning. But on Monday, February 26, 1912, Lawrence had only mayhem to offer.

It was a morning that would see the city turned into a shooting gallery, a tinderbox of revolution, and a theater of class warfare. Before the morning was over, police had arrested sixty-six people on crimes ranging from obstructing a sidewalk to attempted murder. Some stood in the courtroom holding infants[115] while Judge Mahoney lectured them about their role in this "reign of terror."[116] Police wagons ran in shifts from Essex Street to the station and back again, carrying shouting, singing strikers. Police broke up impromptu parades, forming flying wedges[117] that drove hordes down one side street, then another, only to see them emerge—two thousand strong—marching, singing, parading all over again on some unguarded avenue.[118] Massive bloodshed was avoided only by the good graces of bad marksmanship. Strikers hurling bricks,[119] random shots from tenement windows,[120] police firing at their dawn assailants—all missed their targets, all but one. One man was struck in the shoulder by police returning his fire,[121] but dozens more were shot at, clubbed senseless, or cut by strikers' knives. It was a morning when no gesture of defiance—not women dancing and laughing as they were led to jail,[122] not even a woman baring her breasts and daring police to shoot[123]—seemed too extreme. Monday was the day the most feared radicals in America drafted a proclamation freely quoting the Declaration of Independence, citing "a long train of abuses" and denouncing mill owners' "absolute tyranny over these textile workers."[124] It was a day when a U.S. senator visiting Lawrence would call living conditions there "a disgrace to America."[125] It was a day when a rancorous Senate would consider an investigation but deterred by that "chief apostle of protection," Henry Cabot Lodge, finally bury the proposal at the bottom of its calendar.[126] But Monday was also the day when President Taft was shown a copy of the *New York Sun* reporting the clubbing of women in a Massachusetts mill town. Stunned, the president ordered his attorney general to investigate.[127] And before that brutal Monday was done, Enrico Caruso would propose a benefit concert for the strikers,[128] while Haywood would receive a telegram asking him to send children to Washington, DC, for a congressional hearing on the strike that had stirred America's conscience.[129]

Lawrence police had been called spineless. They had proven their mettle, unleashing a city's ravenous fury and repercussions that rippled across the country. Unable to handle their own citizens, the police would now face the judgment of Congress and a public likely to give women and children the benefit of the doubt. Unfazed by the public outcry, authorities stood their ground. On Tuesday, when children and mothers were brought into court, the district attorney charged that parents had been coerced into sending their children away "for the purposes of exploitation."[130] Judge Mahoney revealed that he had been in Manhattan ten days earlier when the children of Lawrence were paraded down Fifth Avenue. "I never saw a more heart-rending sight," the judge said. But although he objected to the exodus, the judge was surprisingly lenient with children and mothers. On the advice of attorneys and child advocates, all but one family was released. Children were taken home,[131] and charges against parents were eventually dropped.[132]

Chaos had arrived as expected. Now came the struggle to capitalize on it. While authorities in Lawrence pointed to Monday's violence as proof that the IWW had unleashed anarchy in their peaceful city, Haywood marshaled his words to control strikers and retain public sympathy. "Every striker must be guarded in his discussion," he told the strike committee on Tuesday. "He must allow no word to pass his lips that can be construed into an encouragement of violence. Now is the time that we want to take the reins and hold this thing steady."[133] Yet as the streets surged with strikers, police also groped for the reins. On Wednesday, hundreds of women swarmed on Essex Street until sent running when mounted police rode down on them.[134] All afternoon, Mayor Scanlon and his aldermen met in Boston with mill owners, pleading with them to concede *something*. No progress was reported.[135] Finally, after several days of widely publicized disorder, a group of magazine writers returned to Lawrence to update their readers.

Arriving from New York, the party set out to "see the strike." First stop was the jail, where journalists were not allowed to see Ettor and Giovannitti but did visit women serving out their sentences. Next they toured the tenements, scribbling impressions. Seeing a dozen people crammed into a kitchen to "save coal by keeping only one room warm,"[136] Ray Stannard Baker observed, "If I were living in one of those miserable tenements . . . I should join any movement, however revolutionary, to put an end to such conditions."[137] Finally, the journalists tried to enter the mill district but were held up at Canal Street, where they could only gawk at the massive mills, "like some strange fortress of industry"[138] guarded by soldiers. The day ended with a dinner hosted by Haywood. As police hustled them off the sidewalk in front of the restaurant, someone recognized an officer who had been at the depot on Saturday morning.

"So, you're the man who clubbed a woman, are you?" one said.

"Now don't you stand talking to me," patrolman Michael Moore replied. "You've got to go along."[139] A crowd gathered as the patrolman tried to disperse the journalists. They refused to move, claiming they had every right to linger on a sidewalk. When a boy told Moore to "go to hell!" the policeman grabbed him. Journalists leaped to the boy's defense and Moore let him go. Finally, the entourage returned to the Needham Hotel, marveling that such conditions could exist in an American city. They were relaxing in the lobby when the hotel manager strode in. He had warned one of the women earlier. Women were not allowed to smoke in public at the Needham. Feeling as if they were in some nightmarish prisoner of war camp where all was "wrong, as wrong as could be,"[140] the journalists left on the next train.[141]

CHAPTER TEN

In Congress, 1912

. . . The sealed-in horizon had never before opened onto as promising a future for these poor people as in their starving state of exaltation. When their eyes began to swim they looked beyond—to the ideal city of their dreams, now close and almost real, with its people of brothers, its golden age of labor, its food shared at a common board. Nothing could shake their conviction that they were at last about to enter it.

—Émile Zola, *Germinal*[1]

In its infancy, Lawrence had been visited by presidents and poets praising its industrial efficiency. Now in its adolescence, the city was forced to suffer more intrusive visitors. The U.S. commissioner of labor. State[2] and federal attorneys general. Professors. Politicians. They came for many reasons: to lecture, to investigate, to grandstand. But none came to settle the strike, a fact Bill Haywood recognized.

Late Tuesday evening, February 27, Haywood was back in the Needham Hotel when he had an unexpected visitor—Congressman Butler Ames. The congressman's name resounded like a bugle through recent history. His father had fought at Gettysburg, winning the Congressional Medal of Honor, then served in the U.S. Senate.[3] The younger Ames was a West Point graduate and Spanish-American War veteran,[4] but Haywood saw him as just another "plute," doubly damned by being both a politician and a mill owner from Lowell. Congressman Ames, a trim, proper man with a neatly clipped mustache, had already met with Mayor Scanlon, Marshal Sullivan, and the Lawrence Citizens' Association when he called on the strike's leader. Haywood sat in the hotel office, his suit coat unbuttoned, his great girth resting heavily in a chair. He had spoken several times in Lawrence that afternoon, but he was never too tired to show his contempt for "the ruling class."

When Ames asked about the strike, Haywood told him that a true representative of the people would not need to ask. He would know the causes, the struggles, the facts about the mills. "You don't represent the working men," Haywood charged.

"I do," the congressman replied in a huff.

"You are an employer, are you not?"

"Yes."

"Then you do not represent the working people. You represent the employers. There is nothing in common between the two classes so you couldn't possibly represent them both." Despite Haywood's belligerence, the congressman warmed to the verbal jousting. Laughing at the charge that he had never done an honest day's work, Ames said he worked longer hours than anyone Haywood knew. This caused Big Bill to snap to attention.

"Do you think six dollars too little pay for a man to work a week for?" Haywood demanded. "Don't you think $7,500 a year too much to pay a man for making laws when only six dollars a week is paid a man for making cloth? Don't you believe that it is more essential to mankind to make cloth than it is to make laws?" The congressman replied that his federal salary was not his chief income and that he gave it, and more, to charity. Haywood said charity would not be needed if workers were given living wages. Ames soon realized he would get nothing but resentment from the strike's leader. Told that his car was waiting, the congressman said goodbye to the Wobbly. Ames said he hoped to attend the strike committee meeting the following morning, and Haywood welcomed him to see the "Congress of the people."[5] The two parted and Haywood went to his room, buoyed by promised publicity from the upcoming congressional hearings on the strike but not expecting much from a Congress he considered "on the bum."[6]

On Friday morning, March 1, a thousand people showed up at the depot to see five adults and thirteen adolescents off on the 7:11 train. Police were present but did nothing more than clear a path.[7] Without incident, the contingent headed for Washington, DC, where hearings were to begin on Saturday. Once the train was out of sight, talk turned to the rumor sweeping the city. A breakthrough had been reached. After a daylong session with Mayor Scanlon and Calvin Coolidge's committee, William Wood had agreed to a 5 percent pay raise.[8] His motives were as elemental as profits and as complex as his own pride. With the peak season of the wool trade coming up, Wood had to pressure cotton manufacturers, whose slack season was starting, to match his offer.[9] But like Wood, all mill owners were frightened by the upcoming hearings and the recent deluge of bad publicity. Each owner had followed Wood's lead, stating emphatically that the offer was *not* a concession to the IWW but was made to his own workers.[10] And having made their move, mill owners invited a representative body of strikers to discuss it with them in Boston. Strikers quickly chose a Committee of Ten to represent them. The city held its breath.

On Friday morning, the Arlington Mill posted a lengthy statement signed by William Whitman and printed in full in the *Lawrence Telegram.* All along Essex Street, the *Telegram* was snatched from newsboys, read in groups, translated into many languages. "During the past two years our business has yielded no profits," Whitman began. These slack years and the likelihood of "adverse tariff legislation" had created "business conditions that do not warrant an increase in wages at the present time." Yet "labor conditions in Lawrence have not been normal." (Strikers reading this must have chuckled.) Because the welfare of the city depended on "the restoration of former contented labor conditions" (more chuckling), the Arlington was offering a 5 percent minimum raise as of Monday, March 4. To ensure that the concession had its desired effect—a stampede to the mills that would end the strike—the raise was offered only through March 6.[11] A narrow window had been opened.

Mayor Scanlon and the press were ecstatic. The mill men had finally spoken. Surely the strike was over. But at Friday's strike committee meeting, the offer was met by utter silence. Throughout Franco-Belgian Hall the "Congress of the people"—grizzled men and women with faces as weathered as winter itself—nervously eyed each other for some sign. No one said a word. Then at the podium, Haywood softly announced, "That isn't fifteen percent." Gaining momentum, he declared that a 5 percent raise "would not yield pennies enough to cover the eyes of babies that have died as a result of the strike."[12] Delegation by delegation, Poles, Italians, Russians, Germans, Jews stood to reveal that their nationalities had already rejected the offer based solely on early rumors.[13] The committee voted unanimously to hold out for all demands and to strike as long as Ettor and Giovannitti were in jail. Then the strains of "The Internationale" echoed through the old hall.[14] The strike was not at an end; it was only starting to distill.

John Golden was in Lawrence that Friday urging his union's members to break the IWW's back by taking the offer.[15] Most striking craftsmen seemed likely to return on Monday. Fifteen thousand unskilled workers, however, had no such intention. They had not come this far just to compromise for a mere third of their proposed increase and no mention of other demands. And that evening, when the strikers' Committee of Ten returned from its first meeting with mill owners, it brought another insult. The breakthrough offer was based on the reduced fifty-four-hour pay scale. Deducting the wage cut that started the strike, the proposed raise was just 1 percent. The committee called this "a joker" and, telling Billy Wood exactly what he could do with it, walked out of the meeting.[16] "The strike is on with more vim and vigor than ever," one member told the press.[17]

Starting the eighth week of impasse, the ground was giving beneath the wage dispute, yet opposing versions of the strike were being set in stone. At public meetings all over Lawrence, Boston, and beyond, strike supporters and opponents peered through their own political prisms to see two different Lawrences. Lawrence was a riotous city incited by radical outside agitators and defended by valiant police and militia. Lawrence was a city besieged by brutal Cossacks. Lawrence was a thriving city with a small "undigested lump"[18] of immigrant workers. Lawrence was a disgraceful slum. Strikers had suffered unspeakable atrocities at the depot. Police had been on their best behavior. Anna LoPizzo was killed by a striker. She was murdered by a cop. The children in exile were happy. They had been kidnapped and desperately wanted to come home. The task of reconciling these refracted viewpoints would fall to an entity decidedly uncomfortable at sticking its nose into any labor dispute—the United States Congress.

By 1912, a few industrialized states had begun tiptoeing into the clash between labor and management. Recent state laws limited working hours for women and children, mandated factory inspections, and provided the first workmen's compensation.[19] Many of these laws were routinely ignored, others barely enforced. Still, William Wood's complaint about Massachusetts's fifty-four-hour law—that his mills could not compete against those in states with no such limit—was not an idle protest. Whenever one state lightened labor conditions, companies took their business elsewhere, pitting states against each other in a scramble to the bottom of the wage ladder. If a law were to truly ease labor's burden without driving jobs elsewhere, it would have to apply nationwide. But Congress was no more inclined to meddle in labor disputes than it was to kill Jim Crow and his "separate but equal" system of segregation. Prior to the New Deal, the federal government entered the labor market only when interstate commerce was involved or when severe violence flared. President Grover Cleveland used injunctions to stop a nationwide railroad strike in 1886 and, eight years later, sent troops to break the Pullman Strike. In 1902, Teddy Roosevelt mediated a five-month anthracite coal strike that threatened to leave the nation without heat during the coming winter.[20] Yet throughout thousands of other strikes that crippled commerce and left dozens dead, the federal government sat coolly above the fray, acting only when some state law violated the Constitution. In the two decades prior to the Lawrence strike, the Supreme Court had struck down nearly every legislative effort to ease labor's load. A law prohibiting blacklisting of organizers. A law banning company "scrip" as payment. A law limiting the workweek to sixty hours. A law restricting court injunctions. Another defining employer liability for injuries. All were declared unconstitutional.[21] Not even bleak tales of child labor could move Congress to act. Six years before the Lawrence strike, a child labor bill languished and died in the Senate when the daily toil of children was considered in Washington to be somebody else's business.[22] So when the House of Representatives agreed to a hearing on the strike in Lawrence, no one knew quite what to expect other than a crowd.

At 10:30 a.m. on Saturday, March 2, an overflow audience crammed into the hearing room of the House Office Building near the Capitol. Hundreds sat or stood along marble-lined walls facing a panel of congressmen seated before tall, curtained windows.[23] Despite public clamor, the proposal for federal hearings on one state's labor troubles had rankled Congress and barely survived strangling by critics and committees. After the Senate had tabled its proposal to investigate, Congressman Victor Berger, a

Socialist, had taken his case to both President Taft and the House Committee on Rules.[24] The latter—eight Democrats and three Republicans—had agreed to hearings provided they be limited to possible violations of constitutional rights or interstate commerce laws.[25] The hearings began quietly. William Wilson, a Pennsylvania Democrat who had been among the founders of the United Mine Workers,[26] explained why he had called for the investigation. America had seen "many conflicts between capital and labor," Wilson stated, "but so far as I know, there has never occurred in the history of trade disputes in this country any conditions approaching or even approximating the conditions which are alleged to exist at Lawrence, Massachusetts."[27] Berger then presented dozens of telegrams he had received urging Congress to investigate. Many were from predictable sources—IWW locals and Socialists. But telegrams had also come from the city council of Thief River Falls, Minnesota; the Central Labor Council of Cincinnati; and the Mattoon, Illinois, Federation of Railroad Employees.[28] Each denounced the police action of February 24, but Berger cautioned against limiting the investigation to a single event. Instead, he attacked American Woolen as the head of "one of the most oppressive trusts in the country," adding, "I have here from Lawrence some of the workers employed by this company and I propose to let them tell their own story."[29] And then, as the first witness was called, what began in chaos on an icy January day came under the most glaring spotlight the nation had to offer.

Grim-faced and resolute, weaver Samuel Lipson took a seat at a long rectangular table strewn with papers. Opening questions were routine. Where do you work? (The Wood Mill.) How long have you worked there? (Three years.) How much do you earn? (Nine to ten dollars a week.)[30] But as Lipson described life in the mills, congressmen became dismayed or skeptical, depending on their politics. Did American Woolen really charge its employees ten cents a week for cold water? Could it be true that mill workers ate meat only on Sunday, living the rest of the week on bread and molasses? "We use a kind of molasses," Lipson told the committee. "We are trying to fool our stomachs with it."[31] Berger led the weaver through a recap of the strike, then asked why he had sent his eight-year-old son to New York. Lipson replied that he had not wanted his son to see the daily violence in Lawrence. Once the boy had asked his father, "Why do the soldiers try to hurt those people and put the bayonets against them?"[32] His son was happy in New York, Lipson said, and he had letters to prove it. Berger then steered Lipson to the events of February 24. Were women and children beaten at the depot? "One policeman took a child and threw her into the wagon, and she got a black eye," Lipson testified. "I saw policemen clubbing women on their hearts and breasts. Women being in a family way were arrested and dragged and pushed into the patrol wagon." Were any of the beaten women in the audience? None were, but Lipson eagerly offered their names and addresses.[33] As he began listing injured children, however, the Massachusetts congressional delegation decided it had heard enough. Men were seen to tiptoe behind the panel, whispering to the chairman and other members. From the audience, Congressman Robert Harris, a Republican from the mill town of Bridgewater, rose to defend "the fair name of Massachusetts" and question the committee's right to interfere in state affairs. More whispering followed, and within minutes, though this was a congressional hearing, a Lawrence city official was allowed to cross-examine the witness.[34]

When city postmaster Louis Cox began questioning Lipson, the courteous hearing, with references to "the gentleman from Georgia" and "the gentleman from Wisconsin," flared up like a fight on a picket line.

Didn't Lipson sometimes earn twenty dollars a week? Cox asked.

"No, never."

Didn't the trouble in Lawrence really begin when Joseph Ettor arrived? And didn't strikers hurl ice and rocks at police?

No, Lipson replied. "Among 20,000 people there must be somebody that takes a snowball," he said. Then turning on Cox, who had served in the militia in January, Lipson asked, "You are the one that was with your soldiers at the city hall, were you not?" Soon the audience was applauding Lipson, causing the committee chairman to warn both men against incendiary statements. Cox and Lipson contained their mutual contempt, even when Cox denied there was any hunger in Lawrence. Could Lipson name a single case of hunger in the city? Lipson asked Cox to repeat the question— "I am a weaver and the ears of the weaver are injured from the noise of the machinery"[35]—then told of soup kitchens serving thousands of hungry people each day.

Lipson's cross-examination was calm, however, compared to the uproar when congressmen had their own "little talk with Golden." Before the panel, John Golden reiterated his claim that the strike was a revolution. The AF of L had tried to organize in Lawrence for years, Golden said, but had been stymied by mill owners. Then came the IWW, which "poisoned the minds of these poor people." At this, Josephine Lis blurted out, "It is a lie!"[36] Lis's words echoed through the room, but Golden continued as if he hadn't heard. The IWW "preached anarchy" in Lawrence, he said. The hearing room rocked with shouts and denials. The chairman banged his gavel and quiet resumed until Golden attacked Ettor. When Golden claimed that Ettor had incited violence and urged workers to buy guns, several in the audience shouted "No! No!" until the chairman threatened to clear the room.[37] Golden finished his testimony in silence. Following an afternoon of methodical talk about the tariff, the hearing was adjourned at 5:30, but no gavel could end its bitterness.

As the crowd dispersed, Lis began taking up a collection to pay the $750 the trip to Washington, DC, was costing the strike delegation. Postmaster Cox put a dollar in her hat but Victor Berger told Lis to give it back. "We don't want any blood money!" the congressman said. At this, Lawrence merchant Robert McCartney began shouting at Berger. The two men stood face-to-face, with McCartney shaking his fist and the congressman bellowing back, demanding Lis return the dollar. She did, but the men continued to posture until Congressman Wilson separated them. And the long day ended.[38] Still to come when hearings resumed on Monday were more witnesses from the depot and thirteen young mill workers. As the teenagers made their way from the hearing room, a woman gave one girl a dollar to buy a souvenir. She bought penny postcards and that night all the young tourists wrote home.[39]

Back in Lawrence, where the hearings were avidly followed in the papers, the two sides fought for moral high ground. On Sunday, Father O'Reilly opened his pulpit to a ringing guest sermon against Socialism. "The Socialist is the shrewdest of all political tacticians," ex-Socialist David Goldstein told St. Mary's parishioners. "He takes advantage of man's discontent, of poverty, and of the evils and sins of the world and makes political capital of them." By advocating both atheism and "free love," Goldstein warned, "the Socialist Party is in conflict with Christian morality."[40] Across town, the strike committee held a rare Sunday meeting. Plans were made for extensive picketing the next day, and Italians announced their soup kitchen would serve coffee at 3:00 a.m. Despite the good cheer, with plenty of singing and Haywood joking at the podium, the meeting broke up early when many left to welcome a cow sent by workers in Lowell. Strikers met the cow as she was being led into the city wearing a yellow blanket adorned with IWW buttons. The cow was taken to a stable to await slaughter for a Tuesday barbecue.[41] The day continued uneventfully, yet the peaceful Sunday could not hide the fact that another Monday was looming.

For fifty-two days, Lawrence had lived in a limbo most cities suffer only in times of war. Yet aside from intermittent flare-ups, much of the strike had been gripped by a numbing sameness, the days themselves marching like pickets beneath skies that hung low and gray. But now, just in time for New England's annual spring tease—crocuses, a shirtsleeve day, then more snow—the strike was poised for one end or another. It could not go on as it had. February's violence had played itself out. The mill men had come out of their monthlong stupor. Haywood and Flynn were rising to new rhetorical heights, and the coming days promised to decide the knock-down, drag-out battle. If enough strikers broke down and took the mill men's small raise, there would be no other offer. If Monday brought more rioting, sympathy would be squandered and the strike would be lost. As both Haywood at his podium and Ettor in his cell knew, most strikes ended not with a bang but with a whimper, as humiliated, starved strikers flowed back to the job. However . . . if strikers could remain strong now, with the whole nation hearing their grievances, then another week might bring the entire edifice of resistance toppling down. Already there was talk that the mills, burdened by a backlog of orders, might close if the strike did not end soon.[42] Perhaps strikes were lost in small surrenders, but they were won in triumph, with everyone returning to work at once, all demands met. And on Monday, March 4, the final test of wills began.

As promised, the Italians served coffee at 3:00 a.m. An hour later, the city's full force of 350 police was on the street.[43] By sunrise, five thousand pickets—the largest number yet—stretched for blocks down Essex. Crossing the Merrimack, they formed their endless chain winding through the maze of mills. When the first whistles blew, almost everyone was already awake, eager to get to the picket line or to work before another Monday broke loose. And as the sun rose, it seemed that every lamppost, every bus stop, every brick wall was plastered with the same poster.

STAND FIRM! STAND FIRM! WIN EVERYTHING!
WIN ALL! NOW IS THE TIME TO STRIKE!

The textile manufacturers are yielding!

The strike is nearly won; it will be won!

The brutality of the agents of the employees, police, militia, courts, and thugs has aroused the whole Nation!

The world is with us! We will, we must win!

All was silent when we suffered!

But now, now, the echo of the industrial struggle for more bread has aroused the citizens of the United States, and all the workers of the world! . . .

Congress, aroused by the fiendish, savage treatment of the pregnant women, of innocent babes, responds to the thunderous voice of an aroused Nation. They are investigating; they are acting, and the sores and wounds of our suffering and brutalized wives and children has laid bare the outrages of capitalist tyranny run mad and amuck!

President Taft, though little affected when we pleaded for redress against the wrongs, has heard the rumblings of a coming revolt, and he has acted only now as the servant of all the people. . . .

Everything is won except your claim for more pay and more rights as producers!

You will win that, too, but you must stand together as in the past!

Don't return to work until complete surrender by the oppressors and industrial czars is assured!

Don't break ranks, else the employers will break your necks and manhood later on!

All together! Let us win! Win all, win everything! Everybody on the fighting line! Everyone a fighter in this industrial war!

Nobody goes back to work until all go back together! Win! Win! Win![44]

The beatings at the depot had slowed the return to work. During the week following the incident, 494 strikers had gone back, less than half the weekly defection rate earlier in February. Still, enough small streams make a river over time, and as the critical eighth week unfolded almost thirteen thousand were back in the mills.[45] With nearly half the workforce back on the job, owners boasted that the strike was breaking down. If numbers seemed on their side, however, sentiment was not. Like the distillate at the bottom of a solution that has been put to the flame, the strike was solidifying. Weaker elements had evaporated, trading hope for a paycheck. Those who stayed out were rock solid. Determined to win, smelling victory in every whiff of change, they marched all morning around the mills, jubilant and united, and did not commit a single act of harassment. The previous Monday, sixty-six had been arrested. The total on Monday, March 4, was zero.[46] Having tamed the beasts among them, some were therefore startled to see evidence of a lingering savagery in the city.

At about 8:00 a.m., as hundreds of strikers came up Broadway just north of the depot, a tall, husky man with a waterfall mustache[47] sprinted out of the Marlboro Chambers Hotel. He was completely naked. Bleeding from his scalp, the man ran into a carriage shop screaming, "For God's sake help a man! They want to kill me!" When the carriage maker realized the man was not insane, he fetched overalls and a horse blanket. Seated and safe now, IWW organizer James P. Thompson told his story. He had been sleeping when a knock came on the door. Opening it, he saw three hulking men in dark coats and derbies. He assumed they were police come to arrest him. Then one man grabbed his arm while another smashed his skull with a blackjack. Dazed, Thompson sprinted from the room and down three flights of stairs while bullets flew past his head. Poor marksmanship again saved a life. The men disappeared, leaving only their weapons—two blackjacks, a .32 revolver, and a "knuckle gun" with a two-inch barrel that allowed it to be concealed in a fist. Thompson was taken to the Needham Hotel, where his wounds were dressed as police questioned him. He insisted he had no idea who might want to kill him. Just then, Haywood entered.

"I wouldn't talk much without counsel," Haywood advised his old friend.

Captain William Proctor, the man who had arrested Ettor, asked, "Has he anything to conceal?"

"Not that I know of," Haywood replied.

"Well, we're doing this in Thompson's interest and you'd better keep out of it," the captain said. He then asked the victim if the "Philadelphia crowd" was after him. Thompson repeatedly denied it, but police continued to claim he had been assaulted by union officials over an internal squabble. Strikers suspected otherwise.[48] Haywood later charged that a New York detective agency had hired the thugs,[49] but police dropped the investigation after a few days.[50]

That same Monday, congressional hearings resumed with the same give-and-take, even the same witness—Samuel Lipson. Cross-examination had been ruled out, however, restoring calm to the committee room. Lipson told of speeded looms and abusive overseers.[51] "The laws in the mills are made by the bosses, you know, and we never see any inspector there to see to it, and they do what they want to. If we dare to say a word they show us the door; they call a watchman to drag us out."[52] Then Samuel Gompers testified, defending John Golden and calling the IWW "an organization that does not organize [with] a leadership that leads nowhere."[53] But just as the hearings were bogging down into a quarrel between unions, the youngest mill workers were called to tell their stories.

The day before, after touring the Capitol, Georgetown, and the Treasury Building, the teenagers had met President Taft at the White House. "He was a nice big man sitting down in a big chair," remembered Rosario Contarino, fifteen at the time. "Big fella, oh yeah, big man, with a mustache, you know. . . . He was asking us where we came from, what part of Italy or what part of Germany." The affable president had shaken hands with each young visitor, then turned to the chaperones and handed them a check for one thousand dollars. For the soup kitchens, he said.[54] Now, as the young mill veterans came before the committee, their size and softened speech commanded attention. These were the "children of Lawrence," the ones the nation had pitied and fed with donations. Now in the crowded hearing room, seated before stern men wearing blue serge made in the Wood Mill, the young workers mumbled and were asked to speak up. When they did, they told Congress and, through the conduit of reporters, the rest of America what the strike was about. Gone were the jousts about wages, trade versus industrial unionism, and who hit whom when. These less volatile voices held forth putting America's industrial system on trial.

Their stories were similar. Each child had quit school at fourteen or slightly younger and gone to work. Each had several siblings to help support. Doffers, carders, bobbin boys working from dawn to dusk, they earned $5.10 to $6.55 a week when they worked a full week, which was not often. Congressmen listened politely but did not comprehend, at first. They asked the factory children if they read books. No, not many. Did they like to play? Well, sometimes on Sunday—baseball or tag. Did they like school? Sure, before they had to quit. And gradually it dawned on the panel that these were not children at all, not even adolescents, but apprentice adults who had left childhood at the mill gates. Then the questioning turned back to work. Repeating answers in disbelief—"They just take off the hour [of pay] because you are late five or ten minutes?"[55]—congressmen finally realized why the children looked so much older than their years.

"Do you have to work at high speed?"

"Sure."

"Why is that? In order to keep up with the machine?"

"I don't know; they make you go quicker and quicker all the time."[56]

Child by aging child, congressmen saw that regardless of whether mothers had been beaten, whether wages were six or nine dollars a week, no American could be proud of conditions in Lawrence. One boy, lamenting that his family survived on bread and water a few days each week, said, "I guess some horses live better than we do."[57] And then just when congressmen thought they understood industrial childhood, one girl gave them another lesson. As the twelfth child to testify, Camella Teoli must have looked much like the rest—small for her age, shy, with downcast eyes. But from their seats, congressmen could not see the bald spot on the back of her head, so they walked right into her testimony, as innocent as she had been when she walked into the Washington Mill at age thirteen.

"Now did you ever get hurt in the mill?"

"Yes."

"Can you tell the committee about that—how it happened and what it was?"

"Well, I used to go to school, and then a man came up to my house and asked my father why I didn't go to work, so my father says, 'I don't know whether she is thirteen or fourteen years old.' So the man says, 'You give me four dollars and I will make the papers come from the old country saying you are fourteen.' So my father gave him the four dollars and in one month came the papers that I was fourteen. I went to work, and about two weeks [later] got hurt in my head."

"Now, how did you get hurt? And where were you hurt in the head? Explain that to the committee."

"I got hurt in the Washington."

"In the Washington Mill?"

"Yes, sir."

"Well, how were you hurt?"

"The machine pulled my scalp off."

"The machine pulled your scalp off?"

"Yes, sir."[58]

The accident had occurred in July 1909. At 5:30 p.m., Teoli had broken a mill rule by letting her hair down before the machines stopped. When a friend called to her, she tossed her hair over her head. Instantly the draft gear of a spinning frame wrenched it. Teoli was rushed to the hospital with two pieces of her scalp wrapped in a newspaper. Doctors were able to restore it, but she spent seven months in the hospital, her bills paid by American Woolen. Though some encouraged her family to sue for more than medical bills, no lawyer would take the case. She had been under the legal age limit.[59]

After Teoli had stunned the hearing room, a congressman asked her, "Do they go around in Lawrence there and find little boys and girls in the schools . . . and urge them to quit school and go to work in the mill?"

"I don't know," she said. Despite further questioning, she preferred to say little else.[60]

On Tuesday morning, a woman from Philadelphia was offering grim details of the beatings at the depot when heads turned to note an arriving celebrity. Wearing a dark, plumed hat, First Lady Helen Taft entered and sat behind the row of congressmen.[61] Mrs. Taft listened attentively as Margaret Sanger told of the malnourished children she had accompanied to New York, and Josephine Lis recounted striking a militiaman with her muff. And then the strikers' case was concluded. During the next two days, city officials would do their best to soften the bleak images of Lawrence, but the children's testimony, indicting the city as one merciless mill where young lives were ground in the gears, was all that lingered as the windows behind the congressmen and the first lady slowly darkened.

Throughout the hearing's final two days, the opposing version of the strike was presented—first by Cornelius Lynch, then by Marshal Sullivan, and on subsequent days by a merchant, a postmaster, mill paymasters, and the Reverend Clark Carter. The latter was the city's missionary to the poor, but all these men were missionaries in a larger sense. They had come to Washington, DC, carrying bulky payroll books or just toting their own self-assurance, eager to rebut "lies" about Lawrence. Yet for all their preparation, their testimony was a delicate web of denial that went far beyond the clubbing of women or the rate of pay. Speaking as if in one voice, the alderman, the marshal, the merchant, the mill men, and the missionary described Lawrence as a typical small American city, perhaps with a few problems but nothing like those of New York or Boston. "We thought we were getting along pretty well until this trouble came upon us," Postmaster Cox said.[62]

None of the city's representatives would admit that poverty existed in Lawrence; none would even say the word *poverty.* Some immigrants were "not wealthy,"[63] others lived in "narrow circumstances."[64] But there were "no slums in Lawrence," according to a written statement submitted by the treasurer of the Broadway Savings Bank.[65] Mill workers were all "well housed, fed, and clothed." Almost all had bank accounts from which immigrant workers sent about two hundred thousand dollars a year to families in Europe.[66] (The sum represented about thirty-five dollars per year for a typical family of seven.) According to the Reverend Clark Carter, when the children were shipped to New York without mittens or gloves, they had left their gloves at home to foster sympathy.[67] Bread and molasses, the reverend testified, was not a meal of desperation, but "a luxury" because working people so often ate bread without molasses. And in Lawrence, he added, "school children have something even better than molasses; they have the Karo corn syrup."[68]

The bayoneting of John Rami drew special scrutiny. Marshal Sullivan did not know much about the killing, but he assured Kentucky Democrat Augustus Stanley that no complaint had been filed by Rami's family. "Well, do you wait there in that country when a man is killed for some complaint from his relatives or friends before you inquire into the nature of the killing?" Stanley asked.[69] The congressman also wondered "what sort of deadly weapon the boy had in his hand at the time he was killed?"

"I did not say he had a deadly weapon," Marshal Sullivan answered. "I said he had a musical instrument."[70] Congressman Stanley later likened the stabbing to the Boston Massacre.[71]

In exhaustive detail, the marshal defended police conduct at the depot. He cited several children sent from the city without consent, starting with Mary Sullivan, the girl who had gone to New York on a whim. Two Italian boys had been taken to Barre, Vermont, without parental permission,[72] three had been allowed to go to New York but asked to come home,[73] and one man, separated from his wife, had denied his children permission to leave but she had sent them anyway.[74] And these seven cases out of more than two hundred, congressmen asked, justified the clubbing of women? But no women were clubbed, the marshal insisted. "I want to say to you here, gentlemen, that I was just as careful that there would be nobody injured, neither women nor children, as I would be at any time or of anybody's children." The only violence that morning, he said, was when an officer grabbed a woman in order to keep from falling off the police truck.[75] Then how did the marshal explain the brutality reported in "practically all the papers"? Newspapers, the marshal replied, "are always looking for the sensational."[76]

Moving on, a congressman held up a wagon spoke like the ones militia had toted in Lawrence. Did the soldiers actually use such bludgeons on people? "Possibly they did," Sullivan replied, "but I don't know of any case where anybody was struck."[77] When the spoke was shown to Postmaster Cox, he blithely assured congressmen that he had seen bigger ones used.

"They are better, are they?" a congressman mocked.

"Yes, sir; they are better because they are longer and they had a smaller head."[78] In a single sentence, Cox then summed up how so many in Lawrence viewed the influx of immigrants. "Those of us who are there and get our living there, and expect to die there are confronted with perhaps as serious a problem as there is in this country, and that is to try to Americanize all of these people."[79]

But the most revealing testimony came from the Reverend Clark Carter. For twenty-five years, the Congregational minister, a graduate of Harvard and Princeton,[80] had run the city's mission to the poor. He had visited people "in narrow circumstances," sharing aid provided by mill owners while encouraging a staunch work ethic and religious conviction.

Now this eminent Victorian, who seemed to have stepped out of a Dickens novel, was grilled by congressmen eager to know how a clergyman viewed the plight of mill workers, especially children. The reverend was polite, referring to congressmen as "my dear sir," and apologizing for rambling. "I am an old man," he said, "and an old man likes to hear himself talk."[81] But the more the old man talked, the more his version of the strike seemed skewed by life in a city where industry hardened people as surely as it sculpted the skyline. It was not just that the reverend saw the strike's early, joyous parades as "mobs," or that he thought mill wages comfortable for all but a few "blundering, untrained, and foreign-tongued" individuals.[82] Questioned at length, the reverend admitted he saw nothing wrong with child labor. Why should Massachusetts raise its minimum working age beyond fourteen? he asked. It would do no good unless older children were "kept occupied at something profitable. . . . Those that are idle until they are sixteen years of age do not amount to much afterwards."[83] And although children needed education, "sometimes it is better that the education be where it is congenial to the child, as it is in many cases in the mill, than where it is uncongenial, as it is in school."[84] The reverend admitted that a ten-hour workday might be "in some cases too severe on the individual." But his own son had worked in a mill, as had "men before us here today of good physique and of good intellect."[85] Finally, Congressman Wilson could take it no longer.

"Are you in sympathy with child labor?" he asked. "Just give us your opinion on this. It is a matter that I think might interest some members of this committee."

"The work that the children do in the mill, most of it, is perfectly proper for children to do," Carter said. "Children have got to be occupied."[86]

Leaving the congressmen nonplussed, the reverend concluded his testimony on Thursday afternoon, March 7. That left only the paymasters. Grimly articulate men armed with sprawling payroll books, they assured congressmen that no looms had ever been accelerated, that every effort was made to avoid hiring underage children, and that no workers were forced to pay for water. Some bought water voluntarily, pooling their pennies. But would they spend their hard-earned money on water, one congressman asked, if the mill's supply were not too warm to drink? "They would be more likely to spend it for molasses and bread, wouldn't they?"[87]

Paymasters consulted their books to prove that Samuel Lipson's average weekly wage was not $10.00 but $11.62,[88] that Josephine Lis also earned more than she claimed, and that the average wage was $9.00. Yet there seemed something pathetic about these men sharing payrolls to prove that workers earned a half dollar or even a dollar more than they claimed when all the testimony about bread and molasses, child labor, and wagon spokes still lingered in memory like the moral of some horrific fairy tale. Finally, under questioning, the cashier of the Ayer Mill revealed that the $9.00 average included "all employees of the mill"—engineers, bookkeepers, carpenters, overseers, cashiers . . .[89] Then, with an ominous threat to pursue further investigation, perhaps of American Woolen's labor practices,[90] the hearings ended.[91] Congressmen, onlookers, and the first lady filed out of the hearing room and went home. Strikers and city officials boarded trains returning them to whichever version of Lawrence they inhabited.

Little unusual had happened in the city during the hearings. Four militia companies had been sent home and were not replaced.[92] Colonel Sweetser, who had worried "the longer we stay here, the more chance there is of someone making a blunder,"[93] finally got his wish and was relieved of duty.[94] Good news for mill stockholders came from New York, where American Woolen was holding its annual meeting. Despite slack times, the company's surplus had risen from $8 million in 1908 to $11.6 million in 1911,[95] about 19 percent of the company's capitalization. Another $2.8 million in dividends had been paid.[96] Good news for strikers came from Elizabeth Gurley Flynn, who telegraphed that she had collected $550 at a "monster" rally in Allegheny, Pennsylvania.[97] On Monday night, the riot call had been sounded when two thousand people filed out of a meeting of the Progressive Women's Club of Lawrence. Fired up by two Wellesley College professors, strikers had spilled into the streets, singing and shouting until scattered by police.[98] All that week, craftsmen returned en masse to the mills, causing the CLU to declare the strike over and close its relief station on Broadway. On Wednesday, police broke up a surly crowd that had waited two hours outside the dark office.[99] And the following morning, carrying permission forms signed by both parents, forty-one children were finally sent to Philadelphia. At the train station, under the watchful eye of the U.S. commissioner of labor,[100] policemen approached chaperones and asked for the names of departing children. "Remember, it is not a command or a demand, but a simple request," one officer said. "You know we are heartily in sympathy with the strikers, but we are only policemen and we have a duty to perform."[101] Mothers again cried as the train pulled out of view.[102] At Boston's South Station, strangers gave children fruit and candy,[103] which they devoured as the train took them south toward the steady approach of spring.

That morning, thousands marched around the mills, but their well of patience had run dry. Someone slashed a scab's neck,[104] and police herded crowds down one street, then another.[105] One of the sixteen arrested,[106] when asked by Judge Mahoney about the charge of disturbing the peace, answered, "What peace?"[107] The strike committee fired off an open letter to Governor Foss and Mayor Scanlon, citing specific instances of women beaten on March 1. One, a twenty-eight-year-old Italian woman who was not a striker, suffered a miscarriage.[108] "We have suffered, we have borne in patience all these atrocities against ourselves and our kin," the letter concluded, "but we will remember, we will never forget, and never forgive."[109] Standing firm, strikers pinned all their hopes on another meeting between mill owners and the Committee of Ten. The committee was due back from Boston on Thursday evening.

CHAPTER ELEVEN

An American Tapestry

A man must always live by his work, and his wages must at least be suf-
ficient to maintain him. They must even upon most occasions be more;
otherwise it would be impossible for him to bring up a family, and the
race of such workmen could not last beyond the first generation.

—Adan Smith, *The Wealth of Nations*[1]

Even while keeping the grueling schedule of an industrial tycoon,
William Wood was a devoted father. He often arrived home in the evening
clutching his thick wool coat and pretending to be a bear while his children
"attacked" him.[2] Arden, his green-trimmed Andover mansion, was a play-
ground for his children, and Wood played with them as often as he could
get away from work. Wood was stern with sons Cornelius and William Jr.,
but he doted on his two daughters. So when, toward the end of his meeting
with strikers on Thursday, March 7, Wood learned that seventeen-year-old
Irene had been hurt in a sledding accident, he brought the discussion to a
hasty end, then took a train to Franconia, New Hampshire.[3] On his way, he
crossed the Merrimack.

Wood may have gone through Lawrence but more probably passed
through Lowell. Either city showed him the fruits of his empire. And although his visit was no more than a stopover, it was the first time "Billy
Wood" had seen a textile mill since the start of the strike. American Woolen
had an office in downtown Lawrence, yet Wood's appearance there would
have incited an uproar, so he had done all his brooding business in Boston.
Now on Thursday evening, as his train crossed the icebound river, Wood

gazed out the window at the realm that had shaped him and the one he had shaped.

What could he have been thinking? Here was the world he had entered a quarter century earlier, arriving to run the wool department of the Washington Mill, then building a kingdom that had woven his wool into gold. Yet now his kingdom was in revolt. For want of just two hours' pay, "fellow workers" had smashed his machinery and marched off their jobs, preferring the leadership of incendiary radicals who had never worked a day in a mill to that of a fellow immigrant risen from their ranks. With a chuckle, Wood may have recalled his prediction on the strike's first day—"I look for an early resumption of work." Nearly two months of deadlock had passed. In his mills, unfilled orders had risen—Wood's steel-trap mind probably knew the exact numbers—from 71,693 to 175,878.[4] These and the impending federal investigation of American Woolen had forced him to make concessions. And now that this inflexible man was bending, he must have wondered how his opponents had done it. How had a miscellaneous mob scraped from the bottom of Europe's cauldron steeled themselves into one cohesive body, defying the world's largest textile conglomerate, bringing it to the bargaining table, then, incredibly, refusing his first offer and holding out for still more? It would not be surprising if Wood hid his face while in the depot, lest his chubby, mustachioed mug be recognized from the platform. But neither would it be surprising if he continued to stare into the streets, seeking answers. The train paused for only a couple of minutes. It took on passengers, then pulled out, taking the dutiful father, the financial genius, the angry and beaten textile king farther north. A few moments later, a train pulled into the depot in Lawrence. From it stepped the Committee of Ten bearing the best news anyone had heard for nearly nine weeks.

On Thursday evening, March 7, Franco-Belgian Hall was jammed shoulder-to-shoulder, its air heavy and humid, so oppressive that a woman at the rear fainted.[5] Striding to the podium, committee members reported on their meeting with mill men in Boston's State House. The meeting had lasted all day. Wood had proposed the same minimum boost in pay, but this time his maximum was higher, much higher—15 percent or more— though exact figures were vague. The committee had asked Wood for a detailed wage schedule. Each striker must know, depending on his job, how much more was in the offing. Wood said this might take two weeks. In the meantime, why didn't strikers go back to work? The committee refused, sending the mill men into conference. Returning, they said an itemized pay schedule could be drafted in a few days. Taking up the bonus system, mill men agreed to cut it in half, making workers toil just two weeks, instead of four, for each premium. Overtime and recriminations were not mentioned, but both sides seemed to think these could be easily negotiated. The package was far more generous than the initial offer, but it was the attitude of the mill men that seemed a revelation.[6]

"Mr. Wood was very nice to us, and was quite ready to do business—not at all as he was last week," one committee member reported. Annie Welzenbach then shared her observations on meeting her boss. The tall, dignified woman in the towering hat was the most optimistic of all. "Be patient," she told the crowd, "and you'll get what you want. I think we've got Mr. Wood's goat."[7] Chatter in a dozen languages rose to a din louder than a mill's, and it was decided to adjourn the meeting. No one could hear the speakers anyway. As Wood sped north toward his daughter, the good news spread. All weekend, while rain[8] gave way to sunshine, the fever of hope infected all sectors of Lawrence. A clothing store on Essex started a "Last Week of the Big Strike Sale." Shirts, normally a dollar, were 50 cents and ladies' spring hats were reduced from $2.00 to $1.19.[9] The *Lawrence Tribune* saw "good signs for a speedy settlement."[10] In ethnic enclaves, strikers tasted the victory within their grasp. A few were disgruntled, worried they might be selling out for less than 15 percent after all,[11] but calmer heads insisted each side must compromise.

On Saturday, March 9, the Committee of Ten was again called to Boston. Expecting an itemized pay schedule, they were instead given a list of wages by department only. When they demanded more details, mill agents told them to expect a call by Monday.[12] That afternoon, fifteen children waving red IWW flags from the back of the train platform were sent to Manchester, New Hampshire.[13] In New York, strike support meetings were held all over the city,[14] including one featuring "stereopticon" photos of Lawrence.[15] Haywood spoke in Union Square, standing on a platform beside two of his celebrated "kiddies" who were staying with an Italian family. "Hello, Mr. Haywood," one boy said. "How are things in Lawrence?"[16] Haywood told the crowd the strike would end within a week, then made a bolder forecast. The coming victory would inspire textile strikes throughout New England, he said. The only way to avoid them would be to raise wages. Even as he spoke, mill men from Maine to Connecticut were taking the hated radical's advice.

All along the rivers of New England, wherever mills had tapped the power of flowing water, fear of another Lawrence inspired sudden wage increases. On Saturday afternoon, mill owners meeting in Boston granted increases of 5 to 7 percent to 125,000 workers.[17] The mill men caved in, one lamented, like "a row of bricks, one falling and knocking down all the others."[18] Some boosted wages without even being asked, others to settle strikes in the making.[19] All that coming week, the bricks fell. In North Adams, Massachusetts. In Greenville, New Hampshire. In Providence, Rhode Island. In Biddeford, Maine.[20] They even knocked over the toughest textile town of all, Fall River, Massachusetts.[21] By the time the last brick fell, some three hundred thousand workers had seen their wages rise thanks to the strikers in Lawrence.[22] The raises would put ten to twelve million dollars into textile workers' pockets in the coming year,[23] yet in mills that granted less than those in Lawrence, they would also stir a demand for parity, leading to copycat strikes.

When one last Monday approached, it brought the promise of a settlement. This being Lawrence, however, there was more twisting in the wind. No one knew whether the promised pay increase would be enough to end it all, nor what mayhem might follow if it wasn't. Meanwhile, nine weeks of a dull, ravenous rage demanded one final release. On Sunday night, as they had on several previous nights, strikers entered tenements and shook terrified scabs in their beds.[24] Five hours later, three shots rang out on the common, the signal for pickets to gather.[25] And then the sun rose on the largest picketing yet, some ten thousand marching in lines that stretched for blocks. Along with IWW ribbons and buttons, many now wore postcard-sized photos of Ettor and Giovannitti.[26] Herded again by police, strikers stood firm, singing, shouting, parading as if this and not mill work were the reason they had come to America. Mill agents reported few gains in workers.[27] Everyone who wanted to go back was already on the job. Another handful was arrested, including one man whose wife clung desperately to his neck to keep him from being dragged away.[28] All that Monday, the Committee of Ten waited for the call to Boston. It never came. Instead, the backlash that had been brewing for two months burst forth with a righteous fury. Lawrence city officials, perhaps the entire city, had been humiliated and defamed. It was time to get even.

Relaxing in the Needham Hotel late Monday night, Haywood, Trautmann, and other IWW leaders were served with subpoenas. They immediately began joking, waving the papers around.[29] The subpoenas called them to Suffolk County Supreme Judicial Court on Friday to defend the use of their relief fund. Three Boston-based contributors—a social worker, a Baptist pastor, and a stockholder in the Pacific Mill[30]—sought an injunction against all remaining IWW strike money. They charged that the fund, advertised as providing hunger relief, had been used instead for legal fees, sending children from the city, and for personal expenses. The following morning, just after the IWW raked in $5,250 in a single day,[31] Haywood defended the expenditures. "It has clearly been said that the funds solicited were for carrying on the war," he told the strike committee, "and to carry on the war means not only the buying of bread but also going into court to see that pickets are properly defended. That is part of this fight."[32] Dimes, dollars, and quarters continued to pour into Franco-Belgian Hall, many in envelopes marked "with no strings attached."[33]

Stronger than subpoenas, however, was the counterattack waged by the Lawrence Citizens' Association and taken up, as if in chorus, by portions of the press. On Monday, March 11, the lead article on the front page of the *New York Tribune* began: "The ease with which an American city of nearly one hundred thousand inhabitants may be seized by a gang of outside agitators and terrorized for weeks is well illustrated in what actually happened in Lawrence during the last two months."[34] Picking up the same speech in the same voice, that same day's *Brooklyn Tablet* continued: "Terrorism was the strongest weapon that the Industrial Workers of the World used in Lawrence. And only as that terror survived, nursed and cultivated"[35]—the *Boston Transcript* chimed in—"by the methods of the Black Hand and Mafia, did any of the strength of the syndicalist strike survive."[36] The identical wording in three separate newspapers was no coincidence. All three articles were reprinted verbatim, without attribution, from pamphlets issued by the Lawrence Citizens' Association. The group that had formed in late February was in full attack mode by mid-March. Grown to five thousand members,[37] the association churned out three pamphlets: *A Reign of Terror in an American City*, *What City after Lawrence?* and *Lawrence as It*

Really Is: Not as Syndicalists, Anarchists, Socialists, Suffragists, Pseudo Philan-
thropists, and Muckraking Yellow Journalists Have Painted It.[38] Each pamphlet seethed with indignation. After detailing the strike's initial violence,
one pamphlet noted the arrival of the IWW, "an organization that few in
Lawrence had ever heard of before."[39] Joseph Ettor "made a fiery address,
in the course of which the city government, the state government, and the
national government were denounced as enemies of the working men, fit
only to be wiped out of existence, along with capitalism, religion of all
kinds, authority of all kinds."[40] Following Ettor's speech, "terrorism of an
undefined, widespread, all pervasive kind spread throughout the city."[41]

The pamphlets defined what would remain for decades the official version of the strike. The planting of dynamite was noted only briefly. There
was no mention of the daily democratic meetings of strikers, the orderly
soup kitchens feeding thousands, the resilient calm that prevailed throughout the tenements. The early parades were described as mobs "that surged
along the streets [in] an irritable, growling, savage state . . . like a wild animal."[42] Each night, "groups of swarthy men [were] detailed to visit the little homes of the working operatives while only the women folks or children
were at home, and the wife and mother [was] told that if she did not prevent the father and bread winner from going to work that he would be
found with his throat cut the next morning."[43] The violence of January 29,
described blow by blow, led to "great headlines blazoning forth" fostering
the image of Lawrence as "a city whose streets had been bathed in the blood
of hundreds of strikers slaughtered by a ruthless capital-controlled militia."[44] The press, or at least "that form of newspaper that caters to the neuras-
thenic or hysterical"[45] was soon abetted by "shoals of theorizing socialists
from the pseudo-philanthropic societies of New York, those under salary
especially, writers of modern studies of the unclean, absinthe drinking fre-
quenters of the imitation cabarets of New York. . . ."[46] These "shoals" descended on Lawrence, "looked over the ground for half an hour and
declared that the Syndicalists were everlastingly right and everyone else
everlastingly wrong."[47] The pamphlets rehashed the wage dispute and defended Lawrence's honor. "There is no brighter looking, more up-to-date
looking industrial city in the country than Lawrence."[48] It was "as prosper-
ous, progressive and contented as any manufacturing city in the United
States until the Syndicalists tried to give birth to a new social era by a cata-

clysm to be started in Lawrence."[49] And above all, the association hammered home its point that no women had been clubbed at the train station.
Such was said to be the sworn testimony of reporters from the *Globe,* other
Boston papers, and the Associated Press. (The pamphlets neglected to
mention that all these news sources had described the clubbing and none
had retracted or corrected their articles in print.) Explaining the widespread reporting of the violence, a pamphlet blamed "certain advanced socialists" who had wired the "fake" to one Boston and one New York paper.
"These papers published the fake under glaring headlines on a Saturday
afternoon. It made rich stuff for the sensational Sunday newspapers 'to
play up,' and they all did 'play it up' to the limit all over the country."[50]

No one will ever know how much the train station incident was "played
up." And there had been unfair attacks in the Socialist press. The *New York
Call* published a poem entitled "Lawrence," which began "City of misery,
want, and greed/Grinding its heel in our brothers' need."[51] *Il Proletario*
continued to romanticize the strike in moralistic black and white: "When a
visitor approaches the police station [in Lawrence] . . . it isn't long before
he feels as if he were in Russia."[52] But the mainstream press reported events
in Lawrence with a steady, unalarmed voice. Contrary to the association's
claims, New York and Boston dailies did not spread false reports of massive bloodshed or widespread anarchy. The press did not "make a goat out
of Lawrence."[53] Instead, the opposite was true. Reeling from recent events
and worried that no one would invest in their tarnished city, the citizens' association was making a goat out of the press. The Lawrence papers
were happy to aid and abet the backlash. The *Tribune,* calling the city's
critics "the sob squad,"[54] excerpted the pamphlets without citing the association as the author. The *Telegram* sneered at "yellow journalists and theorizing college professors" who had made Lawrence out to be "about the
worst city in the country."[55] And with strikers sensing victory and
the backlash rising, Lawrence headed into what seemed certain to be the
strike's final days.

Militia companies had been leaving Lawrence for a week. Most of the
tired troops slipped quietly out of town, yet Lieutenant Colonel Franklin
Joy, Colonel Sweetser's replacement, wanted no such undignified retreat
for his First Corps of Cadets. Just after noon on Tuesday, March 12, the full
corps and its commander marched with shouldered arms out of the castle-

like armory on Amesbury Street, a few blocks north of the mill district. While a lunchtime crowd watched, cadets in starched blue uniforms tramped down Essex,[56] away from the mills where they had been quartered, away from the accusations of butchery, away from this thankless duty, and to the train station. By 1:10 p.m., they were on their way back to Boston when the critical call finally came to the Committee of Ten.

Within minutes, the committee was on its way to the State House to meet with William Wood and American Woolen agents—but no one from any other mills. The meeting dragged on and the committee did not return to Lawrence until it was too late to do anything except hold an executive session with IWW leaders. But the committee chairman made a brief public statement: "We have at last reached an agreement."[57] And by the following morning, everyone knew the end was just a vote away. Beneath a drizzling rain, only three hundred picketed on Wednesday morning. Everyone who could pack beneath its rafters preferred to be in Franco-Belgian Hall, where the crowd spilled onto the stage and out the back door. Haywood called the meeting to order at 10:00 a.m. Strikers may have expected Big Bill to offer a triumphant victory speech but he began like a bureaucrat.

"Your strike committee selected a sub-committee of ten to confer with the American Woolen Company," Haywood announced. "In brief it is said that the workers will receive increases in wages varying from five percent to the highest paid to twenty percent to the lowest paid. The report is that time and a quarter will be paid for overtime work. The premium system will be so modified that it means an adjustment to the premium every two weeks. No discrimination will be shown against any striker and every man will go back to his old job when the strike is declared off."[58] Haywood continued but it is not known how many in the crowd heard or understood what he said. All around the room, terms were being translated, numbers explained, lives taken off hold. In the end, all the numbers came down to one result—victory. Not all strikers would get 15 percent raises, but the poorest would get that much and more. Overtime was not double time as requested, but there had never been any overtime before. The hated premium system had been cut in half. There would be no recriminations. And somewhere in the agreement, perhaps couched in the grudging respect William Wood had given to the Committee of Ten, was the tacit admission

that even in the world's most modern mills, people could not be accelerated as if they were machines.

With all eyes searching Haywood's chunky face for more good news, he
continued. The agreement was with American Woolen only, but similar
terms would be sought from all other mills. Quick compliance was expected. But if the Pacific, Arlington, Atlantic, and the rest refused, the strike
would continue against them. Ettor and Giovannitti remained in jail, but
the legislative committee had promised to lobby for their release. All the
terms would be put before a mass meeting on the common the following
afternoon. And then, having reined in his exuberance long enough, Haywood made the proclamation he had been dreaming of all the previous
week, perhaps for all of his long, laboring life. "You, the strikers of Lawrence,
have won the most signal victory of any body of organized working men in
the world," he said. "You have won the strike for yourselves and by your
strike you have won an increase in wages for over 250,000 other textile
workers in the vicinity, and that means in the aggregate millions of dollars
a year. . . . You are the heart and soul of the working class. Single-handed
you are helpless but united you can win everything. You have won over the
opposed power of the city, state, and national administrations, against the
opposition of the combined forces of capitalism, in face of the armed
forces. You have even won in the face of the partial courts and in face of injunctions. You have won by your solidarity and brains and muscle."[59]

The strike was not over, Haywood cautioned. The final terms had to be
approved by all. But strikers had taken "the first step in your progressive
march towards industrial freedom." At this, the hall erupted. Dozens of
nationalities, yelling, stomping, reveling as one, made the rafters of Franco-
Belgian Hall creak and groan. And then came the songs—"The Internationale," of course, but also a new verse to "In the Good Old Picket Line"
featuring Elizabeth Gurley Flynn and a certain Mr. Lowe, a mill manager:

> In the good old picket line, in the good old picket line
> We'll put Mr. Lowe in overalls and swear off drinking wine,
> Then Gurley Flynn will be the boss,
> Oh gee, won't that be fine,
> The strikers will wear diamonds in the good old picket line.[60]

They sang as if they never wanted to stop. They sang, as every chorus sings, oblivious of the world beyond, keeping it at bay with one song after another. "In the Good Old Picket Line" was followed by Joe Hill's "The Preacher and the Slave," with its chorus mocking the false promises made to workers:

> You will eat, bye and bye
> In that glorious land above the sky;
> Work and pray, live on hay,
> You'll get pie in the sky when you die, and that's a lie.[61]

Strikers sang for a full hour, then filed out into the rain. Walking home along the river and past the mills, hungry for a lunch that might have to wait until dinner, many must have wondered "What now?" Was it really over? In their ragged, shopworn lives, so many loose ends needed mending. Not all were sure they had won enough, and those who were certain now faced the daunting prospect of returning to the mills, enduring all over again the clamor, the pounding pace, the overseers who would be in no mood to treat them any better than before. But for a day at least, perhaps a few more, the city of Lawrence could finally exhale. The only dispute came in city hall.

By order of Colonel Sweetser, public meetings were still forbidden. Urging all to the common the following day, Haywood had told strikers they did not need Mayor Scanlon's approval to exercise "the right of free speech." But Scanlon snapped, "Haywood isn't running this town yet," and insisted on meeting strikers to get their guarantee that any gathering would be peaceful.[62] Then on Wednesday night, alderman and parks commissioner Michael O'Brien, who had earlier donated twenty-five dollars to the strike fund,[63] okayed the use of the common. An outraged mayor read of O'Brien's action in the newspaper and called an emergency meeting Thursday morning. The alderman was sent before the strike committee to order a small delegation to the police station. There Marshal Sullivan was assured that the meeting would be peaceful.[64] Just after lunch on Thursday, the crowds began to gather at the heart of "Immigrant City."

On March 14, 1912, the throng that assembled on the Lawrence Common had come from all over the Western world. They had also come from

just a few blocks away. Beneath hazy skies and merciful spring temperatures, fifteen thousand people[65] clogged streets and alleys as they walked to
their appointed meeting. Men walked with men, women with women,
many carrying babies or holding the hands of small children. They walked
purposefully, just as they had on that morning two months and two days
earlier when they had last trudged to work. Almost all the men wore hats—
bowlers or cloth caps jauntily tipped to one side or pulled back to reveal
expanding foreheads and wisps of hair. The women sported their shawls,
their feathered hats, their shirtwaists. The crowd entered the common
from all directions but quickly crossed snow-patched fields to reach the
octagonal bandstand at the center. There they stood ankle deep in mud,
waiting, talking. Overhearing their chatter, one sociologist was heard to
mutter, "A tower of Babel."[66] But if their languages were many, their purpose was one. They would soon resume quarreling. All the former ani-
mosities, as old as the "old country," would surface. Yet for this singular
afternoon, after sixty-three days without work or pay, surviving on soup
and sandwiches doled out in dingy kitchens, witnessing the death of two
strikers, the beating of dozens, the arrest of hundreds, the marching of
thousands, this cosmopolitan collection of the world's workers had become an American tapestry.

From the raised bandstand, strikers led the throng in more singing.
Banners unfurled: IN STRUGGLE YOU GAIN YOUR RIGHTS. WE FORGIVE YOU
BUT NEVER BE A SCAB AGAIN. RELEASE OUR PRISONERS, ETTOR AND GIO-
VANNITTI.[67] Somewhere in that crowd, probably on tiptoe so he could see,
stood Angelo Rocco. In his pocket was a subpoena calling him to court the
next day to discuss the strike fund.[68] Impromptu speeches and celebrations rippled through the assembly. Occasional cheers rang out as if the
day's vote were a foregone conclusion. Then making his way through the
masses, dressed in a dark suit and tie, came William Dudley Haywood. Son
of a Pony Express rider he never knew, radical sworn to overthrow the
American industrial system yet steeped in his nation's patriotic lore, Big
Bill slogged through the mud in front of the bandstand, climbed the steps,
and stood beside a banner that read I.W.W. At the sight of his face, a great
roar washed over the crowd, loud enough, one reporter guessed, to be
heard by Ettor and Giovannitti in their cells a half mile away.[69] Standing
beside Haywood, called back from scheduled rallies in Pittsburgh,[70] was

Elizabeth Gurley Flynn. Gazing out at the crowd, she smiled and waved again and again. Then Haywood, squinting with his one good eye, called the meeting to order.

On such an auspicious occasion, he might have orated for an hour. Yet like the IWW, which had again toned down its class warfare in order to win a strike, Haywood knew when the people were bigger than he was. "Fellow workers," his baritone boomed, "your strike committee has a report to make." And without another word, he turned the podium over to representatives from each nationality. In the lull, someone shouted, "Joe Ettor and Arturo Giovannitti will be out of jail next week!" Cheers echoed until the crowd quieted. Then language by language, the terms of the settlement were explained in Arabic, Italian, German, Polish, Armenian . . . After they were read in Portuguese, that delegation stepped forward with three brimming bouquets of roses for Haywood, Ettor, and Giovannitti. Haywood sent his bouquet out into the crowd, asking that the petals be taken by those with family members still in jail. The translations continued—in Latvian, Greek, French, and finally Yiddish.[71] Only when the settlement had been laid out in a dozen languages did Haywood speak again. He explained that the terms applied solely to the four American Woolen mills plus the Kunhardt and Atlantic. The strike would continue against all other mills whose agents had refused to meet with a committee of strikers. Then Haywood asked if the crowd was ready to vote. A thunderous "Yes!" swelled across the bandstand. When he asked, "All in favor?" fifteen thousand arms went up at once. All opposed? Five hands were raised.[72]

"By your vote," Haywood bellowed, "you have agreed that the strike on the American Woolen Company, the Kunhardt and the Atlantic Mills is off! You are now ready to go to work tomorrow—"

At this, cries of "No, no!" came from the crowd.

Strikers sensed that they were in control now. They would not go back to the mills before *they* were ready. "The mills are open," Haywood said, "and it is up to you to go to work when you want to." Then taking a shouted suggestion, he called for a vote on when to return. Monday, it was agreed.[73] Haywood said a few more words, urging former strikers to support those still out. And then no one seemed to know what to do. The songs had been sung, the banners waved, the vote taken. After all their previous demonstrations, a parade seemed redundant, so everyone just went home. Within an hour, the streets were clear and several more militia companies were boarding trains back to their hometowns. The strike, at least the great bulk of it, was over. Later that afternoon, several people took roses to the jail but were told they could not leave them for Ettor and Giovannitti. Angered at one more affront, they carried the bouquets back to the strike committee, where it was voted that they be laid on the graves of John Rami and Anna LoPizzo. The flowers found their final resting place on Friday afternoon.[74]

The weekend was chaotic, joyous, anxious, as if the entire city, finally re-covered from a debilitating illness, were scrambling to reassemble its rou-tines. Strikers had voted to go back on Monday, but on Friday morning thousands showed up at the mills asking for work. There was not enough.[75] Whole departments had been idle, and getting them started took more than the raising of hands or the throwing of a switch. Many willing work-ers were sent home, grumbling that scabs somehow had enough work, wondering if they had been swindled. With some four thousand still on strike against six mills—all of them cotton mills—the future of Labor in Lawrence remained on hold.[76] In Boston that rainy morning, Haywood, Trautmann, Rocco, and others testified about their handling of the strike fund. Neither their words nor their numbers said as much as the moment when strike committee treasurer Joseph Bedard lugged a bulky wooden soapbox into court. The box contained a scrap heap of vouchers, receipts, checks, orders for wood, coal, food . . .[77] These, along with one ledger only begun on February 16,[78] were the strike committee's "books," and it would take a Boston accountant several days to make sense of them. Another hearing was set for the following Wednesday.

All that weekend, the rites of spring were as encouraging as the tributes that came from around the country. Steady rains melted ice on the Merri-mack, sending jagged chunks flowing over the Great Stone Dam with a thunder that drew spectators to the river's banks.[79] In New York, Lincoln Steffens proclaimed of Lawrence: "Labor has seldom, if ever, won so com-plete a victory."[80] Eugene Debs, cranking up his presidential campaign, exulted, "The victory at Lawrence [was] one of the most decisive and far-reaching ever won by organized workers."[81] When the rains relaxed, base-ball season heated up. Fans read sports-page stories about Ty Cobb, Honus

Wagner, and Christy Mathewson. The Lawrence Barristers of the New England League, young men in baggy uniforms with tobacco-tinted gloves not much bigger than their own hands, tossed dirty horsehide around the diamond. By Sunday, as the sun rose earlier each morning and higher each noon, women were seen crossing the common carrying bundles of pussy willows.[82] That week, department stores held their annual spring openings, adorning windows and display rooms with the latest in ladies' apparel.[83] Off in Kansas, William Allen White paid strikers the greatest tribute of all. Though they were foreigners, White wrote, "many of them at their mass meetings, in their homes and in their gathering upon the streets reflected to me at least a better Americanism, a clearer vision of what America stands for than did many of those who sneered at them."[84] The weekend concluded with St. Patrick's Day celebrations featuring Irish tenors singing "Mother Macree" and speeches by Father O'Reilly and Mayor Scanlon.[85] And on Monday morning, the whistles blew at dawn. For the first time since January 12, they were not a call to arms but a call to work.

From out of the tenements, the steady stream of Labor flowed again, bustling down Essex Street, crossing the Merrimack, shuffling through the wide gates and into the mills. There was still not enough work. Again many were sent home, but many more were kept on the job, working almost as if nothing had happened. Hands knew by heart the same repetitive motions, the same skills of carding, cleaning, spinning, threading, weaving, all to the accompaniment of the same cacophonous clack-CLACK. There might have been smiles exchanged across looms, shadows of solidarity. And certainly there were the usual insults and ethnic slurs hurled by bosses. But the dreary work for meager pay had never seemed less laborious. The meetings, mobs, and violence were mere memories now. For the first time in nine weeks, Angelo Rocco went to class at Lawrence High School. No one needed to ask him where he'd been. The only items remaining were to settle the strike against other mills, free Ettor and Giovannitti, and bring the children home.

Outside the mills, however, Lawrence remained on edge. One evening, an explosion drew dozens to the armory. It had just been an automobile tire, overinflated.[86] City officials fumed over the reported cost of the strike—$3.2 million in lost wages, revenues, and reimbursement for the militia.[87] The infamy of Lawrence lingered, keeping distinguished visitors

In A Prison Cell Because
They Are Loyal To Their Class

TWO NOBLE FIGHTERS IN THE STRUGGLE OF TWENTY FIVE
THOUSAND STRIKING TEXTILE WORKERS WHOSE WAGES
AVERAGED LESS THAN SIX DOLLARS PER WEEK.

Our Fellow Workers
Arturo Giovannitti & Joseph J. Ettor

INTERNATIONAL PRINTING CO.

At the end of January, strike leaders Arturo Giovannitti *(left)* and Joseph Ettor, though a mile from the scene of the crime, were arrested and charged with being accessories to the murder of a striker. They would remain in jail until their trial that fall, becoming an international cause célèbre.

Following the arrest of Ettor and Giovannitti, the nation's most notorious labor leader, William "Big Bill" Haywood of the Industrial Workers of the World, took command.

Haywood approved another new tactic in American strikes when, on February 10, strikers sent more than a hundred of their children to live with sympathetic families in Manhattan. Here, following a second children's exodus on February 17, children are paraded up Fifth Avenue.

Called by one journalist "the spirit of the strike," twenty-one-year-old Elizabeth Gurley Flynn rallied workers, escorted children out of town, and tirelessly raised money for strike funds.

Father James T. O'Reilly, the spiritual head of Lawrence's many Catholic congregations, returned from a Florida vacation to lead a ferocious backlash against the IWW.

In mid-February, women assumed a prominent role in the strike, marching, parading, and openly defying arrest.

LAW AND ORDER IN LAWRENCE

When Lawrence police beat women trying to send more children out of town, the entire nation was shocked and congressional hearings were scheduled. This cartoon appeared in *Collier's Weekly* and other publications.

With unprecedented solidarity, women kept the strike going despite growing hunger, rage, and violence against strikers.

On March 14, after two months and two days, Big Bill Haywood, with Elizabeth Gurley Flynn by his side, told thousands on the Lawrence Common that the strike was over.

On Columbus Day, tens of thousands carrying flags marched through Lawrence in a "For God and Country" parade protesting the IWW and sparking the greatest peacetime patriotic display in American history.

at arm's length. President Taft visited Boston, then New Hampshire, but steered clear of the city.[88] Teddy Roosevelt came through on a Saturday morning but did not even leave his train car to make a speech, just sat writing while telling a reporter he was "dee-lighted" to be in Lawrence, having heard so much about the city lately.[89] Gradually, the wounds healed into scars. On Sunday, March 24, the strike committee held its final meeting. William Trautmann announced that all remaining mills had met strikers' demands. He declared the strike officially over, and the committee voted itself out of existence.[90] The next day the last militia left,[91] and the bloated police force was soon cut back to its usual numbers.[92] On March 27, the House Rules Committee dropped its pending investigation against American Woolen, its chairman stating that with the strike over, the hearing's publicity had had the desired effect.[93] By then, Haywood, Flynn, and other leaders had left to lead textile strikes breaking out all over New England.

In Barre, Massachusetts, strikers stoned railroad cars carrying woolen goods and slugged it out with club-wielding policemen.[94] A local mill man said his workers had been "crazed by reading about the Lawrence strike."[95] It took ten days, but the strikers got the additional raise they sought.[96] Walkouts started elsewhere, the largest in Lowell, where what looked like a rerun of Lawrence was under way. Angry at raises less than those in their neighboring mill city, workers stormed out of Lowell's cotton mills. A wider strike was threatened, but before it could start, owners staged a lockout.[97] Haywood arrived to a tumultuous crowd at the train station. Soup kitchens were up and running.[98] Ten thousand strikers paraded through the streets[99] demanding 15 to 20 percent raises.[100] Flynn spoke all over the city,[101] and the strike went on into April.

While other textile towns shook, Lawrence was calm again, but beneath its ripples stirred an undercurrent of resentment and resistance. Flush with victory, the IWW rubbed the city's nose in its success. "The Lawrence victory gives the I.W.W. a firm foothold in New England," the union's journal *Solidarity* gloated.[102] The strike had given the IWW an "enormous amount of free advertising . . . largely due to the stupid, blundering brutality of the Lawrence slugging committee."[103] IWW membership in Lawrence now topped ten thousand.[104] "The Little Old Red Button is in Great Demand," Haywood telegrammed *Solidarity*.[105] So popular was the union that one German christened his newborn son Irving William Wilbur, making the boy's initials IWW.[106] "I have no country," an Italian said. "I am I.W.W."[107] Wobblies opened a New England chapter, headquartered in Lawrence and headed by Flynn.[108] But the thought of the "I Won't Work's" taking root in the region's textile industry horrified mill men, mayors, and staunch citizens throughout New England. This peril could not be defeated by pamphlets. A coordinated effort, involving mill agents, overseers, detectives, police, clergymen, and the more respectable craft unions would be needed. Throughout the spring, behind closed doors, the forces of resistance formed a cohesive plan to drive the IWW out of New England.

Before this campaign geared up, the resentment surfaced in mob violence. When Haywood and Flynn spoke in Clinton, Massachusetts, a local organizer dared to criticize the town's militia, just back from Lawrence. Following the meeting, a mob chased the outside agitators through the streets hurling rotten eggs, one hitting Haywood.[109] Articles on the menace of the IWW appeared in newspapers from the *Boston Herald*[110] to the *New York Times,*[111] and in magazines from the AF of L's *American Federationist*[112] to *Atlantic Monthly.*[113] Back in Lawrence, a struggle for workers' loyalty was under way. The AF of L announced a massive campaign to organize New England's textile workers.[114] Meanwhile, the courtroom fight to impound the IWW strike fund ended when a judge ruled that no injunction was necessary against a fund that had dwindled to just forty-nine cents.[115] But the campaign against the Wobblies would continue all summer and flare with a vengeance in the fall.

Workers were not yet embroiled in this backlash, but once on the job, they faced an older adversary. They had not been back much more than a week when a man at the Everett Mill, seated atop an elevator greasing its cables, was crushed to death when the cage suddenly shot to the ceiling.[116] Four days later, while oiling a carding machine in the Wood Mill, a worker got caught in the overhead belt. Whirled to the ceiling, then dropped to the floor, he died that day at Lawrence General Hospital.[117] Smaller injuries were rife, as usual, and workers remained restless. Staging small walkouts at several mills, they complained of being taunted by scabs,[118] not given enough work,[119] or given too much.[120] In all cases, they returned the next day. Considering what the city had survived, these seemed mere aftershocks. Gradually the work caught up with the workforce and the first fifty-four hours on the job passed. Given the pay schedule—each Friday paycheck tied to the previous week's hours—there were no checks for strikers on March 22. Many remained hungry and Joseph Bedard sent out a call for continued relief.[121] But then the second week of work was done, and on Friday, March 29, workers lined up at pay time. Paymasters wheeled carts into the mill rooms to hand out checks. Workers tore them open and saw the harvest of two months' struggle—not just a return of the thirty-two cents that set off the strike but raises of fifty-four cents, eighty-one cents, even $1.08 a week for the lowest paid.[122] And then, without a protest, a cry, or even a yelp of victory, they went back to work. The following afternoon, the "children of Lawrence" came home.

Because their departure had been "a war measure,"[123] it was only fitting that the children return as conquering heroes. One last time, the depot became a theater of anticipation. One last time a crowd began to gather hours before the train was due, thousands choking the streets that led to Essex and Broadway. One last time before ethnic differences returned, workers were one in welcoming their children. Yet the children aboard the train that inched into the station at 5:00 p.m., its bell clanging constantly,[124] were not the same ones who had left Lawrence three, six, or seven weeks earlier. Parents recognized their own, but everyone was startled by the changes. Skinny, half-frozen waifs had left the city toting lunches and little else. But waving from the windows, then stepping from the train into an ocean of outstretched arms were 240 children who looked as if they had come from long visits with rich uncles. They were plump—some had gained a dozen pounds or more[125]—and well clothed. The girls wore new dresses and spring hats; the boys suits with shiny neckties. Girls carried dolls, some of them more than one, and bundles of extra dresses. Boys hefted books, roller skates, and boxes of toys.[126] Many had big bouquets of flowers and all wore badges demanding the release of Ettor and Giovannitti.

They had left New York at 8:00 a.m. that morning, having been gathered there from Philadelphia, Hoboken, and the five boroughs. After singing "The Star-Spangled Banner" to a crowd at Grand Central Station, they boarded two reserved train cars. One boy vowed to return to New York, boasting that he would get his working papers when he was fourteen, then come back and get a job, "you'll see."[127] Many must have sworn the same in secret. And then, bidding good-bye to their surrogate parents, they left these kind strangers alone on the platform to linger for many minutes. The train ride through the rolling green hills of New England was uneventful. Not even Boston had much to show them now. But when the "kiddies" came home to Lawrence, they found a city transformed. Only a dozen police were on hand at the depot, and no militia patrolled the streets. Neither Mayor Scanlon nor Father O'Reilly was anywhere to be seen. The sun was bright, the river flowed freely, the mills were closed until Monday, and they—the children—were the grand marshals of the parade.

Led by Flynn, Annie Welzenbach, and Haywood finally wearing his Stetson hat,[128] seven flatbed furniture vans drawn by horses[129] inched up Broadway past the Arlington Mill. Dozens of children, including those who had arrived earlier from Vermont and New Hampshire, rode in each.[130] They waved to the manic masses. They shouted to people hanging out windows. They saluted the Stars and Stripes and several other national flags, and sang along with marching bands. For two hours, as the sun set and a silver-dollar moon rose to light the way,[131] the mile-long parade[132] wound through Lawrence, finally reaching the common where, at 7:30 p.m., the crowd dispersed. Reunited with parents who had patiently waited to hold them and tell them how they had grown, the children went to Franco-Belgian Hall for a feast. And then, wondering if the skyscrapers, the elevated trains, the generous families lavishing them with gifts had all been a dream, the children went home. On Monday, the youngest returned to school, while the oldest joined the morning march to the mills. Like their parents, they strode with a new pride in their step. It could be seen and sensed in the way people talked to each other, in the way they talked about themselves.

"We are a new people," one worker said. "We have hope. We will never stand again what we stood before."[133]

CHAPTER TWELVE

"The Flag of Liberty Is Here"

A little key, a little key as little as my little finger, a little key of shining brass.
All my ideals, my thoughts, my dreams are congealed in a little key of shiny brass.

—Arturo Giovannitti, "The Walker"[1]

On its joyous route through the city, the parade that welcomed the children back to Lawrence stopped only once. Passing the jail, revelers removed their hats and stood chanting "Ettor!" and "Giovannitti!"[2] Many pointed to an upstairs window, swearing they saw "Smiling Joe,"[3] but he was still in his cell.[4] So was his fellow prisoner, who, after two months behind bars, was widely known as a martyr but not as a man.

When Arturo Giovannitti was arrested on January 30, only the Italians of Lawrence knew anything about him. Everyone else assumed him to be cut from the same cloth as his comrade behind bars. He was anything but. Giovannitti had never joined the IWW.[5] Though he spoke fluent English, Latin, and French,[6] he spoke to crowds solely in a lofty, romantic Italian. And he was not the son of working-class immigrants but came from a family of lawyers and professors back in Italy.[7] How had this man, whose first request for reading material in jail was a four-volume history of literature,[8] come to be accused of inciting murder? It was a descent worthy of Dante.

As he would later tell the jury, Giovannitti was born in "a Godforsaken village up in the Abruzzi,"[9] Italy's harsh, mountainous region east of Rome. Raised to believe in America as "a better and a freer land than my own,"[10] he had followed the flow of Abruzzese peasantry to the Promised Land, crossing the Atlantic in 1900 while still in his teens. His first stop was Canada, where he worked in a coal mine and on a railroad crew.[11] In Montreal, he began preaching in a Presbyterian mission, then moved to Manhattan to enroll in Union Theological Seminary. He never graduated but ran Italian missions in Brooklyn and Pittsburgh before breaking with the church to pursue his own social gospel.[12] His radical politics were forged during lonely nights sleeping on park benches and in animated discussions with fellow members of the Italian Socialist Federation.[13] He began writing for the federation's weekly paper and in 1911 became its editor. Though he had rarely spoken at workers' rallies, his friend Joe Ettor called Giovannitti to Lawrence during the first week of the strike to coordinate relief efforts. Like Ettor, he had been reluctant to come, fearing to enter the volatile city. But his wife urged him to go,[14] and after arriving without the slightest notice, he began holding forth in a powerful voice while holding himself in a manner one observer called "leonine."[15] His most noted address was his "Sermon on the Common." Delivered from the bandstand, its biblical cadences mirrored Jesus's beatitudes—"Blessed are the rebels: for they shall reconquer the earth"—and stirred strikers:

> There is no destiny that the will of man cannot break;
> There are no chains of iron that other iron cannot destroy;
> There is nothing that the power of your arms, lighted by the
>   power of your mind, cannot transform and recast and
>   remake.
> Arise, then, ye men of the plough and the hammer, the helm
>   and the lever, and send forth to the four winds of the earth
>   your new proclamation of freedom which shall be the last
>   and shall abide forevermore.[16]

Giovannitti was in Lawrence only ten days before being arrested. Unlike Ettor, he did not speak at his arraignment nor send letters to strikers. Instead, he maintained a monklike silence. In his cell, while plowing through Byron, Shelley, Kant,[17] and the complete works of Shakespeare, he wrote poems, "blows of my own sledge against the walls of my own jail."[18] The best of them, "The Walker," tells of a prisoner pacing the cell above Giovannitti's own:

For not for the Walker, nor for my heart is there a second, a
    minute, an hour or anything that is in the old clock—there is
    nothing but the night, the sleepless night, the watchful, wistful
    night, and footsteps that go, and footsteps that come and the
    wild, tumultuous beatings that trail after them forever.[19]

When "The Walker" was published that September, critics favorably
compared it with the work of Whitman and Oscar Wilde.[20] Meanwhile, its
author was facing the fate of only a few poets in a century—to be condemned to death by his own words. It would take nearly three more
months to determine whether Giovannitti's eloquence would release him
or send him to the electric chair, and by then his name would have been
chanted in rallies from Rome to Dresden to San Francisco throughout the
shrill seasons that followed the strike.

It was the spring of the *Titanic*, the summer of "Boom Lawrence," and the
autumn of "God and Country."

As spring blossomed, the press and public debated the "lessons of
Lawrence." They were fourfold. One: immigration had reached dangerous
levels. "If the alien influx is permitted to continue," warned the prestigious
North American Review, "it will mean a further degradation of the industrial
worker and the intensifying of the conditions of unrest and dissatisfaction
which offer such fruitful ground to the Socialist and other revolutionary
and radical propagandists."[21] Two: Americans must learn more about labor conditions. "We must understand for Lawrence and for all the industrial communities in America the real facts about labor," wrote *The Survey*.
"We must know wages, hours, conditions. . . . We shall have no time to
discuss fire protection when the house is already ablaze."[22] Three: employers who stifled unionization were fueling class warfare. As the *Atlantic
Monthly* warned, "The way to make anarchism grow in this country is to
refuse to allow organization and collective bargaining."[23] And four: perhaps government might play a role in labor disputes. That summer, Massachusetts adopted the nation's first minimum wage law. It was a hesitant
effort establishing a commission to review women's and children's wages
and recommend a minimum,[24] but it was not declared unconstitutional.

(The following year, the state would limit children under sixteen to an eight-hour workday.)[25] Meanwhile at the urging of President Taft, Congress approved a congressional Commission on Industrial Relations that would eventually take testimony from labor war veterans ranging from John Golden to Bill Haywood.[26]

With the strike's lessons spelled out, its aftermath continued to make news. Then on April 15, the lingering ordeal was overshadowed when an "unsinkable" ocean liner went to the bottom of the Atlantic, filling the rest of the spring with laments, hearings, and recriminations. In Lawrence, one resident was thought to be among the victims until she was discovered, a week after the sinking, among the rescued.[27]

All that spring, the city remained dangerously divided as its old and new powers—the mill men and the IWW—fought for the loyalty of twenty-eight thousand workers. Small, sporadic walkouts continued to roil several mills. Most were settled within a few days, but mill men openly defied the strikers' fourth demand—"no recriminations." Undercover detectives trailed IWW leaders, overseers harassed those handing out IWW leaflets, shop bosses refused to meet with committees containing "IWWs," and mill men compiled blacklists of "agitators" who, once fired, found it impossible to get mill work.[28] Strike fever gradually ebbed in Lawrence but remained epidemic throughout New England. Many mill towns saw walkouts explode into gun battles[29] or uprisings of ten thousand.[30] Mill owners had feared as much, Haywood had predicted it, yet few foresaw that class warfare by other means would be waged in court.

In April, to no one's surprise, a grand jury indicted Ettor and Giovannitti. Their trial was set for May 27. A third man, Joseph Caruso, was indicted for conspiring to kill Anna LoPizzo. The murder itself was charged to another Italian who had fled Lawrence. But that same month, officials determined to purge the IWW from the city fired a shot across the union's bow by indicting Haywood and five other strike leaders for conspiracy to intimidate, incite violence, and strike by "unlawful means."[31] Haywood, speaking out of town when indicted, decided not to return to Lawrence. Come May, strikers were dealt another blow when John Breen was convicted of planting dynamite but merely fined five hundred dollars. Citizens began a campaign that would eventually recall Breen from the school board, while the presiding judge hinted that the former mayor's son had been a pawn in some larger game. "If what I hear is true," the judge said, "it was a foolish attempt on the part of any man to thus help a friend."[32] The judge said no more, leading to wild guesses about what "friend" had put Breen up to the job. Then came the civil suits: Syrians suing Breen for implicating them,[33] John Rami's mother petitioning the state for redress,[34] and a woman beaten at the depot suing Marshal Sullivan. In mid-May, at the request of their attorneys, the trial of Ettor and Giovannitti was postponed until fall. On into summer, while workers across the nation rallied for their release, the prisoners remained in the jail whose poet in residence continued to hear footsteps:

> All this have I heard in the watchful night,
> And the murmur of the wind beyond the walls,
> And the tolls of a distant bell,
> And the woeful dirge of the rain
> And the remotest echoes of the sorrowful city.[35]

Summer had its own theme—"Boom Lawrence." Newspapers told readers to "relate a few of the good things about the city" because "the unpleasant have been magnified tenfold."[36] Caught up in the spirit, Mayor Scanlon made good on his promise to build the city's first municipal playgrounds and in July children were seen soaring in swings and digging in sandboxes along the Merrimack and on the common. By mid-August, the trial was just six weeks away. Preparations were well under way in nearby Salem, where the state had moved the venue, when Lawrence and the entire textile industry were jolted by the most startling news of the entire year. A gunshot set the process in motion.

On August 27, the contractor who had built the Wood and Ayer mills killed himself on his front lawn in Andover. At first, Lawrence was surprised but not suspicious. Said to have been despondent over business affairs, Ernest Pitman was considered a tragedy, not a link to conspiracy.[37] But the following day mill executives were seen slipping into the Suffolk County Courthouse in Boston.[38] Word was soon leaked. Before taking his life, Pitman had confessed. *He* had been the one who procured the dynamite for John Breen. Weeping before a relentless district attorney, the contractor implicated top-level mill men in the plot, then went home to end his life rather than tell the same story to a grand jury. Two days after Pitman's suicide, secret indictments were returned against a Boston businessman and "a prominent, influential and wealthy mill man of Lawrence."[39] The following morning at 10:00 a.m., looking like some summer dandy in a straw boater and checkered sport coat,[40] William Madison Wood was booked on six counts of conspiring to plant dynamite. Considering that his entire meteoric career was in jeopardy, Wood was surprisingly congenial, even posing for photographs. "I cannot conceive what information could have been presented to the jurors which in any way connected me with the so-called 'dynamite plot,' " Wood said. "Beyond this I have nothing to say." After posting five thousand dollars bail, he went to his office.[41]

Leading citizens of Lawrence were stunned[42] but Wobblies were not surprised. Many had suspected such a top-down plot.[43] Recalling that dynamite had been planted in the cobbler's shop next to where Ettor got his mail, they now saw a massive conspiracy to implicate their leader culminating in his arrest on trumped-up charges. Surely the plot was designed to end in his execution. RELEASE ETTOR AND GIOVANNITTI, YOU MILL BARONS, *Industrial Worker* demanded, OR AN AROUSED WORKING CLASS WILL BE FORCED TO TAKE THEM FROM YOUR JAIL![44] Far beyond Lawrence, the same demand, whipped up in the Socialist press, stirred the world's workers. Letters to Governor Foss and President Taft came from trade unionists in Berlin and Dresden,[45] Paris and Bordeaux.[46] A booklet on the case was circulated throughout Italy.[47] *Il Proletario* kept its readers abreast of Ettor-Giovannitti rallies in Switzerland, Germany, Austria,[48] and "the mother country." One of *Il Proletario*'s readers, a Boston-area shoemaker named Nicola Sacco, was consumed by the cause. Sacco had not been an anarchist when he arrived in America, but the Lawrence strike radicalized him. All winter he had gathered money and supplies for strikers. Now, as the trial approached, he tirelessly collected funds for the defense in this cause célèbre whose notoriety would later be surpassed by that of Sacco himself and his friend, Bartolomeo Vanzetti.[49]

As the September 30 trial date approached, Ettor-Giovannitti rallies were held in South Africa and Australia.[50] Labor unions in Sweden and Italy proposed a boycott of American goods if the men were convicted.[51] And money for legal fees flowed into Lawrence, swelling the defense fund to fifty thousand dollars.[52] As leaves began to redden across New England, there was just time for one more rally featuring the return of Big Bill. Since being indicted in April, Haywood had not shown his burly mug in Massachusetts. Instead, he had taken a victory lap around the world of the working stiff. Speaking in textile towns and union halls, he enthralled workers with tales of Lawrence, often praising the women who, he said, "won the strike."[53] Come September, however, Haywood was seen nearer and nearer to Lawrence—first at a protest in Manhattan, then at another in Providence. Finally, on September 15, twenty-five thousand people stood in restless anticipation on the Boston Common. Flyers for the Sunday afternoon rally had promised Haywood would speak. Two trains full of mill workers had come from Lawrence.[54] Police searched for Haywood on these and every other train arriving in Boston. They did not find him. Then as shadows grew long on the common, a portly man in a floppy hat strode through the masses and leaped onto the stage. The crowd went wild, even wilder when Haywood taunted them.

"Are you willing to go on strike?" he shouted, referring to a looming general strike in support of the prisoners.

An ear-splitting "YES!" rocked the rally.

"Do you want Ettor to stay in jail?"

"NO!"

"Do you want Giovannitti to stay in jail?"

"NO!"[55]

Haywood had fooled police, arriving by car. Knowing they wouldn't dare arrest him in front of the crowd, he planned a similar getaway. After finishing his speech, he strode toward where a car was supposed to be waiting. Eager to flee, he followed a call from one of many autos at the edge of the common.

"This way, Bill!"

Haywood hopped in and said, "Step on the gas."[56] Then he noticed the driver—a detective. Three other detectives jumped in beside him. "All right, go ahead," a disgusted Haywood said, and he was taken into custody.[57] The next day, booked on twenty-two counts of conspiracy, he pleaded "guilty of nothing except trying to help the workers of Lawrence get a little more bread."[58] Now that he could show his face, at least he might attend the trial of his friends before his own trial set for January.

With the Ettor-Giovannitti proceeding just days away, Lawrence was again on a hair trigger. This time, however, the man with his finger on that trigger was the most radical leader yet to appear in the city. Following Haywood's indictment, Giovannitti had suggested summoning his friend Carlo Tresca. Tall, flamboyant, and a devout anarchist, Tresca had arrived in Lawrence to lead a May Day parade of five thousand past the jail. Then he had taken up his stock in trade—agitation. "Tresca never makes trouble," wrote Max Eastman, editor of *The Masses*. "He merely goes where it is, cultivates it, cherishes its fine points, props up the weak ends, nurtures it and nurses it along, so that from being a little, mean, and measly trouble, it becomes a fine, big tumultuous catastrophe."[59] For several weeks, Tresca led marches to the grave of Anna LoPizzo until Marshal Sullivan denied him a permit, shouting, "You can't have a funeral every Sunday for that woman."[60] When Tresca tried again, Father O'Reilly barred the gates of Immaculate Conception cemetery.[61] Undeterred, Tresca planned further agitation. He spoke little English—his answer to almost any problem was "I fix"[62]—but he was far more provocative than Haywood. Speaking on the common, his fist flailing, his trim goatee pointing at the crowd, Tresca shouted, "You must swear to fight every day, every minute of your lives, without truce or repose, for the liberation of Ettor and Giovannitti!" And ten thousand people, mostly Italian, shouted back, *"Giuriamo!"* ("We swear!")[63] The battle for the soul of Lawrence intensified. Taking it up con brio, Tresca also fought for the heart of Elizabeth Gurley Flynn. Though he had a wife and son back in New York, he was taken by this "'young, beautiful, and silver-tongued girl' who 'brought a great spiritual element into the battlefields.'"[64] Soon Carlo and "Elisabetta" were exchanging books of poetry and beginning an affair.[65] And by late September, the mood in Lawrence was agitated well beyond the control of two romantic revolutionaries.

Rumors of revenge again consumed Lawrence. A general strike was in the offing. No one knew how many would walk out, but Italians, at least, were fired up in support of their jailed comrades. Marshal Sullivan put extra police on duty. Fire hoses perched outside the largest mills. Another uprising was expected any day. Scorching hatred of the IWW burst forth in the press, the mills, and city hall, yet few recognized how little power the union now had over its minions. Ettor and Haywood had played strikers like a violin, moving them to march, picket, and sing. Tresca, however, was no virtuoso. He tried to maintain order, even getting Ettor and Giovannitti to write letters to workers opposing a general strike in their name. But one last outbreak erupted, one that hastened the demise of the IWW in Lawrence.

On September 27, the Friday before the trial, police squelched an uprising in the mills at pay time, flushing bobbin-throwing mobs outside and herding them across the river.[66] The following afternoon, IWW members overruled Tresca and Flynn to approve a one-day strike for Monday, when the trial would begin.[67] But more trouble flared when Tresca "fixed" another Sunday parade commemorating the eight-month anniversary of Anna LoPizzo's death. As police and marchers collided downtown, two cops were stabbed and several strikers clubbed. Police seized Tresca, but a flying wedge of workers freed him.[68] The mayhem resumed on Monday, making the one-day walkout so volatile that the IWW called it off without a vote lest "hotter heads" prevail and cause more trouble.[69] The havoc had been short-lived, yet to the embattled city, it was a return of exorcised demons. There was, however, a critical difference. During Sunday's march, no American flags were carried, and amid scores of red flags someone held a banner bearing the anarchist slogan "No God, No Master." No one chanted the words; most marchers never even saw them. Yet within a week, Lawrence would rise in righteous rebellion against this slogan. First, however, the trial that had heated Lawrence to its boiling point would finally begin.

Salem, Massachusetts, September 30, 1912, 8:30 a.m. In the city where twenty witches were executed in 1692, everything was ready for the trial the press was calling "second in importance in this country in modern times, perhaps in all time, only to that of the McNamara case."[70] Six additional phone lines and a dozen telegraphs, some linking the courtroom to England and Germany,[71] had been installed. One hundred and fifty witnesses and 350 potential jurors had been summoned. Hundreds of people milled outside the old Romanesque courthouse on the gold-leafed common. Then at precisely 8:45, a horse-drawn carriage pulled up.[72] Stepping from it, Ettor and Giovannitti, the former smiling, the latter waving one hand, walked past cheering crowds and up the steps. They were led into the courtroom, where the state had prepared seats for them—in a cage. A tall iron pen, open at the front, stood in the center of the room and the men sat on a hard bench inside it. Ettor took the indignity with his usual aplomb. Giovannitti used the cage as a metaphor in a poem.

> Like crippled eagles fallen were the three men in the cage, and like children who look into a well to behold the sky were the men that looked down upon them.[73]

The third man in the cage, Joseph Caruso, sat peering sadly through the bars. A lean, lanky mill worker, Caruso spoke little English. He seemed uncertain of why he was even there. Behind him, as she would be every day throughout the trial, was his wife, Rosa. Though her face was partially hidden by a shawl, her anguish was palpable to everyone in the courtroom. Each morning when her husband entered and each afternoon when he left, Rosa Caruso waved and held back tears. She was often seen pacing in front of the courthouse, holding her baby, born while the father was in jail facing the death penalty for conspiring to kill Anna LoPizzo.

Every aspect of the trial was ready except the jury. But in a case expected to last months, with death threats made to the judge and DA, threats to bomb the courtroom,[74] and rumors of ten thousand marching on the jail to tear it down "stone by stone,"[75] who would be willing to sit in judgment? On Monday and Tuesday, a steady succession of men was asked to forgo personal prejudices, judge solely on the facts, etc. Man after man found an excuse not to. Most said they had formed prejudicial opinions; others were opposed to capital punishment, too old, in frail health . . . One man even pleaded insomnia.[76] Judge John Quinn, a squat, bald man with a kindly face,[77] lectured the men about "civic duty" but to no avail. Those few ready to serve were challenged by the prosecution or defense. As a result, after just two days the trial adjourned, having exhausted its jury pool. Disheartened defendants went back to jail and in the ensuing recess, the city of Lawrence rose up as one against the affront of "No God, No Master."[78]

The phrase came from the French Revolution when *Ni Dieu, ni mâitre* was a battle cry at the barricades. The words had little to do with the IWW, whose members did not shun religion, yet in the wake of the latest violence, few in Lawrence cared to debate the differences between Syndicalism and anarchism. Because "No God, No Master" had been slipped into a parade led by Carlo Tresca, the slogan came to stand for everything Lawrence loathed about the IWW.

On Wednesday, October 2, as the trial in Salem ground to a halt, Mayor Scanlon issued an appeal "to the patriotic and law respecting people of Lawrence." He urged citizens to wear small flags in their lapels until Thanksgiving "as a rebuke to those detractors of our National Emblem who would dare carry the red flag of anarchy through our streets on the Lord's Day. Their creed is: 'No God, No Master.' Let ours be: 'For God and Country.'"[79] Simple, even simplistic on its face, Scanlon's was a benign tactic when compared to treatment of the IWW elsewhere. In its seven years of existence, the union had routinely faced vigilante crackdowns and wholesale abuse of members' rights. Wobblies entering strike-torn cities found public halls suddenly closed and free speech—theirs, at least—banned.[80] Jailed en masse, they were tortured with fire hoses,[81] beaten, and exiled by "shotgun brigades."[82] All that spring and summer, San Diego had seen the most savage suppression of an IWW "Free Speech" campaign to date. "Wobs" riding the rails toward the city to fight for their right to recruit members on the street were met by howling mobs, hammered with clubs and ax handles, and left to die in the desert. San Diego's vigilantes were still brutalizing Wobblies[83] when Mayor Scanlon's unique method of handling the IWW caught his city's fancy. What followed was the most spontaneous outburst of peacetime patriotism in American history.

Twenty-four hours after the mayor issued his appeal, Lawrence was festooned in red, white, and blue. Small flags sprouted in home and shop windows. Stars and Stripes flew from horse bridles, fire engines, automobile hoods, and hundreds more impromptu flag posts. Mill workers carried flags to work only to find entire mill rooms decked out in bunting. Stores ran out of free flags. The mayor, who had ordered twenty thousand, soon purchased thirty thousand more.[84] The *Lawrence Tribune* saw "the city ablaze in color,"[85] causing it to boast, "Lawrence has come back."[86] Patriotism swept the streets, becoming a convenient answer to social questions many no longer had the energy to consider. High school students gathered to sing "America," newspapers printed "The Pledge of Allegiance,"[87] and plans were made for a Columbus Day the city would never forget. Preparations were exhaustive. While most of New England rooted for the Red Sox in the World Series or followed the wild four-way presidential race—Taft, Roosevelt, Wilson, and Debs—Lawrence planned a parade. On Saturday, October 12, a cool, gray morning in the city, a star-spangled arch spanned Essex Street bearing a motto chosen by Father O'Reilly:

> **FOR GOD AND COUNTRY**
> **THE STARS AND STRIPES FOREVER. THE RED FLAG NEVER!**
> **A PROTEST AGAINST THE I.W.W.,**
> **ITS PRINCIPLES AND ITS METHODS.**[88]

The parade began at 9:00 a.m. sharp. For the next ninety minutes, downtown Lawrence resembled an Impressionist painting in red, white, and blue. Schoolchildren walked in formation,[89] waving flags. Mill workers followed in step, waving flags. Lodges, ladies' clubs, Boy Scout troops, church groups, German *Turn Vereine,* the Italian Columbus Society, the Syrian Drum Corps, the Irish American Club, various trade unions, whole militia companies— all stepped proudly, waving flags. Alderman Cornelius Lynch was one of many dressed as Uncle Sam,[90] while women costumed themselves as the Statue of Liberty. The parade seemed so all-inclusive that one wondered who would be left to watch it, yet twenty-five thousand cheered beneath decorated downtown facades. The only group not invited was the IWW. Even their buttons were banned, Mayor Scanlon having suggested that volunteers stand along the parade route "and whenever they see a man with an I.W.W. button on, yank him out."[91] The parade wasn't finished long before Mayor Scanlon began receiving telegrams from mayors throughout New England congratulating him on restoring his city's good name.[92]

Wobblies were more dismayed than discouraged. Haywood publicly disassociated the IWW from "No God, No Master," explaining that the slogan had been brought to Lawrence by marchers from Boston having no affiliation with the union. Wobblies spent Columbus Day at a picnic where Haywood somehow managed to win a fifty-yard dash, but many were frightened by what they saw as raw jingoism sweeping Lawrence. Even reputable businessmen now talked of taking matters into their own hands.[93] During a tumultuous city council meeting, Father O'Reilly had labeled the IWW a "band of pirates," adding "those who don't want to work had better take the hint and go."[94] A five-minute ovation followed. Judge Frederic Chandler suggested anarchists be expelled by any means necessary: "Those who have come here to our city to bring destruction should be ejected from our doors, if possible legally, but ejected."[95] Haywood was warned that a hit man had been hired to kill him.[96] Recalling the attempted murder of the IWW's James P. Thompson, Haywood sought a gun permit[97] and several other Wobblies asked Marshal Sullivan for protection.[98] None of these requests was granted, and the IWW soon lay low. Tresca led no more parades. Flynn spoke everywhere except in Lawrence, keeping such a hectic schedule that she was hospitalized with exhaustion.[99] By the time jury selection resumed in Salem, Wobblies were happy to have a distraction, even if they expected the trial to be another witch hunt.[100]

Each trial is an elaborate edifice of words—the word of one witness against another, the well-aimed words of lawyers, the final word, or two, of the verdict. But in the trial of Joseph Ettor and Arturo Giovannitti, words were more than a means to an end. A .38 caliber bullet had killed Anna LoPizzo. A fugitive assailant had allegedly fired it. But in the heat of a tumultuous strike, had words inflamed the murderer? In attempting to prove that a labor organizer and a poet, each a mile from the crime scene, were accessories to murder, the prosecution had one famous legal precedent. In 1887, seven Haymarket martyrs were sentenced to death in Chicago.[101] None was accused of throwing the bomb;[102] only their words—writings in anarchist journals—condemned them to the gallows. The verdict was highly controversial. When Illinois governor John P. Altgeld pardoned three living defendants, he was voted out of office.[103] Several years later, following the McKinley assassination, criminal anarchy laws in many states had further proscribed incendiary speech. Nonetheless, in charging Ettor and Giovannitti with a capital crime, prosecutors were entering little-known legal territory. Not for another seven years would Oliver Wendell Holmes famously rule that certain words—shouting "fire" in a crowded theater, for example—could constitute "a clear and present danger."[104] So on October 16, 1912, with Haymarket as its model, the prosecution began laying out its case. The six-count indictment charged Joseph Caruso and the vanished fourth man with the murder, alleging that Ettor and Giovannitti "did incite, procure, aid, counsel, hire, or command" the killing.[105] The defendants sat in their cage weighing every word of District Attorney Henry Atwill's opening statement.[106]

The jury, 12 men chosen from 506 questioned,[107] consisted entirely of laborers—four carpenters, a sailmaker, a grocer, a driver, a lamp maker, a stock fitter, two leather workers, and a hairdresser.[108] The first witness was Angelo Rocco, but his faulty memory—it seemed he could not remember when he had sent for Ettor nor recall ever seeing him at Franco-Belgian Hall—led prosecutors to seek more useful testimony.[109] Then for the next several days, policemen and reporters recapped the strike, describing Lawrence as the seedbed of anarchy. Ettor's first speech at city hall had led to the January 15 uprising—mobs, fire hoses, shots at the Pacific Mill. These graphic details were followed by scenes from the streetcar riot on January 29, with Ettor spotted all over the city. One officer's testimony, a reporter noted, contained as much action as a half dozen Jack London stories.[110] Jurors heard of women stripped to the waist,[111] passengers bloodied by flying glass, and of a trolley filled with terrorized children.[112] Policemen identified knives, guns, and a cartridge belt taken from strikers.[113] Leaving the city ripe for murder, the DA began to "connect up"[114] the violence with the men who had inspired it.

Certain words burned through the courtroom like lit fuses. "This town won't be very happy in two days," Ettor had predicted just before the stoning of streetcars. "Something is going to happen." He had promised that strikers would "keep the gun shops busy," claiming he would get a gun himself. He had compared the strike to the French Revolution, telling strikers stories of aristocrats hanging from lampposts with grass stuffed in their mouths.[115] And when American Woolen agents combed the tenements spreading the lie that the strike was over, Ettor had drafted a circular urging strikers to take these men and "throw them down the stairs, break their bones and leave them a permanent remembrance."[116] Giovannitti's comments seemed equally inflammatory. Two policemen testified to meeting him in a drugstore. Over hot chocolate, the cops told the poet that the violence had to stop.

"Who's going to stop it?" Giovannitti asked.

"You know perfectly well," Patrolman James Gallagher replied. "We'll have to."

"What the hell do you fellows amount to without your nightsticks and guns?" Giovannitti allegedly replied. Told he could not keep workers out of the mills, Giovannitti shot back, "The hell we can't! If they won't stay out, we'll break their goddamn heads!"[117] Later testimony quoted Giovannitti telling strikers to "prowl around like wild animals looking for the blood of the scabs."[118] Moving beyond speeches, the DA portrayed Ettor as an opportunist who had "rushed to Lawrence"[119] to swell the ranks of the IWW and Giovannitti as coming solely to boost circulation for *Il Proletario*. Both were clever, conniving men with a plan—to foster frightening violence, lull authorities with a false sense of calm, then let hell itself break loose to drive mill owners to the bargaining table.

Through the bars of their courtroom cage, the defendants' contrasting temperaments were etched in their faces. Giovannitti was ashen and nervous; many thought he looked ill.[120] Ettor remained confident, cocky, alert to every word,[121] especially during cross-examination. At first, defense lawyers contented themselves with verbal jousts, insisting that police and reporters call throngs of strikers "crowds," not "mobs." Then as evidence piled up, defense attorneys went on the attack. Had reporters ever supplied inside information to police or mill men? A few admitted they had. Had undercover detectives—several shown to have criminal records—caused the streetcar riot?

"So far as you know," one defense attorney asked a witness about the rioters, "they may have been imported thugs brought to this city at that time?"

The witness, an electrician in the Pacific Mill, agreed.[122] Later, one detective admitted he had been hired by the Essex Savings Bank.[123] The defense then turned to the Italian detective who had quoted Giovannitti's "prowl" speech on the common. Paid fifteen dollars a day to go to "a strange city . . . to fish my way around and see if there was anything," Eugenio Bencordo had gone undercover at strikers' meetings, taking notes. But to protect his family, he had burned those notes.[124] And when Ettor's attorney gave him an Italian test, Bencordo flunked. He defined *giro* (a trip or turn) as "carcass," and translated the incendiary "break their bones" circular into a muddle.[125] Several of Bencordo's other translations caused Ettor and Giovannitti to chuckle.[126] The detective also failed a spelling test, misspelling "develop" and "soldiers."[127] Asked when he had finally left Lawrence, Bencordo replied, "February 31."[128]

After two weeks and nearly seventy-five witnesses, the DA drew the court's attention to a large map hanging above the door to the left of the judge.[129] Posting a map of Union and Garden streets was deemed wiser than taking the jury to the scene of the crime, given the ugly mood in Lawrence. Using the map, the death of Anna LoPizzo was explained with long pointers noting where the "mob" (or "crowd") had gathered, where the police and militia had been, and where the woman had fallen. The dark, riotous evening was replayed again and again, developing before the jurors like a blurred photograph of forensic evidence. Several witnesses pinned Joseph Caruso to the scene.[130] Fifteen shots were fired.[131] No, twenty. No, thirty![132] Just as the DA was about to play his ace, however, a juror's illness forced a postponement.[133] The short break slackened the tension and gave Wobblies back in Lawrence a chance to bury one last victim of the city's inexhaustible rancor.

Threats and exhortations aside, no pack of vigilantes had "ejected" Wobblies from Lawrence, yet in the fervor of "For God and Country," hatred of the IWW festered. Two days after the flag-waving parade, Wobblies were fined for passing out leaflets downtown.[134] Street fights broke out when patriots tried to tear IWW buttons off members' chests.[135] Then on Saturday night, October 19, Jonas Smolskas, a Lithuanian immigrant working in the Arlington Mill, left his home to get a beer. When he entered Ryan's Saloon, someone pointed him out as "one of them damned IWW bastards." A short, stocky man approached Smolskas and asked why he wasn't wearing an American flag like everyone else in Lawrence.[136] Smolskas left the saloon but was followed into his own backyard. There he was knocked to the ground and hit his head on a rock. Out cold for ninety minutes, he was revived and taken to the hospital.[137] He died three days later. Police arrested a local boxer and rumors circulated that one Irish gang or another was involved. The following Saturday police broke up Smolskas's funeral procession. Haywood herded a crowd to opposing sidewalks and led them to the cemetery, where a thousand mourners laid white flowers on the grave of yet another martyr.[138]

When the trial resumed, so did the unfolding murder. A *Boston Post* reporter told of standing just a few feet from Officer Oscar Benoit. As the reporter watched, a hand gripping a revolver rose and aimed at the policeman. The reporter could have grabbed the hand. He regretted that he hadn't.[139] Frozen with fear, he saw a tall Italian fire over the shoulder of another man directly at Benoit. Seconds later, a woman on the far corner collapsed.[140] Officer Benoit then testified to seeing a flash so near it almost burned his face.[141] Two ballistics experts asserted that the fatal bullet was of a foreign make, perhaps French or Italian,[142] and could not have been fired from an American policeman's revolver.[143] The DA had re-created the crime and the words that inspired it. That left only the motive.

Judge Quinn—a novice on the bench to which Governor Foss had appointed him just eight months before[144]—had so far been unpredictable in admitting evidence. Early on, he had excluded the prosecution's questioning about IWW politics.[145] But he also dismissed the defense's frequent attempts to mention workers' wages[146] and the beating of women at the depot.[147] He first excluded but then allowed letters found on Ettor urging strikers to "break into jail and make the county feed them."[148] So when the DA introduced a little red booklet, defense attorneys could only hope it might be ruled inadmissible. The IWW pamphlet had not been found in Ettor's possession, they argued. There was no evidence that any strikers had seen it, let alone those at the scene of the murder. But the little red book came from a building frequented by strikers, and after a half hour of wrangling, it was admitted. The philosophy of the nation's most radical union began to be read aloud in the sonorous, Beacon Hill accent of the district attorney. Beginning with the preamble on the coming class war, DA Atwill read for the rest of one afternoon,[149] then resumed the next morning. Jurors were seen fighting sleep, but spectators were startled by the IWW's warring words: "All peace, so long as the wage system lasts, is but an armed truce." "Failing to force concessions from the employers by the strike, work is resumed and sabotage is used." "For every striker killed by a Cossack, the life of a Cossack would be exacted."[150] After reading the entire booklet, the DA entered one last piece of evidence—a bullet with a sliver of bone attached to it.[151] The bone came from a woman's shoulder shattered by a shot that words had allegedly provoked. The prosecution rested.[152]

In the fall of 1912, a defense fund of fifty thousand dollars bought some first-rate legal talent. It could have purchased the services of Clarence Darrow had he not spent the summer defending himself on charges of bribing a juror in the McNamara dynamiting case.[153] Instead, each defendant had his own estimable attorney. Ettor's was John P. S. Mahoney, a Lawrence lawyer who had represented strikers all year. Giovannitti's was W. Scott Peters, a former DA nicknamed "the fox of the courtroom." Caruso had a well-respected former judge from Lynn,[154] and the team was advised by three more attorneys, including Fred Moore,[155] who had worked with Darrow at the McNamara trial[156] and would later defend Sacco and Vanzetti.[157] On November 1, these men began the last-ditch effort that would either crown the great textile strike or send its leaders to death row.

Giovannitti had said little during his ten days on the street in Lawrence, but it was easy to find witnesses who recalled the words of Joseph Ettor. When they began to testify, the trial that had so far seen mostly Irish or American witnesses now took on an ethnic slant. A goulash of accents[158] filled the courtroom as young girls, boys in knickers, and seasoned mill workers took the witness stand.[159] Each said much the same thing. Ettor had counseled peace. "It was the same all the time," an Arlington Mill worker said. "Keep your hands in your pockets."[160] Ettor's notorious quotes were explained. Yes, he had said strikers should "keep the gun shops busy," testified Annie Welzenbach, but the comment had been a joke, uttered after Ettor had arranged a protest over gun permits given to scabs. When Ettor said he was going to get a gun, Welzenbach had laughed and chimed in, "Me, too!"[161]

The prosecution had reporters on its side; so did the defense. Gertrude Marvin had covered the strike for the *Boston American* until her editor tore up her flattering profile of Haywood, saying "that big two-fisted thug has put it all over you!" Marvin had quit the Hearst paper to write publicity for strikers.[162] Now reporting for the *New York Sun,* she shared Ettor's comments on violence. "He told of incidents of violence in other strikes and said they had 'had it handed to them' so many times that the policy of peace had grown," Marvin said. She and other witnesses explained Ettor's comment, "This town won't be very happy in two days." He had been expecting an impending gas and electrical workers' strike to plunge the city into darkness. Witnesses told of seeing Ettor on January 29 steering crowds *away* from mills and militia. Defense lawyers even tapped the authority of William Wood, with witnesses recalling that Wood, upon first meeting Ettor, had congratulated the "little general" on how well he had controlled crowds. Further testimony asserted that Giovannitti had not told strikers to "prowl around like wild animals" but had cautioned them to watch out because "the soldiers are like wild animals."[163] The DA tried to discredit each witness as a loyal Wobbly recruited by Haywood and coached by Angelo Rocco. He even claimed Annie Welzenbach had been seen kissing Ettor, which Welzenbach vehemently denied.[164] The trial dragged on into its fifth week.

On November 9, the distraught woman so many had noticed in the courtroom offered another snapshot of the murder. In halting Italian, Rosa Caruso told the court that her husband had been home eating dinner—pigs' feet and beans—at 5:30 that evening. She even held out a handful of beans to show the judge. The Carusos had heard shots but did not go outside.[165] Caruso and his landlord corroborated the testimony.[166] Witnesses testified to seeing Officer Benoit shoot Anna LoPizzo. And then, just when exhausted jurors and journalists were expecting the trial to last several additional weeks, the defense announced it would call only a few more witnesses. First among them would be Joseph Ettor.

With his dimples showing as clearly as his innate intelligence, Ettor on the witness stand "was an exhibition worth going a long way to hear,"[167] the *Boston Globe* wrote. Testifying for seven hours, Ettor amazed reporters with a verbatim memory of his own speeches that exactly matched their notes. Jousting with DA Atwill, he explained the differences between Syndicalism and anarchism. He denied ever seeing the "broken bones" circular and chilled the courtroom with a firsthand account revealing how narrowly the strike had avoided a slaughter. One day, when militia had halted paraders, a newspaper photographer had tried to break the standoff by shouting "Fire!" "It was only by a miracle," Ettor said, "that there wasn't a massacre right there."[168] Following Ettor, Giovannitti also impressed the court with his unique blend of aristocratic manners and radical politics. "A gentleman's word is as good as that of twenty-five policemen," he told the DA.[169] He described his long speech on the common as "half a speech, half a sermon," and remembered the conversation with the policemen in the drugstore but insisted that they, not he, had spoken of breaking heads.

The day after Giovannitti's testimony, the defense rested. Lawyers summed up their cases, leaving twelve workingmen to decide which strike Ettor and Giovannitti had led. Had it been the strike portrayed by the prosecution—anarchic, incendiary, carefully crafted as the spark of a workers' revolution? Or had it been a peaceful, even inspiring strike, its only violence triggered by militia, cops, and provocateurs? In the words of both prosecution and defense, each version seemed credible. Something had caused a peaceful city to explode. A woman was dead. Someone had to be responsible.

On Saturday, November 23, as snow flurries fell outside,[170] the grueling trial neared a close. A packed courtroom considered it all over except the verdict when one final surprise emerged. Joseph Ettor wanted to address the jury. It was a calculated risk, one taken against the advice of his lawyers.[171] If Ettor proved a master of persuasion, would it not suggest how his oratory might have stirred strikers to violence? On the other hand, if his speech was too radical, he might lose any sympathy his defense team had engendered. The courtroom fell silent. The judge sat serenely behind his bench. The jury, often inattentive during the repetitive testimony, was riveted on the cage and the man standing deep inside it.[172] Pasty-faced and quivering,[173] Ettor began.

"For my part, I have not been tried on my acts," he stated. "I have been tried here because of my social ideals." He then summed up those ideals in a sentence. They had nothing to do with strikes or two hours' pay. "All wealth is the product of labor," Ettor said, "and all wealth being the product of labor belongs to labor and to no one else."[174] Such an idea might seem radical, he admitted, yet so had the antislavery ideals of abolitionists in Massachusetts only sixty years before. But no matter how unpopular, ideas could not be "choked." Turning to the DA, Ettor cited the examples of Spartacus and Christ, asking, "Does Mr. Atwill believe for a moment that . . . the cross or the gallows or the guillotine, the hangman's noose, ever settled an idea? It never did. If the idea can live, it lives because history adjudges it right. And what has been considered an idea constituting a social crime in one age has in the next age become the religion of humanity."[175] Ettor complained that his speeches had been taken out of context. Hadn't Mayor Scanlon said, "We will either break this strike or break the strikers' heads!" he asked, and was that not an incendiary speech?[176] His voice rising to a crescendo, Ettor insisted he had come to Lawrence solely to help strikers. "Since I was a boy and I could lift my voice for the cause that I thought right, I did. . . . And as I have gone along I have raised my voice on behalf of men, women and children who work in the mines, who work in the mills and who work in the factories of this country, who daily offer their labor and their blood and even their lives in order to make the prosperity of this country. I have carried the flag along . . . I carry it here today, gentlemen; the flag of liberty is here." As Ettor spoke, Giovannitti whispered, "Say it for both," causing Ettor to switch to the plural voice. "The flag that we have carried along and are carrying along—if we have to drop it in the ditch, we will drop it. Gentlemen, I make no threat, but on the moment that we drop the flag because we have been loyal to our calls, hundreds of thousands of wage workers will pick up the flag of labor and carry it forward and cheer it on and sing its song until the flag of the working class shall wave freely and unfurled to the wind over the workshops of the world where free men and women will work and enjoy fully and without trammel the full products of their labor."[177] Offering neither apology nor excuse, asking no favors, Ettor concluded by urging the jury to render justice. He thanked the court and sat.

Judge Quinn then asked, "Do the other defendants wish to address the jury?" Giovannitti stood.

His head held high, his voice calm and assured, Giovannitti looked out at the jury that would decide his fate. In the last dozen years he had come down from the mountains of the Abruzzi and across the Atlantic, through mines and churches, seminary and Socialist circles to arrive in the cage where he stood. Now he called on his own words to save him from execution. It was, he said, "the first time in my life that I speak publicly in your wonderful language, and it is the most solemn moment in my life." He did not know if he would be able to finish, given "the tumult that is going on in my soul." But he began. The jury had seen only one side of "this great industrial question," Giovannitti said. They had seen only methods and tactics. "But what about, I say, the ethical part of this question? . . . What about the better and nobler humanity where there shall be no more slaves, where no man will ever be obliged to go on strike in order to obtain fifty cents a week more, where children will not have to starve any more. . . . It may be, gentlemen of the jury, that you do not believe in that. It may be that we are dreamers. It may be that we are fanatics." But if so, he added, then "so was Socrates a fanatic . . . and so was Jesus Christ a fanatic, who instead of acknowledging that Pilate, or that Tiberius was emperor of Rome . . . preferred the cross between two thieves." Giovannitti then turned to what the DA had called "the New England tradition." Did the prosecutor mean the tradition "of this same town where they used to burn the witches at the stake or . . . the New England traditions of those men who refused to be any longer under the iron heel of the British aristocracy and dumped the tea into Boston Harbor and fired the first musket that was announcing to the world for the first time that a new era had been established?"[178] Each member of the jury had to answer that question, the poet said, but no verdict could stop the progress of humanity. "It is not your verdict that will put a dam before this mighty rush of waves that go forward. It is not the little insignificant cheap life of Arturo Giovannitti offered in holocaust to warm the hearts of the millionaire manufacturers of this town that is going to stop Socialism."[179]

The violence in Lawrence was the fault of neither him nor Ettor, Giovannitti said, but of a system that enabled employers to own a worker's tools, home, and factory, hence own his mind, body, heart, and soul. But now that jurors had seen both him and his "noble comrade" speak, Giovannitti asked, "do you believe for one single moment that we ever preached violence, that a man like me as I stand with my naked heart before you . . . could kill a human being? . . . Gentlemen, if you think that there has ever been a spark of malice in my heart, that I ever said others should break heads and prowl around and look for blood . . . then send me to the chair because it is right and just." Giovannitti then turned to Caruso, sitting silently beside him, not understanding a word. Convinced of his comrade's innocence, he begged the jury to "consider this poor man and his wife. . . ."

As Giovannitti went on, some onlookers and a few journalists brushed back tears.[180] But rather than being unable to finish as he had feared, the poet crafted his words into an impassioned eulogy to life itself. "I am twenty-nine years old," he said. "I have a woman that loves me and that I love. I have a mother and a father that are waiting for me. I have an ideal that is dearer to me than can be expressed or understood. And life has so many allurements and it is so nice and bright and so wonderful that I feel the passion of living in my heart." Willing to be neither a martyr nor a hero, Giovannitti wanted solely to help workers, and he promised to continue his calling. If allowed to go free, he said, "Let me tell you that the first strike that breaks again in this Commonwealth or any other place in America where the work and the help and the intelligence of Joseph J. Ettor and Arturo Giovannitti will be needed and necessary, there we shall go again regardless of any fear and of any threat. We shall return again to our humble efforts, obscure, humble, unknown, misunderstood—soldiers of this mighty army of the working class of the world, which out of the shadows and the darkness of the past is striving towards the destined goal which is the emancipation of human kind, which is the establishment of love and brotherhood and justice for every man and every woman in this earth." Yet if he were convicted and condemned, then "tomorrow we shall go from your presence into a presence where history shall give its last word to us. Whichever way you judge, gentlemen of the jury, I thank you."[181]

Leaving the courtroom moved and motionless, with some onlookers sobbing,[182] Giovannitti finished at 1:50 p.m. Judge Quinn spent the rest of Saturday instructing the jury, then resumed on Monday morning. Shortly after noon, the wait began. Rosa Caruso, with a rosary in her hand, began pacing the sidewalk in front of the courthouse, crying and praying.[183] All afternoon, she walked, joined by hundreds of mill workers.[184] As the sky darkened, a full moon rose over the city. Then suddenly at 6:40 p.m., the jury announced it had reached a decision. Judge Quinn, fearing violence to jurors sent out into the night, insisted the verdict wait until morning. Like Giovannitti's "Walker," Rosa Caruso paced all evening until her husband's interpreter persuaded her to go home. Early the next morning, crowds gathered again outside the courthouse. Finally at 8:20 a.m., court was convened. The defendants, each wearing a red carnation,[185] stood and faced the jury. First Caruso, then Ettor, then Giovannitti raised one hand and stood, ready for the verdict. For all three, it was the same—not guilty.[186]

Within seconds, the courtroom erupted in joy. Smiling, slapping each other's backs, the defendants thanked the jury, Ettor on behalf of "the working class of America," Giovannitti "in the name of justice, truth, and civilization."[187] Caruso, through his interpreter, simply wished to offer thanks and say "that he didn't do it."[188] As the jury filed out, one member said, "If they had taken 1,000 American people and used them the way they did the Italians in Lawrence, there wouldn't be a mill standing there today."[189] Back in the courtroom, the three men were released from the cage. Stepping into freedom, they were smothered with kisses. "Where is Gurley?" Ettor asked as they walked toward the door,[190] and Flynn emerged from the crowd to hug her friend for a long, long time. Caruso and his wife danced like children, and a crowd, many singing "The Marseillaise,"[191] made its way into the street past jubilant mill workers. After a brief party at a local Salvation Army headquarters, the defendants went their separate ways. The Carusos disappeared from history. They were last said to be considering a return to Italy.[192] Ettor said he would travel to Tacoma, Washington, where his father had suffered a stroke. Giovannitti thought he might stay in New England awhile. Having gotten to know only its "cops and detectives," he hoped to "get acquainted with its gentlemen."[193] That afternoon, a telegram from local IWW headquarters promised "to keep the red flag flying in Lawrence." But at 7:00 p.m., when a triumphant crowd met Ettor and Giovannitti at the depot, police broke up a parade, splitting the marching bands from the masses and scattering the ten thousand.[194]

Two days later was Thanksgiving. At 7:00 a.m., noon, and 6:00 p.m., bells rang throughout Lawrence[195] marking the end of Mayor Scanlon's "For God and Country" protest. That afternoon, denied a parade permit,[196] Ettor addressed a huge crowd gathered in a vacant lot. He spoke for ninety minutes, telling workers that the day's thanks should be offered "to you who are good enough to go hungry in order that the bosses may eat." Noting flags all over the city, he added, "This talk of patriotism is a sham and a humbug. The dream of labor is the constant nightmare of the capitalist crew of the world. We need no guns, we need no dynamite to advance our cause, for when we stop work, the capitalist class will starve. When we labor the world goes on." Ettor accepted flowers,[197] then left the city he had come to ten months earlier and headed off to see his father, then home to Brooklyn to find another strike that needed him.

Come evening, citizens held mass meetings throughout the city. Crowds sang "America" and "The Star-Spangled Banner," then settled in to listen to long speeches denouncing anarchy, praising the city's resolve, and urging locals to reach out to immigrants. "The new arrivals are sensitive, as we should learn if we knew them," said a Massachusetts Supreme Court judge who lived in Lawrence. "It is part of wisdom for us to know them as well as to have them know us."[198] And then, after prayers and parting, the people of Lawrence headed home in the waning hours of the holiday. With another winter coming on, many gave thanks that the city's ordeal—the mobs and parades, dynamite and death, rage and resistance, the nationwide notoriety, the long trial and its ultimate acquittal—was finally over. Dawn would bring another workday.

Epilogue

Growing up in Lawrence was a difficult situation. I wouldn't want to go through it again. Oh, God no. We were a developing community, sixty-two different languages and dialects. We were all groping and . . . we had to learn that we were all human. It was a long road, but we've got a history that, when you get it down to a capsule, you've got America.

—Unidentified Lawrence resident[1]

For those raised within earshot of their whistles and drawn by need through their gates, it was never easy to leave the mills. Like some hellish home that is home nonetheless, the mills were always there, ready to take a wayward worker back into the fold. Their predictable grind and steady paychecks kept tens of thousands toiling there for decades and many, looking back with nostalgia, said they were happy to have the work.[2] Others came and went, trying to find better jobs, failing, returning again to the music of the power loom.

When the long year of strike and trial was finally over, the workers of Lawrence trudged on into the future for which they had risked so much. On January 12, 1913, the IWW held anniversary celebrations in Lawrence. It was a Sunday, frigid as usual, but three halls were filled with people eager to welcome back Joseph Ettor. As during the strike, Ettor was all over Lawrence that day, speaking to Italians in the morning, IWW Local 20 in the afternoon, Armenians at night. Everyone wanted to hear Ettor reminisce, but he spoke about his newest strike, one he was running for hotel employees in Manhattan. The Franco-Belgian band and the Italian banjo and mandolin club played, a German glee club sang, and the anniversary was duly noted.[3] But to many, the events of a year earlier—the rage, the struggle, the solidarity—were distant memories. And such memories were even more distant the following morning when dawn broke, whistles screeched, and twenty-eight thousand walked into the mills for another fifty-four-hour week.

But Lawrence was then, as it is now, a city facing forward. As they had in the wake of the Pemberton Mill collapse, the 1890 cyclone, and numerous other calamities, the people of Lawrence sought solace and forgetting in their work. The work continued for the next two decades, when Lawrence thrived as an industrial center. Essex Street blossomed with new department stores, a sparkling theater district, the blare of jazz and big bands, and the roar of automobiles. Lodges and clubs personalized the city, and whenever mill work seemed long and the pay lousy, old-timers recalled that hours had once been much longer, pay much less. And winters had been worse, too.

Lawrence went on, but there would be no more anniversaries of the strike. For a decade after the uprising, further agitation stirred the city. There were dozens of small strikes[4] and two even longer than the 1912 walkout. Union organizers, Socialists, and Communists continued to see Lawrence as fertile ground, bashing heads with mill owners and city officials determined to live down the notoriety of 1912. The shock and shame of that year were felt at all levels. One schoolteacher even had her students write to pen pals across America to tell them something good about Lawrence.[5] The city's spirits were revived by a modest prosperity, the need to face new tragedies—in 1913 eleven boys drowned when a boathouse runway collapsed[6]—and the patriotism fostered by World War I. There was a job to do; there was a war to win. But another key factor was denial.

The citizens' association version of the strike soon became the only version mentioned in Lawrence. Those who accepted this story could not see the strike for what it was—a spontaneous outburst caused by bone-poor conditions among people desperate enough to listen to any leader. Instead of a communal culpability, the people of Lawrence, like many southerners during the civil rights movement, blamed the press, the public, and, above all, outsiders. No matter how much Lawrence might have sympathized with downtrodden workers, it could never forgive their sin of inviting the IWW to the city. The red shirts of radicalism made an easy target, especially during the Red Scare that followed the Bolshevik Revolution. In hindsight, the strikers became a raging mob. The IWW, though its most violent cry was "throw them down the stairs!," became incendiary anarchists, and the militia became saviors of law and order. Anyone who disagreed had clearly been gulled by the sensationalist press. There had been no women beaten at the depot, no hunger, no overwork, no discontent. "Lawrence was all right until Ettor and Haywood came," one man said.[7] Propped on pedestals of denial, Lawrence went on, secure that it had flushed out subversion and was again the home of contented workers. But were workers content? "It was a victory, sure, but what did we really get?" asked Antonietta Capriola in 1981. "So much misery, so much . . . so much hope. My brother he still die the next year. We are still hungry."[8]

As its first anniversary suggested, the IWW remained a force in Lawrence into the winter of 1913. Local membership peaked at sixteen thousand,[9] yet once the trial ended, Ettor, Giovannitti, Haywood, and Flynn were nowhere to be found. In January, prosecutors dropped all charges against Haywood and other strike leaders,[10] but Lawrence had brought them national fame and they meant to use it. Beckoned to run strikes all over the country, the IWW saw its dream about to come true. Its comeuppance came quickly.

Just as generals are prone to fight "the last war," the IWW saw Paterson, New Jersey, as another Lawrence. The silk mill strike there in February 1913 had all the familiar trappings—twenty-five thousand disgruntled workers, a wealth of nationalities, a city besieged. But Paterson's police were far more brutal than the Massachusetts militia, arresting five thousand and firing into an unarmed crowd.[11] Mill owners, learning from mistakes in Lawrence, were wiser. The strike dragged on. Come June, desperate for funds and publicity, the IWW pulled another tactic from its bag of tricks, turning the strike into theater. On June 7, fifteen thousand filled Madison Square Garden to see "The Paterson Strike Pageant." With a backdrop of monstrous mills painted by the noted artist John Sloan and a script written by strikers and journalist John Reed, the pageant replayed the strike onstage. Bringing their own lives across the Hudson River to a New York audience, strikers acted their parts well. They stormed out of the mills, picketed, and roused the audience to its feet. As theater, the strike got rave reviews—"a spectacular production," "a new art form"[12]—but as a fund-raiser it was a debacle, losing almost two thousand dollars and crippling the strike itself. In July, after twenty-two weeks of surviving on a single daily meal, strikers went back to work.[13] IWW tactics had been the same as in Lawrence—children were even sent out of town—yet critics said the union had bungled the strike. The IWW never waged another textile strike nor any other action in the East.[14]

Meanwhile, in Lawrence, the IWW "slowly bled to death," as Flynn recalled.[15] "Most of us were wonderful agitators but poor union organizers," she admitted.[16] Left to organize themselves, sixteen thousand Wobblies splintered into ethnic branches.[17] Divided, they were no match for mill owners. Recriminations that began shortly after the strike—spies, firings, blacklists—took their toll. By the summer of 1913, only seven hundred workers in Lawrence would admit to being Wobblies.[18] The names of these diehards were circulated among mill owners. One blacklist, neatly typed and dated December 14, 1914, singled out seventeen active IWW members. The IWW, noted the list's anonymous compiler, "is now at a complete standstill both in membership and in a financial way. It would have gone out of existence months ago but for the unceasing activity of these men."[19]

Driven out of Lawrence, defeated in Paterson, the IWW soldiered on elsewhere, but internal rifts widened. Haywood's insistence on "direct action" angered cautious Socialists while his brashness—"And I believe in sabotage, that much misunderstood word"[20]—further divided the left. In 1914, Ettor denounced "wild-eyed statements" that helped courts prosecute "alleged 'violent' acts of dozens of our fellow-workers, putting them away in jail to rot."[21] Ettor came once more to Lawrence when, in May 1916, strikers at the Pacific Mill invited him to lead them.[22] This time police were ready. After trailing him around the city, they burst into his room at the Needham Hotel at 5:30 a.m., took him to the depot, and put him on the next train to Boston. "I shall do all in my power to keep him out," the commissioner of public safety said. "We shall get him if he persists in coming to Lawrence."[23] Ettor hired a lawyer,[24] charging police with kidnapping and assault,[25] but Judge Mahoney dismissed the case.[26] After a few brief clandestine visits, "Smiling Joe" never returned. Later that year, he and Haywood had a final falling-out. Following a brutal strike in the iron mines of Minnesota's Mesabi Range, Ettor brokered a plea bargain for two

Wobblies charged with murder.[27] Haywood lashed out, saying the IWW wouldn't have let Ettor plead guilty in Lawrence, "not even for spitting on the sidewalk."[28] Furious, Ettor resigned from the union.[29] Having inherited ten thousand dollars when his father died,[30] he turned from organizing labor to organizing his own wine business in Southern California.[31] He still wrote occasionally for labor publications, but not even time, which saw the Labor movement win major advances—the minimum wage, the industrial unionism of the CIO, the eight-hour day—could douse his fire. In 1945, Ettor penned a four-part article for *Industrial Worker* on the history of American Syndicalism. Though Wobblies were by then mostly a nostalgic memory, Ettor concluded, "To try and try again will show that the I.W.W. is still worthy of its traditions and inheritance."[32] Joseph Ettor died in 1948, forgotten by all but those who remembered the strike in Lawrence. No obituaries ran in any major newspapers.[33]

Like Ettor, Arturo Giovannitti spent only a few more years in IWW circles. Emerging from jail with nationwide fame, he published a volume of poems in 1914. In her introduction, Helen Keller wrote: "Giovannitti is, like Shelley, a poet of revolt against the cruelty, the poverty, the ignorance which too many of us accept."[34] Giovannitti was hailed as Socialism's poetic prophet,[35] yet ten months in jail facing execution left him weary of "direct action." Though he made token appearances in Paterson and Lawrence,[36] he devoted himself to poetry, editing radical journals, and protesting World War I, which claimed two of his brothers. He spoke frequently in defense of Sacco and Vanzetti, and in 1922, he lent his talents to the International Ladies' Garment Workers' Union, heading its education department. For the next three decades, he addressed labor rallies in New York, charming crowds with his Vandyke beard, Lord Byron collar, and flowery Italian and English.[37] But as the workers' revolution became an evanescent dream, Giovannitti sank into depression. In 1950, he was stricken by a paralysis in his legs. He remained bedridden in his home in the Bronx until his death on New Year's Eve in 1959.[38]

Elizabeth Gurley Flynn also bolted from the IWW after the Mesabi strike. She continued her liaison with Carlo Tresca until learning that he had fathered a child with her own sister.[39] Betrayed, "the Rebel Girl" became an even more rebellious woman. "I spoke at the funerals of men and women shot down on the picket line and the iron entered my soul," she wrote.[40] The iron kept her at podiums rallying for Sacco and Vanzetti and antifascist forces during the Spanish Civil War,[41] but the iron also hardened her convictions, blinding her to tyranny in its many guises. Against the advice of Tresca and Giovannitti, Flynn joined the Communist Party in the 1930s.[42] Unlike all but a handful of the party's eighty thousand Depression-era members,[43] she never left. Instead, she became a committed party leader. Blinkered by red-tinted glasses, she refused to admit that the Soviet Union was a totalitarian state,[44] a dogma that led to her ouster from the American Civil Liberties Union, which she had helped to found.[45] In 1952, as the cold war infused iron into American politics, she was charged with advocating the violent overthrow of the government.[46] She defended herself in a nine-month trial and was found guilty. At the age of sixty-four, afflicted with arthritis and high blood pressure,[47] Flynn commenced twenty-eight months in a maximum-security prison. Released in 1957, she remained a Communist even after Nikita Khrushchev shocked the world with revelations of Stalin's tyranny. In 1961, she became chairman of the American Communist Party, which by then had fewer than three thousand members.[48] Flynn spent her last few years speaking—and being denied the right to speak—on American campuses and making junkets to the Soviet Union.[49] As she had in Lawrence, "Gurley" cut quite a figure, a bespectacled, grandmotherly woman[50] sitting at meetings beside Khrushchev, Ho Chi Minh, and Che Guevara. Viewing the Soviet Union through her lifelong struggle against capitalism, she saw nothing that could not be corrected with a little effort. Moscow, she said, reminded her of San Francisco.[51] While on another junket in 1964, Elizabeth Gurley Flynn died in a Soviet hospital. Half her ashes were buried beneath the Kremlin wall, the other half flown back to Chicago where they rested beside those of Big Bill Haywood.[52]

When others had gone their separate ways, Haywood remained loyal to the IWW. After being recalled from the union's board for his reckless statements, he returned in 1916 to mastermind a membership campaign that quadrupled the Wobblies' ranks.[53] But the resurgence came at a cost. First, Haywood saw his friend Joe Hill executed by a Utah firing squad for a murder he did not commit. Dozens of other friends were jailed or beaten as America prepared to enter World War I. During the summer of 1917, soldiers and sailors suspecting Wobblies to be bankrolled by "German gold"[54] ransacked IWW headquarters nationwide.[55] The press fanned the frenzy, branding the IWW as "worse than Germans" (*San Francisco Chronicle*), advocating "Kill them, just as you would kill any other kind of snake" (*Tulsa Daily World*).[56] With America at war, patriots felt they no longer had to tolerate traitors like Bill Haywood. That summer two thousand deputized citizens in Bisbee, Arizona, herded striking copper miners and their IWW leaders onto boxcars and dumped them in the scorching desert across the New Mexico border.[57] In Butte, Montana, Wobbly leader Frank Little was dragged from his jail cell and lynched on a railroad trestle, with a note pinned to his body threatening the same to other "I.W.W.s."[58] Then the federal government took over.

Two months after declaring war, Congress passed the Espionage Act prohibiting the slightest hindrance of the nation's war effort.[59] Socialist publications were banned, Eugene Debs, Emma Goldman, and dozens of others were arrested for speaking against the war, and the Wobblies were crushed. The IWW, President Wilson told his attorney general, "certainly are worthy of being suppressed,"[60] and on September 5, 1917, the suppression went into high gear. Federal agents swarmed through the IWW's Chicago headquarters like "a cloud of Kansas grasshoppers on a field of wheat," Haywood recalled.[61] For three days, agents removed file cabinets, membership lists, paper clips, even the ashes of Joe Hill. Three weeks later, they returned with arrest warrants for 166 Wobblies, including Haywood, Flynn, Ettor, and Giovannitti. The latter three bargained and won separate trials, which were dismissed. But Haywood, placing his faith in a judicial system that had vindicated him in Idaho and Lawrence, dutifully reported to Chicago to be booked and jailed.

The following summer, more than 150 Wobblies were tried on charges ranging from sedition to conspiring to overthrow the government. Prosecutors read mountains of IWW literature aloud to an often-bored jury while defendants told of hard labor and harder lives. In the docket, Haywood contrasted the suffering in textile towns with the mansions of mill owners.[62] After deliberating an hour, the jury found all defendants—except for a few dismissed on technicalities—guilty. Judge Kenesaw Mountain Landis, later the first commissioner of baseball, sentenced them to an aggregate 807 years and fines totaling $2.4 million.[63] Haywood went to Leavenworth for what figured to be the rest of his life. Jail taxed his health.

Though not yet fifty, he had the rotting teeth and ulcers of a much older man, and he developed diabetes that weakened his one eye.[64] Filing an appeal, Haywood was released on bond in 1919, just in time for the Red Scare.

The panic had begun when thirty May Day bombs were mailed to politicians, judges, and industrialists, including William Wood. (Only one went off, blowing the hands off a senator's maid.)[65] That fall, the scare culminated in the infamous Palmer Raids. Some four thousand people,[66] including fifteen in Lawrence,[67] were arrested. To the delight of the public and press, nearly 250 were deported without trial.[68] In this climate, Haywood's appeal stood no chance. He was contemplating life in prison when a Soviet agent offered him an escape. On March 31, 1921, Haywood used a false passport to slip aboard a ship bound for the Soviet Union.[69] Passing the Statue of Liberty, he said, "Goodbye, You've had your back turned on me for too long. I am going to the land of freedom."[70] Hailed as a hero in Moscow, Haywood was nonetheless miserable. As Flynn later wrote: "He longed for the land of baseball and burlesque, big steaks and cigars, cowboys and rodeos, strikes and picket lines, to see the Mississippi and the Rocky Mountains."[71] In 1928, when an American reporter visited him in his small Moscow apartment, Haywood asked, "Do you think I can ever get back? Do you think that guy Coolidge would pass me through. . . . I'd like to die back in the United States. I've done a lot of fighting back there, but I'm an old man now, and I'd like to get back."[72] But that spring he suffered a stroke, then another. He died in May. Like Flynn's, half his ashes were interred beneath the Kremlin wall, the other half shipped to Chicago and buried near a monument to the Haymarket martyrs.[73]

Mayor Michael Scanlon met a more sudden judgment. Having survived what he called "the most difficult year that any city government ever experienced,"[74] Scanlon finally turned to the job of running Lawrence. The recall movement against him went nowhere and he won a narrow reelection in 1913, but the following July, Scanlon felt a throbbing behind his right ear. A specialist found an infection of the mastoid bone. Scanlon underwent an operation and was said to be recovering, but on August 17, a week short of his fiftieth birthday, he died. The next morning, fire bells tolled in Lawrence.[75] "The funeral procession was one of the longest that has ever passed through the streets of the city," the *Telegram* reported.[76] Banks, stores, and newspapers all closed for the morning. The mills churned on.

The men of the Massachusetts militia finally got to fight in a real war. During World War I, all units were mustered into the army. Lawrence's own Battery C fought at Château-Thierry and Saint-Mihiel, losing only one man. Company F fought in the Argonne Forest and the Second Battle of the Marne. By Armistice Day, fewer than a dozen of the company's 80 members were left.[77] In all, 6,000 men from Lawrence served in the war and 196 were killed. But the strike's most curious final act befell William Wood, for of all the major players he alone was truly changed by the events of 1912. The changes transformed him from despised mill mogul into paterfamilias of the textile industry.

On May 19, 1913, Wood's limousine pulled up in front of Superior Court in Boston. Dodging photographers, Wood entered the courtroom to be tried for conspiracy to plant dynamite. As the prosecution made its case, the events of January 1912 were replayed from behind the scenes. The day before the dynamite was found, a local builder testified, he had been approached by Ernest Pitman, Wood's contractor who had killed himself the previous August. Pitman had asked for dynamite to "blow out some boulders on a construction job." With sticks in hand, Pitman and the contractor had gone to Boston, where they handed the explosive to John Breen.[78] Breen testified that he later met "dog fancier" Dennis Collins in a Boston saloon, then took the "bundle" to Washington and Franklin streets. There they were joined by Frederick Atteaux, a longtime business associate of Wood's. The payoff was haphazard. Walking down the sidewalk, Atteaux dropped a bag containing five hundred dollars, quipping to Breen, "Don't say I never gave you anything."[79] That evening, Collins and Breen took the train to Lawrence, where they visited the Italian cobbler's, the Syrian home, and the church cemetery to plant what Breen called "the juice." According to Collins, Breen boasted, "I'll be mayor of this city next year. There is a million back of me."[80]

Along with testimony, prosecutors presented material evidence—American Woolen vouchers made out to Atteaux, signed by Wood,[81] and phone records of calls between American Woolen and Atteaux's office and between Atteaux and Pitman on January 19. A witness testified to seeing Atteaux at Wood's mansion the night "the juice" was planted.[82] A taxi driver had taken a man resembling Atteaux from Wood's house to the street corner where the drop was made. Things did not look good for the president of American Woolen—until his attorneys stirred up reasonable doubt. Wood's chauffeur testified that Atteaux had not been at Wood's house on the key evening, and the taxi driver's written record of his telltale trip turned out to be from 1911. Cross-examined, the driver was unable to recall a single detail of any trip he made the following January 19.[83] American Woolen's vouchers to Atteaux were not itemized; they read, "for expenses occurred during the Lawrence strike."[84] And then there was the credibility of John Breen, further muddied when Atteaux accused him of blackmail.[85]

It seemed the verdict might go either way. Evidence may have been circumstantial, but would American Woolen's longtime contractor have been involved if Wood were not? Would Pitman have killed himself if he didn't have more to hide? Then again, would William Wood have risked all he had accomplished on such a scheme just one week into the strike? The jury deliberated until midnight, then convened early the next morning. The verdict came at 10:00 a.m. Collins—guilty. Atteaux—a hung jury. Wood—acquitted. Friends swarmed around the tycoon. "It has been a long and hard ordeal to pass through," he stated. "I have no bitterness toward anyone that has been connected with the prosecution."[86]

Despite the acquittal, Wood never got over how his "fellow workers" had betrayed him. "From the Atlantic to the Pacific, I was held up to the public as an object of hatred," he said.[87] Wood spent the rest of his life atoning for his insensitivity, or seeming to atone. "In the new social and industrial order on which we have entered, there is no room for the selfish employer or the selfish worker," he stated.[88] His magnanimity may have come from the heart, but it was made possible by the federal government. In October 1913, the fallout Wood had most feared fell upon the textile industry when a Democratic Congress eliminated the wool tariff's Schedule K.[89] The following year, American Woolen lost money for the first time,[90] but Wood regrouped, bought more mills, and saw his fortunes soar during the war. A million Americans in uniform meant a million uniforms and blankets. American Woolen's contract—the largest in the history of the American textile industry—totaled $102 million. Flush with profits[91] and under constant threat of strikes,[92] Wood gave his employees five raises in two years, four of 10 percent and one of 5 percent.[93] "Billy Wood" was no longer a dirty name in Lawrence, and in 1919, when another massive strike began, Wood was not singled out as a target.

Again the issue was a shorter workweek—forty-eight hours with no cut in pay. The strike began on February 3 with a walkout that grew to fifteen thousand.[94] This time, however, the city wanted nothing to do with the militia, parades, or mass meetings on the common. Police from Lawrence and neighboring towns handled crowds. All public assembly was banned.[95] With the IWW reeling, a loose coalition of ministers, ex-Wobblies,[96] and immigrants ran the strike. Amid Red hysteria, charges of "Bolshevism" were fueled by photographs of Marx and Lenin in strikers' meeting halls.[97] Police arrested three hundred strikers and badly beat several. Defending many of them was a recent graduate of Boston University Law School, attorney Angelo Rocco.[98]

Under the slogan "48-54," the strike ground on. One striker was killed and a house bombed.[99] Workers sent their children away, smuggling them out of town in vans.[100] Streetcars were stoned, scabs made miserable,[101] but resistance was more entrenched than in 1912. Church leaders, including both Father O'Reilly and Father Milanese, fought the strike. Finally, as in 1912, the crackdown spun out of control. On May 6, vigilantes dragged two strike leaders from their beds and beat them with blackjacks.[102] Men in flatbed trucks armed with machine guns patrolled the streets,[103] yet with springtime orders piling up,[104] mill owners were forced to concede. After sixteen weeks, workers returned to the mills to toil forty-eight hours for slightly more pay than they had received for fifty-four.[105] Once back on the job, the most active leaders of the strike were fired.[106]

Having endured a second huge strike, Wood finally listened to his son. While studying sociology at Harvard in 1912,[107] William Wood Jr. had heard disparaging comments by professors. Upon graduating to become a director of American Woolen, the younger Wood began lobbying his father for better employee relations.[108] Just after the 1919 strike, American Woolen granted its employees group and accident insurance, maternity benefits, and sick pay. The company formed a Homestead Association to help employees buy their first homes and a Cosmopolitan Club offering lessons in citizenship and English.[109] A new American Woolen summer camp hosted workers' children.[110] In employee relations, the wool industry's trade journal reported, American Woolen became "far-sighted as compared with most of its competitors."[111] Altruism was not Wood's only motive, however. American Woolen's largesse conveniently thwarted textile unions grappling for a hold in Lawrence.[112]

Wood further endeared himself to workers in December 1919, when postwar inflation sent prices soaring. Accusing Lawrence merchants of profiteering, he threatened to open a company store selling goods at cost. The store was never built,[113] but in Lawrence Wood's automobile was hailed by cheering workers as he paraded like a king.[114] The attention went to Wood's head, and workers later complained of being rounded up for more demonstrations of affection[115] dubbed "Songs to Our Captain Billy."[116] Wood's paternalism was embodied in a sign on a company vehicle transporting children: THIS IS ANOTHER OF THE BENEFITS WE RECEIVE FROM OUR GREAT BENEFACTOR, MR. W. M. WOOD.[117] Still, when yet another grinding strike racked Lawrence in 1922, American Woolen's were the only major mills where workers stayed on the job because Wood alone had not cut wages.[118]

From mill worker to mill mogul, Wood's life had taken a rocket's trajectory, but it would also follow a rocket's inevitable descent. The tragedies began in 1918 when Wood's daughter Irene succumbed to the Spanish flu epidemic.[119] Stricken by the loss, Wood often rode in a horse-drawn carriage to his daughter's grave, where he sat holding flowers.[120] Rubbing salt in the wound were lawsuits and indictments that began in 1920, when the federal government prosecuted Wood for wartime profiteering. The case was dismissed on a technicality, yet other indictments waited to be discovered, including a posthumous conviction for having American Woolen pay Wood's personal income tax.[121] Then in 1922, William Wood Jr., who loved to drive his Rolls-Royce at a hundred miles per hour,[122] died when he swerved to avoid an oncoming car and slammed into a telephone pole. "Dad was never the same again," Wood's other son, Cornelius, said. "He remained oppressed with sorrow."[123] Following a stroke in 1924, Wood, now white-haired and bursting the buttons of his spats, lost control of his company, his health, and his will to live. Not even Shawsheen Village could console him. A planned community in Andover, Shawsheen was Wood's attempt to re-create the lost Victorian era. Its 250 Colonial Revival homes surrounded a quaint downtown with shops, a bank, a drugstore, and corporate offices. Wood had his own mansion in Shawsheen, where he hosted huge parties offering cake and ice cream to workers given time off to attend. Shawsheen Village was not popular among executives forced to relocate from Boston, and it infuriated stockholders, who later sued Wood's estate for squandering corporate funds. Then came the final indignity—plummeting profits. In 1924, the world's leading worsted maker lost $6.9 million.[124] Wood resigned that year. "My work has been my life," he told one of his staff. Then pointing in the direction of his son's grave, he added, "Having given that up I fear it will not be long before I shall be over there with Billy."[125]

Wallowing in grief, so befuddled that he often complained about being poor,[126] Wood did not wait for time to fulfill his prophecy. On February 2, 1926, while wintering in Florida, he directed his chauffeur toward a lonely road near Flagler Beach, told him to remain in the car, then walked out of sight, put a .38 revolver in his mouth, and ended his life.[127] Without Wood at the helm, American Woolen, by then a behemoth unable to keep pace with changing fashions, went into a thirty-year death spiral, finally verging on bankruptcy.[128] In 1955, the company merged with Textron, Inc., which closed all the old mills. Back in Lawrence, the world's largest mill sat empty. But by then, it was just another vacant relic in a textile city with no cloth left to weave.

During the 1920s, mills throughout the Northeast had begun moving south to where cotton was king and unions were as weak as peasants. While textile strikes longer and bloodier than those in Lawrence broke out across the South, mill towns from Maine to Pennsylvania became blighted relics of America's industrial past.[129] Some recovered, retooling small mills into factories or warehouses, but as the nation's largest mill town, Lawrence suffered the worst blight. In 1949—a boom year elsewhere in America—the city's unemployment rate was 40 percent.[130] The coup de grâce came in the next few years, which saw the closing of the Ayer Mill (2,657 jobs), the Monomac Mill (3,500 jobs), the Wood Mill (7,000 jobs), and finally, in January 1957, the Pacific Mill (4,100 jobs).[131] From empty weaving rooms to dilapidated tenements, a sad silence fell over the city that had once woven the world's worsteds.

Scrambling to fill fourteen million square feet of industrial space, Lawrence attracted Honeywell and General Electric, yet unemployment remained high and families fled. During the 1960s, urban renewal swept through the city. Tenements[132] and old buildings on Essex fell to the wrecker's ball. One of the Wood Mill's massive wings was leveled, along with much of The Plains. The remaining mills survived to enjoy a modest rebirth in the 1980s. These nineteenth-century behemoths now house a wide mix of concerns—outlets, design firms, artists' studios, high-tech companies, retail stores. Roaming through their subdivided hallways, it's hard to get a sense of the masses that once worked here or of their grueling labor. Yet peer through a closed door. Look out a window at the smokestack skyline. Then climb a creaky wooden stairway to where few visitors go and suddenly the vastness of an unconverted mill room unfolds, its pillars and hardwood floors receding to the vanishing point, its emptiness seeming to echo with distant calls of *"Sciopero!" "Shtrayken!"* and "Strike!"

By the time the mills closed, Lawrence was no longer "Immigrant City." Nationwide quotas imposed in 1921 had cut immigration to a trickle, while citizenship programs established in the wake of the 1912 strike "Americanized" immigrants, teaching them English, civics, and home economics.[133] Gradually, the "old country" was replaced by the new one as grandparents died, foreign newspapers folded,[134] and children grew up speaking English only. But then in the late 1960s, new waves of immigration changed the fabric of Lawrence once again, enlivening the city with languages not heard during the mills' heyday, including Spanish, Vietnamese, and Khmer. Immigrants from the Dominican Republic joined transplants from Puerto Rico and arrivals from Vietnam, Cambodia, and Laos. True to its traditions, "Immigrant City" remains a proud working-class bastion, home to natives of forty different nations.[135] During the 1980s, Lawrence became notorious for drugs, arson, and gangs. Since then, although its social indicators remain some of the region's most alarming, the city has touched bottom and pushed up. A sign of progress came just before Christmas in 1995, when fire gutted several buildings at the Malden Mills, the last functioning mill left in Lawrence. Standing in the parking lot, owner Aaron Feuerstein, whose grandfather founded the mill in 1906, told his employees, "This is not the end." Then in a move that made him a nationwide hero, Feuerstein kept all three thousand workers on his payroll with full pay and benefits while the mill was rebuilt and their jobs were restored.[136] More than eighty years after it became the symbol of corporate greed, Lawrence had given America a symbol of corporate compassion.

Recent immigrants to Lawrence knew little about the city's history, and longtime residents were not about to tell them. For two generations, the strike of 1912 was rarely mentioned and then only in its official version. In a 1950 Pacific Mill "memoir," a fictional boy recalled his father's stories: "Dad was sure they could have won those same pay raises a whole lot quicker if they hadn't let a bunch of outsiders speak for them and work them up into leading off with their fists instead of their brains."[137] In 1962, fiftieth-anniversary newspaper articles said nothing about the planting of dynamite, the children's exodus, the congressional hearings. But that fall, Lawrence commemorated the "For God and Country" movement with another parade of twenty-five thousand, watched by two hundred thousand more. The superintendent of schools recounted how outsiders had taken over the city. "Their methods and thinking were forerunners of many tactics used by modern Communism. They inflamed our working people; there were riots, bloodshed, and even deaths in our streets. . . . The news of this violence in Lawrence gave our city a black name all over the world."[138]

With witnesses dying out, it seemed the sanitized version would forever remain the strike's official story. Then in 1978, the cloud of collective amnesia began to lift. A new mayor encouraged former strikers to speak out. Folk artist Ralph Fassanella displayed his colorful paintings of the strike at the Lawrence Public Library,[139] and a new historical society, the Immigrant City Archives, began an oral history project. Through newspaper articles, radio talk shows, and word of mouth, dozens of strike veterans were found. Many were reluctant to dredge up memories. One man told of his first job in the Arlington Mill, but as he approached the strike, he stopped. "What are you going to do with this story? Are you going to print all this story or what? Well, I don't want too much of it. . . . It was a bad thing and everybody suffered. . . . I'm the only one left of the family and I'd just as soon forget all about it. I don't want to talk any more about 1912."[140] But others talked and talked. The one who talked the most was ninety-eight-year-old Angelo Rocco.

Rocco had practiced law in Lawrence until the Depression, when he went into the contracting business. Retired in 1957, he remained politically active. When asked to remember the strike, he was as sharp as ever. "See, in 1911, the legislature of Massachusetts reduced hours of labor from fifty-six to fifty-four. . . . The mill owners wanted to pay for fifty-four, about twenty cents a week less, you unnerstan'?" Rocco told his tale on tape, then to an audience gathered on the Lawrence Common in 1980 for a commemorative festival. The event included speeches, songs of labor sung by Peter, Paul, and Mary, and reminiscences by strike veterans and their children. A walkway was renamed Camella Teoli Way.[141] The festival soon became an annual event stamped with the strike's new nickname "Bread and Roses." Rocco attended the first few Bread and Roses festivals until, in 1984, he died two months after his one-hundredth birthday.

Over the years, as other strike participants have passed away, succeeding Bread and Roses festivals each Labor Day have become less political, more festive. The 2003 festival was a small affair, just a thousand in attendance. The IWW was there, its representative seated in a booth distributing literature. Just down the walkway on the common, the Lawrence Heritage State Park ran a power loom. In the county fair atmosphere, hardly anyone mentioned bread, roses, or the strike's powerful place in the city's history. The new nickname persists, however, arousing the wrath of locals who cannot figure out how such a lilting phrase became attached to such a bitter strike.

Local legend has it that a photograph from the strike showed a woman holding a picket sign reading WE WANT BREAD, BUT WE WANT ROSES, TOO! No such photograph has ever been found. The phrase, eulogized in James Oppenheim's poem "Bread and Roses," was first published in *American Magazine* one month before the strike. The poem was prefaced: "Bread for all, and Roses, too—a slogan of the women in the West."[142] Oppenheim's poem was published twice more in 1912, once with the phrase attributed to "Chicago Women Trade Unionists." Then in 1916, "Bread and Roses" was indelibly linked to Lawrence when a labor anthology claimed the phrase came from the strike.[143] From there the error grew. An anonymous composer set the words to music and the song was recorded by Judy Collins, among others.[144] By the time Lawrence awoke to its past, it was surprised to find the lovely name attached to its long, bloody strike.[145] No one seemed pleased.

"The strike of 1912, that's what it was," Catherine Simonelli told Immigrant City Archives in 1988. "It was no Bread and Roses. Bread and Roses sounds like something nice. But it wasn't anything nice. . . . That's why the people that saw what was going on, we do not like that name. I wish you'd tell somebody."[146] Many protested in letters to editors, in conversation, in newspaper interviews, but the name stuck. Today, "Bread and Roses" entitles hundreds of social programs across America and Europe. In Lawrence, the Bread and Roses Food Pantry serves hot meals to hungry people. And a single rose carved in granite beside a chaff of wheat adorns a polished headstone laid in 2000 on the grave of Anna LoPizzo.[147] But the quixotic name says little about the struggles of textile workers in Lawrence. Nearly a hundred years after they stormed out of the mills, came together as one, marched, sang, fed and cared for each other to emerge victorious, their struggle should not be poeticized. The strike belongs not to the realms of poetry or politics but to the people who waged or witnessed it. Theirs should be the final word.

July 9, 2003, was a hot summer day in Lawrence. While the world outside blazed on in conflicts that might someday make history, history itself lay in a nursing home a few miles north of the mills. At 101, Domenica Strano could barely hear when an attendant sat her up and shouted in her ear that she had a visitor. He had come to talk about some strike way back in 1912. Did she remember?

Her eyes were hollow and blue; her skin was pale and thin as paper, spotted with age, but her mind was as clear as the riot bells that rang on January 12, 1912, when she was just a week past her tenth birthday. Stretching out a bony finger to tap the hand of the "young man" who asked so many questions, she reached back for memories. "My father gave us orders to put down the shades because the police from Boston had come with guns and horses," she said in a shaky, craggy voice. "If they saw something they didn't like, they'd shoot at you! Father said, 'You stay inside and put down the shade, and if you move from the kitchen, you'll hear about it!' My brothers were a little frisky and he didn't want any of us to have anything to do with it."

Domenica's father, Angelo Laudani, washed wool in the Wood Mill, where she would later work for ten years before getting married. He did not work during the strike. The family had come from Sicily shortly after Domenica was born in 1902. So many questions, so long ago, but she sat in her darkened room, hunched over in a pastel sweater, and tried to answer.

Her wispy white hair contrasted with her unmistakable Sicilian gestures—a baffled shrug of shoulders, the offhand flick of pursed fingers, both hands drawn to her chest in an inverted prayer asking why anyone would deny the strikers two hours' pay. "The only thing I can tell you is they were tough times. Tough times. The workers were looking for a little more pay. That's all they wanted. And Ettor and Giovannitti said, 'You deserve more. You have families.' I remember they killed a woman named Anna LoPizzo. Father Milanese went to the police of Lawrence and said not to do anything to the strikers. They just wanted a little more pay. Isn't it too bad now that the mills are all gone. How could they let them go?"[148]

After a few minutes, the visitor let history lie down and rest with its blanket and its memories. Domenica Strano died in January 2004, shortly after her 102nd birthday. She was the last living person who remembered the great textile strike in Lawrence, Massachusetts, during the winter of 1912.

Acknowledgments

Because this is a work of nonfiction containing no invented scenes or dialogue, I am grateful to the journalists who closely covered the strike, attending meetings, interviewing principals, and providing exceptionally vivid reporting of this most dramatic event. I am also indebted to the librarians and archivists who helped me unearth this primary source material from the following institutions: the W. E. B. DuBois Library at the University of Massachusetts at Amherst, the Beinecke Rare Book and Manuscript Library at Yale University, the Tamiment Library and Robert F. Wagner Labor Archives at New York University, the New York Public Library, the Lawrence Public Library, the Salem (MA) Public Library, and the Boston Public Library.

Special thanks to Terry Billiel at the DuBois Library for digging up the Senate report and transcripts of the House of Representatives hearings. At the Lawrence Public Library, Fabian Rojas, Peter Giannini, Noellia Ramos, and Ingrid Portorreal patiently complied with my requests to pull yet another microfilm reel from their cabinets and helped me overcome my own technical difficulties to make six thick binders of photocopied daily news that provided much of the book's detail. Upstairs at the same library, archivist Louise Sandberg shared my fascination with the strike along with her seemingly bottomless trove of memorabilia. She was also a faithful guide to life in Lawrence in 1912.

Across the city, standing in the shadow of the Everett Mill, is the Lawrence History Center and Immigrant City Archives, whose director, Pat Jaysayne, patiently fulfilled my requests for more and more material, notably the archive's taped interviews with strike veterans. Pat also proved invaluable in digging up strike photographs.

Thanks to the University of Massachusetts Translation Center for translating French and German newspapers. And *mille grazie* to artist and friend Pietro Spica, who helped with Italian translations and insights into Italian immigration and anarchism. All things Lithuanian in the book were provided and translated by Jonas Stundza, a lifelong Lawrence resident who shared both archival material and personal anecdotes about his ancestors and their role in the strike.

I am indebted to historians Bruce Laurie of the University of Massachusetts and Daniel Czitrom of Mount Holyoke College for steering me toward doctoral theses and other sources that I might otherwise have missed. Archivists at the Walter P. Reuther Library, Wayne State University in Detroit, Michigan, and at the American Textile History Museum in Lowell, Massachusetts, assisted in finding photographs. Friend and lawyer Jenny Daniell was helpful in clarifying certain legal terminology. And I owe an odd debt of gratitude to the weather in Lawrence, which managed to be suitably brutal and forbidding almost every time I visited the city, making it easy to envision the winter of 1912.

Finally, I wish to thank those whose emotional and editorial support made the book possible. This list begins with my agent, Jeff Kleinman, who saw the book's potential. Once again my gratitude goes out to my meticulous editor at Viking Penguin, Ray Roberts, for his gentle editing and for setting all this in motion by encouraging me to "chase an interest." My sister, Judith, provided encouragement and advice based on an early reading. Topping the list is my wife, Julie, who along with encouragement and emotional support, served as my first line of defense against stilted phrases and suffocating detail. Finally, I owe more than can be expressed to my children, Elena and Nate, who for nearly two years heard more than they cared to know about a long-ago strike and even walked with me one afternoon through the labyrinth of mills where it all happened. They have only begun to realize how much their future is woven with the past.

Notes

Introduction

1. Philip S. Foner, *History of the Labor Movement in the United States*, vol. 4, *The Industrial Workers of the World, 1905–1917* (New York: International Publishers, 1965), p. 320.

CHAPTER ONE: For Two Hours' Pay

1. Barry Moreno, *Italian Americans* (East Sussex, UK: Ivy Press, 2003), p. 67.
2. *Report on Strike of Textile Workers in Lawrence, Mass., in 1912,* 62nd Cong., 2nd sess., 1912, S. Doc. 870, p. 45. (Hereafter referred to as "Senate Report.")
3. Ibid., p. 11.
4. Elizabeth Shapleigh, "Occupational Disease in the Textile Industry," *New York Call,* December 29, 1912, p. 13.
5. David J. Goldberg, *A Tale of Three Cities: Labor Organization and Protest in Paterson, Passaic, and Lawrence, 1916–1921* (New Brunswick, NJ: Rutgers University Press, 1989), p. 58.
6. Donald B. Cole, *Immigrant City: Lawrence, Massachusetts, 1845–1921* (Chapel Hill: University of North Carolina Press, 1963), p. 75.
7. "Lawrence, Massachusetts: The Strike of 1912," Immigrant City Archives, Lawrence, MA.
8. Thomas R. Brooks, *Toil and Trouble: A History of American Labor* (New York: Delacorte Press, 1971), p. 119.
9. Senate Report, pp. 33–34.
10. Lillian Donohue, oral history interview, tape 246, Immigrant City Archives, Lawrence, MA.
11. "Mob Runs Riot in Mills at Lawrence," *Boston Globe,* January 13, 1912, p. 2.
12. Ibid., and "Frenzied, Armed Mob Descends upon Mills," *Lawrence Daily American,* January 12, 1912, p. 2.
13. "Strikers Force Mills to Close," *Lawrence Telegram,* January 12, 1912, p. 2.
14. Ray Stannard Baker, "The Revolutionary Strike," *American Magazine,* June 1912, p. 20.

15. Ibid.

16. "Strikers Force Mills to Close," *Lawrence Telegram,* January 12, 1912, p. 2.

17. Foner, *History of the Labor Movement,* vol. 4, p. 316.

18. "Heads Battered at Washington Mill," *Lawrence Daily American,* January 12, 1912, p. 1.

19. Foner, *History of the Labor Movement,* vol. 4, p. 307.

20. John Bruce McPherson, "American Woolen Company's Quarter-Century Record," in *Bulletin of the National Association of Wool Manufacturers—1924* (Boston: National Association of Wool Manufacturers, 1924), p. 485.

21. "The Mills Hardly to Blame," *Lawrence Telegram,* January 11, 1912.

22. *Fibre and Fabric,* January 1912, excerpted in "The 54-Hour Law," *Lawrence Sun,* January 8, 1912.

23. "Textile Workers on Anxious Seat," *Lawrence Telegram,* January 5, 1912, p. 4.

24. Foner, *History of the Labor Movement,* vol. 4, p. 314.

25. Melvin Dubofsky, *We Shall Be All: A History of the Industrial Workers of the World* (Chicago: Quadrangle, 1969), p. 235.

26. "Loom Fixers Will Go on Strike," *Lawrence Tribune,* January 4, 1912, p. 1.

27. Ibid.

28. All quotes from Angelo Rocco are from oral history interviews, tape 90, Immigrant City Archives, Lawrence, MA.

29. Moreno, p. 50.

30. Ardis Cameron, *Radicals of the Worst Sort: Laboring Women in Lawrence, Massachusetts, 1860–1912* (Urbana and Chicago: University of Illinois Press, 1993), p. 83.

31. Testimony of John J. Sullivan, in House Committee on Rules, *The Strike at Lawrence, Mass.: Hearings before the Committee on Rules of the House of Representatives on House Resolutions 490 and 433,* 62nd Cong., 2nd sess., March 2–7, 1912, p. 242. (Hereafter referred to as "House Report.")

32. Cole, p. 69.

33. Foner, *History of the Labor Movement,* vol. 4, p. 314.

34. Dubofsky, p. 236.

35. "Lawrence Arms against Anarchy in Textile Strike," *Boston Herald,* January 12, 1912, p. 1.

36. "Mob Runs Riot in Mills at Lawrence," *Boston Globe,* January 13, 1912, p. 2.

37. Testimony of Frank Sherman, House Report, p. 439.

38. "Pay Trucks Were Wheeled into Safe," *Lawrence Daily American,* January 12, 1912, p. 2.

39. "Strikers Force Mills to Close," *Lawrence Telegram,* January 12, 1912, p. 2.

40. "Strikers Rush Mills; Battle with Officers," *Lawrence Evening Tribune,* January 12, 1912, p. 1.

41. Miles Jackson, interviewer, *Lawrence Strike 1912: Viewpoints on American Labor,* oral histories on record (New York: Random House, 1971).

42. "Mob Runs Riot in Mills at Lawrence," *Boston Globe,* January 13, 1912, p. 2.

43. "Foreman Stabbed at Wood Mill," *Lawrence Daily American,* January 12, 1912, p. 1.

44. "Strikers Rush Mills; Battle with Officers," *Lawrence Evening Tribune,* January 12, 1912, p. 1.

45. "Lawrence Mill Workers in Riot over 54-Hour Law," *Boston Herald,* January 13, 1912, p. 1.

46. Edward G. Roddy, *Mills, Mansions, and Mergers: The Life of William M. Wood* (North Andover, MA: Merrimack Valley Textile Museum, 1982), p. 53.

47. Maurice B. Dorgan, *History of Lawrence, Massachusetts* (Lawrence, MA: privately printed, 1924), p. 110.

48. Roddy, p. 15.

49. Ibid., p. 57.

50. Keene Sumner, "A Business Genius Who Has Done What Others Said Was Impossible," *American Magazine,* June 1923, p. 206.

51. Roddy, p. 60.

52. Ibid., p. 40.

53. Ibid., p. 53.

54. Ibid., p. 56.

55. Ibid., p. 22.

56. Ibid., pp. 22–25.

57. Ibid., p. 27.

58. Sumner, p. 203.

59. Roddy, p. 30.

60. Ibid.

61. Sumner, p. 203.

62. Ibid., p. 204.

63. Roddy, p. 33.

64. Ibid., pp. 33–34.

65. Ibid., pp. 34–38.

66. Baker, p. 28.

67. Cameron, p. 118.

68. Jackson, *Lawrence Strike 1912.*

69. Roddy, p. 63.

70. Ibid.

71. "American Woolen Company," in John J. McKone, *Glimpses of Lawrence: The Founding and Progress of a Great Industrial Centre* (Lawrence, MA, 1921).

72. Fred E. Beal, *Proletarian Journey* (New York: Van Rees Press, 1937), p. 32.

73. Goldberg, p. 85.

74. Dexter Philip Arnold, "A Row of Bricks: Worker Activism in the Merrimack Valley Textile Industry, 1912–1922" (PhD diss., University of Wisconsin, Madison, 1985), p. 250.

75. Roddy, p. 46.

76. Ibid., p. 49.

77. Peter Carlson, *Roughneck: The Life and Times of Big Bill Haywood* (New York: W. W. Norton, 1983), p. 161.

78. Roddy, p. 71.

79. Mary Heaton Vorse, "The Trouble at Lawrence," *Harper's Weekly,* March 9, 1912, p. 10.
80. *The Lawrence Directory 1912* (Boston: Sampson and Murdock, 1912), pp. 749–835.
81. Advertisement, *Lawrence Daily American,* January 8, 1912.
82. "Lawrence Women's Club Meets," *Lawrence Evening Tribune,* January 10, 1912.
83. "City Hall Chat," *Lawrence Telegram,* February 17, 1912, p. 4.
84. "Mayor Scanlon Submits Report," *Lawrence Evening Tribune,* August 6, 1912, p. 1.
85. "A Poor Time for Labor Troubles," *Lawrence Tribune,* January 10, 1912, p. 4.
86. Cameron, p. 122, and Arnold, p. 219.
87. Vorse, "The Trouble at Lawrence," p. 11.
88. Cameron, p. 77.
89. Senate Report, pp. 152–53.
90. Cameron, p. 91.
91. Ibid., p. 101.
92. "Elevator Victim Dies in Hospital," *Lawrence Evening Tribune,* January 10, 1912, p. 4.
93. "Attempted Suicide," *Lawrence Evening Tribune,* January 5, 1912.
94. "Mill Operative Dropped Dead," *Lawrence Evening Sun,* January 6, 1912, p. 6.
95. Obituaries, *Lawrence Daily American,* January 5, 8, 12, 1912.
96. Foner, *History of the Labor Movement,* vol. 4, p. 313.
97. Harry Emerson Fosdick, "After the Strike—in Lawrence," *The Outlook,* June 15, 1912, p. 344.
98. "Riot Call Brings Out All Police," *Lawrence Daily American,* January 12, 1912, p. 1.
99. "Frenzied, Armed Mob Descends upon Mills," *Lawrence Daily American,* January 12, 1912, p. 1.

CHAPTER TWO: Immigrant City

1. Steve Dunwell, *The Run of the Mill: A Pictorial Narrative of the Expansion, Dominion, Decline, and Enduring Impact of the New England Textile Industry* (Boston: David R. Godine, 1978), p. 79.
2. Henry David Thoreau, *A Week on the Concord and Merrimack Rivers* (Boston: Houghton Mifflin, 1975), pp. 54–55.
3. U.S. Department of the Interior, *Lowell: The Story of an Industrial City* (Washington, DC, 1992), p. 16.
4. Ibid., p. 15.
5. John Kasson, *Civilizing the Machine: Technology and Republican Values in America, 1776–1900* (New York: Penguin, 1976), p. 78.
6. *U.S. Department of the Interior, Lowell,* p. 50.
7. Arthur L. Eno Jr., *Cotton Was King: A History of Lowell, Massachusetts* (Somersworth, NH: New Hampshire Publishing Company, 1976), p. 95.
8. Charles Dickens, *American Notes* (London: Penguin, 1972), p. 118.
9. Eno, p. 71.
10. Ibid., p. 92.
11. Display at the American Textile History Museum, Lowell, MA.

12. Robert F. Dalzell Jr., *Enterprising Elite: The Boston Associates and the World They Made* (Cambridge, MA: Harvard University Press, 1987), p. 73.

13. The Thomas Jefferson quote is from his *Notes on the State of Virginia.* It appears in Merrill D. Peterson, ed., *The Portable Thomas Jefferson* (New York: Penguin, 1975), p. 217.

14. Barbara M. Tucker, *Samuel Slater and the Origins of the American Textile Industry, 1790–1860* (Ithaca, NY: Cornell University Press, 1984), p. 39.

15. Kasson, p. 68.

16. C. David Heymann, *American Aristocracy: The Lives and Times of James Russell, Amy, and Robert Lowell* (New York: Dodd, Mead, 1980), p. 21.

17. Dunwell, p. 95.

18. Kasson, p. 98.

19. Ibid., p. 72.

20. Dalzell, p. 65.

21. Eno, p. 90.

22. Ibid., p. 101.

23. Dalzell, p. 50.

24. Kasson, p. 75.

25. Cole, p. 17.

26. William Cahn, *Lawrence 1912: The Bread and Roses Strike* (New York: Pilgrim Press, 1980), p. 24.

27. Dunwell, p. 78.

28. Ibid.

29. Hamilton Andrews Hill, *Memoir of Abbott Lawrence* (Boston: privately printed, 1883), pp. 55–56.

30. Dunwell, p. 83.

31. J. F. C. Hayes, *History of the City of Lawrence* (Lawrence, MA: E. D. Green, 1868), p. 11.

32. Cole, p. 17.

33. Hayes, p. 17.

34. Ibid., pp. 18–19.

35. Eartha Dengler, Katherine Khalife, and Ken Skulski, *Images of America: Lawrence, Massachusetts* (Dover, NH: Arcadia, 1995), p. 14.

36. Joseph P. Blanchette, *The View from Shanty Pond: An Irish Immigrant's Look at Life in a New England Mill Town, 1875–1938* (Charlotte, VT: Shanty Pond Press, 1999), p. 8.

37. Dorgan, *History of Lawrence, Massachusetts,* p. 44.

38. Henry Aaron Yeomans, *Abbott Lawrence Lowell—1856–1943* (Cambridge, MA: Harvard University Press, 1948), p. 14.

39. Eno, p. 89.

40. Dengler, Khalife, and Skulski, pp. 22–23.

41. Ibid., p. 24.

42. Ibid., p. 22.

43. Paul S. Boyer, ed., *The Oxford Companion to United States History* (New York: Oxford University Press, 2001), p. 423.

44. Hayes, pp. 65–67, and Cole, pp. 35–36.
45. Hill, p. 28.
46. Ibid., pp. 126–27.
47. Dunwell, p. 97.
48. Cole, p. 29.
49. Ibid., pp. 42–44.
50. Cahn, p. 65.
51. Felix Albert, *Immigrant Odyssey: A French-Canadian Habitat in New England* (Orono: University of Maine Press, 1991), p. 3.
52. Cole, p. 209.
53. Robert Paul McCaffery, *Islands of Deutschtum: German-Americans in Manchester, New Hampshire, and Lawrence, Massachusetts, 1870–1942* (New York: Peter Lang, 1996), pp. 10–11.
54. Kevin Phillips, *Wealth and Democracy: A Political History of the American Rich* (New York: Broadway Books, 2002), p. 34.
55. Dunwell, p. 146.
56. Ibid., p. 101.
57. Mary H. Blewett, *Constant Turmoil: The Politics of Industrial Life in Nineteenth-Century New England* (Amherst: University of Massachusetts Press, 2000), p. 197.
58. Ibid., pp. 121–22.
59. *The Lawrence Gazeteer* (Lawrence, MA: Charles G. Merrill, 1894), p. 43.
60. Cameron, p. 57.
61. Ibid., p. 48.
62. Ibid.
63. Ibid., p. 57.
64. *Lawrence Directory 1896*, p. 532.
65. Blewett, pp. 292–93.
66. Ibid., pp. 45, 59, 61.
67. Roddy, p. 36.
68. Dunwell, p. 11.
69. Cahn, p. 81.
70. Diane Ravitch, ed., *The American Reader: Words That Moved a Nation* (New York: HarperPerennial, 1991), p. 175.
71. Walter Merriam Pratt, "The Lawrence Revolution," *New England Magazine,* March 1912, p. 7.
72. Cole, p. 143.
73. Ibid., p. 52.
74. Goldberg, p. 87.
75. Cole, p. 78.
76. Ibid.
77. Mary Heaton Vorse, *A Footnote to Folly: Reminiscences of Mary Heaton Vorse* (New York: Farrar and Rinehart, 1935), p. 10.

78. Dengler, Khalife, and Skulski, p. 65.

79. Cameron, p. 83.

80. Ibid., p. 96.

81. McCaffery, pp. 50–69.

82. Cole, p. 125.

83. Roddy, p. 48.

84. Baker, p. 29.

CHAPTER THREE: **The Battle of the Merrimack**

1. *Lawrence Directory 1912*, pp. 30–31.

2. "Strikers Force Mills to Close," *Lawrence Telegram,* January 12, 1912, p. 2, and "Mob Runs Riot in Mills at Lawrence," *Boston Globe,* January 13, 1912, p. 2.

3. "Foreman Stabbed at Wood Mill," *Lawrence Daily American,* January 12, 1912, p. 2.

4. "Lawrence Mill Workers in Riot over 54–Hour Law," *Boston Herald,* January 13, 1912, p. 1.

5. "Foreman Stabbed at Wood Mill," *Lawrence Daily American,* January 12, 1912, p. 1.

6. "Strikers Force Mills to Close," *Lawrence Telegram,* January 12, 1912, p. 2.

7. "Mob Runs Riot in Mills at Lawrence," *Boston Globe,* January 13, 1912, p. 3.

8. "Scenes of Riot and Disorder," *Lawrence Daily American,* January 12, 1912, p. 1.

9. "Frenzied, Armed Mob Descends upon Mills," *Lawrence Daily American,* January 12, 1912, p. 1.

10. "Strikers Rush Mills; Battle with Officers," *Lawrence Evening Tribune,* January 12, 1912, p. 1.

11. "Strike Riots Close Big Lawrence Mills," *New York Times,* January 13, 1912, p. 7.

12. "Strikers Rush Mills; Battle with Officers," *Lawrence Evening Tribune,* January 12, 1912, p. 1.

13. "Lawrence Mill Workers in Riot over 54–Hour Law," *Boston Herald,* January 13, 1912, p. 2.

14. "A Statement by Pres. Wood," *Lawrence Daily American,* January 12, 1912, p. 1.

15. "Mob Runs Riot in Mills at Lawrence," *Boston Globe,* January 13, 1912, p. 2.

16. "Girls Beaten Down by a Lawrence Mob," *Boston Herald,* January 12, 1912, p. 2.

17. "Merely as Precaution, Says Scanlon," *Boston Globe,* January 15, 1912, p. 2.

18. "Scenes of Riot and Disorder," *Lawrence Daily American,* January 12, 1912, p. 2.

19. Ibid.

20. "Translation of Italian Circular," *Lawrence Daily American,* January 14, 1912, p. 1.

21. "Searchlight on Mill," *Boston Globe,* January 13, 1912, p. 2.

22. "The Weather," *Lawrence Telegram,* January 13, 1912, p. 1.

23. "Ayer Clock Tower," in McKone.

24. "Strikers Force Mills to Close," *Lawrence Telegram,* January 12, 1912, p. 1.

25. "Searchlight on Mill," *Boston Globe,* January 13, 1912, p. 2.

26. Arnold, p. 208.

27. Dorgan, *History of Lawrence, Massachusetts,* pp. 73–74.

28. *Views of Lawrence* (Portland, ME: L. H. Nelson, 1903).

29. Cole, p. 154.

30. Ibid., p. 161.

31. Ibid., pp. 79–80.

32. Ibid., p. 172.

33. "Lawrence in Arms against Anarchy Talk," *Boston Herald,* January 14, 1912, p. 2.

34. "Strikers Hold Mass Meeting," *Lawrence Telegram,* January 13, 1912, p. 3.

35. "Lawrence in Arms against Anarchy Talk," *Boston Herald,* January 14, 1912, p. 2.

36. "Mill Agents Interviewed," *Lawrence Evening Tribune,* January 13, 1912, p. 1.

37. "President Wood Is Optimistic," *Lawrence Telegram,* January 13, 1912, p. 2.

38. Dorgan, *History of Lawrence, Massachusetts,* p. 72.

39. "Mill Officials Hissed," *Lawrence Daily American,* January 13, 1912, p. 1.

40. Testimony of John J. Sullivan, House Report, p. 285.

41. Rocco, oral history.

42. "Everett Shuts Down," *Lawrence Telegram,* January 13, 1912, p. 8.

43. Senate Report, p. 35.

44. "Lawrence in Arms against Anarchy in Textile Strike," *Boston Herald,* January 14, 1912, p. 2.

45. "Ettor Hearing," *Lawrence Evening Tribune,* February 19, 1912, p. 3.

46. "New Police Head for Lawrence," *Boston Globe,* February 20, 1912, p. 2.

47. Rocco, oral history.

48. Ravitch, p. 129.

49. Carlson, pp. 161–62.

50. Elizabeth Gurley Flynn, *The Rebel Girl: An Autobiography, My First Life (1906–1926)* (New York: International Publishers, 1955), p. 54.

51. Norma Fain Pratt, *Morris Hillquit: A Political History of an American Jewish Socialist* (Westport, CT: Greenwood Press, 1979), p. 106.

52. Carlson, pp. 161–62.

53. "Haywood on the Ettor-Giovannitti Case," *Industrial Worker,* June 22, 1912, p. 1.

54. Flynn, *Rebel Girl,* p. 87.

55. "Lawrence Strikers to Vote on Raise," *Boston Globe,* March 14, 1912, p. 5.

56. Rocco, oral history.

57. "Strikers Hold Mass Meeting," *Lawrence Telegram,* January 13, 1912, p. 3.

58. Vorse, *Footnote to Folly,* p. 7.

59. "Meeting Held in the City Hall This Afternoon," *Lawrence Evening Telegram,* January 13, 1912, p. 1.

60. "Lawrence in Arms against Anarchy in Textile Strike," *Boston Herald,* January 14, 1912, p. 2.

61. Brooks, p. 119, and Louis Adamic, *Dynamite: The Story of Class Violence in America,* rev. ed. (Gloucester, MA: Peter Smith, 1963), p. 162.

62. Foner, *History of the Labor Movement,* vol. 2, p. 106.

63. Justus Ebert, "Who Joseph J. Ettor Is," *Industrial Worker,* May 23, 1912, p. 1.

64. "Ettor a Resourceful Strike Leader," *Boston American*, January 28, 1912, p. 9.

65. "Urged Peace, Ettor Says," *Boston Globe*, November 12, 1912, p. 4.

66. Dubofsky, p. 236.

67. *Ettor and Giovannitti before the Jury at Salem, Massachusetts* (Chicago: Industrial Workers of the World, 1912), p. 12.

68. Foner, *History of the Labor Movement*, vol. 4, p. 294.

69. Dubofsky, p. 207.

70. "Militia Called at Lawrence," *Boston Globe*, January 15, 1912, p. 2.

71. Rocco, oral history.

72. Foner, *History of the Labor Movement*, vol. 4, p. 165.

73. Ibid., pp. 147 and 348. The figure of fifteen thousand represents the 1912 end-of-the-year total of twenty-five thousand members minus the ten thousand dues-paying members who joined in Lawrence during the strike.

74. Dubofsky, p. 349.

75. Foner, *History of the Labor Movement*, vol. 4, pp. 86, 245, 353, 361.

76. Ibid., p. 155.

77. Ibid., p. 80.

78. William D. Haywood, *The Autobiography of Big Bill Haywood* (New York: International Publishers, 1974), p. 181.

79. Foner, *History of the Labor Movement*, vol. 4, p. 29.

80. Elliott J. Gorn, *Mother Jones: The Most Dangerous Woman in America* (New York: Hill and Wang, 2001), pp. 96–97.

81. Ibid., pp. 33–34.

82. Foner, *History of the Labor Movement*, vol. 4, pp. 40–48.

83. Ibid., p. 70.

84. Joyce L. Kornbluh, ed., *Rebel Voices: An IWW Anthology* (Ann Arbor: University of Michigan Press, 1964), pp. 405–8.

85. Philip S. Foner, *Women and the American Labor Movement: From the First Trade Unions to the Present* (New York: Macmillan, 1979), p. 192.

86. Foner, *History of the Labor Movement*, vol. 2, p. 209.

87. J. Anthony Lukas, *Big Trouble* (New York: Simon and Schuster, 1997), p. 142.

88. Bruce Laurie, *Artisans into Workers: Labor in Nineteenth Century America* (New York: Farrar, Straus, and Giroux, 1989), p. 174.

89. Brooks, p. 105.

90. Samuel Gompers, "Those 'World Redeemers' at Chicago—Their Plight," *American Federationist*, August 1905, p. 515.

91. Brooks, p. 115.

92. Haywood, *Autobiography*, p. 186.

93. Barbara Mayer Wertheimer, *We Were There: The Story of Working Women in America* (New York: Pantheon, 1977), p. 354.

94. Kornbluh, p. 84.

95. Ibid., p. 65.

96. Foner, *History of the Labor Movement*, vol. 4, p. 131.
97. Dubofsky, p. 166.
98. William Moran, *The Belles of New England: The Women of the Textile Mills and the Families Whose Wealth They Wove* (New York: St. Martin's Press, 2002), p. 202.
99. Dubofsky, p. 170.
100. Ibid., p. 94.
101. Foner, *History of the Labor Movement*, vol. 4, p. 163.
102. Ibid., p. 157.
103. Dubofsky, p. 123.
104. Foner, *History of the Labor Movement*, vol. 4, p. 84.
105. Ibid., p. 160.
106. "Strikers Firm and Mills May Close," *Boston Globe*, January 14, 1912, p. 2.
107. Ibid.
108. Foner, *History of the Labor Movement*, vol. 4, p. 318.
109. Tom Herriman, "Angelo Rocco: A Rank and File Union Leader Remembers the 1912 Lawrence Textile Strike," *Labor Unity*, April 1980, p. 10.
110. Cole, pp. 184–86.
111. "Militia Called at Lawrence," *Boston Globe*, January 15, 1912, p. 2.
112. Cole, p. 164.
113. "Father O'Reilly Goes South," *Lawrence Tribune*, January 12, 1912, p. 1.
114. "Return of Fr. J.T. O'Reilly," *Lawrence Tribune*, February 15, 1912, p. 1.
115. "Prepare Militia for Lawrence Rioters," *New York Times*, January 15, 1912, p. 7.
116. Mary K. O'Sullivan, "The Labor War at Lawrence," *The Survey*, April 6, 1912, p. 72.
117. "Order Militia to Arm for Lawrence Strike," *Boston Herald*, January 15, 1912, p. 1.
118. "Militia Called at Lawrence," *Boston Globe*, January 15, 1912, p. 2.
119. "Strikers Rush Wood Mill," *Lawrence Tribune*, January 16, 1912, p. 2.
120. "Martial Law in Mills," *Lawrence Telegram*, January 15, 1912, p. 3.
121. "Strikers Rush Wood Mill," *Lawrence Tribune*, January 16, 1912, p. 2.
122. Ibid.
123. Ibid.; see also "Militia Assembles," *Lawrence Telegram*, January 15, 1912, p. 3.

CHAPTER FOUR: Stars, Stripes, and Bayonets

1. Brooks, p. 50.
2. "Strikers in Big Parade," *Lawrence Tribune*, January 17, 1912, p. 3.
3. "Militia Bars Strikers from the Mill District," *Lawrence Tribune*, January 18, 1912, p. 2.
4. Dengler, Khalife, and Skulski, p. 89.
5. *Historical and Pictorial Review: National Guard of the Commonwealth of Massachusetts 1939* (Baton Rouge, LA: Army and Navy, 1939), pp. xxiv–xxxiv.
6. "Militia Guarding Lawrence Mills," *Boston Globe*, January 16, 1912, p. 3.
7. "Bayonet Charge on Lawrence Strikers," *New York Times*, January 16, 1912, p. 7.
8. Nell Irwin Painter, *Standing at Armageddon: The United States 1877–1919* (New York: W. W. Norton, 1987), p. 16.
9. Brooks, p. 53.

10. Nick Salvatore, *Eugene V. Debs: Citizen and Socialist* (Urbana and Chicago: University of Illinois Press, 1982), p. 31.
11. Brooks, p. 97.
12. Ibid., p. 96.
13. Laurie, p. 207.
14. Foner, *History of the Labor Movement,* vol. 4, pp. 286–87, 290.
15. "Militia Guarding Lawrence Mills," *Boston Globe,* January 16, 1912, p. 3.
16. "Militia in Charge at the Mills," *Lawrence Telegram,* January 15, 1912, p. 6.
17. "Bayonet Charge on Lawrence Strikers," *New York Times,* January 16, 1912, pp. 7–8.
18. "Militia in Charge at the Mills," *Lawrence Telegram,* January 15, 1912, p. 6.
19. Ibid.
20. "Tribute Is Paid to Late Justice," *Lawrence Telegram,* February 5, 1927, p. 1.
21. "Strikers in Police Court," *Lawrence Tribune,* January 18, 1912, p. 1.
22. "Heavy Sentences Given Rioters," *Lawrence Telegram,* January 16, 1912, p. 1.
23. "Striker Sentenced to Two Years," *Lawrence Tribune,* January 15, 1912, p. 1.
24. "Strikers in Police Court," *Lawrence Tribune,* January 18, 1912, p. 6, and Cahn, p. 138.
25. Photograph in *Boston Herald,* January 19, 1912, p. 2.
26. Fosdick, p. 341.
27. "Jos. Ettor Advises Serenading 'Scabs,' " *Lawrence Daily American,* January 18, 1912, p. 2.
28. "Joseph Ettor, Strike Leader, Surrounded by Admirers" (photograph), *Boston Globe,* January 16, 1912, p. 2.
29. "Strike Situation Peaceful," *Lawrence Telegram,* January 16, 1912, p. 4.
30. "Bayonet Charge on Lawrence Strikers," *New York Times,* January 16, 1912, p. 7.
31. "Mass Meeting in City Hall," *Lawrence Telegram,* January 16, 1912, p. 8.
32. Ibid.
33. Flynn, *Rebel Girl,* p. 134.
34. Goldberg, p. 91.
35. Cahn, p. 118.
36. Justus Ebert, *The Trial of a New Society* (Cleveland: IWW Publishing Bureau, 1913), pp. 57–58.
37. John Golden, "Trade Unionism Only Solution of Strike, Says Golden," *Boston American,* January 21, 1912, pt. 2, p. 1.
38. William F. Hartford, *Where Is Our Responsibility: Unions and Economic Change in the New England Textile Industry, 1870–1960* (Amherst: University of Massachusetts Press, 1996), p. 41.
39. Moran, p. 199.
40. John Golden, "Trade Unionism Only Solution of Strike, Says Golden," *Boston American,* January 21, 1912, pt. 2, p. 1.
41. "Strike Situation Peaceful," *Lawrence Telegram,* January 16, 1912, p. 2.
42. Foner, *History of the Labor Movement,* vol. 4, p. 338.
43. "Devoted to Violence," *Lowell Courier,* reprinted in *Lawrence Telegram,* January 18, 1912, p. 6.
44. "Order Militia to Arm for Duty in Lawrence Strike," *Boston Herald,* January 15, 1912, p. 1.

45. "Rioters Are Sent to Jail," *Boston American,* January 16, 1912, p. 1.
46. "City Pays Tribute to Its Dead Mayor," *Lawrence Telegram,* August 18, 1914, p. 6.
47. "Strikers Driven Back by Troops but Close Mills," *Boston Globe,* January 16, 1912, p. 3.
48. Ebert, *Trial of a New Society,* p. 122.
49. "Mass Meeting in City Hall," *Lawrence Telegram,* January 16, 1912, p. 8.
50. "Agree to Confer," *Boston Globe,* January 17, 1912, p. 2.
51. "Lawrence Hopes Strikers Win Fight for a Living," *Boston American,* January 21, 1912, p. 3B.
52. Foner, *History of the Labor Movement,* vol. 4, p. 323.
53. Ibid., p. 322.
54. "Strikers Issue Fervid Appeal," *Lawrence Evening Tribune,* January 17, 1912, p. 10.
55. "Militia Bars Strikers from the Mill District," *Lawrence Tribune,* January 18, 1912, p. 5.
56. "300 Armenians Join Strikers," *Lawrence Daily American,* January 18, 1912, p. 2.
57. "100 Hebrews Join Strikers," *Lawrence Daily American,* January 18, 1912, p. 2.
58. "Militia Bars Strikers from the Mill District," *Lawrence Tribune,* January 18, 1912, p. 1.
59. "Militia Fights 3,000 in Lawrence Mob," *Boston Evening Globe,* January 17, 1912, p. 1.
60. "Fear Dynamite in Lawrence Strike," *New York Times,* January 18, 1912, p. 7.
61. "Conditions Quiet," *Lawrence Tribune,* January 19, 1912, p. 3.
62. "Strikers in Big Parade," *Lawrence Tribune,* January 17, 1912, p. 3.
63. "Militia Bars Strikers from the Mill District," *Lawrence Tribune,* January 18, 1912, p. 2.
64. "Mass Meeting in City Hall," *Lawrence Tribune,* January 16, 1912, p. 8.
65. Foner, *Women and the American Labor Movement,* p. 206.
66. "Strikers Driven Back by Troops but Close Mills," *Boston Globe,* January 16, 1912, p. 2.
67. "Mill Strikers Will Confer with Owners," *New York Times,* January 17, 1912, p. 7.
68. "Companies Refuse to Arbitrate," *Boston Evening Globe,* January 17, 1912, p. 2.
69. "Mill Strikers Will Confer with Owners," *New York Times,* January 17, 1912, p. 7, and Cahn, p. 109.
70. "Wood Cannot Raise Wages," *Boston Globe,* January 19, 1912, p. 2.
71. "The Great Strike in Retrospect," *Bulletin of the National Association of Wool Manufacturers—1912* (Boston: National Association of Wool Manufacturers, 1912), p. 141.
72. "Strikers Issue Fervid Appeal," *Lawrence Evening Tribune,* January 17, 1912, p. 10.
73. "Two Views of a Striker's Pay Envelope," *Boston Globe,* January 28, 1912, p. 2.
74. "Wages Received by Strikers at Old Rate," *Lawrence Tribune,* January 18, 1912, p. 1.
75. Lewis E. Palmer, "A Strike for Four Loaves of Bread," *The Survey,* February 3, 1912, p. 1695.
76. Ibid., p. 1696.
77. Mildred Gwin Andrews, *The Men and the Mills: A History of the Southern Textile Industry* (Macon, GA: Mercer University Press, 1987), p. 83.
78. Foner, *History of the Labor Movement,* vol. 4, p. 173.
79. Ken Skulski, *Images of America: Lawrence, Massachusetts,* vol. 2 (Charleston, SC: Arcadia, 1997), p. 50.
80. "Living Conditions of the Lawrence Strikers," *Boston Post,* February 11, 1912, p. 4.

81. "The Cost of Living," in "Lawrence, Massachusetts: The Strike of 1912," Immigrant City Archives, Lawrence, MA.

82. "Lawrence, Massachusetts: The Strike of 1912," Immigrant City Archives, Lawrence, MA.

83. "Genuine Lockhart Mill-End Sale," *Lawrence Evening Tribune,* January 12, 1912, p. 4.

84. "Living Conditions of the Lawrence Strikers," *Boston Post,* February 11, 1912, p. 4.

85. "Lessons of the Strike," *Lawrence Telegram,* January 19, 1912, p. 9.

86. Henry F. Pringle, *The Life and Times of William Howard Taft* (New York: Farrar and Rinehart, 1939), p. 456.

87. Ida M. Tarbell, "The Mysteries and Cruelties of the Tariff: The Passing of Wool," *American Magazine,* October 1910, p. 742.

88. Ibid., p. 741.

89. Ida M. Tarbell, "The Mysteries and Cruelties of the Tariff: The Bulwark of the Wool Farce," *American Magazine,* November 1910, pp. 59–60.

90. Ron Chernow, *Titan: The Life of John D. Rockefeller, Sr.* (New York: Vintage, 1998), p. 358.

91. "Can the Wool Trust Gag the Press?" *Collier's,* March 18, 1911, p. 11.

92. Tarbell, "The Bulwark of the Wool Farce," p. 52.

93. "Symphony in K Flat," *The Nation,* March 13, 1911, p. 360.

94. Tarbell, "The Bulwark of the Wool Farce," pp. 52–54.

95. Richard Washburn Child, "The Making of 'K,' the Wool Schedule," *Everybody's Magazine,* March 1910, p. 344.

96. "Wool Tariff," in *Reader's Guide to Periodical Literature,* 1910–1914 (Minneapolis: H. W. Wilson, 1915).

97. Kathleen Brady, *Ida Tarbell: Portrait of a Muckraker* (New York: Seaview/Putnam, 1984), p. 193.

98. "Can the Wool Trust Gag the Press?" p. 11.

99. "Symphony in K Flat," p. 360.

100. "Can the Wool Trust Gag the Press?" p. 12.

101. Ibid.

102. Tarbell, "The Passing of Wool," p. 742.

103. Pringle, p. 600.

104. Ibid., p. 448.

105. "The Wool Bill Veto," *The Outlook,* August 26, 1911, pp. 910–11.

106. *Bulletin of the National Association of Wool Manufacturers—1912,* p. 139, and "Socialism behind Lawrence Strike," *Journal of Commerce and Commercial Bulletin,* February 1, 1912.

107. Pratt, "Lawrence Revolution," p. 9.

108. "Strikers Meet at City Hall," *Lawrence Daily American,* January 16, 1912, p. 2.

109. Pratt, "Lawrence Revolution," p. 9.

110. "Strikers in Big Parade," *Lawrence Tribune,* January 17, 1912, p. 1.

111. "Legislature Called On to Investigate," *Lawrence Tribune,* January 19, 1912, p. 3.

112. "Militia Guarding Lawrence," *Boston Globe,* January 16, 1912, p. 3.

113. "Settlement Is Far Off," *Boston Globe*, January 19, 1912, p. 2.

114. "Saloons Are Closed Today," *Lawrence Telegram,* January 16, 1912, p. 8.

115. "Sharpshooters Are Stationed in Mill Towers," *Lawrence Daily American*, January 15, 1912, p. 1.

116. "Militia Bars Strikers from the Mill District," *Lawrence Tribune*, January 18, 1912, p. 2.

117. "Officials Taking Every Precaution" (photograph), *Lawrence Telegram*, January 13, 1912, p. 3.

118. "Monster Parade of Strikers Peaceful," *Lawrence Daily American*, January 18, 1912, p. 2.

119. Photograph in *Boston Globe*, January 19, 1912, p. 1.

120. "Battle Feared at Duck Bridge," *Boston Globe*, January 18, 1912, p. 2.

121. "Refusal to Arbitrate Ettor Announced," *Lawrence Evening Tribune*, January 17, 1912, p. 3.

122. "Battle Feared at Duck Bridge," *Boston Globe*, January 18, 1912, p. 5.

123. "Fear Dynamite in Lawrence Strike," *New York Times*, January 18, 1912, p. 7.

124. "Three Lots of Dynamite Unearthed at Lawrence," *Boston Globe*, January 21, 1912, p. 2.

125. "American Woolen Company Pays Off Strikers," *Lawrence Daily American*, January 19, 1912, p. 3.

126. "Pres. Wood Asks Operatives to Return," *Lawrence Tribune*, January 20, 1912, p. 3.

127. "Plot to Blow Up Mills Unearthed; Seven Arrested," *Lawrence Daily American*, January 20, 1912, p. 1.

128. "Dynamite Discovered!" *Lawrence Evening Tribune*, January 20, 1912, p. 1.

129. Director of the Bureau of Statistics, *42nd Annual Report on the Statistics of Labor for the Year 1911* (Boston: Wright and Potter, 1913), p. 3.

130. "Seven Dynamite Arrests Made," *Lawrence Telegram*, January 20, 1912, p. 1.

131. "Three Lots of Dynamite Unearthed at Lawrence," *Boston Globe*, January 21, 1912, p. 1, and "Cache of Dynamite in Lawrence Strike," *New York Times*, January 21, 1912, p. 9.

CHAPTER FIVE: Dynamite

1. Clarence Darrow, *The Story of My Life* (New York: Da Capo Press, 1996), p. 60.

2. Henry Fredette, tape 90, interview in Immigrant City Archives, Lawrence, MA.

3. Cole, pp. 30–31.

4. *An Authentic History of the Lawrence Calamity* (Boston: J. J. Dyer, 1860), p. 1.

5. "Lawrence Fears Reign of Terror," *Boston Herald*, January 21, 1912, p. 2.

6. "Three Lots of Dynamite Unearthed at Lawrence," *Boston Globe*, January 21, 1912, p. 8.

7. "Dynamite Plots Fail in Lawrence," *New York Sun*, January 21, 1912, p. 2.

8. "Lawrence Fears Reign of Terror," *Boston Herald*, January 21, 1912, p. 2.

9. "Three Lots of Dynamite Unearthed at Lawrence," *Boston Globe*, January 21, 1912, p. 8.

10. "Dynamite Discovered!" *Lawrence Evening Tribune*, January 20, 1912, p. 1.

11. "Lawrence Fears Reign of Terror," *Boston Herald,* January 21, 1912, p. 2.
12. "Dynamite Discovered!" *Lawrence Evening Tribune,* January 20, 1912, p. 1.
13. "Three Lots of Dynamite Unearthed at Lawrence," *Boston Globe,* January 21, 1912, p. 8.
14. U.S. Department of Commerce, Bureau of the Census, "Work Stoppages, Workers Involved, Man-Days Idle, Major Issues, and Average Duration: 1881–1970," in *Historical Statistics of the United States: Colonial Times to 1970* (Washington, DC, 1976), p. 179. Note that the average covers only the years 1901–1905. The federal government did not keep statistics on work stoppages from 1906 to 1913.
15. Foner, *History of the Labor Movement,* vol. 5, pp. 7–8.
16. "Seeking More Dynamiters" and "Pueblo Laundry Blown Up," *New York Times,* January 20, 1912, p. 4.
17. David Halberstam, *The Powers That Be* (New York: Dell, 1979), p. 158.
18. Adamic, p. 210.
19. Halberstam, p. 147.
20. Adamic, p. 211.
21. Foner, *History of the Labor Movement,* vol. 5, p. 15.
22. Ibid., p. 13.
23. Adamic, p. 218.
24. Foner, *History of the Labor Movement,* vol. 5, p. 20.
25. Halberstam, pp. 159–60.
26. Adamic, p. 229.
27. Ibid., p. 236.
28. "Strike Leader Declares Dynamite Was 'Planted,'" *Lawrence Daily American,* January 22, 1912, p. 8.
29. "Three Lots of Dynamite Unearthed at Lawrence," *Boston Globe,* January 21, 1912, p. 8.
30. "Father Milanese to Help Strikers," *Lawrence Tribune,* January 22, 1912, p. 10.
31. Ibid.
32. "Lawrence Strikers Reject Mill Plan," *New York Times,* January 22, 1912, p. 3.
33. "Father Milanese to Help Strikers," *Lawrence Tribune,* January 22, 1912, p. 10.
34. "Cause of Industrial Turmoil—'Way of Cain,' Says Preacher," *Lawrence Daily American,* January 22, 1912, p. 2.
35. Foner, *History of the Labor Movement,* vol. 4, p. 333.
36. "Pastor Praises Troops," *Boston Globe,* January 22, 1912, p. 2.
37. "Want to Settle All Along the Line," *Boston Globe,* January 22, 1912, p. 2.
38. "Colonel Sweetser Warns," *Lawrence Tribune,* January 23, 1912, p. 3.
39. Cahn, p. 152.
40. "Strike Yet Unchanged," *Lawrence Tribune,* January 25, 1912, p. 1.
41. Ibid.
42. "Colonel Sweetser Warns," *Lawrence Tribune,* January 23, 1912, p. 1.
43. "Strike Yet Unchanged," *Lawrence Tribune,* January 25, 1912, p. 1.
44. Vorse, *Footnote to Folly,* p. 7.

45. "Was without Result," *Lawrence Tribune,* January 27, 1912, p. 1.

46. "Hunger Drives Strikers' Children to Soup Kitchens," *Boston American,* January 28, 1912, p. 3B.

47. Leslie H. Marcy and Frederick Sumner Boyd, "One Big Union Wins," *International Socialist Review,* April 1912, p. 618.

48. James Ford, "The Co-Operative Franco-Belge of Lawrence," *The Survey,* April 6, 1912, p. 68.

49. Marcy and Boyd, p. 618.

50. Jackson, *Lawrence Strike 1912.*

51. Baker, p. 30A.

52. Kornbluh, p. 180.

53. "Strikers Indorse Plan to Meet Their Employers," *Boston Globe,* January 23, 1912, p. 2.

54. "Dynamite Cases Heard," *Lawrence Tribune,* February 2, 1912, p. 2.

55. "Agree to Confer with Mill Men," *Boston Globe,* January 22, 1912, p. 2.

56. Cahn, p. 145.

57. "Strikers Indorse Plan to Meet Their Employers," *Boston Globe,* January 23, 1912, p. 2.

58. "Three Lots of Dynamite Unearthed at Lawrence," *Boston Globe,* January 21, 1912, p. 2.

59. "Agree to Confer with Mill Men," *Boston Globe,* January 22, 1912, pp. 1–2.

60. "Doubt Dynamite Case," *Boston Globe,* January 23, 1912, p. 2.

61. "Lawrence Dynamite 'Plant' by Sleuths," *New York Call,* January 24, 1912, p. 1.

62. "Pres. Wood Asks Operatives to Return," *Lawrence Tribune,* January 20, 1912, p. 3.

63. Photograph in collection of Immigrant City Archives, Lawrence, MA.

64. "Strikers Indorse Plan to Meet Their Employers," *Boston Globe,* January 23, 1912, p. 1.

65. "Globe Woman in Lawrence," *Boston Globe,* January 23, 1912, p. 2.

66. "Hunger Drives Strikers' Children to Soup Kitchens," *Boston American,* January 28, 1912, p. 3B.

67. Senate Report, p. 33.

68. Dengler, Khalife, and Skulski, p. 56.

69. "Ice Cutting on the River," *Lawrence Telegram,* January 22, 1912, p. 5.

70. "Seek Work in Lowell," *Lawrence Telegram,* January 16, 1912, p. 12.

71. "Fred Nyham Wounded by Bayonet at Lawrence," *Boston Globe,* January 23, 1912, p. 13.

72. Dengler, Khalife, and Skulski, p. 52.

73. "Ovation for Haywood," *Lawrence Tribune,* January 24, 1912, p. 1.

74. "Inspires Her Fellow Workers," *Boston Globe,* January 25, 1912, p. 2.

75. "About Haywood," *Literary Digest,* June 14, 1913, p. 135.

76. Carlson, p. 164.

77. Ibid., p. 23.

78. Ibid., p. 109.

79. Haywood, *Autobiography,* p. 10.

80. Ibid., p. 341.

81. Ibid., p. 8.

82. Ibid., p. 12.
83. Ibid.
84. Ibid., p. 29.
85. Ibid., p. 15.
86. Ibid., p. 31.
87. Carlson, pp. 40–42.
88. Haywood, *Autobiography,* p. 52.
89. Ibid., p. 62.
90. Carlson, p. 146.
91. Ibid., p. 58.
92. Lukas, *Big Trouble,* pp. 201–2.
93. Carlson, p. 69.
94. Ibid., p. 86.
95. Ibid., p. 100.
96. Lukas, p. 278.
97. Ibid., p. 284.
98. Ibid., p. 474.
99. Adamic, p. 149.
100. Lukas, p. 538.
101. Darrow, p. xiv.
102. Lukas, pp. 296, 334.
103. Ibid., p. 711.
104. Carlson, p. 130.
105. Lukas, pp. 753–54.
106. Carlson, pp. 138–39, and Lukas, p. 729.
107. Carlson, p. 68.
108. Ibid., p. 146.
109. Flynn, *Rebel Girl,* p. 73.
110. "A Radical Assault upon Trade Unions," *Current Literature,* April 1912, p. 384.
111. Carlson, epigraph page.
112. "'Hold Reins Tight,' Advises Haywood," *Lawrence Daily American,* January 23, 1912, p. 1.
113. "Ovation for Haywood," *Lawrence Tribune,* January 24, 1912, p. 1.
114. "Will Meet Mill Owners," *Boston Globe,* January 25, 1912, p. 2.
115. "Concerned Move to Stop the Strike," *Boston Globe,* January 25, 1912, p. 2.
116. Ibid, p. 1.
117. "Ovation for Haywood," *Lawrence Tribune,* January 24, 1912, p. 1.
118. "Strike Yet Unchanged," *Lawrence Tribune,* January 25, 1912, p. 2.
119. "One Man Is Responsible," *Lawrence Evening Tribune,* January 24, 1912, p. 1.
120. "Wood Scores Holman," *Lawrence Tribune,* January 25, 1912, p. 10.
121. "Attempt to Settle Strike Fizzles Out," *Boston Globe,* January 25, 1912, pp. 1–2, and "Strike Yet Unchanged," *Lawrence Tribune,* January 25, 1912, pp. 1–2.
122. "Foss Urges Inquiry into Mill Strike," *New York Times,* January 26, 1912, p. 6.

123. "For Recall of Scanlon," *Lawrence Tribune,* January 24, 1912, p. 1.
124. Benoit Clothing Company ad, "Our Contribution to the Strikers," *Lawrence Evening Tribune,* January 26, 1912, p. 8.
125. "Settlement in Sight!" *Lawrence Evening Tribune,* January 26, 1912, p. 1.
126. "Use of Force Not Advised," *Boston Evening Globe,* November 2, 1912, p. 2.
127. "Ultimatum to Ettor Issued," *Lawrence Telegram,* January 27, 1912, p. 3.
128. Ibid.
129. "Ovation for Haywood," *Lawrence Tribune,* January 24, 1912, p. 3.
130. "Exploding the Dynamite," *Boston Globe,* January 28, 1912, p. 2.
131. "Ettor Promises Mill Owners Something Big," *Lawrence Tribune,* January 26, 1912, p. 2.
132. "President Wood Meets Strike Committee," *Lawrence Evening Tribune,* January 27, 1912, p. 3.
133. "Ultimatum to Ettor Issued," *Lawrence Telegram,* January 27, 1912, p. 3.

CHAPTER SIX: Spinning Out of Control

1. "Ettor Speaks in Faneuil Hall," *Boston Globe,* January 27, 1912, p. 4.
2. "Shift in Plans of Workers' Chief," *Boston Globe,* January 28, 1912, p. 2.
3. "Never Urged Violence," *Boston Evening Globe,* November 13, 1912, p. 3.
4. "Shift in Plans of Workers' Chief," *Boston Globe,* January 28, 1912, p. 2.
5. "Ettor Puts in Busy Sunday," *Lawrence Tribune,* January 29, 1912, p. 3.
6. Arnold, p. 266.
7. "Tells Kunhardt Employees How They Can Get Square," *Lawrence Daily American,* January 29, 1912, p. 8.
8. "Leader Threatens Lawrence Looms," *New York Times,* January 29, 1912, p. 4.
9. "More Troops and Police to Protect Lawrence," *Boston Evening Globe,* January 29, 1912, p. 1.
10. "Woman Slain by Shot in Lawrence Strike Excitement," *New York Call,* January 30, 1912, p. 1.
11. Ibid.
12. "Bullet Kills Woman; Officer Benoit Stabbed," *Lawrence Evening Tribune,* January 29, 1912, p. 1.
13. Ibid.
14. Ibid.
15. "More Rioting by Strikers Today," *Lawrence Telegram,* January 29, 1912, p. 2.
16. "More Troops and Police to Protect Lawrence," *Boston Evening Globe,* January 29, 1912, p. 2.
17. "Strikers Destroy Cars," *Lawrence Tribune,* January 29, 1912, p. 1.
18. "Woman Slain in Lawrence Riot," *Boston Globe,* January 30, 1912, p. 4.
19. "Real Labor War Now in Lawrence," *New York Times,* January 30, 1912, p. 1.
20. "Agree to Confer with Mill Men," *Boston Globe,* January 22, 1912, p. 2.
21. "Burns Detective Agency Assists," *Lawrence Daily American,* January 29, 1912, p. 1; see also Foner, *History of the Labor Movement,* vol. 4, pp. 331–32.

22. "Drop Charge of Inciting Riots," *Boston Globe*, October 22, 1912, p. 1.
23. Arnold, p. 267.
24. Ibid., p. 273.
25. "Battle Waged an Hour," *Boston Herald*, January 30, 1912, p. 2.
26. Cameron, p. 106.
27. "Battle Waged an Hour," *Boston Herald*, January 30, 1912, p. 2.
28. Ellis Island On-Line, http:www.ellisisland.org/.
29. Cameron, p. 78.
30. "Woman Slain in Lawrence Riot," *Boston Globe*, January 30, 1912, p. 4.
31. Arnold, p. 271.
32. "Scouted Offer of Foss," *Lawrence Tribune*, January 30, 1912, p. 2.
33. "Woman Slain in Lawrence Riot," *Boston Globe*, January 30, 1912, p. 4.
34. Ibid.
35. "One Side Near End," *Lawrence Tribune*, October 31, 1912, p. 3.
36. "Scouted Offer of Foss," *Lawrence Tribune*, January 30, 1912, p. 2.
37. "Woman Killed by Shot Meant for Policeman," *Lawrence Tribune*, January 30, 1912, p. 8.
38. "Real Labor War Now in Lawrence," *New York Times*, January 30, 1912, p. 1; "Woman Slain by Shot in Lawrence Strike Excitement," *New York Call*, January 30, 1912, p. 1; and "Woman Killed by Shot Meant for Policeman," *Lawrence Tribune*, January 30, 1912, p. 1.
39. "Woman Slain in Lawrence Riot," *Boston Globe*, January 30, 1912, p. 4.
40. *Lawrence Gazeteer*, p. 57.
41. Ibid.
42. Arnold, p. 248.
43. "Pitman's Confession Implicates Four Men," *Lawrence Evening Tribune*, August 28, 1912, p. 2.
44. Rocco, oral history.
45. "The New John Breen School Ready for Formal Opening," *Lawrence Daily American*, January 18, 1912, p. 8.
46. "Breen Pleads Not Guilty," *Lawrence Tribune*, January 30, 1912, p. 1.
47. "Woman Slain in Lawrence Riot," *Boston Globe*, January 30, 1912, p. 4.
48. "Strikers Destroy Cars," *Lawrence Tribune*, January 29, 1912, p. 3.
49. "Ettor Puts in Busy Sunday," *Lawrence Tribune*, January 29, 1912, p. 3.
50. "Militia Quick to Arm When Call Sounds," *Boston Herald*, January 30, 1912, p. 3.
51. Ibid.
52. "Arms and the 'Exams,'" *Boston Globe*, January 31, 1912, p. 10.
53. Heymann, cover inset.
54. "Scouted Offer of Foss," *Lawrence Tribune*, January 30, 1912, p. 1.
55. "Strike Leaders Are Held without Bail," *Lawrence Telegram*, January 31, 1912, p. 4.
56. "Woman Killed in Lawrence Riot—Foss Rushes More Troops to City," *Boston Globe*, January 30, 1912, p. 1.
57. Ibid., p. 2.

58. "Will Shoot If Necessary," *Lawrence Daily American,* January 30, 1912, p. 1.
59. "Scouted Offer of Foss," *Lawrence Tribune,* January 30, 1912, p. 1.
60. Foner, *History of the Labor Movement,* vol. 4, p. 331.
61. "Dead Number Two—Ettor and His Right Hand Man Arrested on Murder Charges," *Boston Globe,* January 31, 1912, p. 5.
62. "Militia Check a Lawrence Mob," *Boston Evening Globe,* January 30, 1912, p. 1.
63. "Strike Leaders Are Held without Bail," *Lawrence Telegram,* January 31, 1912, p. 2.
64. "Great Test Comes Today," *Boston Globe,* February 1, 1912, p. 1.
65. "High Rents behind Lawrence Strike," *New York Times,* February 1, 1912, p. 3.
66. "Textile Mills Increase Force," *Boston Evening Globe,* January 31, 1912, p. 2.
67. "Arrest of Jos. J. Ettor," *Lawrence Tribune,* January 31, 1912, p. 3.
68. "Dead Number Two—Ettor and His Right Hand Man Arrested on Murder Charges," *Boston Globe,* January 31, 1912, pp. 1, 5.
69. "Arrest of Jos. J. Ettor," *Lawrence Tribune,* January 31, 1912, p. 3.
70. Skulski, p. 94.
71. Photograph in *Boston Globe,* February 10, 1912, p. 2.
72. "Man About Town," *Lawrence Telegram,* February 2, 1912, p. 6.
73. "Arrest of Jos. J. Ettor," *Lawrence Tribune,* January 31, 1912, p. 3.
74. Rocco, oral history, and "Militia in Lawrence Brings Greater Confidence," *Boston Evening Globe,* January 31, 1912, p. 1.
75. "Strike Leaders Are Held without Bail," *Lawrence Telegram,* January 31, 1912, p. 2.
76. Ibid.
77. "Ettor in Police Court," *Lawrence Tribune,* January 31, 1912, p. 1.
78. "5000 Loaves of Bread Given Away," *Lawrence Tribune,* January 31, 1912, p. 5.
79. "Haywood Back in the City," *Lawrence Tribune,* February 1, 1912, p. 2.
80. "Notes and Comments," *Lawrence Telegram,* February 1, 1912, p. 6.
81. Christine Stansell, *American Moderns: Bohemian New York and the Creation of a New Century* (New York: Henry Holt, 2000), p. 58.
82. Donohue, oral history.
83. "No Arbitration, No Compromise," *Lawrence Tribune,* January 31, 1912, p. 1.
84. "Crowd Forced from Street," *Boston Globe,* February 1, 1912, p. 8.
85. "Strikers Planning to Release Ettor," *Boston Globe,* February 2, 1912, p. 4.
86. "Man About Town," *Lawrence Telegram,* February 2, 1912, p. 6.
87. "Arrest of Jos. J. Ettor," *Lawrence Tribune,* January 31, 1912, p. 3.

CHAPTER SEVEN: A Nation Divided

1. Walter Weyl, *The New Democracy* (New York: Macmillan, 1912), p. 1.
2. "Man About Town," *Lawrence Telegram,* January 31, 1912, p. 4.
3. "Haywood Back in City," *Lawrence Tribune,* February 1, 1912, p. 1.
4. Internet Movie Database, http:www.imdb.com/.
5. Harold Evans, *The American Century* (New York: Alfred A. Knopf, 1998), p. 116.
6. Ibid., p. 117.

7. Michael E. Hennessy, *Twenty-five Years of Massachusetts Politics: 1890–1915* (Boston: Practical Politics, 1917), p. 273.

8. "Ice Covers the Sound," *New York Times,* February 6, 1912, p. 1.

9. "Niagara Ice Bridge Out; Three Drown," *New York Tribune,* February 5, 1912, p. 1.

10. "May Intervene in Cuba Again," *New York Times,* January 17, 1912, p. 1.

11. "Denounces Czarina's Mystic," *New York Times,* February 8, 1912, p. 1.

12. Eric Foner and John A. Garraty, eds., *The Reader's Companion to American History* (Boston: Houghton Mifflin, 1991), p. 691.

13. The *Tribune* also came out in a slightly different version called the *Eagle,* while the *American* had a sister daily called the *Sun* that reprinted most of its copy.

14. "15,000 Strikers Wreck Mills in Lawrence Riot," *Boston American,* January 12, 1912, p. 1.

15. "Big Dynamite Plot Exposed," *Boston American,* January 18, 1912, p. 1.

16. "Strike Committee at State House," *Lawrence Telegram,* February 3, 1912, p. 2.

17. "Fair Play at Lawrence," *Boston American,* February 2, 1912, p. 12.

18. "The Facts about the Lawrence Strike," *Boston American,* January 27, 1912, p. 12.

19. "The Laborer Is Worthy of His Hire," *Lawrence Tribune,* January 27, 1912, p. 4.

20. Dorgan, *History of Lawrence, Massachusetts,* pp. 134–35.

21. "Pointing the Finger," *Lawrence Telegram,* January 19, 1912, p. 6.

22. *Lawrence Daily American,* January 24, 1912, p. 1.

23. *Lawrence Daily American,* January 17, 1912, p. 1.

24. Cole, p. 234.

25. "La greve," *Le Courrier de Lawrence,* February 1, 1912, p. 1.

26. "La fortune des millionaires et les pauvres," *Le Courrier de Lawrence,* February 22, 1912, p. 4.

27. "Zum streik in Lawrence," *Anzeiger und Post,* January 27, 1912, p. 1.

28. Foner, *History of the Labor Movement,* vol. 4, p. 318.

29. "Jeder arbeiter seine lohne," *Anzeiger und Post,* February 24, 1912, p. 1.

30. "The Animal Behavior of the State with the Striking Lawrence Workers," *Keleivis,* February 29, 1912, p. 1.

31. "Aukos," *Keleivis,* March 7, 14, and 21, 1912, p. 1.

32. "A Discussion between Mikey and His Father," *Keleivis,* February 29, 1912, p. 4.

33. "Weavers' Strike in Lawrence," *Keleivis,* February 8, 1912, p. 1.

34. "Universal Strikes," *New York Tribune,* February 6, 1912, p. 6.

35. "The Lawrence Strike: A Poll of the Press," *The Outlook,* February 17, 1912, p. 357.

36. "'Smash the Machinery!'" *New York Times,* January 30, 1912, p. 8.

37. "Trouble Makers," *Los Angeles Times,* February 8, 1912, p. 4.

38. "Eugene Foss's Nemesis," *Los Angeles Times,* February 8, 1912, p. 4.

39. "Bloodshed at Lawrence," *Appeal to Reason,* February 3, 1912, p. 2.

40. "The Lesson of Lawrence," *The Masses,* April 1912, p. 3.

41. "The Contrast in Lawrence," *New York Call,* February 1, 1912, p. 6.

42. "I ladroni" and "I parassiti," *Il Proletario,* January 26, 1912, p. 2.

43. "Un'altra grandiosa insurrezione proletaria," *Il Proletario*, January 19, 1912, p. 1; on January 16, the *New York Call* also reported strikers gunned down at the Pacific Mill.
44. "La grandiosa lotta di Lawrence," *Il Proletario*, February 1, 1912, p. 1.
45. Walter Weyl, "The Strikers at Lawrence," *The Outlook*, February 10, 1912, p. 310.
46. Vorse, *Footnote to Folly*, p. 5.
47. Vorse, "Trouble at Lawrence," p. 10.
48. Baker, p. 23.
49. *Boston Post*, February 12, 1912, p. 4.
50. Vorse, "Trouble at Lawrence," p. 10.
51. "Tribune Topics," *Lawrence Tribune*, February 6, 1912, p. 4.
52. Weyl, *New Democracy*, p. 1.
53. "Man About Town," *Lawrence Telegram*, February 13, 1912, p. 4.
54. "Big Bill Haywood Returns to Scene of Lawrence Fight," *New York Call*, February 2, 1912, p. 1, and "Williams Helps Ettor," *Lawrence Telegram*, February 2, 1912, p. 4.
55. "Man About Town," *Lawrence Telegram*, February 2, 1912, p. 6.
56. "Haywood Says Ettor's Arrest Helped Strike," *Lawrence Tribune*, February 2, 1912, p. 3.
57. Arthur Regan, tape 181, oral history interview, Immigrant City Archives, Lawrence, MA, March 12, 1992.
58. "Stick of Dynamite Dropped near Tracks," *Lawrence Evening Tribune*, February 3, 1912, p. 1.
59. "Strikers Disappointed," *Boston Evening Globe*, February 3, 1912, p. 2.
60. Jackson, *Lawrence Strike 1912*.
61. "Ministers Discuss Lawrence Strike," *Lawrence Evening Tribune*, February 6, 1912, p. 2.
62. "Local Pastor Threatened," *Lawrence Tribune*, February 6, 1912, p. 1.
63. "Rev. Barber Denies Certain Statements," *Lawrence Tribune*, February 9, 1912, p. 12.
64. "Call New Troops," *Boston Globe*, February 6, 1912, p. 1.
65. "Strikers Disappointed," *Boston Evening Globe*, February 3, 1912, p. 2.
66. "'We Are Gaining,' Say the Strikers," *Lawrence Tribune*, February 2, 1912, p. 1.
67. Senate Report, p. 33.
68. Palmer, p. 1697.
69. "Haywood Says Ettor's Arrest Helped Strike," *Lawrence Tribune*, February 2, 1912, p. 3.
70. "Down to Grind at Lawrence," *Boston Globe*, February 9, 1912, p. 4.
71. "Lodge and Club," *Lawrence Evening Tribune*, February 5, 1912, p. 5.
72. "South Lawrence," *Lawrence Evening Tribune*, February 6, 1912, p. 2.
73. "Factory Girl Gives Up" (advertisement), *Lawrence Tribune*, January 27, 1912, p. 8.
74. "Legislators to See Strikers," *Boston Globe*, February 9, 1912, p. 4.
75. "John Breen Held for Grand Jury," *Lawrence Tribune*, February 3, 1912, p. 10.
76. "Habeas Corpus Hearing Tuesday," *New York Call*, February 4, 1912, p. 2.
77. "Haywood Says Ettor's Arrest Helped Strike," *Lawrence Tribune*, February 2, 1912, p. 3.
78. "New England Mill Tie-Up Threatened," *Boston Globe*, February 4, 1912, p. 2.

79. Stansell, p. 111.

80. Ibid.

81. Todd Brewster and Peter Jennings, *The Century* (New York: Doubleday, 1998), p. 30.

82. Phillips, p. 122.

83. Ibid., p. 338.

84. "Tribune Topics," *Lawrence Tribune,* February 10, 1912, p. 4.

85. Painter, p. 270.

86. Salvatore, p. 221.

87. Ibid., p. 242.

88. Ibid., pp. 208–9.

89. Painter, p. 266.

90. "Socialist Party of America," in Boyer, p. 727.

91. Ibid.

92. J. N. Larned, "Prepare for Socialism," *Atlantic Monthly,* May 1911, p. 578.

93. H. G. Wells, "Socialism, Parts I and II," *Harper's Monthly,* January and February 1912, pp. 197–204, 403–9.

94. Ronald Steel, *Walter Lippmann and the American Century* (New York: Vintage, 1980), p. 25.

95. *Appeal to Reason,* January 20, 1912, p. 1.

96. David Von Drehle, *Triangle: The Fire That Changed America* (New York: Atlantic Monthly Press, 2003), pp. 3, 68.

97. "The Trend of Things," *The Survey,* March 23, 1912, p. 1981.

98. Joseph J. Ettor, *Industrial Unionism the Road to Freedom,* IWW Pamphlet, June 1913, from University of Arizona, Special Collections AZ 114 box 1, folder 3A, exhibit 131, http://digital.library.arizona.edu/bisbee/docs/131.php.

99. Max Weber, *The Protestant Ethic and the Spirit of Capitalism and Other Writings* (New York: Penguin, 2002), p. 28.

100. Ibid., p. 120.

101. Ibid., p. 121.

102. *Who's Who in America, 1912–1913,* vol. 7 (Chicago: A. N. Marquist, 1913), s.vv. "Amory, Charles"; "Ayer, Frederick"; "Ayer, Frederick Fanning"; "Foss, Eugene"; "Greene, Edwin"; "Hobbs, Franklin"; "Lawrence, Amory"; "Lyman, Arthur"; "Whitman, William"; "Wigglesworth, George"; and "Wood, William."

103. Arnold, pp. 42–44.

104. Ibid., pp. 48–53.

105. Ibid., p. 345.

106. Roddy, p. 122.

107. Merle Crowell, "78—and Still at the Head of a Tremendous Concern," *American Magazine,* December 1920, p. 37.

108. *Arlington Mills 1865–1925* (Norwood, MA: Plimpton Press, 1925), p. 24.

109. Crowell, p. 120.

110. Ibid., p. 119.

111. Baker, p. 28.

112. Samuel Gompers, "The Lawrence Strike," *American Federationist,* April 1912, pp. 292–93.
113. Baker, p. 26.
114. McPherson, "American Woolen Company's Quarter-Century Record," in *Bulletin of the National Association of Wool Manufacturers—1924,* p. 485.
115. Fosdick, p. 345.
116. Baker, p. 22.
117. Richard Hofstadter, *The Age of Reform* (New York: Random House, 1955), p. 218.
118. Evans, p. 68.
119. Henry F. May, *The End of American Innocence: A Study of the First Years of Our Own Time—1912–1917* (Chicago: Quadrangle, 1959), pp. 54–55.
120. David Brian Robertson, *Capital, Labor, and State: The Battle for American Labor Markets from the Civil War to the New Deal* (Lanham, MD: Rowman and Littlefield, 2000), p. 9.
121. "Four Murdered in Lawrence," *New York Times,* February 3, 1912, p. 1.
122. "New England Mill Tie-Up Threatened," *Boston Globe,* February 4, 1912, p. 8.
123. "Robbery the Motive for Four Lawrence Murders," *Boston Globe,* February 3, 1912, p. 1.
124. "Four Murdered in Lawrence," *New York Times,* February 3, 1912, p. 1.
125. "Slayer of Four Still at Large," *Boston Globe,* February 4, 1912, p. 8.
126. "Four Murdered in a Lawrence Home," *Boston Globe,* February 3, 1912, p. 1.
127. Foner, *History of the Labor Movement,* vol. 4, p. 88.
128. "Resents Move of the A.F. of L.," *Boston Globe,* February 7, 1912, p. 1.
129. Ibid.
130. Lincoln Steffens, "Playing Our Game," *Industrial Worker,* March 28, 1912, p. 4.
131. "Working for a Settlement," *Lawrence Tribune,* February 8, 1912, p. 1.
132. "Investigators Find This City a Fertile Field," *Lawrence Telegram,* February 5, 1912, p. 3.
133. "To Settle Strike," *Lawrence Tribune,* February 7, 1912, p. 3.
134. "La greve," *Le Courrier de Lawrence,* February 1, 1912, p. 1.
135. "Bread to Be Given Away," *Lawrence Tribune,* February 7, 1912, p. 1, and "Helping the Needy," *Lawrence Telegram,* February 3, 1912, p. 2.
136. Testimony of Rev. Clark Carter, House Report, p. 368.
137. "Appeal to All Unions," *Lawrence Tribune,* February 5, 1912, p. 3.
138. "Mayor Fitzgerald Sends Check," *Lawrence Tribune,* February 5, 1912, p. 3.
139. Central Labor Union contributions and expenses, Immigrant City Archives, Lawrence, MA.
140. "To Settle Strike," *Lawrence Tribune,* February 7, 1912, p. 3.
141. "How Boston Women Aid Strike Victims," *Boston American,* February 11, 1912, p. 3B.
142. "Many Asking for Assistance," *Boston Globe,* February 7, 1912, p. 2.
143. "Hungry Man Is Assailant," *Lawrence Tribune,* February 7, 1912, p. 1.
144. "Habeas Corpus Petition Dismissed," *Lawrence Tribune,* February 6, 1912, p. 1.
145. "Rocco Case Disposed Of in Court," *Lawrence Tribune,* February 8, 1912, p. 1.

146. "To Be Called in Morning," *Boston Globe*, February 6, 1912, p. 2.

147. "Legislators Move to End Mill Strike," *New York Times*, February 9, 1912, p. 1.

148. "Fail to Reach a Settlement," *Boston Globe*, February 10, 1912, p. 2.

149. Robert Sobel, *Coolidge: An American Enigma* (Washington, DC: Regnery, 1998), p. 77.

150. Senate Report, pp. 48–49.

151. Foner, *History of the Labor Movement*, vol. 4, p. 339.

152. "Yates Says Crisis Is Near," *Lawrence Tribune*, February 9, 1912, p. 2.

153. "Strikers Are Leaving City," *Lawrence Tribune*, February 4, 1912, p. 1.

CHAPTER EIGHT: The Children's Exodus

1. Mary Harris Jones, *The Autobiography of Mother Jones* (Chicago: Charles H. Kerr, 1925; rep., New York: Arno Press, 1969), p. 236. Citations are to the Arno edition.

2. "Strikers Send Children Away," *Lawrence Tribune*, February 10, 1912, p. 1.

3. Margaret Sanger, "The Fighting Women of Lawrence," *New York Call*, February 18, 1912, p. 15.

4. "Juveniles as Help to Strikers' Cause," *Boston Evening Globe*, February 10, 1912, p. 2.

5. "Strikers Send Children Away," *Lawrence Tribune*, February 10, 1912, p. 1.

6. Ibid.

7. "Juveniles as Help to Strikers' Cause," *Boston Evening Globe*, February 10, 1912, p. 2.

8. Ibid.

9. "Haywood Predicts State-Wide Strike in Massachusetts," *New York Call*, February 4, 1912, p. 1.

10. William D. Haywood, "When the Kiddies Came Home," *International Socialist Review*, May 1912, p. 716.

11. "Courts Aid Bosses against Strikers in Big Lawrence Fight," *New York Call*, February 7, 1912, p. 1.

12. "150 Strike Waifs Find Homes Here," *New York Times*, February 11, 1912, p. 1.

13. "Children of a Strike," *The Survey*, February 24, 1912, p. 1791.

14. "Sian figli nostri," *Il Proletario*, February 9, 1912, p. 1.

15. "150 Strike Waifs Find Homes Here," *New York Times*, February 11, 1912, p. 1.

16. "Juveniles as Help to Strikers' Cause," *Boston Evening Globe*, February 10, 1912, p. 2.

17. Sanger, "Fighting Women," p. 15.

18. "Children Shout and Sing in New York for Strike," *Boston Herald*, February 11, 1912, p. 2.

19. "150 Strike Waifs Find Homes Here," *New York Times*, February 11, 1912, p. 1.

20. Sanger, "Fighting Women," p. 15.

21. "Children of a Strike," p. 1791.

22. "Lawrence Children in New York Given Passionate Ovation," *New York Call*, February 11, 1912, p. 1.

23. Testimony of Margaret Sanger, House Report, p. 227.

24. Ibid.

25. Glenn W. Miller, *American Labor and the Government* (New York: Prentice-Hall, 1948), p. 147.

26. "Little Exiles, Strikers' Children Tagged for Shipment," *Boston American*, February 18, 1912, pt. 2, p. 1.

27. "150 Strike Waifs Find Homes Here," *New York Times*, February 11, 1912, p. 1.

28. "Whole City Mourns Sudden Death of Mayor Scanlon," *Lawrence Telegram*, August 18, 1914, p. 6.

29. "'Outrage,' Scanlon Calls the Parade," *Boston American*, February 11, 1912, pt. 2, p. 2B.

30. "Ministers Condemn Parade of Children," *Boston American*, February 11, 1912, pt. 2, p. 2B.

31. "Two I.W.W. Leaders Give Strikers Advice," *Lawrence Tribune*, February 14, 1912, p. 6.

32. "Exploiting Children Insane Foolishness, Says Dr. Berle," *Boston American*, February 11, 1912, pt. 2, p. 1.

33. "Officials Unable to Prevent Parade of the Children," *Boston American*, February 11, 1912, pt. 2, p. 3B.

34. "Strikers Send Children Away," *Lawrence Tribune*, February 10, 1912, p. 1.

35. "Seemed Like Fairyland," *Boston Globe*, February 12, 1912, p. 4.

36. Ibid., and "Strikers Send Children Away," *Lawrence Tribune*, February 10, 1912, p. 1.

37. Flynn, *Rebel Girl*, p. 137.

38. Ibid.

39. "Workers Everywhere Rally to Aid of 22,000 Strikers in Lawrence," *New York Call*, February 15, 1912, p. 2.

40. "Sullivan in Control of Police Department," *Lawrence Evening Tribune*, February 20, 1912, p. 3.

41. "To Send Away More Children," *Boston Globe*, February 13, 1912, p. 9.

42. "Philadelphia Will Take 200 Children from Mill Strikers," *New York Call*, February 12, 1912, p. 1.

43. "Little Girl's Story," *Lawrence Daily American*, February 13, 1912, p. 1.

44. "Strikers Send Children Away," *Lawrence Tribune*, February 10, 1912, p. 1.

45. Flynn, *Rebel Girl*, p. 130.

46. Dubofsky, p. 161.

47. Carlson, p. 291.

48. "Police Warn W. D. Haywood," *Lawrence Tribune*, February 12, 1912, p. 2.

49. "By William D. Haywood," *New York Call*, February 16, 1912, p. 2.

50. "Mass Meeting in Boston," *Lawrence Telegram*, March 1, 1912, p. 3.

51. Flynn, *Rebel Girl*, p. 132.

52. "About Haywood," *Literary Digest*, June 14, 1913, pp. 135–36.

53. Palmer, "Strike for Four Loaves," p. 1691.

54. "Down to Long, Hard Fight at Lawrence," *Boston Globe*, February 11, 1912, p. 9.

55. Senate Report, p. 33.

56. "Detectives Employed," *Lawrence Telegram*, February 15, 1912, p. 2.

57. Goldberg, p. 88.

58. Senate Report, p. 33.

59. "No Clash from New Picket Plan," *Lawrence Tribune*, February 12, 1912, p. 3.

60. "Proclamation to Be Issued," *Lawrence Tribune*, February 16, 1912, p. 1.

61. "Received Black Hand Letter," *Lawrence Tribune,* February 15, 1912, p. 2.
62. "Strike Spirit Badly Shaken," *Boston Globe,* February 14, 1912, p. 2.
63. "Ettor Makes His Demands," *Salem Evening News,* November 1, 1912, p. 5.
64. "Soldiers Turning 'Big Bill' Haywood's 'Afternoon Walk' Paraders off Essex St. at Franklin St., Lawrence" (photograph), *Boston Globe,* February 15, 1912, p. 1.
65. "Resents Move of the A.F. of L.," *Boston Globe,* February 7, 1912, p. 2.
66. Gibbs M. Smith, *Labor Martyr: Joe Hill* (New York: Grosset and Dunlap, 1969), p. 27.
67. Joe Hill, "John Golden and the Lawrence Strike," in Kornbluh, p. 180.
68. "Cannot Make Concessions Now," *Lawrence Evening Telegram,* February 17, 1912, p. 1.
69. "Fail to Reach a Settlement," *Boston Globe,* February 10, 1912, p. 2.
70. "Strikers Send Children Away," *Lawrence Tribune,* February 10, 1912, p. 1.
71. "Col. Sweetser's Warning," *Lawrence Telegram,* February 10, 1912, p. 1.
72. "Hit with Bayonet," *Lawrence Tribune,* February 14, 1912, p. 3.
73. "Proclamation to Be Issued," *Lawrence Tribune,* February 16, 1912, p. 1.
74. "Complain of Militia," *Boston Evening Globe,* February 16, 1912, p. 2.
75. "Uses Air Gun on Troops," *Lawrence Telegram,* February 12, 1912, p. 3.
76. Senate Report, p. 496.
77. "Down to Long, Hard Fight at Lawrence," *Boston Globe,* February 11, 1912, p. 9.
78. "Lawrence Soldiers Will Not Obey Orders," *Lawrence Tribune,* February 16, 1912, p. 12, and "Fifth Avenue Sees Lawrence Children," *New York Call,* February 18, 1912, p. 2.
79. "Statements by People Who Took Part: A Militia Man's Experiences," *The Survey,* April 6, 1912, p. 76.
80. Weyl, "Strikers at Lawrence," p. 310.
81. "Strikers to Defy Police," *Boston Evening Globe,* February 23, 1912, p. 4.
82. "Man About Town," *Lawrence Telegram,* February 10, 1912, p. 4.
83. Ibid.
84. Ibid.
85. "Both Cases Continued until Monday Morning," *Lawrence Tribune,* February 10, 1912, p. 5.
86. "Great Number of Witnesses," *Lawrence Tribune,* February 12, 1912, p. 1.
87. Ibid.
88. "Letters to Ettor and Haywood Are Produced in Police Court," *Lawrence Telegram,* February 9, 1912, p. 1.
89. "Charge Policeman with Shooting Woman," *Lawrence Evening Tribune,* February 20, 1912, p. 1.
90. "Letter Is Offered," *Boston Globe,* February 10, 1912, p. 2.
91. "Monster Parade to Boston Is Planned," *Boston Globe,* February 14, 1912, p. 2.
92. "To Send Away More Children," *Boston Globe,* February 13, 1912, p. 1.
93. "Woman Organizer Is Given Big Reception," *Lawrence Daily American,* January 22, 1912, p. 8.
94. Ibid.

95. "Man About Town," *Lawrence Telegram,* January 24, 1912, p. 4.
96. Richard Washburn Child, "Industrial Revolt at Lawrence," *Collier's,* March 9, 1912, p. 14.
97. Flynn, *Rebel Girl,* p. 110.
98. Kornbluh, p. 145.
99. Flynn, *Rebel Girl,* p. 53.
100. Helen C. Camp, *Iron in Her Soul: Elizabeth Gurley Flynn and the American Left* (Pullman: Washington State University Press, 1995), p. 5.
101. Flynn, *Rebel Girl,* p. 36.
102. Ibid., p. 46.
103. Ibid., p. 65.
104. Ibid., p. 64.
105. Ibid., p. 97.
106. Camp, p. 17.
107. Dubofsky, p. 179.
108. Camp, p. 23.
109. Flynn, *Rebel Girl,* p. 110.
110. Ibid., p. 134.
111. Ibid., p. 136.
112. Vorse, *Footnote to Folly,* pp. 8–9.
113. Cameron, p. 78.
114. Ibid., p. 48.
115. Elizabeth Gurley Flynn, "Women in Industry Should Organize," in Rosalyn Fraad Boxandall, *Words on Fire: The Life and Writing of Elizabeth Gurley Flynn* (New Brunswick, NJ: Rutgers University Press, 1987), p. 95.
116. Flynn, *Rebel Girl,* p. 132.
117. Cameron, p. 1.
118. "Strike Committee Meeting," *Lawrence Telegram,* January 26, 1912, p. 4.
119. Cameron, p. 135.
120. Baker, p. 30A.
121. Haywood, *Autobiography,* p. 249, and Cameron, p. 148.
122. Cameron, p. 161.
123. Ibid., p. 148.
124. Ibid., p. 159.
125. Foner, *Women and the American Labor Movement,* p. 211.
126. "More Women before Court," *Lawrence Evening Tribune,* February 28, 1912, p. 1.
127. "Congressman Ames at Meeting," *Lawrence Evening Tribune,* February 28, 1912, p. 1.
128. Cameron, p. 109.
129. Ibid., p. 159.
130. Ibid., p. 156.
131. House Report, p. 246.
132. "Strikers to Defy Police," *Boston Evening Globe,* February 23, 1912, p. 4.
133. "Murder Held to Be Proved," *Boston Globe,* February 22, 1912, p. 2.

134. House Report, p. 242.

135. "Took Gun Away from Soldier," *Lawrence Sun,* February 22, 1912, p. 4.

136. "Three Sisters Appear in Court," *Lawrence Tribune,* February 16, 1912, p. 1.

137. "Denies Kissing Defendant Ettor," *Lawrence Tribune,* November 6, 1912, p. 9.

138. Fosdick, p. 345.

139. Moran, p. 195.

140. "Complain of Militia," *Boston Evening Globe,* February 16, 1912, p. 1.

141. "Sweetser Issues Order to Strikers," *Lawrence Tribune,* February 17, 1912, p. 1.

142. "Women Are Awakening," *Industrial Worker,* July 25, 1912, p. 7.

143. "Protest of Lawrence Women," *Lawrence Evening Tribune,* February 20, 1912, p. 4.

144. Fosdick, p. 344.

145. Cameron, p. 154.

146. "Funds Pouring In," *Boston Globe,* February 11, 1912, p. 9, and Central Labor Union contributions and expenses, Immigrant City Archives, box 4, Lawrence, MA.

147. "Children of a Strike," p. 1791.

148. "Suit for Inquiry into Strike Fund," *Boston Herald,* March 11, 1912, p. 2.

149. Senate Report, pp. 66–67.

150. Central Labor Union contributions and expenses, Immigrant City Archives, box 4, Lawrence, MA.

151. "Conciliation Abandoned," *New York Call,* February 11, 1912, p. 2.

152. Baker, p. 30.

153. "Picketing Abandoned," *Boston Evening Globe,* February 12, 1912, p. 2.

154. "More Police for Lawrence," *Boston Globe,* February 16, 1912, p. 1.

155. "To Stop Exodus of Strikers' Children," *Boston Evening Globe,* February 17, 1912, p. 1.

156. "Cheering Throngs Greet Children of Textile Strikers," *New York World,* February 18, 1912, p. 3.

157. "Strikers' Children and Escorts in New York Parade" (photograph), *Boston American,* February 19, 1912, p. 1.

158. "Strikers' Children Parade Fifth Ave.," *New York Times,* February 18, 1912, p. 4.

159. "Fifth Avenue Sees Lawrence Children," *New York Call,* February 18, 1912, p. 1.

160. "Children Taken from the City," *Lawrence Evening Tribune,* February 17, 1912, p. 1.

161. Ernesto Calderone, oral history interview, tape 154, Immigrant City Archives, Lawrence, MA.

162. "To Stop Exodus of Strikers' Children," *Boston Evening Globe,* February 17, 1912, p. 1.

163. "Children Taken from City," *Lawrence Evening Tribune,* February 17, 1912, p. 1.

164. "Philadelphia Will Take 200 Children from Mill Strikers," *New York Call,* February 12, 1912, p. 1.

165. "Defends Exodus of Children," *Lawrence Telegram,* February 14, 1912, p. 3.

166. Child, "Industrial Revolt," p. 15.

CHAPTER NINE: Crackdown

1. Joseph Conrad, *Heart of Darkness* (New York: W. W. Norton, 1988), p. 42.

2. "Man About Town," *Lawrence Telegram,* February 17, 1912, p. 4.

3. "Eugene Foss's Nemesis," *Los Angeles Times,* February 8, 1912, p. 4.

4. Richard M. Abrams, *Conservatism in a Progressive Era: Massachusetts Politics 1900–1912* (Cambridge, MA: Harvard University Press, 1964), p. 254.

5. Dubofsky, p. 245.

6. Ibid., pp. 135, 154.

7. "State Authorities Severely Criticize Local Government," *Lawrence Daily American,* February 14, 1912, p. 1.

8. "Textile Strike a Revolution," *Industrial Worker,* February 29, 1912, p. 1.

9. "Soldiers May Be Withdrawn," *Boston Globe,* February 13, 1912, p. 1.

10. "Militia Will Stay," *Boston Globe,* February 14, 1912, p. 2.

11. "Civic Authorities Spineless, Says Adjt. Gen. Pearson," *Lawrence Daily American,* February 14, 1912, p. 1.

12. "During Strike Trouble," *Lawrence Tribune,* February 15, 1912, p. 1.

13. Dorgan, *History of Lawrence, Massachusetts,* pp. 183–84.

14. "Mahoneys Figure Large in Lawrence Murder Hearing" (photograph), *Boston Globe,* February 14, 1912, p. 2.

15. Testimony of George Roewer, in House Report, p. 250.

16. "Sullivan Is Marshal," *Boston Globe,* February 20, 1912, p. 2.

17. Testimony of John J. Sullivan, in House Report, p. 290.

18. Photograph in *Boston Evening Globe,* February 24, 1912, p. 5.

19. Ibid.

20. "Defense Scores," *Boston Globe,* February 21, 1912, p. 1.

21. "Rule Due Today," *Boston Globe,* February 24, 1912, p. 2.

22. "More Children to Leave the City," *Boston Globe,* February 16, 1912, p. 9.

23. "Fall River Weavers Strike," *Boston Globe,* February 15, 1912, p. 4; "Submit Demands," *Boston Globe,* February 15, 1912, p. 4; and "Strike in New Bedford," *Lawrence Telegram,* February 26, 1912, p. 10.

24. "Children and Mothers Taken Away by Police," *Boston Evening Globe,* February 24, 1912, p. 1.

25. Ibid.

26. Robert E. Gilbert, *The Tormented President: Calvin Coolidge, Death, and Clinical Depression* (Westport, CT: Praeger, 2003), p. 69.

27. "Meeting," *Lawrence Evening Tribune,* February 24, 1912, p. 1.

28. "Man Shot by a Rioter," *Lawrence Tribune,* February 26, 1912, p. 6.

29. Senate Report, p. 33.

30. "Children to Be Kept at Home," *Lawrence Tribune,* February 22, 1912, p. 1.

31. "Defense Scores," *Boston Globe,* February 21, 1912, p. 1.

32. "Charge Policeman with Shooting Woman," *Lawrence Evening Tribune,* February 20, 1912, p. 1.

33. "Say Police Killed Woman," *Boston Evening Globe,* February 20, 1912, p. 2.

34. "Murder Held to Be Proved," *Boston Globe,* February 22, 1912, p. 2.

35. Ibid., and Testimony of Cornelius F. Lynch, in House Report, pp. 263, 276.

36. Testimony of Tema Camitta, ibid., p. 201.

37. "Stops Exodus of Children," *Boston Globe,* February 23, 1912, p. 4.

38. "200 Children Are Shipped to New York to Exploit Strike," *Boston American,* February 11, 1912, p. 1.

39. "Mill Strikers Forced to Part with Children," *Boston American,* February 12, 1912, p. 1.

40. "Letters from Children," *Lawrence Telegram,* February 19, 1912, p. 8.

41. "Women Strike Picket Is Fined at Lawrence," *Boston American,* February 19, 1912, p. 2.

42. "Wm. D. Haywood Makes Reply," *Lawrence Evening Tribune,* February 20, 1912, p. 3.

43. "Complained to Police," *Lawrence Evening Tribune,* February 23, 1912, p. 1.

44. "Rule Due Today," *Boston Globe,* February 24, 1912, p. 2.

45. "Plans for Children," *Lawrence Tribune,* February 24, 1912, p. 3.

46. "Police Prevent Children's Exile," *Lawrence Evening Tribune,* February 24, 1912, p. 1.

47. "Children and Mothers Taken by Police," *Boston Evening Globe,* February 24, 1912, p. 1.

48. "The Lawrence Strike: A Review," *The Outlook,* March 9, 1912, p. 531.

49. Ibid.

50. Ibid.

51. "Police and the Strikers Clash," *Lawrence Evening Telegram,* February 24, 1912, p. 1.

52. "Children and Mothers Taken by Police," *Boston Evening Globe,* February 24, 1912, p. 1.

53. "Police and the Strikers Clash," *Lawrence Evening Telegram,* February 24, 1912, p. 1 For further testimony to the clubbing of women, see also *Boston Evening Globe* and *Lawrence Evening Tribune,* February 24, 1912, p. 1; *Boston Post,* February 25, 1912, p. 1; *New York Times, New York Herald,* and *New York Call,* February 25, 1912, p. 1; *New York American,* February 25, 1912, p. 3; *New York World,* February 26, 1912, p. 6; and *New York Sun,* quoted in "The Lawrence Strike Children," *Literary Digest,* March 9, 1912, p. 471. Newspapers that covered the event but did not mention the clubbing of women include *Lawrence Sun,* February 24, 1912, p. 1; *Le Courrier de Lawrence,* February 29, 1912, p. 6; *Boston American,* February 24, 1912, p. 1; and *Boston Herald,* February 25, 1912, p. 4.

54. Testimony of Tema Camitta, in House Report, p. 196.

55. "Police Prevent Children's Exile," *Lawrence Evening Tribune,* February 24, 1912, p. 3.

56. "Angry Women Attack Police," *Boston Globe,* February 25, 1912, p. 6.

57. "Police and the Strikers Clash," *Lawrence Evening Telegram,* February 24, 1912, p. 1.

58. "Children and Mothers Taken by Police," *Boston Evening Globe,* February 24, 1912, p. 1.

59. "Disturbance at Strike Meeting," *Lawrence Evening Tribune,* February 24, 1912, p. 3.

60. "Claim Police Clubbed Women in Riot," *Boston Post,* February 25, 1912, p. 9.

61. "Disturbance at Strike Meeting," *Lawrence Evening Tribune,* February 24, 1912, p. 3.

62. "Police and the Strikers Clash," *Lawrence Evening Telegram,* February 24, 1912, p. 1.

63. "Arrest 50 in Strike Rioting," *Boston American,* February 24, 1912, p. 2.

64. "Children and Mothers Taken by Police," *Boston Evening Globe,* February 24, 1912, p. 1.

65. "Philadelphia to Get 100 Strikers' Children Today," *New York Call,* February 24, 1912, p. 1.
66. "Many Pickets Arrested," *Lawrence Evening Tribune,* February 24, 1912, p. 3.
67. "Angry Women Attack Police," *Boston Globe,* February 25, 1912, p. 1.
68. "The Embargo on Strike Children," *The Survey,* March 2, 1912, p. 1822.
69. Testimony of George Roewer, in House Report, p. 251.
70. Photograph of the City Home, Immigrant City Archives, Lawrence, MA.
71. "Angry Women Attack Police," *Boston Globe,* February 25, 1912, p. 6.
72. "Women Fined in Court," *Boston Globe,* February 25, 1912, p. 6.
73. "Angry Women Attack Police," *Boston Globe,* February 25, 1912, p. 6.
74. "Police Clubs Keep Lawrence Waifs In," *New York Times,* February 25, 1912, p. 2.
75. Ibid.
76. "Appeal to Soldiers," *Boston Globe,* February 25, 1912, p. 6.
77. "Policemen Draw Their Revolvers," *Lawrence Evening Tribune,* February 26, 1912, p. 1.
78. "General Strike Appeal," *Boston Globe,* February 25, 1912, p. 6.
79. "Police Clubs Keep Lawrence Waifs In," *New York Times,* February 25, 1912, p. 2.
80. Mary Peccerillo Lynch, tape 95, oral history interview, Immigrant City Archives, Lawrence, MA.
81. Cole, p. 164.
82. Alice L. Walsh, *A Sketch of the Life and Labors of Rev. James T. O'Reilly, O.S.A.* (Lawrence, MA: Free Press Printing, 1924), p. 12.
83. Cole, p. 164.
84. Lynch, oral history.
85. Cole, p. 55.
86. Ibid., p. 166.
87. Walsh, p. 55.
88. "Fr. O'Reilly States View," *Lawrence Evening Tribune,* February 26, 1912, p. 7.
89. Arnold, p. 315.
90. "Clash at Lawrence," *Boston Globe,* February 26, 1912, p. 8.
91. "Blundering at Lawrence," *New York Tribune,* February 26, 1912, p. 6.
92. "The Lawrence Outrage," *New York World,* February 26, 1912, p. 6.
93. "This, in Free America," *Miami Herald,* February 28, 1912, p. 2.
94. "Lawrence Strike Children," p. 471.
95. "The Lawrence Strikers and Their Children," *Springfield* (MA) *Republican,* February 29, 1912, p. 10.
96. "The Strike in the Woolen Mills," *Current Literature,* April 1912, p. 384.
97. Kornbluh, p. 161.
98. "Mill Murderers of Massachusetts," *Appeal to Reason,* March 2, 1912, p. 1.
99. "Les Etats-Unis s'acheminent vers la revolution," *Le Courrier de Lawrence,* February 29, 1912, p. 4.
100. "The Animal Behavior of the State with the Striking Lawrence Workers," *Keleivis,* February 29, 1912, p. 1.
101. William E. Borah, "Unconstitutional," *New York Call,* February 25, 1912, p. 1.

102. Newton Baker, "Uncivilized," *New York Call,* February 25, 1912, p. 1.

103. "Mill Officials Offer Concessions," *Lawrence Evening Tribune,* March 1, 1912, p. 10.

104. Testimony of Honorable Victor L. Berger, in House Report, pp. 11–24.

105. Mrs. Joseph Ellis, "Misuse of Power," *New York Call,* February 25, 1912, p. 1.

106. "Cole Raps Officials," *Boston Globe,* February 28, 1912, p. 2.

107. "Perilous Literature," *Lawrence Telegram,* February 3, 1912, p. 8, and Lawrence Citizens' Assocation, *A Reign of Terror in an American City* (pamphlet), March 1912.

108. Lawrence Citizens' Association, *Lawrence as It Really Is* (pamphlet), March 1912, p. 1.

109. "For City's Welfare," *Boston Evening Globe,* February 28, 1912, p. 1.

110. "The Police and the Public," *Lawrence Telegram,* February 26, 1912, p. 4.

111. "Man Held in $14,000 after Shots at Police," *Boston Evening Globe,* February 26, 1912, p. 1.

112. "Rioters Boldly Shoot," *Lawrence Evening Tribune,* February 26, 1912, p. 1.

113. "Fire 30 Shots at Lawrence," *Boston Globe,* February 27, 1912, p. 3.

114. "Man Held in $14,000 after Shots at Police," *Boston Evening Globe,* February 26, 1912, p. 1.

115. "Sixty-Six Tried in Police Court," *Lawrence Evening Tribune,* February 27, 1912, p. 6.

116. "Fire 30 Shots at Lawrence," *Boston Globe,* February 27, 1912, p. 3.

117. "Lawrence Police Charge Strikers as Bus Is Fired Upon," *Christian Science Monitor,* February 26, 1912, p. 1.

118. "Man Held in $14,000 after Shots at Police," *Boston Evening Globe,* February 26, 1912, p. 1.

119. Ibid.

120. "Lawrence Strikers Fire upon the Police," *New York Times,* February 27, 1912, p. 20.

121. "Man Held in $14,000 after Shots at Police," *Boston Evening Globe,* February 26, 1912, p. 1.

122. "4 Women Pickets Arrested," *Lawrence Evening Telegram,* February 26, 1912, p. 4.

123. "Man Held in $14,000 after Shots at Police," *Boston Evening Globe,* February 26, 1912, p. 1.

124. "Strikers Proclaim," *Lawrence Tribune,* February 27, 1912, p. 1.

125. "No Excuse for Action," *Boston Globe,* February 27, 1912, p. 3.

126. "Taft Starts Probe in Lawrence Case," *Boston Globe,* February 27, 1912, p. 3.

127. "Reign of Terror in Full Swing at Lawrence, Mass. as Police Beat Up Strikers," *New York Call,* February 27, 1912, p. 1.

128. "Caruso for Strikers," *Lawrence Evening Tribune,* February 26, 1912, p. 1.

129. "Child Cases Up in Court," *Boston Globe,* February 28, 1912, p. 2.

130. "Children Are Lured Away," *Lawrence Evening Tribune,* February 27, 1912, p. 1.

131. "Exile of Children," *Lawrence Evening Tribune,* February 29, 1912, p. 1.

132. "Court Dismisses Children's Cases," *Lawrence Evening Tribune,* March 12, 1912, p. 1.

133. "May Be Compelled to Rise in Revolt," *Boston Evening Globe,* February 27, 1912, p. 1.

134. "Women in Skirmish," *Lawrence Evening Tribune,* February 28, 1912, p. 1.

135. "Confer with Mill Men," *Lawrence Evening Tribune,* February 29, 1912, p. 10.

136. Baker, p. 26.

137. Ibid., p. 22.
138. Vorse, "Trouble at Lawrence," p. 10.
139. "Probers Pry into Lawrence Strike," *Boston Globe,* February 29, 1912, p. 1.
140. Baker, p. 21.
141. "Probers Pry into Lawrence Strike," *Boston Globe,* February 29, 1912, p. 1.

CHAPTER TEN: In Congress, 1912

1. Émile Zola, *Germinal* (New York: New American Library, 1970), p. 182.
2. "Attorney General in Lawrence," *Lawrence Tribune,* February 27, 1912, p. 1.
3. *Who's Who in America, 1912–1913,* s.v. "Ames, Adelbert."
4. Ibid., s.v. "Ames, Butler."
5. "Congressman Ames at Meeting," *Lawrence Evening Tribune,* February 28, 1912, p. 1.
6. Ibid.
7. "Strikers Depart for Washington," *Lawrence Evening Tribune,* March 1, 1912, p. 1.
8. "Did William M. Wood Break Deadlock?" *Lawrence Evening Tribune,* March 1, 1912, p. 16.
9. "Offer Wage Raise to End Strike," *Boston Globe,* March 1, 1912, p. 2.
10. "Mayor Goes into Detail," *Lawrence Telegram,* March 2, 1912, p. 1.
11. "Statement by the Arlington Mills," *Lawrence Telegram,* March 1, 1912, p. 1.
12. "Women Once More Beaten and Kicked in Lawrence City," *New York Call,* March 3, 1912, p. 1.
13. "No Action at Morning Session," *Lawrence Telegram,* March 1, 1912, p. 1, and "Five Percent Not Enough," *Boston Evening Globe,* March 2, 1912, p. 1.
14. "Women Once More Beaten and Kicked in Lawrence City," *New York Call,* March 3, 1912, p. 1.
15. "Golden Is Satisfied," *Lawrence Tribune,* March 5, 1912, p. 10.
16. "Strikers Hear Plan of Raise," *Boston Globe,* March 2, 1912, p. 1.
17. "Strike Leaders Are Not Satisfied with Concessions," *Lawrence Tribune,* March 2, 1912, p. 8.
18. "Discussed the Strike," *Lawrence Telegram,* March 1, 1912, p. 2.
19. Robertson, p. 9.
20. Edmund Morris, *Theodore Rex* (New York: Random House, 2001), pp. 156–69.
21. *Final Report of the Commission on Industrial Relations* (Washington, DC, 1915), pp. 48–49.
22. Robertson, pp. 155–56.
23. Cahn, p. 201.
24. "Reign of Terror in Full Swing at Lawrence, Mass., as Police Beat Up Strikers," *New York Call,* February 27, 1912, p. 1.
25. "Will Arouse Washington," *Boston Globe,* March 1, 1912, p. 2.
26. *Who's Who in America, 1912–1913,* s.v. "Wilson, William B."
27. Testimony of Honorable William B. Wilson, in House Report, p. 3.
28. Testimony of Honorable Victor L. Berger, in ibid., pp. 11–25.
29. Ibid., pp. 11, 29.

30. Testimony of Samuel Lipson, in House Report, pp. 31–32.

31. Ibid.

32. Ibid., p. 44.

33. "Won't Return until All Go Together," *Lawrence Telegram,* March 8, 1912, p. 5.

34. "Lawrence Strikers See Victory Now Smiling on Them," *New York Call,* March 10, 1912, p. 2.

35. Testimony of Samuel Lipson, in House Report, pp. 66, 70.

36. "Woes of Strikers Told to Congress," *Boston Globe,* March 3, 1912, p. 4.

37. Testimony of John Golden, in House Committee on Rules, *Strike at Lawrence, Mass.,* pp. 75, 86–87.

38. "Woes of Strikers Told to Congress," *Boston Globe,* March 3, 1912, p. 4.

39. "Lawrence Alert for a Strike Test Today," *Boston Globe,* March 4, 1912, p. 2.

40. "Socialism Feeds on Discontent," *Lawrence Evening Telegram,* March 4, 1912, p. 1.

41. Ibid., and "Raid Textile Men's Meeting," *New York Times,* March 6, 1912, p. 6.

42. "No Sign of Break among the I.W.W. Strikers," *Boston Evening Globe,* March 4, 1912, p. 2.

43. Ibid.

44. Senate Report, p. 505.

45. Ibid., p. 33.

46. "No Sign of Break among the I.W.W. Strikers," *Boston Evening Globe,* March 4, 1912, p. 2.

47. Photograph of James P. Thompson, *Boston Evening Globe,* March 4, 1912, p. 1.

48. "No Sign of Break among the I.W.W. Strikers," *Boston Evening Globe,* March 4, 1912, p. 2.

49. "Thursday's Strike Meeting," *Lawrence Evening Tribune,* March 15, 1912, p. 1.

50. "Police Investigation," *New York Call,* March 8, 1912, p. 2.

51. Testimony of Samuel Lipson, in House Report, pp. 114–15.

52. Ibid.

53. Testimony of Samuel Gompers, in House Report, pp. 126–28.

54. Rosario Contarino, oral history interview, tape 95, Immigrant City Archives, Lawrence, MA, and letter to editor, *Lawrence Eagle Tribune,* September 1987, Lawrence, MA, Strike 1912, box 2.

55. Testimony of Samuel Goldberg, in House Report, p. 140.

56. Testimony of Auguste Waite, in ibid., p. 148.

57. Testimony of John Bodelar, in ibid., pp. 154–55.

58. Testimony of Camella Teoli, in ibid., pp. 169–70.

59. Testimony of C. H. Kitchin, in ibid., p. 429.

60. Testimony of Camella Teoli, in ibid., pp. 171–73.

61. "Police Say Women Led Lawrence Mobs," *New York Times,* March 7, 1912, p. 6.

62. Testimony of Louis Cox, in House Report, p. 411.

63. Testimony of John J. Sullivan, in ibid., p. 340.

64. Testimony of Rev. Clark Carter, in ibid., p. 380.

65. Statement of Louis Cox, in ibid., p. 407.

66. Testimony of C. O. Andrews, in ibid.

67. Testimony of Rev. Clark Carter, in ibid., p. 358.

68. Ibid., p. 381.

69. Testimony of John J. Sullivan, in House Report, p. 326.

70. Ibid., p. 297.

71. Ibid., p. 321.

72. Ibid., p. 297.

73. Ibid., p. 298.

74. Ibid., p. 309.

75. Ibid., p. 304.

76. Ibid., p. 342.

77. Ibid., p. 344.

78. Testimony of Louis Cox, in House Report, p. 419.

79. Ibid., p. 411.

80. "Rev. Clark Carter Dies at Andover," *Lawrence Tribune,* April 1920, p. 1.

81. Testimony of Rev. Clark Carter, in House Report, p. 385.

82. Ibid., p. 382.

83. Ibid., p. 393.

84. Ibid., p. 392.

85. Ibid.

86. Ibid., p. 396.

87. Testimony of C. H. Kitchin, in House Report, p. 431.

88. Testimony of Frank Sherman, in ibid., p. 438.

89. Testimony of August P. Wade, in ibid., p. 444.

90. "Settlement Is Possible," *Boston Globe,* March 8, 1912, p. 1.

91. "To Investigate Situation," *Lawrence Evening Tribune,* March 8, 1912, p. 2.

92. "Congressmen Hear Strikers' Children," *New York Times,* March 5, 1912, p. 5.

93. Owen R. Lovejoy, "Right of Free Speech in Lawrence," *The Survey,* March 9, 1912, p. 1904.

94. "Sweetser Going Today," *Lawrence Tribune,* March 5, 1912, p. 10.

95. "Mills Are Insured against Riots," *Lawrence Telegram,* March 5, 1912, p. 1.

96. McPherson, "American Woolen Company's Quarter-Century Record," in *Bulletin of the National Association of Wool Manufacturers—1924,* p. 485.

97. "Told to Carry Pepper," *Boston Evening Globe,* March 4, 1912, p. 2.

98. "Riot Call at Lawrence," *New York Times,* March 5, 1912, p. 5.

99. "Relief Station Is Closed," *Lawrence Evening Tribune,* March 7, 1912, p. 6.

100. "Police Intimidation," *New York Call,* March 8, 1912, p. 2.

101. "Children Made Happy," *Boston Evening Globe,* March 7, 1912, p. 6.

102. "Police Get Facts about Children," *Lawrence Evening Tribune,* March 7, 1912, p. 1.

103. "Children Made Happy," *Boston Evening Globe,* March 7, 1912, p. 6.

104. "Man Stabbed, Arms Pinioned," *Boston Evening Globe,* March 7, 1912, p. 1.

105. "Attempt Made to Stab Policeman," *Lawrence Evening Tribune,* March 7, 1912, p. 5.

106. "Man Stabbed, Arms Pinioned," *Boston Evening Globe,* March 7, 1912, p. 1.

107. "Tribune Topics," *Lawrence Tribune*, March 8, 1912, p. 4.

108. "Describes Alleged Clubbing," *Lawrence Telegram*, March 9, 1912, p. 12; see also Marcy and Boyd, p. 625, and Haywood, *Autobiography*, p. 251.

109. "Open Letter to Authorities," *Lawrence Evening Telegram*, March 8, 1912, p. 6.

CHAPTER ELEVEN: An American Tapestry

1. Adam Smith, *The Wealth of Nations*, vol. 1 (New York: G. P. Putnam and Sons, 1904), pp. 69–70.

2. Roddy, p. 47.

3. "Miss Irene Wood Injured Coasting," *Lawrence Telegram*, March 8, 1912, p. 7.

4. Fosdick, p. 343.

5. "Settlement Is Possible," *Boston Globe*, March 8, 1912, p. 2.

6. Ibid.

7. Ibid.

8. "Fewer Pickets Were on Duty This Morning," *Lawrence Evening Telegram*, March 9, 1912, p. 1.

9. "Last Week of the Big Strike," *Lawrence Evening Tribune*, March 8, 1912, p. 4.

10. "Things Talked About," *Lawrence Evening Tribune*, March 11, 1912, p. 4.

11. "To Lift Strike Partly," *Boston Evening Globe*, March 14, 1912, p. 5.

12. "Will Submit New Schedule," *Boston Globe*, March 10, 1912, p. 1.

13. "Fifteen Children Leave for Manchester," *Lawrence Evening Telegram*, March 9, 1912, p. 1.

14. "Parade Today for Lawrence Strikers," *New York Call*, March 9, 1912, p. 1.

15. "Lecture on the Lawrence Strike," *New York Call*, March 9, 1912, p. 2.

16. "Haywood Sees End of Lawrence Strike," *New York Call*, March 10, 1912, p. 2.

17. "Textile Mills Raise Wages," *Boston Globe*, March 10, 1912, p. 8.

18. Arnold, p. 343.

19. "Strike Just Before Raise," *Boston Globe*, March 13, 1912, p. 2.

20. "Pepperell to Readjust," *Boston Globe*, March 10, 1912, p. 8.

21. "Raise by 35 Corporations," *Boston Globe*, March 13, 1912, p. 2.

22. "Big Textile Strike in This City Is Over," *Lawrence Telegram*, March 25, 1912, p. 4.

23. "300,000 Benefited by Local Strike," *Lawrence Evening Tribune*, March 25, 1912, p. 1.

24. "Await Fifth Conference," *Boston Evening Globe*, March 11, 1912, p. 2.

25. "Will Not Obey Injunction," *Boston Globe*, March 12, 1912, p. 2.

26. "More Strike Literature," *Lawrence Tribune*, March 11, 1912, p. 8.

27. Ibid.

28. "Await Fifth Conference," *Boston Evening Globe*, March 11, 1912, p. 2.

29. "Leaders Summoned," *Lawrence Evening Tribune*, March 12, 1912, p. 3.

30. Arnold, p. 340.

31. "Over $5,000 in One Day," *Lawrence Tribune*, March 12, 1912, p. 10.

32. "To Keep Up Distribution," *Boston Evening Globe*, March 12, 1912, p. 2.

33. "Vote to Work in Six Mills," *Boston Globe*, March 15, 1912, p. 2.

34. "Reign of Terror in an American City," *New York Tribune*, March 11, 1912, p. 1.

35. Reprinted in "Another View of the Great Strike," *Lawrence Tribune*, March 12, 1912, p. 2.

36. "Catholic Scores Strike," *Boston Evening Transcript*, March 11, 1912, p. 8.

37. Dorgan, *History of Lawrence, Massachusetts*, pp. 156–57.

38. Lawrence Citizens' Association, *A Reign of Terror in an American City, What City after Lawrence?* and *Lawrence as It Really Is* (Lawrence, MA: March 1912).

39. *Lawrence as It Really Is*, p. 2.

40. Ibid.

41. Ibid.

42. *A Reign of Terror in an American City*, p. 2.

43. Ibid., p. 3.

44. *Lawrence as It Really Is*, p. 2.

45. Ibid., p. 3.

46. Ibid.

47. Ibid.

48. Ibid., p. 4.

49. Ibid.

50. *What City after Lawrence?* pp. 1–2.

51. "Lawrence," *New York Call*, March 10, 1912, p. 15.

52. "Dal teatro della lotta," *Il Proletario*, March 1, 1912, p. 1.

53. *What City after Lawrence?* p. 2.

54. "Sob Squad at Lawrence," *Lawrence Tribune*, March 14, 1912, p. 2.

55. "Reaction Is Sure," *Lawrence Telegram*, March 14, 1912, p. 4.

56. "Notes and Comments," *Lawrence Telegram*, March 13, 1912, p. 4.

57. "Raises for 175,000 in New England, Likely 100,000 More," *Boston Globe*, March 13, 1912, p. 1.

58. "Accept Wage Increase," *Lawrence Evening Tribune*, March 13, 1912, p. 1.

59. "Acceptance Is Recommended," *Lawrence Evening Telegram*, March 13, 1912, p. 2.

60. Kornbluh, p. 180.

61. *Songs of the Workers*, 34th ed. (Chicago: Industrial Workers of the World, 1980), p. 64.

62. "Conflict of Authority," *Lawrence Evening Tribune*, March 14, 1912, p. 8.

63. "Working for a Settlement," *Lawrence Evening Tribune*, March 8, 1912, p. 1.

64. "Going to Work Monday," *Lawrence Evening Tribune*, March 15, 1912, p. 9.

65. "Great Strike Settled," *Lawrence Evening Tribune*, March 14, 1912, p. 1.

66. "Vote to Work in Six Mills," *Boston Globe*, March 15, 1912, p. 2.

67. "Going to Work Monday," *Lawrence Evening Tribune*, March 15, 1912, p. 9.

68. "Served with Summons," *Lawrence Evening Telegram*, March 14, 1912, p. 1.

69. "Vote to Work in Six Mills," *Boston Globe*, March 15, 1912, p. 2.

70. "New Castle Aids Lawrence," *Solidarity*, March 23, 1912, p. 1.

71. "Going to Work Monday," *Lawrence Evening Tribune*, March 15, 1912, p. 9.

72. Ibid.

73. "Vote to Work in Six Mills," *Boston Globe*, March 15, 1912, p. 2.

74. "Bouquets Put on Graves," *Lawrence Evening Tribune*, March 15, 1912, p. 16.

75. "Mills Want Former Strikers to Return," *Lawrence Tribune*, March 16, 1912, p. 1.

76. "Strikers Back to Looms," *New York Times,* March 16, 1912, p. 2.

77. "Man About Town," *Lawrence Telegram,* March 16, 1912, p. 6.

78. "Suit for Inquiry into Strike Fund," *Boston Herald,* March 11, 1912, p. 2.

79. "Tribune Topics," *Lawrence Tribune,* March 19, 1912, p. 4.

80. "The Lawrence Labor Victory," *Literary Digest,* March 23, 1912, p. 575.

81. Cahn, p. 216.

82. "Man About Town," *Lawrence Telegram,* March 19, 1912, p. 4.

83. "Spring Openings Held," *Lawrence Tribune,* March 20, 1912, p. 1.

84. Foner, *History of the Labor Movement,* vol. 4, p. 347.

85. "Tributes to St. Patrick," *Lawrence Tribune,* March 18, 1912, p. 8.

86. Ibid.

87. "Loss by the Strike," *Lawrence Telegram,* March 13, 1912, p. 3.

88. "President Taft Starts for New Hampshire," *Lawrence Evening Tribune,* March 19, 1912, p. 1.

89. "Colonel Roosevelt Was in This City," *Lawrence Evening Tribune,* March 20, 1912, p. 1.

90. "Big Textile Strike in This City Is Over," *Lawrence Telegram,* March 25, 1912, p. 4.

91. "Militia Has Gone Away," *Lawrence Evening Tribune,* March 25, 1912, p. 1.

92. "Police Force Much Pared," *Lawrence Evening Tribune,* March 27, 1912, p. 1.

93. "No Federal Probe of Local Strike," *Lawrence Evening Tribune,* March 27, 1912, p. 1.

94. "Rioting Begins in Strike at Barre," *New York Times,* March 17, 1912, p. 7.

95. "Crazed by Lawrence Affair," *Lawrence Tribune,* March 12, 1912, p. 4.

96. "Barre Strike Ends," *Lawrence Tribune,* March 22, 1912, p. 1, and Arnold, p. 360.

97. Arnold, pp. 361–62.

98. "Nation-Wide Aid Promised to Lowell Mill Strikers," *Lawrence Evening Tribune,* March 27, 1912, p. 1.

99. "Lowell Strikers Parade Peaceably," *New York Call,* March 29, 1912, p. 1.

100. "Great Textile Strike Threatens Lowell," *Lawrence Evening Tribune,* March 25, 1912, p. 1.

101. Flynn, *Rebel Girl,* pp. 144–45.

102. "Victory in Lawrence," *Solidarity,* March 23, 1912, p. 1.

103. "Advertising the I.W.W.," *Solidarity,* March 23, 1912, p. 4.

104. Fosdick, p. 340.

105. "Latest from Lawrence," *Solidarity,* March 23, 1912, p. 1.

106. John J. Maginnis, "A City Transformed by Turmoil," *Lawrence Eagle-Tribune,* April 27, 1980, sec. D, pp. 1–2.

107. "Haywood on the Ettor-Giovannitti Case," *Industrial Worker,* June 27, 1912, p. 4.

108. "Organize Textile District," *Lawrence Tribune,* March 18, 1912, p. 10.

109. "I.W.W. Organizer Pelted in Clinton," *Lawrence Evening Tribune,* March 29, 1912, p. 1.

110. "Handling the Lawrence Strike," *Boston Herald,* March 16, 1912, p. 4.

111. "The New Socialism That Threatens the Social System," *New York Times,* March 17, 1912, pt. 5, p. 1.

112. Samuel Gompers, "The Lawrence Strike," *American Federationist,* April 1912, pp. 281–93.

113. Lorin F. Deland, "The Lawrence Strike: A Study," *Atlantic Monthly,* May 1912, pp. 694–705.

114. "A.F. of L. Plans Campaign," *Lawrence Tribune,* March 27, 1912, p. 2.

115. "Dismisses Petition to Enjoin I.W.W. Fund," *Lawrence Evening Tribune,* March 27, 1912, p. 1.

116. "Man's Spine Broken," *Lawrence Tribune,* March 22, 1912, p. 1, and "Wm. Todd Dies of Injuries," *Lawrence Evening Tribune,* March 30, 1912, p. 1.

117. "Man Whirled around Shafting," *Lawrence Tribune,* March 26, 1912, p. 1.

118. "Walkout at Wood Mill," *Lawrence Telegram,* March 20, 1912, p. 4.

119. "Workers Charge Discrimination," *Lawrence Evening Tribune,* March 18, 1912, p. 1.

120. "Strikers Return to Work," *Lawrence Telegram,* March 26, 1912, p. 1.

121. "Lawrence Workers Still Need Help to Complete Victory," *New York Call,* March 19, 1912, p. 1.

122. "The Increase," *Lawrence Evening Tribune,* March 14, 1912, p. 1.

123. Haywood, "When the Kiddies Came Home," p. 716.

124. "Monster Parade Welcomes Exiled Children Home," *Boston Globe,* March 31, 1912, p. 1.

125. "Story of the Lawrence Children," *New York Call,* March 31, 1912, p. 10.

126. "Pass through Boston," *Boston Herald,* March 31, 1912, p. 2.

127. "Story of the Lawrence Children," *New York Call,* March 31, 1912, p. 10.

128. Cahn, p. 221.

129. "10,000 Parade in Lawrence to Greet 'Kiddies,'" *Boston Herald,* March 31, 1912, p. 1.

130. "Children Paraded through Streets," *Lawrence Tribune,* April 1, 1912, p. 2.

131. "Monster Parade Welcomes Exiled Children Home," *Boston Globe,* March 31, 1912, p. 1.

132. "10,000 Parade in Lawrence to Greet 'Kiddies,'" *Boston Herald,* March 31, 1912, p. 2.

133. Fosdick, p. 345.

CHAPTER TWELVE: "The Flag of Liberty Is Here"

1. Kornbluh, p. 186.

2. "Children Paraded through Streets," *Lawrence Tribune,* April 1, 1912, p. 2.

3. "10,000 Parade in Lawrence to Greet 'Kiddies,'" *Boston Herald,* March 31, 1912, p. 2.

4. "Monster Parade Welcomes Exiled Children Home," *Boston Globe,* March 31, 1912, p. 2.

5. Camp, p. 27.

6. "Who Arturo Giovannitti Is," *Industrial Worker,* May 30, 1912, p. 4.

7. "The Social Significance of Arturo Giovannitti," *Current Opinion,* January 1913, p. 24.

8. Ibid., p. 26.

9. Ebert, *Trial of a New Society,* p. 70.

10. *Ettor and Giovannitti before the Jury,* p. 60.

11. Helen Keller, introduction, in Arturo Giovannitti, *The Collected Poems of Arturo Giovannitti* (Chicago: E. Clemente and Sons, 1962), p. vii.

12. "Social Significance of Arturo Giovannitti," p. 24.
13. "Who Arturo Giovannitti Is," *Industrial Worker,* May 30, 1912, p. 4.
14. Interview with Len Giovannitti, in Jackson, *Lawrence Strike 1912.*
15. *Ettor and Giovannitti before the Jury,* p. 49.
16. Giovannitti, *Collected Poems,* pp. 193, 197–98.
17. "Social Significance of Arturo Giovannitti," p. 26.
18. Kenneth Macgowan, "Giovannitti: Poet of the Wop," *The Forum,* October 1914, p. 611.
19. Kornbluh, p. 185.
20. "Social Significance of Arturo Giovannitti," p. 25.
21. W. Jett Lauck, "Lessons from Lawrence," *North American Review,* May 1912, p. 672.
22. Walter Weyl, "The Lawrence Strike from Various Angles: It Is Time to Know," *The Survey,* April 6, 1912, p. 66.
23. Deland, p. 705.
24. *Acts and Resolutions Passed by the General Court of Massachusetts in the Year of 1912* (Boston: Wright Potter, 1912), pp. 782–83.
25. Moran, p. 219.
26. "President Names Industrial Board," *New York Times,* December 18, 1912, p. 6.
27. "20 Year Old Lawrence Woman Found Alive," *Lawrence Evening Tribune,* April 23, 1912, p. 3.
28. Arnold, pp. 407–13.
29. "Police Shoot Down Strikers," *Lawrence Evening Tribune,* June 3, 1912, p. 1.
30. "13,000 Will Quit Mills," *Boston Globe,* July 15, 1912, p. 1.
31. "W. D. Haywood Is Indicted," *Lawrence Evening Tribune,* April 22, 1912, p. 1, and "Haywood Indicted in April on Charge of Conspiracy," *Boston Globe,* September 16, 1912, p. 4.
32. "Pitman Preferred Death to Inquiry," *Lawrence Evening Tribune,* August 28, 1912, p. 3.
33. "Dynamite Plant Grows Civil Suit," *Lawrence Evening Tribune,* June 15, 1912, p. 1.
34. "Chief Sullivan Sued," *Lawrence Evening Tribune,* May 21, 1912, p. 1.
35. Kornbluh, p. 185.
36. "The Lawrence Point of View," *Lawrence Evening Tribune,* September 11, 1912, p. 4.
37. "Kills Himself with Revolver," *Lawrence Evening Tribune,* August 27, 1912, p. 1.
38. "Charge Plot to Big Mill Men," *Boston Evening Globe,* August 28, 1912, p. 1.
39. "Collins Arrested and Two Other Men Indicted," *Boston Evening Globe,* August 29, 1912, p. 1.
40. "Pres. Wood of American Woolen Co. Surrenders," *Boston Evening Globe,* August 30, 1912, p. 1.
41. Ibid.
42. "Shock to Lawrence," *Boston Evening Globe,* August 30, 1912, p. 3.
43. "I.W.W. Makes a Statement," *Lawrence Evening Tribune,* August 30, 1912, p. 1.
44. "Capitalist Dynamiter Commits Suicide," *Industrial Worker,* September 5, 1912, p. 1.
45. "Giant Labor Awakening," *Industrial Worker,* July 25, 1912, p. 1.
46. "Whole World Protests against Crime," *Industrial Worker,* July 3, 1912, p. 1.

47. "Italian Unions Act for Ettor-Giovannitti," *New York Call*, September 15, 1912, p. 2.
48. "In Italia," "Da Napoli," "In Germania," "Nella Svizzera," "Da Ginevra," "In Austria," "In Francia," *Il Proletario*, July 20, 1912, p. 4.
49. Paul Avrich, *Sacco and Vanzetti: The Anarchist Background* (Princeton, NJ: Princeton University Press, 1991), p. 26.
50. "Editorial Points," *Boston Globe*, September 17, 1912, p. 12.
51. "Haywood's Arrest," *Literary Digest*, September 28, 1912, p. 503, and "Meetings for Ettor," *Lawrence Evening Tribune*, September 10, 1912, p. 3.
52. "To Make Move Today at Salem," *Boston Globe*, September 23, 1912, p. 4.
53. Cahn, p. 214.
54. "Thousands at the Meeting," *Lawrence Evening Tribune*, September 16, 1912, p. 3.
55. Ibid.
56. Haywood, *Autobiography*, p. 256.
57. "Haywood for General Strike," *Boston Globe*, September 16, 1912, p. 4.
58. Haywood, *Autobiography*, p. 256.
59. Camp, p. 186.
60. Ibid., p. 34.
61. "I.W.W. Turns Out Strong," *Lawrence Evening Tribune*, May 31, 1912, p. 5.
62. Flynn, *Rebel Girl*, p. 147.
63. Dorothy Gallagher, *All the Right Enemies: The Life and Murder of Carlo Tresca* (New Brunswick, NJ: Rutgers University Press, 1988), p. 37.
64. Camp, p. 34.
65. Gallagher, p. 39.
66. Ibid.
67. "Mass Meeting Held This Afternoon," *Lawrence Evening Tribune*, September 28, 1912, p. 10.
68. "Police Stabbed and Beaten in Street Riot in Lawrence," *Boston Globe*, September 30, 1912, p. 1.
69. "Fierce Fighting in Lawrence Riot," *New York Times*, October 1, 1912, p. 1.
70. "One Juror Is Chosen," *Salem Evening News*, September 30, 1912, p. 7.
71. "Trial of I.W.W. Leaders Opens," *Boston Evening Globe*, September 30, 1912, p. 1.
72. "Must Call More Jurors," *Salem Evening News*, October 1, 1912, p. 2.
73. "A Poet of the I.W.W," *The Outlook*, July 5, 1913, p. 505.
74. "Face Serious Problem in Getting Ettor Case Jury," *Boston Globe*, October 2, 1912, p. 2.
75. "Make Threat to Burn Lawrence," *Boston Globe*, October 7, 1912, p. 8.
76. Ibid.
77. *Salem Evening News*, September 30, 1912, p. 7.
78. "Two Policemen Stabbed by Crowd," *Lawrence Tribune*, September 30, 1912, p. 5.
79. "Patriotism Is Rampant," *Lawrence Tribune*, October 3, 1912, p. 1.
80. Dubofsky, p. 185.
81. Ibid., p. 188.
82. Foner, *History of the Labor Movement*, vol. 4, pp. 222–23.
83. Ibid., pp. 194–206.

84. "Citizens Committee Bars I.W.W. Buttons," *Lawrence Evening Tribune*, October 8, 1912, p. 2.

85. "The City Ablaze in Color," *Lawrence Evening Tribune*, October 4, 1912, p. 1.

86. "Conditions Are Changed," *Lawrence Tribune*, October 7, 1912, p. 5.

87. "Allegiance to Our Flag," *Lawrence Tribune*, October 5, 1912, p. 1.

88. "Motto of the City Decided," *Lawrence Evening Tribune*, October 11, 1912, p. 1.

89. "Cheer Flag and Sing," *Boston Evening Globe*, October 12, 1912, p. 2.

90. Photograph in Immigrant City Archives, Lawrence, MA.

91. "Citizens Committee Bars I.W.W. Buttons," *Lawrence Evening Tribune*, October 8, 1912, p. 2.

92. "Parade Created Big Impression," *Lawrence Tribune*, October 16, 1912, p. 1.

93. "Tension in Lawrence," *Boston Evening Globe*, October 4, 1912, p. 1.

94. "City Aroused by Red Flag," *Boston Globe*, October 4, 1912, p. 4.

95. "Down with Anarchy Cry Aroused Citizens," *Lawrence Tribune*, October 3, 1912, p. 4.

96. "Truce to Be Maintained," *Boston Globe*, October 3, 1912, p. 2.

97. "Haywood and Heselwood Wanted to Carry Pistols," *Salem Evening News*, October 3, 1912, p. 1.

98. "I.W.W. Leaders in Lawrence Demand Police Protection from Vigilance Committee," *Salem Evening News*, October 7, 1912, p. 1.

99. "In Hospital for Rest," *Boston Globe*, October 13, 1912, p. 2.

100. "Salem Witchcraft, Case No. 2," *New York Call*, October 13, 1912, p. 6.

101. Henry David, *The History of the Haymarket Affair* (New York: Russell and Russell, 1936), p. 316.

102. Ibid., p. 300.

103. Ibid., p. 493.

104. Franklin S. Haiman, *Speech and Law in a Free Society* (Chicago: University of Chicago Press, 1981), p. 269.

105. "The Indictment against the Three Defendants, Caruso, Ettor, Giovannitti," *Salem Evening News*, September 30, 1912, p. 7.

106. "The Completed Jury," *Salem Evening News*, October 16, 1912, p. 5.

107. "Ettor Jury Empaneled," *Boston Globe*, October 16, 1912, p. 1.

108. "The Completed Jury," *Salem Evening News*, October 16, 1912, p. 1.

109. "Prominent Men Commend City," *Lawrence Evening Tribune*, October 17, 1912, p. 1.

110. "Said He Heard Ettor Appeal to Crowd to Rescue a Prisoner," *Salem Evening News*, October 22, 1912, p. 5.

111. Ibid.

112. Ibid.

113. "Tells of Threats," *Boston Globe*, October 22, 1912, p. 5.

114. "Taken Out of the Record," *Boston Globe*, October 23, 1912, p. 10.

115. "More Testimony about Rioting at Lawrence Given by Witnesses," *Salem Evening News*, October 18, 1912, p. 5.

116. "The Prosecution Spring Surprise This Morning; Italian Detective Called," *Salem Evening News*, October 24, 1912, p. 1.

117. "Swear to Threats," *Boston Globe*, October 17, 1912, p. 2.
118. "The Prosecution Spring Surprise This Morning; Italian Detective Called," *Salem Evening News*, October 24, 1912, p. 1.
119. "Ettor Makes Plea to Jury," *Boston Evening Globe*, November 23, 1912, p. 5.
120. "Tells of Threats," *Boston Globe*, October 22, 1912, p. 5.
121. *Salem Evening News*, October 16, 1912, p. 5.
122. "Tells of Threats," *Boston Globe*, October 22, 1912, p. 5.
123. "Caruso near the Scene of the Murder," *Lawrence Tribune*, October 25, 1912, p. 1.
124. "Incendiary Talk Given by Giovannitti," *Boston Globe*, October 25, 1912, p. 11.
125. *Salem Evening News*, October 26, 1912, p. 5.
126. *Boston Globe*, October 30, 1912, p. 5.
127. "Saw Firing of Fatal Shot," *Boston Evening Globe*, October 30, 1912, p. 5.
128. "Trial Resumes," *Boston Globe*, October 30, 1912, p. 5.
129. *Salem Evening News*, October 16, 1912, p. 1.
130. "Down to Killing of Anna LoPizzo," *Boston Globe*, October 26, 1912, p. 1.
131. "Caruso near the Scene of the Murder," *Lawrence Tribune*, October 25, 1912, p. 1.
132. "The Prosecution Spring Surprise This Morning; Italian Detective Called," *Salem Evening News*, October 24, 1912, p. 1.
133. "Down to Killing of Anna LoPizzo," *Boston Globe*, October 26, 1912, p. 9.
134. "Men Punished for Distributing Cards," *Lawrence Evening Tribune*, October 14, 1912, p. 1.
135. "Street Fight," *Lawrence Tribune*, October 8, 1912, p. 2.
136. "Lawrence I.W.W. Man Fined $5," *New York Call*, October 27, 1912, p. 1.
137. "A Lithuanian Killed in Lawrence," *Keleivis*, October 31, 1912, p. 1.
138. "Police Stop I.W.W. Parade at Funeral," *Lawrence Tribune*, October 28, 1912, p. 2.
139. "Tall Man Fired Shot," *Boston Globe*, October 31, 1912, p. 1.
140. "Saw Firing of Fatal Shot," *Boston Evening Globe*, October 30, 1912, p. 5.
141. "At the Scene of Fatal Riot Shot, He Testifies," *Boston Evening Globe*, October 25, 1912, p. 8.
142. "Wants Both Men in Court," *Boston Evening Globe*, October 31, 1912, p. 3.
143. Ibid.
144. Hennessy, *Twenty-five Years of Massachusetts Politics: 1890–1915*, p. 276.
145. "City Marshal Sullivan of Lawrence Testifies about Violence in Lawrence Strike," *Salem Evening News*, October 21, 1912, p. 1.
146. "Said He Heard Ettor Appeal to Crowd to Rescue a Prisoner," *Salem Evening News*, October 22, 1912, p. 1.
147. "City Marshal Sullivan of Lawrence Testifies about Violence in Lawrence Strike," *Salem Evening News*, October 21, 1912, p. 5.
148. "Boast of Stabbing," *Boston Globe*, November 1, 1912, p. 4.
149. Ibid.
150. "Ettor Makes His Demands," *Salem Evening News*, November 1, 1912, p. 5.
151. "Opening for the Defense," *Boston Evening Globe*, November 1, 1912, p. 1.

152. Ibid., p. 6.
153. Arthur and Lila Weinberg, *Clarence Darrow: A Sentimental Rebel* (New York: G. P. Putnam's Sons, 1980), pp. 222–49.
154. Ebert, *Trial of a New Society*, p. 87.
155. "Many Lawyers in the Case on Both Sides," *Salem Evening News*, September 30, 1912, p. 7.
156. "Tells of Threats," *Boston Globe*, October 22, 1912, p. 5.
157. Avrich, p. 160.
158. "State Ettor Urged Peace," *Boston Evening Globe*, November 5, 1912, p. 16.
159. Ibid.
160. "Many Witnesses Declare That Ettor and Giovannitti Counseled Peace in Strike," *Salem Evening News*, November 5, 1912, p. 6.
161. "Denies Kissing Defendant Ettor," *Lawrence Tribune*, November 6, 1912, p. 9.
162. Haywood, *Autobiography*, p. 251.
163. "Clergymen Testified," *Lawrence Tribune*, November 7, 1912, p. 9.
164. "Denies Kissing Defendant Ettor," *Lawrence Tribune*, November 6, 1912, p. 9.
165. "Mrs. Caruso Is a Witness," *Boston Evening Globe*, November 9, 1912, p. 2.
166. Ibid.
167. "Exact in Details," *Boston Globe*, November 13, 1912, p. 5.
168. "Never Urged Violence," *Boston Evening Globe*, November 13, 1912, p. 10.
169. "Half Speech, Half Sermon," *Boston Evening Globe*, November 18, 1912, p. 5.
170. "Ettor Case with Jury," *Boston Evening Globe*, November 25, 1912, p. 1.
171. "Defendant Ettor Addresses Jurors," *Lawrence Evening Tribune*, November 23, 1912, p. 1.
172. "Ettor Makes Plea to the Jury," *Boston Evening Globe*, November 23, 1912, p. 5.
173. "Prisoners' Pleas Stir Labor Trial," *New York Times*, November 24, 1912, p. 1.
174. Ebert, *Trial of a New Society*, p. 36.
175. Ibid., p. 38.
176. Ibid., p. 32.
177. Ibid., p. 45.
178. Ibid., p. 62.
179. Ibid., p. 63.
180. "Social Significance of Arturo Giovannitti," p. 24.
181. Ebert, *Trial of a New Society*, pp. 71–72.
182. "Social Significance of Arturo Giovannitti," p. 24.
183. "All Night Duty," *Boston Evening Globe*, November 26, 1912, p. 2.
184. "Ettor Case Verdict Waits until Morning," *New York Times*, November 26, 1912, p. 9.
185. "Ettor, Giovannitti, and Caruso Are Free," *New York Call*, November 27, 1912, p. 1.
186. "10,000 Hail Ettor and Comrades Free," *New York Times*, November 27, 1912, p. 1.
187. Ibid.
188. "Acquit Ettor, Caruso and Giovannitti," *Boston Evening Globe*, November 26, 1912, p. 1.

189. "Ettor, Giovannitti and Caruso Found Not Guilty," *Salem Evening News,* November 26, 1912, p. 2.
190. "Ettor, Giovannitti, and Caruso Are Free," *New York Call,* November 27, 1912, p. 1.
191. Elizabeth Balch, "Songs for Labor," *The Survey,* January 3, 1914.
192. "Acquit Ettor, Caruso and Giovannitti," *Boston Evening Globe,* November 26, 1912, p. 2.
193. "10,000 Hail Ettor and Comrades Free," *New York Times,* November 27, 1912, p. 1.
194. "Police Break Up Attempt at Parade," *Boston Globe,* November 27, 1912, p. 4.
195. "Citizens End Protest Period," *Lawrence Tribune,* November 29, 1912, p. 5.
196. "I.W.W. Plans for Meeting Today," *Boston Globe,* November 28, 1912, p. 1.
197. "Ettor Says No Guns Needed," *Boston Globe,* November 29, 1912, p. 3.
198. "Citizens End Protest Period," *Lawrence Tribune,* November 29, 1912, p. 5.

Epilogue

1. Jackson, *Lawrence Strike 1912.*
2. Jeanne Schinto, *Huddle Fever: Living in the Immigrant City* (New York: Alfred A. Knopf, 1995), p. 19.
3. "Presents for Ettor," *Lawrence Evening Tribune,* January 13, 1913, p. 4.
4. Goldberg, p. 97, and Arnold, p. 529.
5. Marion Barker, tape 55, oral history interview, Immigrant City Archives, Lawrence, MA.
6. Dorgan, *History of Lawrence, Massachusetts,* p. 58.
7. Baker, p. 21.
8. Cameron, p. 163.
9. Foner, *History of the Labor Movement,* vol. 4, p. 348.
10. Ebert, *Trial of a New Society,* p. 151.
11. Foner, *History of the Labor Movement,* vol. 4, pp. 358–60.
12. Robert Rosenstone, *Romantic Revolutionary: A Biography of John Reed* (Cambridge, MA: Harvard University Press, 1990), pp. 127–29.
13. Foner, *History of the Labor Movement,* vol. 4, pp. 360–68.
14. Ibid., pp. 371–72.
15. Flynn, *Rebel Girl,* p. 151.
16. Ibid., p. 150.
17. *Lawrence Directory 1912,* pp. 48–49.
18. Foner, *History of the Labor Movement,* vol. 4, p. 349.
19. Anonymous blacklist from Strike of 1912, box 2, Immigrant City Archives, Lawrence, MA.
20. Foner, *History of the Labor Movement,* vol. 4, p. 408.
21. Ibid., p. 171.
22. "Ettor Talks to Loomfixers," *Lawrence Tribune,* May 22, 1916, p. 12.
23. Arnold, p. 554.
24. "As Boston Sees Ettor," *Lawrence Evening Tribune,* May 24, 1916, p. 2.
25. "Complain of Police," *Lawrence Tribune,* May 26, 1916, p. 1.
26. Arnold, p. 555.

27. Carlson, p. 237.

28. Haywood, *Autobiography,* p. 292.

29. Carlson, p. 237.

30. Flynn, *Rebel Girl,* p. 221.

31. *American National Biography,* vol. 7 (New York: Oxford University Press, 1999), s.v. "Ettor, Joseph James."

32. Joseph J. Ettor, "The Light of the Past," *Industrial Worker,* July 28, 1945, p. 2.

33. *American National Biography,* vol. 7, s.v. "Ettor, Joseph James."

34. Helen Keller, "Introduction to *Arrows in the Gale,*" reprinted in Giovannitti, *Collected Poems,* pp. 135–36.

35. "Social Significance of Arturo Giovannitti," pp. 24–26.

36. Goldberg, p. 156.

37. "Arturo Giovannitti Dies at 75; Poet, Long-Time Labor Leader," *New York Times,* January 1, 1960, p. 19.

38. Ibid.

39. Camp, p. 113.

40. Ibid., epigraph.

41. Ibid., p. 111.

42. Ibid., p. 143.

43. Ibid., p. 141.

44. Ibid., p. 161.

45. "Elizabeth Gurley Flynn Is Dead; Head of U.S. Communist Party," *New York Times,* September 6, 1964, p. 56.

46. Camp, p. 220.

47. Ibid., p. 257.

48. "Communist Party—USA," in *Boyer,* p. 149.

49. Camp, p. 291.

50. "Elizabeth Gurley Flynn Is Dead; Head of U.S. Communist Party," *New York Times,* September 6, 1964, p. 1.

51. Camp, p. 308.

52. Ibid., p. 322.

53. Carlson, pp. 236, 244.

54. Ibid., p. 251.

55. Dubofsky, p. 383.

56. Carlson, p. 246.

57. Dubofsky, p. 386.

58. Ibid., p. 392.

59. David Kennedy, *Over Here: The First World War and American Society* (New York: Oxford University Press, 1980), p. 26.

60. Carlson, p. 251.

61. Ibid., p. 253.

62. Haywood, *Autobiography,* p. 323.

63. Carlson, p. 285.

64. Ibid., p. 293.
65. Kennedy, p. 288.
66. Ibid., p. 290.
67. "'Reds' Taken to Boston Today," *Lawrence Evening Tribune*, January 3, 1920, p. 1.
68. Kennedy, p. 290.
69. Ibid., p. 315.
70. Haywood, *Autobiography*, p. 361.
71. Carlson, p. 323.
72. Ibid., p. 324.
73. Ibid., p. 325.
74. Philip A. Laudani, *Mayors of Lawrence* (Lawrence, MA: privately printed, 1996), p. 5.
75. "City Mourns Death of Mayor," *Lawrence Telegram*, August 18, 1914, p. 1.
76. "City Pays Tribute to Its Dead Mayor," *Lawrence Telegram*, August 19, 1914, p. 1.
77. Dorgan, *History of Lawrence, Massachusetts*, pp. 208, 217, 233–36.
78. "Rice Called as a Witness," *Lawrence Telegram*, May 22, 1913, p. 1.
79. "Breen Testifies in Dynamite Trial," *Lawrence Telegram*, May 21, 1913, p. 5.
80. "Collins a Witness for the Prosecution," *Lawrence Telegram*, May 20, 1913, p. 1.
81. "Strike Expense Account Figures," *Lawrence Telegram*, May 23, 1913, p. 1.
82. "State's Case Now Nearly Completed," *Lawrence Telegram*, May 28, 1913, p. 12.
83. "Government Rests in Dynamite Case," *Lawrence Telegram*, June 3, 1913, p. 2.
84. "Strike Expense Account Figures," *Lawrence Telegram*, May 23, 1913, p. 1.
85. "Defense Rests in Dynamite Trial," *Lawrence Telegram*, June 4, 1913, p. 5.
86. "President Wood Is Acquitted," *Lawrence Telegram*, June 7, 1913, pp. 1–3.
87. Sumner, p. 207.
88. "Editorial: Wm. M. Wood," *Lawrence Telegram*, February 3, 1926, p. 4.
89. Arthur Walworth, *Woodrow Wilson: American Prophet* (New York: Longmans, Green, 1958), p. 299.
90. McPherson, "American Woolen Company's Quarter-Century Record," in *Bulletin of the National Association of Wool Manufacturers—1924*, p. 485.
91. Ibid.
92. Arnold, p. 567.
93. "Mill Pay Again Increased," *Lawrence Evening Tribune*, October 4, 1917, p. 1.
94. Goldberg, p. 107.
95. Ibid., p. 110.
96. Ibid., p. 103.
97. Ibid., p. 118.
98. Cole, p. 200.
99. McKone.
100. Goldberg, p. 112.
101. Ibid., p. 111.
102. Arnold, p. 685.
103. Goldberg, p. 121, and McKone.
104. Goldberg, p. 121.

105. Arnold, p. 693.

106. Ibid., p. 736.

107. Roddy, p. 74.

108. John Bruce McPherson, "William Madison Wood—A Career of Romance and Achievement," in *Bulletin of the National Association of Wool Manufacturers—1926* (Boston: National Association of Wool Manufacturers, 1926), p. 252.

109. "American Woolen Success Due Largely to W. M. Wood," *Lawrence Telegram,* February 3, 1926, p. 5.

110. Arnold, p. 186.

111. Roddy, p. 76.

112. Goldberg, p. 149.

113. Roddy, p. 77.

114. "The Cost of Living in Lawrence," *The Outlook,* January 7, 1920, p. 7.

115. Beal, p. 55.

116. Goldberg, p. 151.

117. Roddy, p. 76.

118. Arnold, p. 189.

119. McPherson, "William Madison Wood," *Bulletin of the National Association of Wool Manufacturers 1926,* p. 251.

120. Roddy, p. 116.

121. Ibid., p. 129.

122. "A $28,600,000 Loss," *Fortune,* June 1935, p. 70.

123. Roddy, p. 117.

124. "A $28,600,000 Loss," p. 70.

125. McPherson, "William Madison Wood," *Bulletin of the National Association of Wool Manufacturers 1926,* p. 257.

126. "William M. Wood Will Be Buried in West Parish," *Lawrence Evening Tribune,* February 3, 1926, p. 1.

127. Roddy, p. 120.

128. "American Woolen," *Fortune,* March 1954, p. 93.

129. Roddy, p. 157.

130. Janet E. Duncan, "An Investigation into the Characteristics and Development of Replacement Industries in Lawrence, Massachusetts" (PhD diss., Boston University, 1971), p. 119.

131. Ibid., p. 121.

132. Skulski, p. 123.

133. Cameron, pp. 175–79.

134. Arnold, p. 736.

135. Lawrence Heritage State Park.

136. Moran, p. 222, and Lance Secretan, "Spirit at Work," *Industry Week,* December 16, 1998.

137. Josef Berger, *Memoirs of a Corporation: 1850–1950—Weaving a Century* (Boston: Pacific Mills, 1950), p. 19.

138. "200,000 Watch Lawrence's 'God and Country' Parade," *Lawrence Eagle-Tribune,* September 24, 1962, p. 1.

139. Paul Cowan, "Introduction," in Cahn, n.p.

140. Name withheld, oral history interview tape 212, Immigrant City Archives, Lawrence, MA.

141. Gayle Pollard, "For 'Bread and Roses, Too,'" *Boston Globe,* April 28, 1980, p. 1.

142. James Oppenheim, "Bread and Roses," *American Magazine,* December 1911, p. 242.

143. Upton Sinclair, ed., *The Cry for Justice: An Anthology of the Literature of Social Protest* (Philadelphia: John C. Winston, 1916), p. 247.

144. Jim Zwick, "Behind the Song: Bread and Roses," *Sing Out!* Winter 2003, pp. 92–93.

145. Ibid.

146. Catherine Simonelli, oral history interview tape 215, Immigrant City Archives, Lawrence, MA.

147. "Slain Striker Finally Gets Gravestone," *Lawrence Eagle-Tribune,* August 30, 2000.

148. Domenica Strano, personal interview, July 9, 2003.

Bibliography

Magazine and Journal Articles and Pamphlets

"About Haywood." *Literary Digest,* June 14, 1913, pp. 135–36.

"American Woolen." *Fortune,* March 1954, pp. 91–96, 198–200, 204–5.

Baker, Ray Stannard. "The Revolutionary Strike." *American Magazine,* May 1912, pp. 19–30c.

Balch, Elizabeth. "Songs for Labor." *The Survey,* January 3, 1914, pp. 408–12.

"Can the Wool Trust Gag the Press?" *Collier's,* March 18, 1911, pp. 11–12.

Child, Richard Washburn. "Industrial Revolt at Lawrence." *Collier's,* March 9, 1912, pp. 14–15.

———. "The Making of 'K,' the Wool Schedule." *Everybody's Magazine,* March 1910, pp. 338–49.

"Children of a Strike." *The Survey,* February 24, 1912, p. 1791.

"The Cost of Living in Lawrence." *The Outlook,* January 7, 1920, p. 7.

Crowell, Merle. "78—and Still at the Head of a Tremendous Concern." *American Magazine,* December 1920, pp. 37, 113–20.

Deland, Lorin F. "The Lawrence Strike: A Study." *Atlantic Monthly,* May 1912, pp. 694–705.

"The Embargo on Strike Children." *The Survey,* March 2, 1912, p. 1822.

Ford, James. "The Co-Operative Franco-Belge of Lawrence." *The Survey,* April 6, 1912, pp. 68–70.

Fosdick, Harry Emerson. "After the Strike—in Lawrence." *The Outlook,* June 15, 1912, pp. 340–46.

Giovannitti, Arturo. "Syndicalism—the Creed of Force." *Independent,* October, 30, 1913, pp. 209–11.

Gompers, Samuel. "The Lawrence Strike." *American Federationist,* April 1912, pp. 281–93.

———. "Those 'World Redeemers' at Chicago—Their Plight." *American Federationist,* August 1905, pp. 514–16.

Haywood, William D. "When the Kiddies Came Home." *International Socialist Review,* May 1912, pp. 716–17.

"Haywood's Arrest." *Literary Digest,* September 28, 1912, pp. 502–3.

Heaton, James. "Legal Aftermath of Lawrence Strike." *The Survey,* July 6, 1912, pp. 503–10.

Herriman, Tom. "Angelo Rocco: A Rank & File Union Leader Remembers the 1912 Lawrence Textile Strike." *Labor Unity,* April 1980, pp. 10–12.

Larned, J. N. "Prepare for Socialism." *Atlantic Monthly,* May 1911, pp. 577–80.

Lauck, W. Jett. "Lessons from Lawrence." *North American Review,* May 1912, pp. 665–72.

Lawrence Citizens' Association. *Lawrence as It Really Is* (pamphlet). Lawrence, MA, March 1912.

———. *A Reign of Terror in an American City* (pamphlet). Lawrence, MA, March 1912.

———. *What City after Lawrence?* (pamphlet). Lawrence, MA, March 1912.

"The Lawrence Labor Victory." *Literary Digest,* March 23, 1912, pp. 575–76.

"Lawrence, Massachusetts: The Strike of 1912." Immigrant City Archives, Lawrence, MA.

"The Lawrence Strike Children." *Literary Digest,* March 9, 1912, pp. 471–72.

"The Lawrence Strike: A Poll of the Press." *The Outlook,* February 17, 1912, pp. 357–58.

"The Lawrence Strike: A Review." *The Outlook,* March 9, 1912, p. 531.

Lovejoy, Owen R. "Right of Free Speech in Lawrence." *The Survey,* March 9, 1912, p. 1904.

Macgowan, Kenneth. "Giovannitti: Poet of the Wop." *The Forum,* October 1914, pp. 609–11.

Marcy, Leslie H., and Frederick Sumner Boyd. "One Big Union Wins." *International Socialist Review,* April 1912, pp. 613–30.

O'Sullivan, Mary K. "The Labor War at Lawrence." *The Survey,* April 6, 1912, pp. 72–74.

Palmer, Lewis E. "A Strike for Four Loaves of Bread." *The Survey,* February 3, 1912, pp. 1690–97.

"A Poet of the I.W.W." *The Outlook,* July 5, 1913, pp. 504–6.

"The Poetry of Syndicalism." *Atlantic Monthly,* June 1913, pp. 853–54.

Pratt, Walter Merriam. "The Lawrence Revolution." *New England Magazine,* March 1912, pp. 7–16.

"A Radical Assault upon Trade Unions." *Current Literature,* April 1912, pp. 381–84.

Rowell, Wilbur E. "The Lawrence Strike." *The Survey,* March 23, 1912, pp. 1958–60.

"Socialism behind Lawrence Strike." *Journal of Commerce and Commercial Bulletin,* February 1, 1912, p. 4.

"The Social Significance of Arturo Giovannitti." *Current Opinion,* January 1913, pp. 24–26.

"Statements by People Who Took Part." *The Survey,* April 6, 1912, pp. 75–82.

"The Strike in the Woolen Mills." *Current Literature,* April 1912, pp. 381–84.

Sumner, Keene. "A Business Genius Who Has Done What Others Said Was Impossible." *American Magazine,* June 1923, pp. 16–17, 203–20.

"Symphony in K Flat." *The Nation,* March 13, 1911, p. 360.

Tarbell, Ida M. "The Mysteries and Cruelties of the Tariff: The Bulwark of the Wool Farce," *American Magazine,* November 1910, pp. 51–60.

———. "The Mysteries and Cruelties of the Tariff: The Passing of Wool." *American Magazine,* October 1910, pp. 735–43.

"The Trend of Things." *The Survey,* March 23, 1912, pp. 1981–82.

"A $28,600,000 Loss." *Fortune,* June 1935, pp. 65–72, 122–32.

Vorse, Mary Heaton. "The Trouble at Lawrence." *Harper's Weekly,* March 9, 1912, p. 10.

Wells, H. G. "Socialism, Parts I and II." *Harper's Monthly,* January and February 1912, pp. 197–204, 403–9.

Weyl, Walter. "The Lawrence Strike from Various Angles: It Is Time to Know." *The Survey,* April 6, 1912, pp. 65–67.

————. "The Strikers at Lawrence." *The Outlook,* February 10, 1912, pp. 309–12.

"The Wool Bill Veto." *The Outlook,* August 26, 1911, pp. 910–11.

"Work Stoppages, Workers Involved, Man-Days Idle, Major Issues, and Average Duration: 1881–1970." *Historical Statistics of the United States: Colonial Times to 1970.* U.S. Department of Commerce, Bureau of the Census. Washington, DC, 1976.

Zwick, Jim. "Behind the Song: Bread and Roses." *Sing Out!* Winter 2003, pp. 92–93.

Books

Abrams, Richard M. *Conservatism in a Progressive Era: Massachusetts Politics 1900–1912.* Cambridge, MA: Harvard University Press, 1964.

Acts and Resolutions Passed by the General Court of Massachusetts in the Year of 1912. Boston: Wright and Potter, 1912.

Adamic, Louis. *Dynamite: The Story of Class Violence in America.* Rev. ed. Gloucester, MA: Peter Smith, 1963.

Albert, Felix. *Immigrant Odyssey: A French-Canadian Habitat in New England.* Orono: University of Maine Press, 1991.

American National Biography. Vols. 7, 9, 16. New York: Oxford University Press, 1999.

Andrews, Mildred Gwin. *The Men and the Mills: A History of the Southern Textile Industry.* Macon, GA: Mercer University Press, 1987.

Arlington Mills 1865–1925. Norwood, MA: Plimpton Press, 1925.

An Authentic History of the Lawrence Calamity. Boston: J. J. Dyer, 1860.

Avrich, Paul. *Sacco and Vanzetti: The Anarchist Background.* Princeton, NJ: Princeton University Press, 1991.

Baxandall, Rosalyn Fraad. *Words on Fire: The Life and Writing of Elizabeth Gurley Flynn.* New Brunswick, NJ: Rutgers University Press, 1987.

Beal, Fred E. *Proletarian Journey.* New York: Van Rees Press, 1937.

Bedford, Henry F. *Socialism and the Workers in Massachusetts 1886–1912.* Amherst: University of Massachusetts Press, 1966.

Berger, Josef. *Memoirs of a Corporation: 1850–1950—Weaving a Century.* Boston: Pacific Mills, 1950.

Bird, Steward, Dan Georgakas, and Deborah Shaffer. *Solidarity Forever: An Oral History of the I.W.W.* Chicago: Lake View Press, 1985.

Blanchette, Joseph P. *The View from Shanty Pond: An Irish Immigrant's Look at Life in a New England Mill Town, 1875–1938.* Charlotte, VT: Shanty Pond Press, 1999.

Blewett, Mary H. *Constant Turmoil: The Politics of Industrial Life in Nineteenth-Century New England.* Amherst: University of Massachusetts Press, 2000.

Boyer, Paul S., ed. *The Oxford Companion to United States History.* New York: Oxford University Press, 2001.

Brady, Kathleen. *Ida Tarbell: Portrait of a Muckraker.* New York: Seaview/Putnam, 1984.

Brewster, Todd, and Peter Jennings. *The Century.* New York: Doubleday, 1988.

Brooks, Thomas R. *Toil and Trouble: A History of American Labor.* New York: Delacorte Press, 1971.

Bulletin of the National Association of Wool Manufacturers—1912. Boston: National Association of Wool Manufacturers, 1912.

Bulletin of the National Association of Wool Manufacturers—1924. Boston: National Association of Wool Manufacturers, 1924.

Bulletin of the National Association of Wool Manufacturers—1926. Boston: National Association of Wool Manufacturers, 1926.

Cahn, William. *Lawrence 1912: The Bread and Roses Strike.* New York: Pilgrim Press, 1980.

Cameron, Ardis. *Radicals of the Worst Sort: Laboring Women in Lawrence, Massachusetts, 1860–1912.* Urbana and Chicago: University of Illinois Press, 1993.

Camp, Helen C. *Iron in Her Soul: Elizabeth Gurley Flynn and the American Left.* Pullman: Washington State University Press, 1995.

Carlson, Peter. *Roughneck: The Life and Times of Big Bill Haywood.* New York: W. W. Norton, 1983.

Chernow, Ron. *Titan: The Life of John D. Rockefeller, Sr.* New York: Vintage, 1998.

Clifton, Daniel, ed. *Chronicle of the Twentieth Century.* Mount Kisco, NY: Chronicle Publications, 1982.

Cole, Donald B. *Immigrant City: Lawrence, Massachusetts, 1845–1921.* Chapel Hill: University of North Carolina Press, 1963.

Dalzell, Robert F., Jr. *Enterprising Elite: The Boston Associates and the World They Made.* Cambridge, MA: Harvard University Press, 1987.

Darrow, Clarence. *The Story of My Life.* New York: Da Capo Press, 1996.

David, Henry. *The History of the Haymarket Affair.* New York: Russell and Russell, 1936.

Dengler, Eartha, Katherine Khalife, and Ken Skulski. *Images of America: Lawrence, Massachusetts.* Dover, NH: Arcadia, 1995.

Dickens, Charles. *American Notes.* London: Penguin, 1972.

Director of the Bureau of Statistics. *42nd Annual Report on the Statistics of Labor for the Year 1911.* Boston: Wright and Potter, 1913.

Dorgan, Maurice B. *History of Lawrence, Massachusetts.* Lawrence, MA: privately printed, 1924.

———. *Lawrence—Yesterday and Today (1845–1918).* Lawrence, MA: privately printed, 1918.

Dubofsky, Melvyn. *We Shall Be All: A History of the Industrial Workers of the World.* Chicago: Quadrangle, 1969.

Dunwell, Steve. *The Run of the Mill: A Pictorial Narrative of the Expansion, Dominion, Decline, and Enduring Impact of the New England Textile Industry.* Boston: David R. Godine, 1978.

Ebert, Justus. *The Trial of a New Society.* Cleveland: I.W.W. Publishing Bureau, 1913.

Eno, Arthur L., Jr. *Cotton Was King: A History of Lowell, Massachusetts.* Somersworth, NH: New Hampshire Publishing, 1976.

Ettor and Giovannitti before the Jury at Salem, Massachusetts. Chicago: Industrial Workers of the World, 1912.

Evans, Harold. *The American Century.* New York: Alfred A. Knopf, 1998.

Final Report of the Commission on Industrial Relations. Washington, DC, 1915.

Flynn, Elizabeth Gurley. *The Rebel Girl: An Autobiography, My First Life (1906–1926).* New York: International Publishers, 1955.

Foner, Eric, and John A. Garraty, eds. *The Reader's Companion to American History.* Boston: Houghton Mifflin, 1991.

Foner, Philip S. *History of the Labor Movement in the United States.* 5 vols. New York: International Publishers, 1965–1980.

———. *Women and the American Labor Movement: From the First Trade Unions to the Present.* New York: Macmillan, 1979.

Gallagher, Dorothy. *All the Right Enemies: The Life and Murder of Carlo Tresca.* New Brunswick, NJ: Rutgers University Press, 1988.

Gilbert, Robert E. *The Tormented President: Calvin Coolidge, Death, and Clinical Depression.* Westport, CT: Praeger, 2003.

Giovannitti, Arturo. *The Collected Poems of Arturo Giovannitti.* Chicago: E. Clemente and Sons, 1962.

Goldberg, David J. *A Tale of Three Cities: Labor Organization and Protest in Paterson, Passaic, and Lawrence, 1916–1921.* New Brunswick, NJ: Rutgers University Press, 1989.

Gorn, Elliott J. *Mother Jones: The Most Dangerous Woman in America.* New York: Hill and Wang, 2001.

Haiman, Franklin S. *Speech and Law in a Free Society.* Chicago: University of Chicago Press, 1981.

Halberstam, David. *The Powers That Be.* New York: Dell, 1979.

Hartford, William F. *Where Is Our Responsibility: Unions and Economic Change in the New England Textile Industry, 1870–1960.* Amherst: University of Massachusetts Press, 1996.

Hayes, J. F. C. *History of the City of Lawrence.* Lawrence, MA: E. D. Green, 1868.

Haywood, William D. *The Autobiography of Big Bill Haywood.* New York: International Publishers, 1974.

Hennessy, Michael E. *Four Decades of Massachusetts Politics: 1890–1935.* Norwood, MA: Norwood Press, 1935.

———. *Twenty-five Years of Massachusetts Politics: 1890–1915.* Boston: Practical Politics, 1917.

Heymann, C. David. *American Aristocracy: The Lives and Times of James Russell, Amy, and Robert Lowell.* New York: Dodd, Mead, 1980.

Hill, Hamilton Andrews. *Memoir of Abbott Lawrence.* Boston: privately printed, 1883.

Historical and Pictorial Review: National Guard of the Commonwealth of Massachusetts 1939. Baton Rouge, LA: Army and Navy, 1939.

Hofstadter, Richard. *The Age of Reform.* New York: Random House, 1955.

Income in the United States: Its Amount and Distribution, 1909–1919. New York: National Bureau of Economic Research, 1922.

Jackson, Miles, interviewer. *Lawrence Strike 1912: Viewpoints on American Labor.* New York: Random House, 1971. Oral histories on record.

Jones, Mary Harris. *The Autobiography of Mother Jones.* Chicago: Charles H. Kerr, 1925. Reprint, New York: Arno Press, 1969.

Kasson, John. *Civilizing the Machine: Technology and Republican Values in America, 1776–1900.* New York: Penguin, 1976.

Kennedy, David. *Over Here: The First World War and American Society.* New York: Oxford University Press, 1980.

Kornbluh, Joyce L., ed. *Rebel Voices: An I.W.W. Anthology.* Ann Arbor: University of Michigan Press, 1964.

La Sorte, Michael. *La 'Merica: Images of Italian Greenhorn Experience.* Philadelphia: Temple University Press, 1985.

Laudani, Philip A. *Mayors of Lawrence.* Lawrence, MA: privately printed, 1996.

Laurie, Bruce. *Artisans into Workers: Labor in Nineteenth Century America.* New York: Farrar, Straus, and Giroux, 1989.

The Lawrence Directory 1896, 1899–1900, 1910, 1911, 1912, 1913. Boston: Sampson and Murdock.

The Lawrence Gazeteer. Lawrence, MA: Charles G. Merrill, 1894.

Lukas, J. Anthony. *Big Trouble.* New York: Simon and Schuster, 1997.

McCaffery, Robert Paul. *Islands of Deutschtum: German-Americans in Manchester, New Hampshire, and Lawrence, Massachusetts, 1870–1942.* New York: Peter Lang, 1996.

McKone, John J. *Glimpses of Lawrence: The Founding and Progress of a Great Industrial Centre.* Lawrence, MA, 1921.

May, Henry F. *The End of American Innocence: A Study of the First Years of Our Own Time— 1912–1917.* Chicago: Quadrangle, 1959.

Miller, Glenn W. *American Labor and the Government.* New York: Prentice-Hall, 1948.

Moran, William. *The Belles of New England: The Women of the Textile Mills and the Families Whose Wealth They Wove.* New York: St. Martin's Press, 2002.

Moreno, Barry. *Italian Americans.* East Sussex, UK: Ivy Press, 2003.

Morris, Edmund. *Theodore Rex.* New York: Random House, 2001.

Painter, Nell Irvin. *Standing at Armageddon: The United States 1877–1919.* New York: W. W. Norton, 1987.

Peterson, Merrill D., ed. *The Portable Thomas Jefferson.* New York: Penguin, 1975.

Phillips, Kevin. *Wealth and Democracy: A Political History of the American Rich.* New York: Broadway Books, 2002.

Pratt, Norma Fain. *Morris Hillquit: A Political History of an American Jewish Socialist.* Westport, CT: Greenwood Press, 1979.

Pringle, Henry F. *The Life and Times of William Howard Taft.* New York: Farrar and Rinehart, 1939.

Ravitch, Diane, ed. *The American Reader: Words That Moved a Nation.* New York: Harper-Perennial, 1991.

Robertson, David Brian. *Capital, Labor, and State: The Battle for American Labor Markets from the Civil War to the New Deal.* Lanham, MD: Rowman and Littlefield, 2000.

Roddy, Edward G. *Mills, Mansions, and Mergers: The Life of William M. Wood.* North Andover, MA: Merrimack Valley Textile Museum, 1982.

Rosenstone, Robert. *Romantic Revolutionary: A Biography of John Reed.* Cambridge, MA: Harvard University Press, 1990.

Salvatore, Nick. *Eugene V. Debs: Citizen and Socialist.* Urbana and Chicago: University of Illinois Press, 1982.

Schinto, Jeanne. *Huddle Fever: Living in the Immigrant City.* New York: Alfred A. Knopf, 1995.

Sinclair, Upton, ed. *The Cry for Justice: An Anthology of the Literature of Social Protest.* Philadelphia: John C. Winston, 1916.

Skulski, Ken. *Images of America: Lawrence, Massachusetts.* Vol. 2. Charleston, SC: Arcadia, 1997.

Smith, Adam. *The Wealth of Nations.* Vol. 1. New York: G. P. Putnam's Sons, 1904.

Smith, Gibbs M. *Labor Martyr: Joe Hill.* New York: Grosset and Dunlap, 1969.

Sobel, Robert. *Coolidge: An American Enigma.* Washington, DC: Regnery, 1998.

Songs of the Workers. 34th ed. Chicago: Industrial Workers of the World, 1980.

Stansell, Christine. *American Moderns: Bohemian New York and the Creation of a New Century.* New York: Henry Holt, 2000.

Steel, Ronald. *Walter Lippmann and the American Century.* New York: Vintage, 1980.

Sullivan, Mark. *Our Times: The United States 1900–1925.* Vol. 4, *The War Begins— 1909–1914.* New York: Charles Scribner's Sons, 1946.

Thoreau, Henry David. *A Week on the Concord and Merrimack Rivers.* Boston: Houghton Mifflin, 1975.

Tarbell, Ida M. *All in the Day's Work: An Autobiography.* New York: Macmillan, 1939.

Tucker, Barbara M. *Samuel Slater and the Origins of the American Textile Industry, 1790–1860.* Ithaca, NY: Cornell University Press, 1984.

U.S. Congress. House. Committee on Rules. *The Strike at Lawrence, Mass.: Hearings before the Committee on Rules of the House of Representatives on House Resolutions 490 and 433.* 62nd Cong., 2nd sess., March 2–7, 1912.

U.S. Congress. Senate. *Report on Strike of Textile Workers in Lawrence, Mass. in 1912.* 62nd Cong., 2nd sess., 1912. S. Doc. 870.

U.S. Department of Commerce. *Statistical Abstract of the United States: The National Data Book.* Washington, DC, 2002.

U.S. Department of the Interior. *Lowell: The Story of an Industrial City.* Washington, DC, 1992.

Views of Lawrence. Portland, ME: L. H. Nelson, 1903.

Von Drehle, David. *Triangle: The Fire That Changed America.* New York: Atlantic Monthly Press, 2003.

Vorse, Mary Heaton. *A Footnote to Folly: Reminiscences of Mary Heaton Vorse.* New York: Farrar and Rinehart, 1935.

Walsh, Alice L. *A Sketch of the Life and Labors of Rev. James T. O'Reilly, O.S.A.* Lawrence, MA: Free Press Printing, 1924.

Walworth, Arthur. *Woodrow Wilson: American Prophet.* New York: Longmans, Green, 1958.

Weber, Max. *The Protestant Ethic and the Spirit of Capitalism and Other Writings.* New York: Penguin, 2002.

Weinberg, Arthur and Lila. *Clarence Darrow: A Sentimental Rebel.* New York: G. P. Putnam's Sons, 1980.

Wertheimer, Barbara Mayer. *We Were There: The Story of Working Women in America.* New York: Pantheon, 1977.

Weyl, Walter. *The New Democracy.* New York: Macmillan, 1912.

Who's Who in America, 1912–1913. Vol. 7. Chicago: A. N. Marquist, 1913.

Wilkie, Richard W., and Jack Tager. *Historical Atlas of Massachusetts.* Amherst: University of Massachusetts Press, 1991.

Yeomans, Henry Aaron. *Abbott Lawrence Lowell—1856–1943.* Cambridge, MA: Harvard University Press, 1948.

Newspapers

Anzeiger und Post

Appeal to Reason

Boston American

Boston Globe

Boston Herald

Boston Post

Boston Transcript

Christian Science Monitor

Le Courrier de Lawrence

Harvard Crimson

Industrial Worker

Keleivis

Lawrence Daily American/Sun

Lawrence Telegram

Lawrence Tribune

Los Angeles Times

Miami Herald

New York Call

New York Herald

New York Sun

New York Times

New York Tribune

New York World

Il Proletario

Salem (MA) Evening News

Solidarity

Springfield Republican

CD-ROMS and Web Sites

Ellis Island On-Line. http:www.ellisisland.org/.

Internet Movie Database. http:www.imdb.com/.

Rosenzweig, Roy, Steve Brier, and Josh Brown. *Who Built America? From the Centennial Celebration of 1876 to the Great War of 1914.* CD-ROM. Voyager, American Social History Productions, 1993, 1994.

University of Arizona, Special Collections AZ 114 box 1, folder 3A, exhibit 131. Ettor, Joseph J. *Industrial Unionism the Road to Freedom.* IWW Pamphlet, June 1913. http://digital.library.arizona.edu/bisbee/docs/131.php.

Dissertations

Arnold, Dexter Philip. "A Row of Bricks: Worker Activism in the Merrimack Valley Textile Industry, 1912–1922." PhD diss., University of Wisconsin, Madison, 1985.

Duncan, Janet E. "An Investigation into the Characteristics and Development of Replacement Industries in Lawrence, Massachusetts." PhD diss., Boston University, 1971.

Index

Atlantic Mill, 17, 61, 210
Atlantic Monthly, 133, 219
Atteaux, Frederick, 249–50
Atwill, Henry, 230, 233
Auden, W. H., 102
Axelrod, Sara "the egg woman," 157
Ayer, Ellen, 22
Ayer, Frederick, 22
Ayer Mill
  accosting of scabs at, 60
  building of, 24
  closing of, 253
  flight of workers from, 44
  laborers on strike at, 46

Baker, Ray Stannard, 127, 135, 179
Barre, Massachusetts, 213
Barre, Vermont, 159–60
Bastany, Gabriel, 117
Bedard, Joseph, 211, 215
Beers, Robert W., 86
"Bell Time," 36
Bencordo, Eugenio, 231
Benoit, Oscar, 109, 152, 165, 166, 233
Berger, Victor, 184–85, 187
Berry, Louis, 18, 60
Black Hand death threats, 130, 149, 203
Blesky, John, 73
boardinghouse system in mill towns, 30,
  32–33, 35
bombing at *Los Angeles Times,* 84–85
bomb plot. *See* dynamite plot
bonus system of rewards, 23, 70, 201, 206
Borah, William, 175
Boston American, 67, 124, 166–67, 234
"Boston Associates," 33
Boston Globe
  blaming of foreign operatives for
    strike, 47
  detachment in reporting, 124
  on Ettor's trial testimony, 235
  on Lawrence after train station beatings,
    175

on phantom workers at Washington
  Mill, 112
on spirit of strike, 149
on Sullivan's promotion to city marshal,
  164
Boston Herald, 67, 124, 214
Boston Transcript, 124, 203
Brandeis, Louis, 74
"Bread and Roses"
  Oppenheim poem, 119, 256
  origin and symbolism of phrase, 3,
    256–57
Breen, John
  and conspiracy in dynamite plot,
    109–10, 131, 220, 249–50
  as first Irish mayor in Lawrence, 40
  sued by Syrians, 221
British immigrants, 36
British textile cities, 31–32
Broadway Magazine, 154
Brooklyn Tablet, 203
Burns, William, 84, 85
Burns Detective Agency, 106

Calderone, Ernesto, 160
Cameron, Ardis, 157
capitalism
  Capital versus Labor, in building of
    American West, 56
  and class divide in America, 132–33
  IWW as threat to, 58
  popular call for reform of, 123,
    125–26
  public wariness of, 74
  stockholding in mills, 135–36, 197
  tycoons in New England, 33
  Weber's essay on, 134
Capriola, Antonietta, 243
Carter, Clark, 166, 194, 195–96
Caruso, Enrico, 178
Caruso, Joseph, 220, 226, 240. *See also*
  Ettor-Giovannitti trial
Caruso, Rosa, 226, 235, 239, 240